Folk Songs
from
Uttar Pradesh

Folk Songs from Uttar Pradesh

Laxmi Ganesh Tewari

D.K. Printworld (P) Ltd.
New Delhi

Cataloging in Publication Data — DK
Courtesy: D.K. Agencies (P) Ltd. <docinfo@dkagencies.com>

Tewari, Laxmi Ganesh, 1938 -
Folk songs from Uttar Pradesh / Laxmi Ganesh Tewari.
x, 333 p. 23 cm.
In Hindi (Devanagari and roman); translation and introductory matter in English.
Includes bibliographical references (p.)
ISBN 8124603545

1. Folk songs, Hindi — India — Uttar Pradesh. 2. Folk songs, Hindi — Translations into English. I. Title.

DDC 782.421 629 143 009 542 22

ISBN 81-246-0354-5
First published in India 2006

Published and printed by:
D.K. Printworld (P) Ltd.
Regd. office : *'Sri Kunj'*, F-52, Bali Nagar
New Delhi - 110 015
Phones : (011) 2545-3975; 2546-6019; *Fax* : (011) 2546-5926
E-mail: dkprintworld@vsnl.net
Web : www.dkprintworld.com

to my Mother

Bitti

विषय-सूची — Contents

Acknowledgements

My thanks to Messrs. Balmukund Bajpai, Ram Sewak Pandey, Kaushal Kishore Misra, Durga Charan Shukla, and many others who helped me during my field trips, organizing musical gatherings, introducing me to musicians, and taking me to villages so that I might observe the daily lives of the people.

To all the musicians, my profound thanks for being so generous with their time sharing their traditional art with me.

My wife, Carolyn Yogini Tewari, has been infinitely patient in helping me in proofreading the manuscript numerous times and offering improvements.

Finally, I offer my respect to my late *guru* Dr. Lalmani Misra, who always pointed out the natural beauty in folk music.

Thanks to Mr. Susheel K. Mittal for accepting to publish this manuscript.

Key to Transliteration

VOWELS

अ *a* (but)	आ *ā* (palm)	इ *i* (it)	ई *ī* (beet)	उ *u* (put)	ऊ *ū* (pool)
ऋ *ṛ* (rhythm)	ए *e* (play)	ऐ *ai* (air)	ओ *o* (toe)	औ *au* (loud)	

CONSONANTS

Guttural	क *ka* (skate)	ख* *kha* (blockhead)	ग *ga* (gate)	घ *gha* (ghost)	ङ *ṅa* (sing)
Palatal	च *ca* (chunk)	छ* *cha* (catch him)	ज *ja* (john)	झ *jha* (hedgehog)	ञ *ña* (bunch)
Cerebral	ट *ṭa* (start)	ठ* *ṭha* (anthill)	ड *ḍa* (dart)	ढ* *ḍha* (godhead)	ण* *ṇa* (under)
Dental	त *ta* (path)	थ *tha* (thunder)	द *da* (that)	ध* *dha* (breathe)	न *na* (numb)
Labial	प *pa* (spin)	फ* *pha* (philosophy)	ब *ba* (bin)	भ *bha* (abhor)	म *ma* (much)
Semi-vowels	य *ya* (young)	र *ra* (drama)	ल *la* (luck)	व *va* (vile)	
Sibilants	श *śa* (shove)	ष *ṣa* (bushel)	स *sa* (so)	ह *ha* (hum)	
Others	क्ष *kṣa* (*kṣatriya*)	त्र *tra* (*triśūla*)	ज्ञ *gya* (*gyānī*)	ळ* *ḷ* (*play*)	ॠ* *ṝ*

HINDI LETTERS (extras)

ँ = *ñ* (*candrabindu*)	ं = ṅ (*anusvāra*)	ड़ = *ṛa*	ढ़ = *ṛha*

* No exact English equivalents for these letters.

Introduction

DURING the first thirty years of my life, I often heard the folk songs which are presented here, for they were sung when I, my brothers, and neighbourhood boys were born and when other ceremonies were celebrated for us. Somehow, although I grew up in India in this rich cultural environment, I never paid any attention to the songs which soothed my ears everyday. Ceremonies and festivals seemed to be part of the daily routine.

In 1972, by an accident of fate, circumstances forced me to go back to these songs and listen to their messages. In the beginning, I had no idea what I might uncover. Now, almost thirty-three years later, I present the fruits of my field trips to Indian villages, with my sincere personal respect for the "folk" who have performed and preserved these songs. These trips were among the most rewarding experiences of my life: they made me realize the depth of the traditions in which I was raised and the process through which musical traditions are transmitted from one generation to the next. These experiences were additionally humbling to me as a musician, when I recognized the high level of skill among village musicians and their sensitivity towards musical renderings of utmost brilliance, nurtured by a "listen, participate and learn" oral tradition.

Imagine this scene (a recurrent memory I have of my childhood days): It is early dawn (*brahma belā*); birds have just started chirping in their nests, and bells around domestic animals' necks jingle with the movement of their heads. Here and there, one hears prayers recited in husky, subdued voices. Small groups of women chat on their way to fetch water from the well. Inside the houses, other women are busy sweeping, cleaning pots and pans, and grinding grain into flour on a *cakiyā* (stone-mill) as they sing, accompanied by rhythm from the bangles on their wrists and the scraping sound of the *cakiyā* (Song Nos. 244, 245 and 246).

By the time one sees the first sunlight on the eastern horizon, the men have reached the fields, and smoke from dried cowdung fires pours out of every house, as if a great sacrifice was being performed in praise of the sun. It is refreshing to be in this rural atmosphere: soft singing blends with animal sounds and the noises of people at work, creating a heavenly feeling that fills one with delight.

This is how each day started in a traditional Indian village. Additionally, village people celebrated some festival, religious rite, ceremony, or social function almost every other day, for ceremonies, performed from cradle to funeral pyre, were the backbone of Hindu society. The Hindu "... is born religious, and dies religious .... religion attends him in antenatal ceremonies long before his birth, and follows him in endless offerings for the good of his soul long after death." (Williams 1916: ii). These ceremonies were designed to purify human beings physically, mentally, and intellectually, and have been observed from very early times. Today, most orthodox Hindus know of sixteen ceremonies (Pandeya 1966 and Prasad 1962) related to the human life- cycle. These ceremonies can be classified into five groups, according to the occasions for their celebration:

I. Ceremonies prior to birth:

(1) *Garbhādhān* — performed when it is known that a woman has become pregnant.

(2) *Puṁsavan* — performed in the third month of pregnancy, in order to assure that a male child will be born.

(3) *Sīmantonayan* — performed in the fourth, sixth, or eighth month of pregnancy, to protect the pregnant woman from evil spirits.

II. Ceremonies related to birth and childhood:

(4) *Jātakarm* — birth of the child.

(5) *Nāmakaraṇa* — naming the child: time varies.

(6) *Niṣkramaṇ* — taking the child out of the house for the first time, at the age of four months.

(7) *Annaprāśan* (commonly known as *pasanī*) — first feeding of solid food (most often *khīr*-rice and sugar cooked in milk), usually when a child is six months old.

(8) *Cūḍākaraṇ* (commonly known as *muṇḍan*) — shaving of the child's hair, between one and three years of age. Many families maintain the traditional time and place practised in their household.

(9) *Karṇavedh* (commonly knwon as *chedan*) — piercing of the child's ears: time varies.

III. Ceremonies related to the commencement of education:

(10) *Vidyārambh* — commencement of reading and writing the alphabet: time varies.

(11) *Yajñopavīt* (commonly known as *upanayan* or *janeū*) — the sacred thread ceremony, which is performed by the three upper castes of Hindus; time varies.

(12) *Vedārambh* — beginning of Vedic studies, performed by the three upper castes of Hindus: number of years varies for each caste.

(13) *Keśānt* or *Godān* — shaving of the beard and/or giving the gift of a cow as a token fee to a spiritual preceptor, near the end of Vedic studies.

(14) *Samāvartan* or *Snān* — end of Vedic studies, performed when a son returns home after finishing his studies.

IV. Marriage and related ceremonies:

(15) *Vivāh* (commonly known as *śādī*) — marriage.

V. Death and related ceremonies:

(16) *Antakarm* — death.

Only a few of the above ceremonies are observed in Indian society today. All of the ceremonies prior to birth have lost their significance and are rarely performed. Celebration of the birth of a child is popular, although the mode of celebration now tends towards Western-style parties with birthday cake. Many families observe the head-shaving ceremony, but other childhood ceremonies are rarely performed. Except for sacred-thread observances by a few families, all the ceremonies associated with the beginning of education have become endangered species. Marriage is the most important and significant event in a Hindu's life and as such is performed with great pomp and show. Death ceremonies are still observed (with modifications to conserve time).

Songs such as those reproduced here were a very important part of life-cycle ceremonies. With the demands of nuclear family units, universal education, and the working schedules of both husband and wife, ceremonial observances have been condensed to suit the time and space of modern

Indian households' changing lifestyles. The sweet melodies of womens' singing, accompanied by *ḍholak* and *mañjīrā,* are less frequent today.

From early times, society preferred the birth of a male child (see Song No. 65), for ". . . by looking at the face of the new born son the father is absolved from all debts and attains immortality" (Pandeya 1966: 73). Upon a male child's birth, a man is freed from *pitṛ ṛṇa* (one of the three debts of a man according to Hindu religion).[1] Only a son can perform funeral rites. It is believed that by begetting a son a man saves himself (and seven preceding and seven future generations) from the spirit world. A funeral ceremony performed by a son protects him from Yama, King of the Dead.

Moreover, the dowry system imposes great hardship on a girl's family. At the time of marriage, the bride's family has to give the groom's family a large amount of money and goods, often so much that the family goes deep into debt. This system can bring a family unending unhappiness, and thus, the birth of a daughter may mean eventual humiliation, worries, and debts.

Sanskrit literature has always depicted the birth of a male child with music and merry-making. At the time of Rām's birth:

> ". . . gandharvas [celestial musicians] played divine melodies, nymphs danced, celestial drums were heard and the gods showered flowers from the sky. . . . The king gave gifts to the bards and ballad singers."
> — Shastri (1692: 43)

When Kṛṣṇa was born:

> ". . . festivities were held in Braja to celebrate the birthday ceremony of Krishna . . . musical instruments were struck up, songs were sung and *mantras* and benedictions were pronounced by the Brāhmaṇas."
> — Sanyal: n.d.: 29

Once it is known that a woman is pregnant, the news spreads all over the neighbourhood and among her husband's relatives. At the moment the child is born, a conch is blown and bells and gongs are played, so

1. The three debts of a man are *pitṛ-ṛṇa,* a debt from which a man is freed when he begets a son; *deva-ṛṇa*, the debt of religious rites and sacrifices; and *ṛṣi-ṛṇa*, the obligation which one owes to a *guru* (teacher).

that everyone knows of the child's birth. These auspicious sounds are supposed to clear the air of evil spirits. "This also accounts for the music played at weddings, when the young pair are in special danger from the attacks of spirits." (Crooke 1896 : I : 167-69).

Relatives and neighbourhood women gather before and after the birth to sing congratulatory songs. The texts of ceremonial songs are concerned mainly with the household environment: *nanad*'s (sister-in-law's) teasing jests, husband's desire for a son, distribution of gifts, and the preparation and performance of different traditional roles and rituals by family relatives, as well as overall happiness. One hears songs describing the cravings of a pregnant woman. These songs are commonly called *sohar* or *badhāī*. Other childbirth-related songs, sung during domestic rituals performed after birth, are often named after spices used in foods specially prepared for a new mother[2] or after ceremonies (such as *caruā* and *kājal*) performed by specific relatives. A few songs, like *pālanā* (cradle) and *jhunjhunā* (a child's rattle), describe the child's activities. Songs related to Rām's and Kṛṣṇa's births are popular: every boy-child is personified as Rām or Kṛṣṇa and his parents as Daśarath and Kauśalyā or Nand and Yaśodā. The most common form of ceremonial song-texts is the repetition of lines with individual relatives performing specific rituals, with his or her name or relationship inserted into the song-text.

Songs sung during ceremonies tell us about the everyday life of a household. In Song No. 48, a woman has to do cleaning work by herself, even during her final stage of pregnancy. The sister-in-law's taunts reveal that the birth of a female child can bring great misery upon a woman. If the child is a boy, singing and rejoicing go on and professional musicians (*śahanāī* players) and/or *gaunihārin* (professional ceremonial song singers)[3]

2. Spices such as *jīrā* (cumin seed), *pīpar* (a kind of long pepper), *ajavāin* (an aromatic seed), *soṁṭh* (dry ginger), and *haldī* (turmeric) are mixed with dried fruit in a syrup of *gur* (jaggery) to make *harīra*, a special dish made for a mother after the delivery of her child.

3. Many women (usually poor widows) in the three upper caste groups take up the profession of singing ceremonial songs, to supplement their incomes.

are called in. All the female members of the family prepare special food for the *jaccā* (mother of the newborn child); making *harīrā* involves many stages of grinding, sifting, drying, and cooking.

Muṇḍan (also called *cuḍākaraṇ*) is the ceremony performed at the time of shaving the child's hair. The nearest relatives are invited. In the morning, the child is taken to the River Gaṅgā (or at the bank of a nearby river) or to the courtyard of a religious place or temple, accompanied by women and men of the household. The barber shaves the child's hair, while the child's *buā* (father's sister) sits nearby with bread dough in her hand, collecting all the shorn hair before it falls to the ground, and kneading it into the dough. At the conclusion of the shaving, the child's *buā* throws the lump of dough into the river or pond. In return, she pertly demands a present from the child's mother; many *muṇḍan* songs include an affectionate exchange of dialogue between a *jaccā* and her *nanad* (Song No. 75). Women of the household sing ceremonial songs at the house, going to and from the selected place for shaving, and in the afternoon at home.

Generally speaking, women are more religious, superstitious and tradition-minded than men are; as a result, women's folk songs focus on the customs of ceremonies and gift-giving: who should perform what, when, where, and with what reward. Since the River Gaṅgā is the most sacred body of water to the Hindus, it is a blessing for the whole family to perform *muṇḍan* ceremonies on the banks of the River Gaṅgā. Homage to the River Gaṅgā is a part of almost every ceremony; if the ceremony cannot be performed on the banks of the River Gaṅgā itself, water from the River Gaṅgā (kept in many Hindu households for religious occasions) will be used in the ceremony.

Marriage is the most important and significant ceremony. Today, although one frequently hears about love marriages, intercaste (and intercontinental) marriages, and occasional elopements, the most common practice approved by the society is a marriage arranged by the parents of the bride and groom. The girl's father and other relatives take the initiative to search for a suitable groom. Once the girl's family finds a suitable groom, the first step is to obtain the boy's horoscope, which is then compared to the girl's horoscope. Only if the two horoscopes are compatible will the girl's family approach the groom's side for further negotiations (dowry and other details). Upon agreement of the two sides, a *varīkṣā* (*var* = groom; *ikṣā* = consent) ceremony takes place. The second stage is known as *phaladān* (gift of fruits). Close relatives of the girl's side go to the groom's house with gifts (and the agreed-upon sum of dowry money), to finalize the dates of the marriage ceremony. Numerous ceremonies take place, and preparations begin in both houses.[4] Household ceremonies are often condensed into one celebration, symbolically observed on the day of the marriage party's departure from the groom's house anḍ the day of its arrival at the bride's house.

On the appointed day, the groom's party arrives at the girl's home. The number of guests is usually agreed upon in advance by both parties. In the evening, the procession of the groom arrives with decorated elephants, horses, fireworks, bands of musicians, and the groom seated in an elaborately decorated automobile turned into a throne; members of the groom's party dance to music played by an accompanying band. The groom's party and the bride's guests are treated to a big feast, after which most of the guests leave. The groom and a few close relatives remain behind to perform various ceremonies, culminating in the final marriage ceremony. In the morning, they depart with the bride.

Each relative has a specific title by which he or she is addressed. The most important relations, who are invariably mentioned during the singing of these ceremonial songs, are given in the "Table of Relationships."

A woman's *sasur* is depicted as calling for the musicians, going to market to purchase specific ingredients, organizing the wedding party and being welcomed at the bride's home upon arrival. In a role of *bappā*,

---

4. Such as *dhan dareti* (a ceremony which begins with an odd number of invited married women grinding whole grains of lentils and chickpeas into split grains and then winnowing them); *ubaṭan* (rubbing a girl's body with a paste made of flour, mustard oil, and turmeric); *maṇḍap* (setting up the area where the marriage ceremony will be performed); *mātṛ pūjan* (worship of household goddesses); *Gaurī pūjā* (worship of Goddess Pārvatī); *piyarī* (when the bride-to-be, wearing a yellow *sārī*, is taken to the local goddess' shrine by her mother and other invited women).

he distributes gifts and bestows affection and comfort of his *bahū*. Being the head of the household, he officiates and is consulted about details for all ceremonies.

A *sās* welcomes her *bahū* into her home and makes sure that all customary celebrations occur and gifts are given to relatives. For the rest of her life, a *bahū* treats her *sās* with great reverence, as a figure of authority. At the birth of a grandson, the *sās* performs a specific ritual of preparing a baked clay pot with ceremonial designs; she fills the pot with water and spices and sets it to boil, to prepare a medicinal drink for the *jaccā*. The ceremony is known as *caruā caḍhānā* (lit. to put the clay pot on the fire). As *ammā*, she gives the first alms to the son undergoing his sacred thread ceremony; she prepares her son as a groom and receives him, along with her new *bahū*. Being the female head of the household she officiates and is consulted about all ceremonies.

The relations of *nanad* and *buā*, are very important and are required to be present during all ceremonies. The squabbling between a *bahū* and *nanad* are an important topic in most ceremonial songs. A young *nanad* is usually the close confidant of a *bahū*.

Jeṭh and *jeṭhānī* are next in line in the hierarchy and are prominently mentioned in ceremonial songs. The *jeṭh* is engaged in providing the ingredients and *jeṭhānī* in preparing special food for the *jaccā*. In the social order, the *jeṭhānī* is next in line after the *sās*.

A *devar* is a close confidant to the *bahū*. He consoles her when she is distressed. He has the social right to joke with her.

The other relatives in the Table (p. 14) are also honoured in the songs as they perform their ritual obligations.

Much has changed regarding marriage ceremonies. In earlier times, a Hindu marriage took anywhere from three to five days, with a few ceremonies performed each day. Appropriate congratulatory songs were sung by the women during each ceremony. A traditional band of musicians used to travel with the groom's party, playing music at the beginning of each ceremony and when they returned home with the bride; these musicians left only after the welcoming of the bride at the groom's house and receiving goods and fees for their services. Nowadays such elaborate, musically traditional marriages are rarely seen. Many of them are observed by families as token gestures: most of the traditional women's songs and band music with traditional instruments have been replaced by amplified movie songs and Western-style bands playing popular movie melodies on Western instruments.

The most common style of singing ceremonial songs is by a group of women, with one singer leading the song and the rest of the group singing along with the leader, to the accompaniment of *ḍholak* and *mañjīrā* and/ or without any instrumental accompaniment.

Besides life-cycle ceremonies, Indian society traditionally celebrated festivals welcoming seasonal changes or honouring gods and goddesses. Picture this scenario: after the burning hot summer months, the sky is full of dark clouds, announcing the coming of the monsoon season, to everyone's relief. The air is full of sweet, earthy odors and everyone is happy; this happiness begins the chain of festivals. There is a saying that the *Tīj* festival comes and sows the seeds of festivals; *Holī* comes and takes away the festivals in her shawl. *Tīj, Sāvan, Jhūlā, Kajarī, Guḍiyā, Nāg Pañcamī, Janmāṣṭmī, Rāmanavamī, Śivarātri, Daśaharā, Jhoñjhī, Ṭesū, Dīpāvalī, Katakī, Makar Saṁkrānti, Holī* and so forth are performed with rejoicing. Singing of *bhajan-kīrtan, devī gīt, caitī, kajarī, phaguā, bārahamāsā, caumāsā* become routine in neighbourhood temples and households.

Sāvan is the fifth month of the Hindu calander and heralds the coming of the monsoon in its full force, to everyone's relief. The air is full of sweet, earthy odors and the countryside is lush and green. It is customary that a *bahū* be taken to her paternal home during this time. During this season, a swing is hung inside the house or outside on the trees, so that men, women and children can enjoy swinging. A *bahū* returning to her paternal home enjoys the freedom to sing and swing with her friends and relatives. The songs sung at this time are called *Kajarī* and *Sāvan*. Many of the women's *Sāvan* songs refer to the custom of *gaunā*;[5] the ceremony of taking a bride to her husband's home for the first time after marriage. Song No. 182 expresses the fears of a girl who is about to leave

5. Early marriage was (and still is to some extent) common in India. After marriage, the girl used to remain in her parents' home until the age of puberty, after which she was taken to her husband's house. *Gaunā*, therefore, is called second marriage.

her childhood's familiar faces and the house in which she grew up, to go to her husband's home, a strange and unknown world. The last two lines of the sung suggest a dual meaning. One meaning could be traced to the time when travelling was not easy; once a girl left her parent's home, it was uncertain whether she would ever see them again. Another meaning is that whoever comes into this world dies and after death there is no reunion. Other songs depict the impatient *bahū* waiting for her brother to come to take her back home for the festive time.

During the rainy season, a farmer has little work to do in the fields, therefore, menfolk idle away their time doing repair work, making ropes, and singing traditional songs into the late hours of the night.

Another song form, *Bārahamāsā* (songs of the twelve months) and *Caumāsā* (the four months of the rainy season) are also common during the rainy season. *Bārahamāsā* is a song in which the longing of a wife separated from her husband is depicted with sentimentality. Some of the *Caumāsā* songs describe the four months of the rainy season in detail, while others are composed of four couplets, each couplet describing three months, thus covering all twelve months of the year.

Another popular festival with lots of singing and merry-making is *Holī* (also called *Phāg* or *Phaguā*). A common theme of *Holī* songs (as well as other folk songs) is Kr̥ṣṇa and his exploits with cowgirls.

The yearly cycle of religious festivals is an important part of Indian family life. Ceremonies and festivals are means for teaching children religious lore, family customs, and social etiquette as everyone participates in preparing for and observing each occasion.

Besides the frequent festivals, Indian day-to-day life is full of entertainment, including traditional *naṭ* (acrobats), *saperā* (snake charmers), *madārī* (bear and monkey charmers), *kaṭhaputalī* (puppeteers), *sādhū-sant* (saint-musicians), and theatrical performances (*Nauṭaṅkī, Rāmalīlā,* and *Kr̥ṣṇlīlā*). Singing and instrumental playing were predominant in all of these presentations.

Singing of *bhajans* (devotional songs) is a popular way of expressing devotion as well as entertainment. The *bhakti* (devotion) movement became particularly strong during the fourteenth-sixteenth centuries, when numerous saint-musicians (Raidās, Tulsīdās, Sūrdās, Kabīr, Mīrābāī and others) sang out their hearts to god. Their *bhajans*, as well as many written by unknown writers, old and contemporary, are a significant part of the folk song repertoire.

Rural life is full of singing folk songs to pass time. Some of the songs are typically labelled as belonging to distinct caste groups, such as boatmen's songs (Nos. 240, 241, 242 and 243), washermen's songs (Nos. 7, 8, 9, 10, 11, 12 and 13), and Dhanuk's songs (Nos. 247, 248 and 249). They are sung to specific instrumental accompaniment by a caste group. For example, the washermens song's are sung to the accompaniment of *sup* (winnowing basket).

Belavariyā, lacak and *lacarī*, songs given in the miscellaneous section are so labelled by a few musicians; they are recent additions to the folk traditions with social themes. *Hahu* (Song No. 261) is a term used for songs to scare young children so that they will behave properly.

Folk songs can be grouped into three main categories: (1) *Rāmāvatārī* (songs pertaining to the incarnation of Rām), (2) *Kṛṣṇāvatārī* (songs pertaining to the incarnation of Kṛṣṇa), and (3) other songs (including domestic scenes, songs in praise of other gods and goddesses, mythological, and modern). The image of Kṛṣṇa as a child or youth is particularly dear to the people and thus, *Kṛṣṇāvatārī* focus on the Kṛṣṇa's birth, childhood, and amorous exploits, neglecting his adulthood. Rām, on the other hand, is eulogized as the ideal man, fulfilling perfectly the roles of son, husband, brother, warrior and ruler. *Rāmāvatārī* therefore, focus on Rām's marriage, his wanderings in the forest, and his triumphant return to his rightful throne, while his birth and childhood are not often mentioned in the songs. The legends of Rām and Kṛṣṇa are so deeply rooted in folk culture that even folk songs which do not describe anything related to them have their names inserted in them.

In general, folk songs are anonymous. Nevertheless, the name of a famous saint poet such as Tulsīdās, Kabīr, or Sūrdās is often inserted in the signature line of a song. It is difficult to determine whether famous saint-poets got inspiration for their poems from folk songs popular in their own day and age, whether the folk poets copied their ideas, or whether the folk songs which have come down to us with their signature lines are indeed their original songs, changed by time, travel and the effects of oral tradition.

It is common to find similar songs popular in different areas, with slight changes. The reason for this is marriage, which binds two families in close contact. Through marriage, a girl from one area is established in another area and the songs she knows migrate to that area also. Children, who often travel with their mothers, pick up the songs of both areas. If the child is a girl, she goes to a third area when she marries, forming a triangle within which her songs rotate. Thus, like waves in a pond, folk songs travel from one area to another.

Unfortunately, much of the ceremonial, festival and occasional music is being forgotten in the name of modernity. The faint memories of my childhood have become a dream in present-day Indian society. Economic inflation has destroyed the generosity of households, which in turn has affected wandering minstrels and folk singers; these musicians have left their traditional arts to join professional musical groups geared towards attracting and impressing audiences with film tunes and new song-texts. Under these circumstances, the spirit of folk music has died and "the folks" in the audience no longer participate in the music themselves. Many folk forms have disappeared and many are in the process of disappearing. Such is the case with instruments like the *kaṇḍāl* and the *turahī*, which were popularly played at wedding processions in the state of Uttar Pradesh. When I was a child, I heard them often in the villages; during all of 1972-73, however, I didn't hear them even once. Members of the young generation are ignorant of these musical instruments.

The growing popularity of band music has forced village musicians to give up playing their folk instruments in order to play in Westernized bands. Marching bands with Western instruments (trumpets, clarinets, tubas, etc.) are in great demand today, since they play popular film tunes (while members of the procession dance). Even small towns have organized these kinds of bands. It doesn't matter if the music played by such bands is generally cacophonous and out of tune; having a band is prestigious and a sure sign of the family being modern.

Before the advent of radio, television, and movie houses, ceremonies and festivals were virtually the only source of entertainment, especially for women. Older women say that they learned ceremonial songs from elderly women of their own and neighbouring households while they were young, merely by participating in singing during the ceremonies. "Such occasions were a pleasure to us as young girls, as we were encouraged to sing in such gatherings, which gave us a good excuse for attending all the ceremonies that happened in the area." At present there are many distractions in both urban and rural areas. Values are changing because of increased education and contact with the outside world; most young people are attracted by modern things.

Although village life is changing slowly than life in the cities, the movement of people moving from village to cities, and vice versa, has had an adverse effect on the maintenance of ceremonial traditions. Chances are that a city girl who moves to a village because of marriage will not participate in ceremonial singing, either because she is not familiar with the tradition or because she feels it is a waste of time. A village girl who moves to the city may find it difficult to celebrate ceremonies and festivals, even if she wishes to, simply because of the lack of a homogeneous society there. Relatives required to participate in certain ceremonies may not be available, she may not be able to remember the details of the ceremonies, or there may not be enough women from her area or caste group who know the songs she knows.

The fast pace of city life does not normally allow enough time to celebrate ceremonies and festivals on the scale traditionally called for. Marriage, for instance, are often shortened to one or two days of ceremonies, instead of the customary three or four. This is happening more often in the villages, too, because many of the relatives who attend must travel from the cities and often have trouble getting leave from their jobs for a full week.

In cities, more and more births are occurring in hospitals rather than at home. This in itself is diminishing the number of childbirth ceremonies performed and precludes the possibility of singing songs. Western customs are becoming more prevalent instead, with friends bringing flowers and gifts to the mother at the hospital, rather than relatives and neighbours performing ceremonies.

All in all, there is an increasing lack of opportunity for ceremonial songs to be transmitted orally. Most young people do not appreciate the rich traditions of ceremonies and festivals and folk songs. Many of the older people watch the dying of these traditions with sadness. One time, during a recording session I observed a few young girls being encouraged by an elderly woman to sing while she helped them with the text. Upon my asking her why she herself did not sing, she told me: "I am too old now to sing and I am suffering from asthma, but I am forced to sing whenever there are ceremonies among my people. If these girls learn the songs, they can maintain the tradition; otherwise, I will cary the *purukhan kī cīj* (the heritage of my ancestors), with me upon my death."

Folk music is the mirror of people's everyday lives and family customs, and a link in the continuous chain of Indian culture which connects the present to the ancient past. As a student of music approaching this mountain of riches, I find myself in a forest of precious beauty, precariously situated between traditional values and today's modern technological world. Changes in patterns of living are affecting India as a whole, transforming it from agrarian to industrial to technological and gradually undermining many aspects of village culture. This publication is an attempt to generate the interest of young scholars and educators in traditions that exist under their very noses.

Table of Relationships

Son's / Daughter's	*Daughter-in-law (Sons' wife)*	*Grandson's/ Granddaughter's*
Bāppā (father)	*Sasur* (father-in-law)	*Bābā* (grandfather)
Āmmā (mother)	*Sās* (mother-in-law)	*Dādī* (grandmother)
Baḍe Bhaiyā (elder brother)	*Jeṭh* (husband's elder brother)	*Tāu* (father's elder brother)
Bhābhī/Bhaujī (elder brother's wife)	*Jeṭhānī* (husband's elder brother's wife)	*Tāī* (father's elder brother's wife)
Bhāī (younger brother)	*Devar* (husband's younger brother)	*Cācā* (father's younger brother)
Bahinī (sister)	*Nanad* (husband's sister)	*Buā* (father's sister)
Jījā (sister's husband)	*Nandoī* (husband's sister's husband)	*Fūfā* (father's sister's husband)
Māmā (mother's brother)		

Note: Younger relations are usually addressed by their names by the elders. Besides these common address terminology, there are numerous variables from family to family and in different regions.

अध्याय १
भजन

भजन

१.

दिन के दीपक सुरज हैं रात के दीपक चाँद।
कुल के दीपक पुत्र हैं और सुख के दीपक राम॥
भजु मन राम चरण सुखदाई॥
जिन चरणों से निकरी सुरसरी, शंकर के जटा समाई
जटाशंकरी नाम परो, त्रिभुवन को तारन आई॥
सोई चरनन की चरण पादुका, भरत रह्यो लौ लाई जी
सोई चरनन केवट धो लीनो, तब हरि नाव चढ़ाई॥
सोई चरनन संतन जन सेवें, सदा रहें सुखदाई
सोई चरनन गौतम ऋषि नारी, पग से परम पद पाई॥
दंडक बन प्रभु पावन कीनो, ऋषियों के त्रास मिटाई
तुम ही प्रभु तिरलोक के स्वामी, कनक मृगा सन धाई॥
कपि सुग्रीव बन्धु भये ब्याकुल, तिन जा छत्र फिराई
रिप को अनुज बभीसन निशचर, कंचन लंका पाई॥
शिव सनकादिक और ब्रह्मादिक, शेष सहस मुख गाई
तुलसीदास मारुत सुत की प्रभु, निज मुख करैं बड़ाई॥

din ke dīpak suraj haiṅ rāt ke dīpak cāṅda,
kul ke dīpak putr haiṅ aur sukh ke dīpak rām.
bhaju man rām caraṇ sukhadāī.
jin caraṇoṅ se nikarī surasarī, śaṅkar ke jaṭā samāī;
jaṭāśaṅkarī nām paro, tribhuvan ko tāran āī.
soī caranan kī caraṇ pādukā, bharat rahyo lau lāī jī.
soī caranan kevaṭ dho līno, tab hari nāv caṛhāī.
soī caranan santan jan seveṅ, sadā raheṅ sukhadāī.
soī caranan gautam ṛṣi nārī, pag se param pad pāī.
daṇḍak ban prabhu pāvan kīno, ṛṣiyoṅ ke trās miṭāī.
tum hī prabhu tiralok ke svāmī, kanak mṛgā san dhāī.

kapi sugrīv bandhu bhaye byākul, tin jā chatr phirāī.
rip ko anuj babhīsan niśacar, kañcan laṅkā pāī.
śiva sanakādik aur brahmādik, śeṣa sahas mukh gāī.
tulsīdās mārut sut kī prabhu, nij mukh karaiṅ baṛāī.

The lamp of the day is the sun and the lamp of the night is the moon;
The lamp of the lineage is a son and Rām is the lamp of happiness.
O dear mind, recite the name of Rām, the mine of happiness.
Out of whose feet the Ganges came and submerged in Śaṅkar's hair.
Gaṅgā was thus called Jaṭāśaṅkarī; she came down to free the three worlds from future transmigration.
Bharat received with great reverance the sandals of those feet.
Kevaṭ washed those feet before taking Him on his boat.
Saints serve these same feet and thus always remain blissfull.
The wife of Gautam was liberated by the same feet.
O God, you purified Daṇḍak forest and wiped away the saint's troubles.
You are the master of the three worlds; You chased after the golden deer.
The monkey Sugrīv was troubled by his brother and you helped him regain his throne.
The brother of your enemy, Vibhiṣan, was blessed with the throne of Golden Laṅkā.
God Śiva, Brahmā and their sons, along with the hundred hooded snake sang your glory.
Tulsīdās says: "God himself praised the son of the wind, Hanumān."

(CYT: 237C: 1975, Kanpur, Sadhu)

२.

राम नाम धन पाया मैंने, घट में हरि को पाया मैंने ॥
ना कोई गंगा गये ना यमुना, ना कोई तीर्थ नहाया मैंने ॥
ना कोई जंगल गये ना बन में, ना कोई जज्ञ रचाया मैंने ॥
ना कोई मन्दिर, गये ना मस्जिद, ना कोई शँख बजाया मैंने, ना कोई आरती उतारा मैंने ॥
मीरा के प्रभु गिरधर नागर, चरण कमल रज पाया मैंने ॥

rām nām dhan pāyā mainne; ghaṭ men hari ko pāyā mainne.
nā koī gangā gaye nā yamunā; nā koī tīrth nahāyā mainne.
nā koī jangal gaye nā ban men; nā koī jagy racāyā mainne.
nā koī mandir gaye nā masjid, nā koi śankh bajāyā mainne, nā koī āratī utārā mainne.
mīrā ke prabhu giradhar nāgar, caraṇ kamal raj pāyā mainne.

I received the treasure of Rām's name; I found Hari within me.
I didn't go [to bathe] to the Ganges nor Yamunā rivers; I did't go to bathe at any religious place.
I didn't go to any forest nor did I organize any religious sacrifice.
I didn't go to any temple or mosque nor did I blow any conch-shell nor did I perform *āratī*.
Mīrā's lord is Kṛṣṇa and [she] has received the dust from His feet.
(LGT: 5R: 1972-73, Dhanabad, Brāhmaṇ Women)

३.

भजु मन मदन गोपाल भजु मन श्री राधे ॥
आवो आवो कृष्ण मुरारी बीच भँवर में नाव हमारी
पार लगाओ घनश्याम भजु मन श्री राधे ॥
द्रोपदी सुता की लज्जा राख्यो राख्यो लाज करेव न देरी
चीर बढ़ायो घनश्याम भजु मन श्री राधे ॥
दुरयोधन घर मेवा त्याग्यो सूखा साग बिदुर घर खायो
भोग लगायो घनश्याम भजु मन श्री राधे ॥
गज और ग्राह लड़ैं जल भीतर गज की टेर सुन्यो छड़ माहीं
प्राण बचायो घनश्याम भजु मन श्री राधे ॥
खम्भ तोड़ि हिरणाकुश मारेव ध्रुव ने अनल अटल फल पायो
वैसे उबारेव हमें श्याम भजु मन श्री राधे ॥

bhaju man madan gopāl bhaju man śrī rādhe.
āvo āvo kṛṣṇ murārī bīc bhañvar men nāv hamārī.
pār lagāo ghanśyām bhaju man śrī rādhe.
dropadī sutā kī lajjā rākhyo rākhyo lāj karev n derī.
cīr baṛhāyo ghanśyām bhaju man śrī rādhe.

durayodhan ghar mevā tyāgyo sūkhā sāg bidur ghar khāyo.
bhog lagāyo ghanśyām bhaju man śrī rādhe.
gaj aur grāh laṛaiṅ jal bhītar gaj kī ṭer sunyo chaṛ māhīṅ.
Prāṇ bacāyo ghanśyām bhaju man śrī rādhe.
khambh toṛi hiraṇākuś mārev dhruv ne anal aṭal phal pāyo.
vaise ubārev hameṅ śyām bhaju man śrī rādhe.

O mind, recite the name of Kṛṣṇa and Rādhā.
Come, O Kṛṣṇa as my boat is in the middle of a whirlpool.
O Kṛṣṇa, take me ashore. O mind, recite the name of the Śrī Rādhe.
You saved the honour of Draupadi by not delaying.
You extended the cloth. O mind, recite the name of Śrī Rādhe.
You refused Duryodhan's great feast, instead eating simple food at Vidur's house.
You did partake of food. O mind, recite the name of Śrī Rādhe.
The elephant and the crocodile fought under water and you heard the elephant's call.
You saved his life. O mind, recite the name of Śrī Rādhe.
You killed Hiraṇyakuś; Dhruv received steadfast bliss.
Similarly, liberate me Kṛṣṇa. O mind, recite the name of Śrī Rādhe.

(LGT: 6R: 1972-73, Dhanabad, Brāhmaṇ, Women)

४.

सीताराम सीताराम करलो मन में जो सुख चाहो जीवन में ॥
राजा दशरथ के चार पुत्र हैं, राम लक्ष्मण भरत शत्रुघन
राम हैं सबसे दुलारे हों, जो सुख चाहो जीवन में ॥
राम सिया को ब्याहन गये हैं, नौमत बजत अवधपुर में, जो सुख चाहो जीवन में ॥
राम सिया जब द्वारे गये हैं, ससुरा ने अरति उतारी है, जो सुख चाहो जीवन में ॥
राम सिया जब घर में गये हैं, माता ने उनको लियो गोद में, जो सुख चाहो जीवन में ॥
माता कैकेई दशरथ से बोलीं, राम को चौदह वर्ष बनवास में, जो सुख चाहो जीवन में ॥

sītārām sītārām karalo man meṅ jo sukh cāho jīvan meṅ.
rājā daśarath ke cār putr haiṅ, rām lakṣmaṇ, bharat, śatrughan;
rām haiṅ sabase dulāre ho, jo sukh cāho jīvan meṅ.

rām siyā ko byāhan gaye haiṅ, naumat bajat avadhapur meṅ, jo sukh cāho jīvan meṅ.
rām siyā jab dvāre gaye hain, sasurā ne arati utārī hai, jo sukh cāho jīvan meṅ.
rām siyā jab ghar meṅ gaye haiṅ, mātā ne unako liyo god meṅ, jo sukh cāho jīvan meṅ.
mātā kaikeī daśarath se bolīṅ, rām ko caudah varṣ banavās meṅ, jo sukh cāho jīvan meṅ.

Recite the name of Sītārām if you want happiness in this life.
King Daśarath has four sons, Rām, Lakṣmaṇ, Bharat and Satrughan.
Rām is dearest of all.
Rām has gone to wed Sītā; the musical ensembles are playing at Avadha.
When Rām arrived at this gate, his sasur performed āratī to him.
When Rām arrived back home with Sītā, his mother took them on her lap.
Mother Kaikeyī said to Daśarath that Rām should go to the forest for fourteen years.

(LGT: 12R : 1972-73, Dhanabad, Brāhmaṇ, Women)

५.

ए हो नहिं जन पिया कौने भेष न अंता हमरे लागि रहे ॥
पहिला पहरा पड़ा पिया का पिया चले असनान का
सोने के गेडुवा मा जल भरि लायों,
मोरे पिया घर ही मा करौ असनान न अंता हमरे लागि रहे ॥
दुसरा पहरा पड़ा पिया का पिया चले ज्योनार का
सोने के थारा मा ज्योना बनायों
मोरे पिया घर ही मा जेंवौ जेउनार न अंता हमरे लागि रहे ॥
तिसरा पहरा पड़ा पिया पर पिया चले शिकार का
फूल निवड़ि कलि सेज लगायों
मोरे पिया घर ही मा सोवौ सेउनार न अंता हमरे लागि रहे ॥

तुलसीदास भजौ भगवानैं
अरे पिया कतहूँ न लागैं अब शिकार न अंता हमरे लागि रहे ॥[1]

e ho nahiṅ jan piyā kaune bheṣ n aṅtā hamare lāgi rahe.
pahilā paharā paṛā piyā kā piyā cale asanān kā;
sone ke geḍuvā mā jal bhari lāyoṅ;
more piyā ghar hī mā karau asanān n aṅtā hamare lāgi rahe.
dusarā paharā paṛā piyā kā piyā cale jyonār kā;
sone ke thārā mā jyonā banāyoṅ;
more piyā ghar hī mā jeṅvau jeunār n aṅtā hamare lāgi rahe.
tisarā paharā paṛā piyā par piyā cale śikār kā;
phūl nivaṛi kali sej lagāyoṅ;
more piyā ghar hī mā sovau seunār n aṅtā hamare lāgi rahe.
tulsīdās bhajau bhagavānaiṅ.
are piyā katahūñ n lāgaiṅ ab śikār n aṅtā hamare lāgi rahe.

I do not know my husband but he is my infinity.
Early in the morning, my husband went to bathe;
I drew water in a golden pot:
O my dear husband, take bath in the house.
The next hour, my husband prepared to eat;
I prepared and arranged food on a golden plate;
O my dear husband, eat food at home.
In the evening, my husband prepared to go hunting;
I prepared a bed and decorated it with flowers;
O my dear husband, sleep at home.
Tulsīdās says: "Worship the Lord."
O my dear husband, there is no game anywhere.
(LGT:31 & 32R: 1972-73, Dhanabad, Camār Women)

---

1. The singers were unable to explain the meaning of न अंता हमरे लागि रहे. I am reading this phrase as अनंता हमरे लागि रहे ("my husband [God] is my infinite").

६.

पिया गवना न लीन्हेंव हमार जवानी बरबाद भई ॥
सदा उमर नैहर मा बीती उजले पड़ि गये केश
पिया अपने का मुख ना देख्यों मोरे रामा कबहूँ न दीख्यों ससुरारि ॥
आप नहीं आवैं पत्र नहिं भेजैं हुवन से करैं ब्यवहार
सेज माज के गोरिया बैठी अरे रामा पचरंग पड़े हैं ओहार ॥
माया र्वावय बप्पा र्वावय र्वावय जग संसार
गलिन गलिन के आड़े र्वावय अरे रामा है कोई राखन हार ॥
तुलसीदास भजौ भगवानै अरे रामा हरि के चरन चित ध्यान ॥
पिया गवना न लीन्हेंव हमार जवानी बरबाद भई ॥

piyā gavanā n līnheṅv hamār javānī barabād bhaī.
sadā umar naihar mā bītī ujale paṛi gaye keś;
piyā apane kā mukh nā dekhyoṅ more rāmā kabahūñ n dīkhyoṅ sasurāri.
āp nahīṅ āvaiṅ patr nahiṅ bhejaiṅ huvan se karaiṅ byavahār
sej māj ke goriyā baiṭhī are rāmā pacaraṅg paṛe haiṅ ohār.
māyā rvāvay bappā rvāvay rvāvay jag saṅsār;
galin galin ke āṛe rvāvay are rāmā hai koī rākhan hār.
tulasīdās bhajau bhagavānai are rāmā hari ke caran cit dhyān.
piyā gavanā n līnheṅv hamār javānī barabād bhaī.

O dear husbad, you never came for *gavanā* and my whole youth wasted away.
I spent my entire life at my parents' home and my hair is white;
I never saw the face of my husband nor my in-law's place.
You do not come nor send any letter and maintain relationship from far.
All dressed and complete with makeup, the woman sat on a multicoloured spread.
My mother and father are crying; so is the whole world;
[All are crying] at the corners of lanes saying, is there anyone to care for us?
Tulsīdās says: "Recite the name of Rām and meditate on His feet."
(LGT: 33R: 1972-73, Dhanabad, Chamar, Women)

७.

आज सभा मा गणपति आये राखौ लाज हमारी ॥
वेद पुरान की पूजा प्रथमैं दुनिया करै तुम्हारी
गजनायक गजवदन विनायक गजमुख हैं भुज चारी ॥
चौदा विद्या के तुम मालिक संग शारधा माई
आउ सुरसती बैठु कण्ठ मा सब देउतन झनकारी ॥
हाथ चक्र तिरशूल बिराजै कुंडल कै छबि न्यारी
आठौ सिद्ध साथ मा लीन्हें मूसन करी सवारी ॥
गौरी के पूत महादेव के पायक पूजा करौं तुम्हारी
तुलसीदास भजौ भगवाने सबके दुख निवारी ॥

āj sabhā mā gaṇapati āye rākhau lāj hamārī.
ved purān kī pūjā prathamaiṅ duniyā karai tumhārī.
gajanāyak gajavadan vināyak gajamukh haiṅ bhuj cārī.
caudā vidyā ke tum mālik saṅg śāradhā māī.
āu surasatī baiṭhu kaṇṭh mā sab deutan jhanakārī.
hāth cakr tiraśūl birājai kuṇḍal kai chabi nyārī.
āṭhau siddh sāth mā līnheṅ mūsan karī savārī.
gaurī ke pūt mahādev ke pāyak pūjā karauṅ tumhārī.
tulsīdās bhajau bhagavāne sabake dukh nivārī.

God Gaṇeś has come to our meeting. Keep my honour.
The world worships you prior to worshipping Ved Purān.
You are Gajanāyak, Gajavadan, Vināyak and Gajamukh, having four arms.
You are the master of fourteen sciences and Goddess Śāradā accompanies you.
Çome, O Goddess Sarasvatī and reside on my throat so that I can sing to all the gods.
With discus and trident in your hands and earrings, you are adorable.
You possess all eight successes and ride on a mouse.
O, son of Goddess Gaurī and attendant of God Mahādev, I worship thee.
Tulsīdās says: "Recite the name of God; he will remove all our sorrows."
(LGT: 50R: 1972-73, Dhanabad, Dhobī Men)

८.

ए बम्हनी सुदामा तुमका भलि कै समुझावा ॥
जब ते ब्याह घरे तुम लायो साथ दलिद्दुर आवा
कपड़ा फाट वस्त्र दाँतन मा अन्न पेट भर ना खावा ॥
तावा फूट कठैली नाहीं कोरे बर्तन ना पावा
मलत मलत मोरे हाथ खियाने पनवरियन मा परसावा ॥
छपरा पुरान बिरनि भई बाती टपकै बूँद धरनिया मा
चारि महीना वर्षा के बीते बैठैं का ठौर नहीं पावा ॥
जब से आयों नगर अयोध्ये कंचन कै ढेरी पावा
तुलसीदास भजौ भगवाने प्रेम सहित दर्शन पावा ॥

e bamhanī sudāmā tumakā bhali kai samujhāvā.
jab te byāh ghare tum lāyo sāth daliddur āvā;
kapaṛā phāṭ vastr dāñtan mā ann peṭ bhar nā khāvā.
tāvā phūṭ kaṭhailī nāhīṅ kore bartan nā pāvā;
malat malat more hāth khiyāne, panavariyan mā parasāvā.
chaparā purān birani bhaī bātī ṭapakai būñd dharaniyā mā;
cāri mahīnā varṣā ke bīte baiṭhaiṅ kā ṭhaur nahīṅ pāvā.
jab se āyoṅ nagar ayodhye kaṅcan kai ḍherī pāvā;
tulsīdās bhajau bhagavāne prem sahit darśan pāvā.

O brāhmaṇ Sudāmā, how I have tried to make you understand.
From the moment your brought me to your home after marriage, poverty has followed;
My clothes are torn and I never have enough to eat.
The griddle is broken, there is no large wooden tub or any new utensils;
My hands are scraped from rubbing and we eat on leaf plates.
The thatched roof is old and leaking, the wick is damp, and the ground is wet.
In four months of rain, I didn't find any place to rest.
Upon visiting the city of Ayodhyā, I saw mounds of gold;
Tulsīdās says: "Recite the name of God, by whose grace I was blessed with divine sight."

(LGT: 52R: 1972-73, Dhanabad, Dhobī Men)

९

आज मैं हरि से अस्त्र गहइहौं ॥
मोहें शपथ गंगा जननी की सवतिन सुत न कहइहौं
महाभारत पारथ के ऊपर हरि के परन छुड़इहौं ॥
खण्डय खण्ड महारथ तोड़ौं कपि ध्वज सहित धहइहौं
महाभारत पारथ के ऊपर हरि के परन छुड़इहौं ॥
मोंहिं शपथ है रामचन्द्र की क्षत्री जल्म न पइहौं
सूरश्याम रण समर भूमि मा जियत न पीठ दिखइहौं ॥

Āj maiṅ Hari se astr gahaihauṅ;
moheṅ śapath gaṅgā jananī kī savatin sut n kahaihauṅ;
mahābhārat pārath ke ūpar hari ke paran chuṛaihauṅ.
khaṇḍay khaṇḍ mahārath toṛauṅ kapi dhvaj sahit dhahaihauṅ;
mahābhārat pārath ke ūpar hari ke paran chuṛaihauṅ.
moṅhiṅ śapath hai rāmacandr kī kṣtrī jalm n paihauṅ;
sūraśyām raṇ samar bhūmi mā jiyat n pīṭh dikhaihauṅ.

Today I will force Kṛṣṇa to bear arms.
I vow on my mother Gaṅgā and I will not be a son of King Śāntanu.
On the battlefield of the Mahābhārat, I will force Kṛṣṇa to break his vow.
Piece by piece I will break the great chariot and will ruin it along with its flag.
On the battlefield of the Mahābhārat, I will force Kṛṣṇa to break his vow.
I take an oath in the name of Rām that I may not be blessed with a warrior's birth in the next life;
Sūrdās says: "As long as I live, I will not turn my back on the battlefield"
(LGT: 53R, 1972-73, Dhanabad, Dhobī Men)

१०.

अब ख्रावति हैं राम गोद मा लीन्हें भाई ॥
रामचन्द्र लक्ष्मण का लइके गोदि मा लिये लगाई
तुम तो मरे हमहू मर जइबे सीता मरिहैं जहर बिष खाई ॥
कबहूँ खबर अजोध्ये जइहै सुनिहैं भारत भाई

जो सुनि पइहैं मात सुमित्रा खाई जहर हुवैं मर जाई ॥
जामवंत हनुमत से बोले अब कुछ करो उपाई
वैद सुखैन हवैं लंका मा उनका लियो मंगाई ॥
रामचन्द्र हनुमत से बोले लावौ वैद बुलाई
तुलसीदास भजौ भगवाने चले हैं हनुमत हरि का शीश नवाई ॥

ab rvāvati haiṅ rām god mā līnheṅ bhāī.
rāmacandr lakṣmaṇ kā laike godi mā liye lagāī;
tum to mare hamahū mar jaibe sītā marihaiṅ jahar biṣ khāī.
kabahūñ khabar ajodhye jaihai sunihaiṅ bhārat bhāī;
jo suni paihaiṅ māt sumitrā khāī jahar huvaṅ mar jāī
jāmavaṅt hanumat se bole ab kuch karo upāī;
vaid sukhain havaiṅ laṅka mā unakā liyo maṅgāī.
rāmacandr hanumat se bole lāvau vaid bulāī;
tulasīdās bhajau bhagavāne cale haiṅ hanumat hari kā śīś navāī.

Rām is crying as he holds his [mortally wounded] brother on his lap.
Rām took Lakṣmaṇ on his lap.
You are dying and I will die too and hearing this Sītā will die from eating poison.
Soon this news will reach Ayodhyā and brother Bharat will hear it;
Once your mother Sumitrā hears this news, she will also die from eating poison.
Jāmavant said to Hanumān: "Figure out some remedy."
Bring doctor Sukhain who lives in Laṅkā.
Rām instructed Hanumān to get the doctor;
Tulsīdās says: "Recite the name of God, Hanumān left after bowing to Rām."
(LGT: 54R: 1972-73, Dhanabad, Dhobī Men)

११.

अब लावौ संजीवन अंजनी के हनुमाना ॥
सीता के हरन मरन दशरथ के लछिमन लागे बाना
इतना संकट काटौ पवनसुत राखि लियो तीनों के प्राना ॥
लछिमन मरे हमहू मरि जइबे सिय सुनि तजिहैं प्राना

इतना संकट काटौ पवनसुत राखि लियो तीनों के प्राना ॥
यतना बचन जब सुनै पवनसुत तनिकौ न करैं गुमाना
मूरि संजीवन हम लै अइबै उवइ न पइहैं भामा ॥
हनुमत लाये मूरि संजीवन रघुबर घोटि पियाना
तुलसीदास भजौ भगवाने लछिमन भेंटि रहे भगवाना ॥

ab lāvau sañjīvan Añjanī ke hanumānā.
sītā ke haran maran daśarath ke lachiman lāge bānā;
itanā saṅkaṭ kāṭau pavanasut rākhi liyo tīnoṅ ke prānā.
lachiman mare hamahū mari jaibe siy suni tajihaiṅ prānā;
itanā saṅkaṭ kāṭau pavanasut rākhi liyo tīnoṅ ke prānā.
yatanā bacan jab sunai pavanasut tanikau n karaiṅ gumānā;
mūri sañjīvan ham lai aibai uvai n paihaiṅ bhāmā.
hanumat lāye mūri sañjīvan raghubar ghoṭi piyānā;
tulasīdās bhajau bhagavāne lachiman bheṅṭi rahe bhagavānā.

O, Añjanī's son, Hanumān, go and bring the *sañjīvanī* plant.
Sītā is abducted, Daśarath is dead, and Lakṣmaṇ is unconscious from the arrow's blow;
O, Pavan's son, help me in my distress and save the lives of us three.
If Lakṣmaṇ dies, I too will die, and Sītā will die as soon as she hears the news;
O, Pavan's son, help me in my distress and save the lives of us three.
Hearing these words, Hanumān did not feel proud;
He said: "I will bring the *sañjivanī* plant before sunrise."
Hanumān brought the *sañjīvanī* plant and Rām applied it to Lakṣmaṇ's wound;
Tulsīdās says: "Recite the name of God, Lakṣmaṇ is embracing Rām."
(LGT: 55R: 1972-73, Dhanabad, Dhobī Men)

१२.

मैया मोरि मैं नाहीं दधि खायो ॥
होत भोर भिनही के पहरे मधुबन मोंहि पठाई
चारि पहर वंशीवन भटक्यों साँझ भये घर आई ॥

मैं तो ढोटा पायन का छोटा सिकहर कै बिधि पाई
ब्रज की सखी सब बैर किये हैं मोरे मुँह मा दही लगाई ॥
हमरे मन मा ऐसी आवै की कतहूँ चल जाई
दै देव माता लकुटि कमरिया कितनेव नाच नचाई ॥
बिहँसत बदन निकरि आई दतियाँ सूरदास जस गाई
सूरश्याम बलि जाऊँ चरनि की जसुमति अंग लगाई ॥

maiyā mori maiṅ nāhīṅ dadhi khāyo.
hot bhor bhinahī ke pahare madhuban moṅhi paṭhāī;
cāri pahar vaṅśīvan bhaṭakyoṅ sāñjh bhaye ghar āī.
maiṅ to ḍhoṭā pāyan kā choṭā sikahar kai bidhi pāī;
braj kī sakhī sab bair kiye haiṅ more muṅh mā dahī lagāī.
hamare man mā aisī āvai kī katahūñ cal jāī;
dai dev mātā lakuṭi kamariyā kitanev nāc nacāī.
bihañsat badan nikari āī datiyāñ sūradās jas gāī;
sūraśyām bali jāūñ carani kī jasumati aṅg lagāī.

O my dear mother, I did not eat yoghurt.
At day break you send me to the forest;
For a whole day I roam the forest and return home in the evening.
I am a child with small feet, how could I reach the hanging net;
All my friends in Braj are envious of me and have pasted yoghurt in my mouth.
I am thinking that I should go away somewhere;
O mother, give me my black blanket, I have suffered a lot.
Hearing this, mother laughed and poet Sūrdās sang this incident;
Sūrdās sacrifices himself at His lotus feet; Jasoda hugged child Kṛṣṇa.
(LGT: 57R: 1972-73, Dhanabad, Dhobī Men)

१३.

मैया मोरी चन्द्र खिलौना लेहौं ॥
सौ जोजन मा बसै चन्द्रमा ताको कौने बिधि पइहौं
मचलि लाल पलना मा र्‌वावैं कौने जतन समझइहौं ॥
भुइँ मा गिरौं धूरि मा ल्वाटौं तुम्हरी गोद न अइहौं

ढोटा होइहौं नन्द बबा का तुम्हरा सुत न कहइहौं
आओ लाल बलैया लेहौं बलदेवै न बतइहौं
अति कुमार याहू ते निरमल निरमल दुलहिन लइहौं ॥
मैया री मैं दूल्हा बनिहौं अबहीं ब्याहन जइहौं
सूरश्याम रण समर बराती आनन्द मंगल गइहौं ॥

maiyā morī candr khilaunā lehauṅ.
sau jojan mā basai candramā tāko kaune bidhi paihauṅ;
macali lāl palanā mā rvāvaiṅ kaune jatan samajhaihauṅ.
bhuiñ mā girauṅ dhūri mā lvāṭauṅ tumharī god n aihauṅ.
ḍhoṭā hoihauṅ nand babā kā tumharā sut n kahaihauṅ.
āo lāl balaiyā lehauṅ baldevai n bataihauṅ;
ati kumār yāhū te niramal niramal dulahin laihauṅ.
maiyā rī maiṅ dūlhā banihauṅ abahīṅ byāhan jaihauṅ;
sūraśyām raṇ samar barātī ānand maṅgal gaihauñ.

O my mother, I want the moon as a toy.
How am I going to get the moon for you as it is miles away?
Stubbornly, my child is crying in his crib and how can I reason with him?
"I will fall on the ground and welter in dirt and will not come to your lap;"
"I will become the son of father Nand and will not call myself your son."
"Come dear child, I sacrifice to you, and will not tell Baldev;"
"I will get a delicate wife, better than his, for you."
O mother, I want to become a groom and be wed right away.
Sūrdās says, "in the company of the groom's party, I will sing auspicious songs."

(LGT: 57AR: 1972-73, Dhanabad, Dhobī Men)

१४.

उमर तोरी धोखे मा बीति गयो ॥
दस बरस तक बालापन है बिसवें मा जोर कियो
तीस बरस में चढ़ी जवानी घर घर झगरा कियो ॥
चालीस में निख्खालिस होबा नयनों से ज्योति घटो
पूरे पचास आई सफेदी दिन दिन तनवा बुढ़ी ॥

साठ बरस में काठा के तन होइ हाड़ से माँस फुटो
घर के परानी याही मनावैं बुढ़ऊ मरि न गयो ॥
सत्तर में निखत्तर भइला रामा का नाम न लियो ॥
अस्सी में तन खस्सी का होइहैं पानी न कोई दियो ॥
नब्बे में जब नाश भये हो बिरथा जनम कियो
कहत कबीर सुनो भाई साधो एकहु ओर के न भयो ॥

umar torī dhokhe mā bīti gayo.
das baras tak bālāpan hai bisaveṅ mā jor kiyo;
tīs baras meṅ caṛhī javānī ghar ghar jhagarā kiyo.
cālīs meṅ nikhkhālis hobā nayanoṅ se jyoti ghaṭo.
pūre pacās āī saphedī din din tanavā buṛhī;
sāṭh baras meṅ kāṭhā ke tan hoi hāṛ se māñs phuṭo.
ghar ke parānī yāhī manāvaiṅ buṛhaū mari n gayo.
sattar meṅ nikhattar bhailā rāmā kā nām n liyo;
assī meṅ tan khassī kā hoihaiṅ pānī n koī diyo.
nabbe meṅ jab nāś bhaye ho birathā janam kiyo;
kahat kabīr suno bhāī sādho ekahu or ke n bhayo.

Your life passed in delusion.
Ten years passed in childhood and around the age of twenty, life was in full bloom.
At thirty, with full youth, you quarrelled from house to house.
At forty, your teeth began to fall out and your eyesight became dull.
At fifty, all your hair was white and day by day your body began to grow old.
At sixty, the body became stiff and meat began to detach from its bones.
All the people in the family wish that this old man will die soon.
At seventy, you have become completely wasted and haven't recited the name of Rām.
At eighty, your body became impotent and nobody gave you even water.
Now at ninety, when you have wasted all your life;
Kabīr says, "Listen brother, good souls, you belong no where."

(LGT: 92AR: 1972-73, Varanasi, Street Blind Musician)

१५

बजाय हरि बीना कौने बन श्यामा ॥
अन्न बिना ये लोग दुखित हैं जल बिन तड़पै मीना
पती बिना पतिबरता दुखित भइलीं, दिन दिन रहति मलीना ॥
गंगा नहाई सूरज सर डारी बहुति अरजि हम कीन्हा
हे बिधना तोरा का मैं बिगारूँ, छोटा पुरुष लिखि दीन्हा ॥
लाल पलँग पर लाल बिछौना चादर तानै झीना
धीरे से पाँव धरौ पलँगे पर, सूतलि नार नगीना ॥
दुख हरन गुरु कै समुझावै शिव नरायन चीन्हा
धन बिधिना धन बेद तिहारो गावत राम नगीना ॥

bajāy hari bīnā kaune ban śyāmā.
ann binā ye log dukhit haiṅ jal bin taṛapai mīnā;
patī binā patibaratā dukhit bhailīṅ, din din rahati malīnā.
gaṅgā nahāī sūraj sar ḍārī bahuti araji ham kīnhā;
he bidhanā torā kā maiṅ bigāruñ, choṭā puruṣ likhi dīnhā.
lāl palañg par lāl bichaunā cādar tānai jhīnā;
dhīre se pāñv dharau palañge par, sūtali nār nagīnā.
duhkh haran guru kai samujhāvai śiv narāyan cīnhā.
dhan bidhinā dhan bed tihāro gāvat rām nagīnā.

In which forest is Kṛṣṇa playing the flute?
People are sad without food and fish are fluttering without water;
Without her husband the faithful wife is suffering and heart-broken.
After bathing in the Ganges, I worshipped the sun and prayed;
But, O fate, what wrong have I done that I have a mediocre man in my life?
There is a red bed with red linen and a thin sheet;
Be careful while getting on the bed, because the beautiful woman is sleeping.
For all this sorrow, there is only one remedy, the Guru;
Rām Nagīnā sings: "O God, your ways and means are beyond understanding."

(LGT: 157R: 1972-73, Varanasi, Blind Street Musician)

१६.

दौड़ो दौड़ो कृष्ण मुरारी पति राखो न हमारी ॥
अर्जुन भीम नकुल सहदेवा, सभवा मा बैठे मनवा मारी हो पति राखो न हमारी ॥
दुष्ट दुशासन चीर खिंचत है, जुरयोधन ललकारी हो पति राखो न हमारी ॥
कवन कसूर हमें सभा में बुलवला, लूटल जात इज्जत हमारन हो पति राखो न हमारी ॥

dauṛo dauṛo kṛṣṇa murārī pati rākho n hamārī.
arjun bhīm nakul sahadevā, sabhavā mā baiṭhe manavā mārī ho pati rākho n hamārī.
duṣṭ duśāsan cīr khiṅcat hai, jurayodhan lalakārī ho pati rākho n hamārī.
kavan kasūr hameṅ sabhā meṅ bulavalā, lūṭal jāt ijjat hamāran ho pati rākho n hamārī.

Run, O Kṛṣṇa, and save my honour.
Broken hearted, Arjun, Bhīm, Nakul and Sahadev sat at the assembly.
Wicked Duḥśāsan is pulling my sārī and Duryodhan is encouraging him.
By what failing was I called to the assembly? My honour is being robbed.
(LGT: 159R: 1972-73, Varanasi, Mixed Men)

१७.

ठाढ़े जमुनवा के तीर राजा मिरगवा मारैं ॥
राम लखन दूनो भइया, ऊहो चलनि बनवास राजा मिरगवा मारैं ॥
चाँद सुरज दूनो बहिना, ऊहो उगैंला आकाश राजा मिरगवा मारैं ॥
गंगा जमुना दूनो बहिना, ऊहो बहेली पताल राजा मिरगवा मारैं ॥

ṭhāṛhe jamunavā ke tīr rājā miragavā māraiṅ
rām lakhan dūno bhaiyā, ūho calani banavās rājā miragavā māraiṅ.
cāñd suraj dūno bahinā, ūho ugaiṅlā ākāś rājā miragavā māraiṅ.
gaṅgā jamunā dūno bahinā, ūho bahelī patāl rājā miragavā māraiṅ.

On the bank of the Jamunā, King is hunting deer.
Rām and Lakṣmaṇ are two brothers and they proceeded towards the forest.

Moon and Sun are two sisters, they grow in the sky.
Gaṅgā and Jamunā are two sisters, they flow in the underworld.
(LGT: 160R: 1972-73, Varanasi, Mixed Men)

१८

अभै दुवारे हँसत खेलत थे रमि रहे जोगिया किनारे
मात कौशिला ढूँढन निकसीं अन्त खोज ना पैया, बन की रहियै रहियै न
बन का डगर चले दोउ भैया बन की रहियै रहियै न ॥
आगू आगू राम चलत हैं पीछे लछमन भैया
बीच जानकी अति बल सोहैं चित्रकोट ला जइया ॥
राम बिना मोरी सूनी अजोध्या लछमन बिन ठकुरैया
सीता बिन मोरी सूनी रसोंइयाँ को परसै को खइया ॥
सावन गरजै भादौं बरसै पवन चलै पुरवैया
कौन बिरछ तरे भीजत होइहैं राम लखन दोउ भैया ॥
भीतर रोवय मात कौशिला बाहर भारत भैया
तुलसीदास भजौ भगवाने लंका की राज भभीसन पैया ॥

abhai duvāre hañsat khelat the rami rahe jogiyā kināre.
māt kauśilā ḍhūñḍhan nikasīṅ ant khoj nā paiyā, ban kī rahiyai rahiyai n.
ban kā ḍagar cale dou bhaiyā ban kī rahiyai rahiyai n.
āgū āgū rām calat haiṅ pīche lachaman bhaiyā;
bīc jānakī ati bal sohaiṅ citrakoṭ lā jaiyā.
rām binā morī sūnī ajodhyā lachaman bin ṭhakuraiyā;
sītā bin morī sūnī rasoṅiyāñ ko parasai ko khaiyā.
sāvan garajai bhādauṅ barasai pavan calai puravaiyā;
kaun birach tare bhījat hoihaiṅ rām lakhan dou bhaiyā.
bhītar rovay māt kauśilā bāhar bhārat bhaiyā;
tulsīdās bhajau bagavāne laṅkā kī rāj Bhabhīsan paiyā.

Just a while ago, they were playing outside, but now they have taken the path of ascetics.
Mother Kauśalyā came out to search for them, but couldn't find them.
Both brothers have gone to the forest following the long forest paths.
Rām leads the way and Lakṣmaṇ is behind;

In the middle, Sītā looks beautiful; thus they proceed towards Citrakūṭ.
Without Rām my Ayodhyā is desolate, without Lakṣmaṇ there is no lordliness;
Without Sītā, my kitchen is empty. Who is there to serve and who will eat?
In the month of Sāvan and Bhādauṅ, clouds thunder and rain and the easterly wind blows hard;
Perhaps both brothers, Rām and Lakṣmaṇ, are soaking wet under a tree.
Inside mother Kauśalyā is crying, outside brother Bharat;
Tulsīdās says: "Recite the name of God, Vibhīṣan became the king of Laṅkā."

(LGT 92R: 1972-73, Tahirapur, Camār Men)

भजन (अचरी)

१९.

असिया कोस मइया तेरी फुलबगिया, कौन रखावन रे जाय मा
जैहै तो जैहै मइया भइया लँगुरवा, जाके हाथे गुलेल मा
काहे की मइया गुला रे गुफनिया, काहे की फटकार हो मा
रूपे की मइया गुला रे गुफनिया, रेशम की फटकार हो मा
पहली गुलिनिया मारी बीरा लँगुरा, लागी आम की री डार मा
दूजी गुलिनिया मारी बीरा लँगुरा, कोहिल मार गिराई हो मा
कोयल मार हाथ में लै लई, जाय भुवनन दरवार हो मा
हँस हँस पूँछे मैया देवी शारदा, कोयल काहे मारी हो मा
सुआ हरामी को काहे न मार दओ, काटे है लोटन रे आम मा
जो हम जानै तोय मैया के लँगुरवा, कोयल देवौ जियाय मा
लेत भभूत देत पैकरमा, कोयल दई है जिआय मा
देवी के भुवन में दै पैकरमा, अटल छत्र जै रे बोल मा

asiyā kos maiyā terī phulabagiyā, kaun rakhāvan re jāy mā.
jaihai to jaihai maiyā bhaiyā lañguravā, jāke hāthe gulel mā.
kāhe kī maiyā gulā re guphaniyā, kāhe kī phaṭakār ho mā.
rūpe kī maiyā gulā re guphaniyā, reśam kī phaṭakār ho mā.
pahalī guliniyā mārī bīrā lañgurā, lāgī ām kī rī ḍār mā.

dūjī guliniyā mārī bīrā lañgurā, kohil mār girāī ho mā.
koyal mār hāth meṅ lai laī, jāy bhuvanan daravār ho mā.
hañs hañs pūñchai maiyā devī śāradā, koyal kāhe mārī ho mā.
suā harāmī ko kāhe n mār dao, kāṭe hai loṭan re ām mā.
jo ham jānai toy maiyā ke lañguravā, koyal devau jiyāy mā.
let bhabhūt det paikaramā, koyal daī hai jiāy mā
devī ke bhuvan meṅ dai paikaramā, aṭal chatr jai re bol mā.

O Mother your garden is eighty *kos*. Who will keep watch?
If there is anyone who will, it will be Mother's lañgur. He keeps a pellet bow in his hand.
Of what are pellet balls made and what is a pellet bow made of?
The pellet balls are made of silver and the pellet bow is made of silk.
The first pellet ball thrown by the *lañgur* struck a mango branch.
The second pellet ball thrown by the *lañgur* killed a cuckoo.
The *lañgur* carried the dead cuckoo to his mother's sanctuary.
Laughingly, Mother Śāradā asked: "Why did you kill the cuckoo?"
Why didn't you kill the wicked parrot that is biting all the mangoes?
"I will know that I am truly your *lañgur* only if you bring the cuckoo back to life."
As he applied ashes and circumambulated the sanctum, the cuckoo came back to life.
Uttering, "Victory to Mother's permanent protection," he circumambulated once more out of gratitude.

(LGT: 31R: 1976, Sandalpur, Mix~d Men)

२०.

बम्हन का लड़का पोथी बाँचे पूजे ठाकुर द्वार का
क्षत्री का लड़का रण में जूझे काम करे तलवार का
कायश्थ का लड़का कलम चलावै सूबे थानेदार का
धोबी धानुक करे सफाई नौवा बार बनाइ का
मनवा काहे ना भजौ श्री भगवान का ॥
बढ़ई का लड़का पलँग बनावै कारीगर कुम्हार का
लोहार का लड़का जड़ै कढ़इया भुजवा झोंकै भार का

माली का लड़का मलवा गूँधै सीधा काम चमार का
भँगी धानुक सड़क बटोरे काम करे सरकार का॥
काछी कुरमी करे किसानी कुँजड़ा है तकरार का
दर्जी का लड़का जामा सींवै बरई कतरै पान का
सुनार का लड़का पँहुची गूँधै जोड़ा बिके मनिहार का॥
अहीर गड़रिया लोद बौरिया मीजा मिलाया चारों का
मैला लड़का है तेली का साफ लड़का कहार का
दर्जी का लड़का जामा सींवै बरई कतरै पान का
लगा के लासा मैनें फाँसा ख्याल ये खासा चिड़ीमार का॥

bamhan kā laṛakā pothī bāñce pūje ṭhākur dvār kā;
kṣtrī kā laṛākā raṇ meṅ jhūjhe kām kare talavār kā;
kāyaśth kā laṛakā kalam calāvai sūbe thānedār kā;
dhobī dhānuk kare saphāī nauvā bār banāi kā;
manavā kāhe nā bhajau śrī bhagavān kā?
baṛhaī kā laṛakā palañg banāvai kārīgar kumhār kā;
lohār kā laṛakā jaṛai kaṛhaiyā bhujavā jhoṅkai bhār kā;
mālī kā laṛakā malavā gūñdhai sīdhā kām camār kā;
bhañgī dhānuk saṛak baṭore kām kare sarakār kā;
kāchī kuramī kare kisānī kuñjaṛā hai takarār kā;
darjī kā laṛakā jāmā sīṅvai baraī katarai pān kā;
sunār kā laṛakā pañhucī gūñdhai joṛā bike manihār kā;
ahīr gaṛariyā lod bauriyā mījā milāyā cāroṅ kā;
mailā laṛakā hai telī kā, sāph laṛakā kahār kā;
darjī kā laṛakā jāmā sīṅvai baraī katarai pān kā;
lagā ke lāsā maineṅ phāñsā khyāl ye khāsā ciṛīmār kā.

The priest's son recites religious texts and worships in the temple;
The warrior's son holds the sword and fights in battles;
The businessman's son writes and works in the office.
The washerman *dhanuk* does the cleaning, the barber trims the hair;
O, my mind, why don't you just sing the name of God?
The carpenter's son makes bed, and potter's son does pottery;
The blacksmith's son makes iron tools and parcher's son parches grains;

The gardener's son makes garlands and leather worker's job is to work with leather.
Bhaṅgī and *dhanuk* clean the roads and toilets and work for the government;
Kāchī, Kuramī do the farming, Kuñjara are quarrelsome.
The tailor's son sews the garments, the Barai clips the betel leaves.
The goldsmith's son makes ornaments, the bangleseller makes and sells bangles.
The milkman, Gaṛariya, Lod, and Bauriyās' work is interrelated;
The oil presser's son is dirty and the potter's son is clean;
The tailor's son sews the garments, the Baraī clips the betel leaves;
The bird catcher always thinks to catch birds with bird-lime.[2]
(LGT: 114R: 1972-73, Ganj Muradabad, Dhobī Men)

२१.

दया करु माई दया करु माई, तू जग जननी दया करु माई॥
आठ मास नौ गरभ बास में, सुरसरि दुधवा पिलाई॥
तुलसीदास प्रभु आस चरण की, प्रभु जी से रहो चित लाई॥

dayā karu māī dayā karu māī, tū jag jananī dayā karu māī.
āṭh mās nau garabh bās meṅ, surasari dudhavā pilāī.
tulasīdās prabhu ās caraṇ kī, prabhu jī se raho cit lāī.

O mother of the universe, bestow the kindness on us.
We lived in your womb for eight to nine months and later you fed us milk.
Tulsīdās says, "I hope for your blessed feet; devote yourself to god."
(LGT: 160AR: 1972-73, Varāṇasī, Mixed Men)

2. This song refers to different castes and sub-castes that have traditionally performed specific services for the community; some of the sub-castes are also traditionally associated with performing certain tasks and providing music at ceremonial/festive occasions.

भजन (देवी गीत)

२२.

कला तेरी काहू से बरनी ना जाय ॥
नारायण के मुख से निकली, ज्वालामुखी तेरो नाम ॥
गढ़ पर्वत एक नदिया बहति है, मानों गंगा हहराई ॥
पाँच पाण्डवन होम रचो है, अर्जुन छत्र तनाय ॥
पाँच सुपारी मैया ध्वजा नारियल, या लेव भेंट हमारी ॥
दीपक बारि धरौ मठ भीतर, ज्योत चहूँ जग जाई ॥
जो जो ध्यावे मैया सो फल पावै, बेमुख कोऊ न जाय ॥

kalā terī kāhū se baranī nā jāy.
nārāyaṇ ke mukh se nikalī, jvālāmukhī tero nām.
gaṛh parvat ek nadiyā bahati hai, mānoṅ gaṅgā haharāī.
pāñc pāṇḍavan hom raco hai arjun chatr tanāy.
pāñc supārī maiyā dhvajā nāriyal, yā lev bheṅṭ hamārī.
dīpak bāri dharau maṭh bhītar, jyot cahūñ jag jāī.
jo jo dhyāvai maiyā so phal pāvai bemukh koū n jāy.

No one can describe your attributes.
You came out of Viṣṇu's mouth and are named Jvālāmukhī.
Amidst mountains a river flows; it seems like Ganges in full force.
The five Pāṇḍavas have arranged a fire sacrifice and Arjun is hanging a tent.
O Mother accept my gifts of five betelnuts, a flag and a coconut.
Light a lamp in the inner sanctum so that the light can reach the four corners of the universe.
Whoever worships you receives your blessings; no one becomes disheartened.

(CYT: 240C: 1975, Sheoli, Brāhmaṇ Woman)

२३.

माग्यों वरदान देवी के शिवाले भीतर ॥
माग्यों मैं पाँच बिरनवाँ, बहिनी अकेल ॥

माग्यों मैं पाँच दिवरवा, ननदी अकेल ॥
माग्यों मैं पाँच बलकवा, कन्या अकेल ॥
माग्यों मैं हरी पीरी चुड़ियाँ, मोतियन भरी माँग ॥

māgyoṅ varadān Devī ke śivāle bhītar.
māgyoṅ maiṅ pāñc biranavāñ, bahinī akel.
māgyoṅ maiṅ pāñc divaravā, nanadī akel.
māgyoṅ maiṅ pāñc balakavā, kanyā akel.
māgyoṅ maiṅ harī pīrī cuṛiyāñ, motiyan bharī māñg.

In the inner sanctum of the temple of Mother Goddess, I pleaded for blessings.
I begged for five brothers but only one sister.
I begged for five *devar* but only one *nanad*.
I begged for five sons but only one daughter.
I begged for gold and yellow bangles and part of my hair filled with pearls.
(CYT: 242C: 1975, Sheoli, Brāhmaṇ Woman)

२४.

कैसे के दर्शन पाऊँ मैया तेरा सँकरा दुवरवा ॥
मैया के दुवारे एक अँधा पुकारे, दीहो नयन घर जाई ॥
मैया के दुवारे एक कोढ़ी पुकारे, दीहो कया घर जाई ॥
मैया के दुवारे एक निर्धन पुकारे, दीहो मया घर जाई ॥
मैया के दुवारे एक लँगड़ा पुकारे, दीहो पयर घर जाई ॥
मैया के दुवारे एक भूखा पुकारे, दीहो दया घर जाई ॥
मैया के दुवारे एक कन्या पुकारे, दीहो वर घर जाई ॥

kaise ke darśan pāūñ maiyā terā sañkarā duvaravā.
maiyā ke duvāre ek añdhā pukāre, dīho nayan ghar jāī.
maiyā ke duvāre ek koṛhī pukāre, dīho kayā ghar jāī.
maiyā ke duvāre ek nirdhan pukāre, dīho mayā ghar jāī.
maiyā ke duvāre ek lañgaṛā pukāre, dīho payar ghar jāī.
maiyā ke duvāre ek bhūkhā pukāre, dīho dayā ghar jāī.
maiyā ke duvāre ek kanyā pukāre, dīho var ghar jāī.

How could I see you, O Mother? Your doorway is narrow.
A blind person is calling at the Mother's doorway: "Grant me eyes, so that I may go home."
A leper is calling at the Mother's doorway: "Grant me good body, so that I may go home."
A pauper is calling at the Mother's doorway: "Grant me wealth, so that I may go home."
A lame person is calling at the Mother's doorway: "Grant me legs, so that I may go home."
A hungry person is calling at the Mother's doorway: "Grant me food, so that I may go home."
A maiden is calling at the Mother's doorway: "Grant me a groom, so that I may go home."

(LGT: 9/118R: 1972-73, Dhanabad, Brāhmaṇ Women)

२५.

दर्शन देउ माइ मोर मन लागा दरश कइहाँ ॥
अरि ए सहेली कहाँ तुम्हारा जल्म हुआ, कहना अवतार ॥
अरि ए सहेली नीमशार मेरा जल्म हुआ, पाटन अवतार ॥
अरि ए सहेली कहाँ तुम्हारी बैठक है, कहना सुख सेज ॥
अरि ए सहेली नीम तरे मेरा बैठक है, मन्दिर सुख सेज ॥
अरि ए सहेली जो ध्यावै फल पावेगा बेमुख ना जाय ॥

darśan deu māi mor man lāgā daraś kaihāñ.
ari e sahelī kahāñ tumhārā jalm huā kahanā avatār.
ari e sahelī nīmaśār merā jalm huā pāṭan avatār.
ari e sahelī kahāñ tumhārī baiṭhak hai, kahanā sukh sej.
ari e sahelī nīm tare merā baiṭhak hai, mandir sukh sej.
ari e sahelī jo dhyāvai phal pāvegā, bemukh nā jāy.

O Mother show your sight, my mind is set on seeing you.
O girl-friend tell us where were you born and what's the story of your incarnation.
O girl-friend, I was born at Nirmaśār, the city of my incarnation.

O girl-friend tell us where you live and where you sleep.
O girl-friend my sitting place is under neem trees and I sleep in my temples.
O girl-friend, whoever meditates on me receives fruit; no one goes away empty handed.

(LGT: 10R: 1972-73, Dhanabad Brāhmaṇ Women)

२६.

देवी दयाल भई भई मेरी मैया॥
देवी की माँग में सेंदुर सोहै, हो गई दयाल भरी मेरी मंगिया॥
देवी के हाथ में चूड़ी सोहै, हो गई दयाल भरी मेरी बहियाँ॥
देवी के हाथ में लल्ला सोहै, हो गई दयाल भरी मेरी गोदी॥

devī dayāl bhaīṅ bhaīṅ merī maiyā.
devī kī māñg meṅ seṅdur sohai, ho gaī dayāl bharī merī maṅgiyā.
devī ke hāth meṅ cūṛī sohai, ho gaī dayāl bharī merī bahiyāñ.
devī ke hāth meṅ lallā sohai, ho gaī dayāl bharī merī godī.

O my mother goddess is kind to us.
The *sindūr* on goddess's part is beautiful; similarly the goddess filled my part too.
There are bangles on goddess's hand; similarly she filled my hands with bangles too.
A baby boy looks beautiful in goddess's lap; similarly she also blessed my lap.

(LGT: 11R: 1972-73, Brāhmaṇ Women)

२७.

अँगना मा आईं महरानी लपटि के पैंया लागौं॥
चन्दन चौकी आसन दीन्हों, देवा के चरन पखारे, अम्बे के चरन पखारे॥
बीरा बतासा फूलों का गजरा, देवा के गले पहिनाये, अम्बे के गले पहिनाये॥
काहे के कारन बीरा बतासा, काहे के कारन हार॥
पूता के कारन बीरा बतासा, दूधा के कारन हार॥
दूध तो दियो मैया भरि के दुधाड़ी, पूता दियो भरि गोद॥

दुध जो आवै मैया अलकत झलकत, खेलति आवैं नन्दलाल ॥
जो जो ध्यावै अम्बे सो फल पावै, बेमुख कोई न जाय ॥

añganā mā āīṅ maharānī lapaṭi ke paiṅyā lāgauṅ.
candan caukī āsan dīnhoṅ, devā ke caran pakhāre, ambe ke caran pakhāre.
bīrā batāsā phūloṅ kā gajarā, devā ke gale pahināye, ambe ke gale pahināye.
kāhe ke kāran bīrā batāsā, kāhe ke kāran hār.
pūtā ke kāran bīrā batāsā, dūdhā ke kāran hār.
dūdh to diyo maiyā bhari ke dudhāṛī, pūtā diyo bhari god.
dūdh jo āvai maiyā alakat jhalakat khelati āvaiṅ nandalāl.
jo jo dhyāvai ambe so phal pāvai bemukh koī n jāy.

The goddess has come to our courtyard; throw yourself at her feet.
We gave a sandalwood stool for her to sit on and washed her feet.
We offer her betel leaves, sweets, and a garland of flowers; the garland of flowers we put around her neck.
Why did you offer betel leaves, sweets and a garland?
I offered betel leaves and sweets to beget a son and a garland to have plenty of milk.
O mother, give us a milkpot filled with milk and a son to fill my lap.
The milk is overflowing and a son is coming playfully.
Whoever worships you Mother Ambe, receives fruit; no one goes away empty handed.

(LGT: 58R: 1972-73, Ganj Muradabad, Mixed Women)

२८.

आनन्दी बन बोलि रहे बन मोर ॥
ठाढ़ी मोरिनिया अरज करति है, बच्चा भये चकचूर ॥
की तोरे मोरिनि अनुधन थोरो की तेरे हरि परदेश ॥
न मेरे शीतला अनुधन थोरो, न मेरे हरि परदेश ॥
राजा नल की फौजें निकरीं, बच्चा भये चकचूर ॥
बच्चा होते तो लइ उड़ि जातिंव, अण्डा भये चकचूर ॥
मठ के बाहर निकरी मोरिनिया, बच्चा करत किलोल ॥
जैसे देवा मोरी हमहीं निवारेव, वैसे निवारौ सब कोय ॥

ānandī ban boli rahe ban mor.
ṭhāṛhī moriniyā araj karati hai, baccā bhaye cakacūr.
kī tore morini anudhan thoro kī tere hari parades.
n mere śītalā anudhan thoro, n mere hari parades.
rājā nal kī phaujaiṅ nikarīṅ, baccā bhaye cakacūr.
baccā hote to lai uṛi jātiṅv, aṇḍā bhaye cakacūr.
maṭh ke bāhar nikarī moriniyā baccā karat kilol.
jaise devā morī hamahīṅ nivārev vaise nivārau sab koy.

Peacocks are crowing in the forest at the temple of Ānandī.
Standing, the peahen is praying that all my eggs are broken.
"Do you, peahen, have little money or is your husband abroad?"
O Śītalā, I am not short of money nor is my husband abroad.
King Nal's army was marching and they broke all my eggs.
If I had chicks I would have flown away with them but the eggs broke.
As peahen came out of the shrine, she found her chicks clicking.
O goddess, help everyone as you have protected me.

(LGT: 59R: 1972-73, Ganj Muradabad, Mixed Women)

भजन (निर्गुण)

२९.

इस काया पर गुमान मत करिये यह तन बिल्कुल मट्टी है
इसका भरोसा कभी न करना यह धोखे की टट्टी है ॥
बोला बोला जब तक बोला ना बोला हो गया खतम
दम इस तन से निकल गया और जाके पहुँचा मुल्के अदम
जीते दम पर सभी कोई है भाई बन्धु और लोक कुटुम्ब
चलने वाला चला गया एक खाली ठाठ रह गया सनम
सबने मिलकर जला दिया यो मानो काँच की भट्टी है ॥
दौलत दुनियाँ और माल खजाना कोई काम न आवेगा
जिसके दम पर फूल रहा है पड़ा वो भी रह जावेगा
दो दिन वास्ते हाथ लगा उठ गया तो फिर पछतावेगा

ए हाथों से करेंगे सौदा वो हाथों से पावेगा
भगवान भजन के सौदे पर नफा छोड़ ना घट्टी है॥
जिसको कहते अपना अपना बना वही तेरा दुश्मन
एक लँगोटी पहना करके घर से निकालेंगे फौरन
होते नहीं किसी के जग में जीते दम पे सभी भरम
माया मोह में पड़ करके बरबाद कर दिया अपना धन
अभी सचेतो भजन करो क्यों बाँधे आँख में पट्टी है॥
याद करोगे उस दिन को जब लेने फरिश्ते आँवेंगे
धन और दौलत नहीं छुवेंगे फकत तुझे ले जावेंगे
जैसी करनी करेंगे बन्दे वैसी दफा लगावेंगे
भूल जाय बस्ती का रहना जँगल मकाँ बँधावेंगे
अभी से चेत ले बन्दे मरना है काल के फन्दे
बोले कबीर मिल सतगुरु जहाँ लगी ज्ञान की सट्टी है॥

is kāyā par gumān mat kariye yah tan bilkul maṭṭī hai.
isakā bharosā kabhī n karanā yah dhokhe kī ṭaṭṭī hai.
bolā bolā jab tak bolā nā bolā ho gayā khatam.
dam is tan se nikal gayā aur jāke pahuñcā mulke adam.
jīte dam par sabhī koī hai bhāī bandhu aur lok kuṭumb.
calane vālā calā gayā ek khālī ṭhāṭh rah gayā sanam.
sabane milakar jalā diyā yo māno kāñc kī bhaṭṭī hai.
daulat duniyāñ aur māl khajānā koī kām n āvegā.
jisake dam par phūl rahā hai paṛā vo bhī rah jāvegā.
do din vāste hāth lagā uṭh gayā to phir pachatāvegā.
e hāthoṅ se kareṅge saudā vo hāthoṅ se pāvegā.
bhagavān bhajan ke saude par naphā choḍ nā ghaṭṭī hai.
jisako kahate apanā apanā banā vahī terā duśman.
ek lañgoṭī pahanā karake ghar se nikāleṅge phauran.
hote nahīṅ kisī ke jag meṅ jīte dam pe sabhī bharam.
māyā moh meṅ paṛ karake barabād kar diyā apanā dhan.
abhī saceto bhajan karo kyoṅ bāñdhe āñkh meṅ paṭṭī hai.
yād karoge us din ko jab lene phariśte āñveṅge.
dhan aur daulat nahīṅ chuveṅge phakat tujhe le jāveṅge.
jaisī karanī kareṅge bande vaisī daphā lagāveṅge.

bhūl jāy bastī kā rahanā jañgal makāñ bañdhāveṅge.
abhī se cet le bande maranā hai kāl ke phande.
bole kabīr mil sataguru jahāñ lagī jñān kī saṭṭī hai.

Don't take pride in this body as this body is absolute mud.
Don't count on it as it is a trap of deception.
It is all good as long as it is living but it could cease without warning.
After leaving this body the soul arrives at the abode of god.
Everybody, brother, family, and clan, is yours as long you are living.
The driving force, the soul, has departed and what is left is a stiff body.
They burned you as if this body was a glass boiler.
This wealth, and worldly possessions none are of any use.
All that you are proud of will remain here.
This life is for two days; you will regret it, if you don't take advantage of it.
Whatsoever you do in this life is what you will reap in the after life.
There is no loss but only gain in reciting the name of god.
The one whom you call your friend today will become your enemy.
They will drive you out of your house with only a loincloth.
Nothing is yours' it is all illusion as you live.
In the net of worldly ignorance, you lost all your wealth.
Be mindful and sing devotional songs. Why are you keeping a bandage of ignorance on your eyes?
You will remember that day when the messenger of god will come to take you away.
They will not touch your wealth but will take you away.
According to your actions in this world is how they will treat you there.
Forget about living in an inhabited place, instead make your shrine in the forest.
Become conscious right now as you will get a noose of death one day.
Kabīr says: "You will find the true teacher in the market of knowledge."

(CYT: 238C: 1975, Kanpur, Sādhu)

३०.

कौन समय की राँधूं मैं तरकारी प्यारे बलमूँ ॥
देवरा माँगै रंग रंग की तरकारी प्यारे बलमूँ
नेनुआ में नारद जी बिराजैं तरोई में तुलसी ज्ञानी
लौकी में लक्ष्मी बिराजैं श्री कृष्ण की पटरानी
सेम में सीता सती बिराजैं कोहणा में हैं कल्याणी
सुरपतिये में सुरसती जो विद्या देती बुधमानी
गोभी में हैं गोबरधन्य गिरधारी प्यारे बलमूँ ॥
भिंडी में भगवान बिराजैं ककरी में हैं कान्धैया
परवर में हैं पारबती कारैला में काली मैया
टेन्डू में ठाकुर जी बिराजैं ग्वाल बाल लीन्हें गैया
सूरन में हैं श्री सरोहण सुर काते चारो भैया
आलू में तो अलख मुनी तैयारी प्यारे बलमूँ ॥
चौरे में चतुनागर स्वामी रचे वेद की करें कथन
बंडा में हैं विश्वनाथ लो विश्वनाथ का भोलापन
भरी गाँठ गोभी में गंगाजल जिनका जल है शीश बरन
कुँदरूक में कुबेर जी बैठे बाची में तो बाँच करन
मूरी में मगसूदन लाल मुरारी प्यारे बलमूँ ॥
अरुई में नर्मदा बिराजैं रक्षा की करने वाली
चीचिन्दा चौराद सिद्ध हैं नाथ बने धूमी डाली
भाँटे में तो भैरोंनाथ की शान प्यारे बलमूँ ॥

kaun samay kī rāñdhūṅ maiṅ tarakārī pyāre balamūñ.
devarā māñgai raṅg raṅg kī tarakārī pyāre balamūṅ.
nenuā meṅ nārad jī birājaiṅ taroī meṅ tulsī jñānī
laukī meṅ lakṣmī birājaiṅ śrī kṛṣṇa kī paṭarānī.
sem meṅ sītā satī birājaiṅ kohaṇā meṅ haiṅ kalyāṇī.
surapatiye meṅ surasatī jo vidhyā detī budhamānī.
gobhī meṅ haiṅ gobaradhany giradhārī pyāre balamūñ.
bhiṅḍī meṅ bhagavān birājaiṅ kakarī meṅ haiṅ kāndhaiyā.
paravar meṅ haiṅ pārabaṭī kārailā meṅ kālī maiyā.
ṭnḍū meṅ ṭhākur jī birājaiṅ gvāl bāl līnheṅ gaiyā.
sūran meṅ haiṅ śrī sarohaṇ sur kāte cāro bhaiyā .
ālū meṅ to alakh munī taiyārī pyāre balamūñ.

caure meṅ catunāgar svāmī race ved kī kareṅ kathan.
baṅḍā meṅ haiṅ viśvanāth lo viśvanāth kā bholāpan.
bharī gāñṭh gobhī meṅ gaṅgājal jinakā jal hai śīś baran.
kuñdarūk meṅ kuber jī baiṭhe bācī meṅ to bāñc karan.
mūrī meṅ magasūdan lāl murārī pyāre balamūñ
aruī meṅ narmadā birājaiṅ rakṣā kī karane vālī.
cīcindā caurād siddh haiṅ nāth bane dhūmī ḍālī.
bhāñṭe meṅ to bhairoṅnāth kī śān pyāre balamūñ.

O dear husband, what kind of vegetable should I make?
My *devar* asks for different kinds of vegetables.
Sage Nārad lives in *nenuā* and learned Tulsīdās lives in *zuccini.*
Goddess Lakṣmī, Queen of Śrī Kṛṣṇa, lives in *laukī.*
Chaste Sītā lives in kidney-bean and Goddess Kalyānī lives in pumpkin.
Goddess Sarasvatī, the giver of learning and intelligence, lives in *surapatiyā*(?)
Dear Kṛṣṇa resides in cauliflower.
God resides in okra and Kṛṣṇa in *kakarī.*
Goddess Pārvatī lives in *paraval* and Mother Kālī in bitter gourd.
Kṛṣṇa, along with cowherds and cows, lives in *ṭenḍu.*
Among gods Sarohaṇ (?) is greatest; all four brothers are embodiment of Gods.
Sage Alakh lives in potato.
Sage Catunagar, who composes and recites Vedas, lives in *caurai.*
Lord Śiva resides in *baṇḍā.*
The sacred water of Gaṅgā is in cabbage.
God Kuber lives in *kundaru.*
Dear Kṛṣṇa, as Murārī, lives in *mūrī.*
River Narmadā, the protector of all, lives in *arui.*
God Bhaironāth proudly lives in eggplant.[3]

(CYT: 239C: 1975, Kanpur, Sādhu)

---

3. This unusual song refers to the many vegetables found in India and mentions that different gods and goddesses of the Hindu pantheon reside in each vegetable. Since there are many vegetables unknown in other areas (besides their botanical names), I have given the vernacular names in italics.

भजन (संध्या)

३१.

मन सँझा सुमिरन कै लियो रे॥
काहे की चौकी काहे के आसन, काहे का माला जपि लियो रे॥
अरे सोने की चौकी कुसन के आसन, तुलसी का माला जपि लियो रे॥
अरे चुगली चवाई पराई निन्दा, ई सबहुन का तजि दियो रे॥
अरे तुलसीदास भजौ भगवानै, राम चरन चित धरि लियो रे॥

man sañjhā sumiran kai liyo re.
kāhe kī caukī kāhe ke āsan, kāhe kā mālā japi liyo re.
are sone kī caukī kusan ke āsan, tulsī kā mālā japi liyo re.
are cugalī cavāī parāī nindā, ī sabahun kā taji diyo re.
are tulasīdās bhajau bhagavānai, rām caran cit dhari liyo re.

O dear mind, remember the evening prayer.
What is your seat made of and what kind of rosary are you telling.
My sitting stool is made of gold, my mat is made of *kuś* grass and my telling beads are made of basil wood.
Backbiting and criticizing others, abandon all such acts.
Tulsīdās says: "Recite god's name and keep Rām in your heart."
(LGT: 48R: 1972-73, Dhanabad, Brāhmaṇ, Women)

भजन (सुमिरनी)

३२.

सुमिरौं खेड़ेपती अगवानी महाबीर ललना॥
कण्ठ पर बैठ मेरी ज्वाला, ज्वाला गले में पहिने माला
माला लिये हाथ में भाला, भाला मार रही दुश्मन के शमशीरे ललना॥
सुमिरौं गौरा मात भवानी, भवानी जो पर्वत की रानी

रानी हरिश्चन्द्र थे दानी, दानी हुये जगत में कमती धरौ धीर ललना ॥
सुमिरौं तपेश्वरी मैया, मैया पार करौ मोरी नैया
नैया की हौ तुम्हीं खिवैया, मैया तोरे भवन मा लागी बड़ी भीर ललना ॥
माता कर भैरों का ख्याल, ख्याल में रहते मेवालाल
लाल हैं सब सैदिन के काल, गाते बाबूपुरवा वाले लै जँजीरे ललना ॥

sumirauṅ kheṛepatī agavānī mahābīr lalanā.
kaṇṭh par baiṭh merī jvālā, jvālā gale meṅ pahine mālā;
Mālā liye hāth meṅ bhālā, bhālā mār rahī duśman ke śamaśīre lalanā.
sumirauṅ gaurā māt bhavānī, bhavānī jo parvat kī rānī;
rānī hariścandr the dānī, dānī huye jagat meṅ kamatī dharau dhīr lalanā.
sumirauṅ tapeśvarī maiyā, maiyā pār karau morī naiyā;
naiyā kī hau tumhīṅ khivaiyā, maiyā tore bhavan mā lāgī baṛī bhīr lalanā.
mātā kar bhairoṅ kā khyāl, khyāl meṅ rahate mevālāl;
lāl haiṅ sab saidin ke kāl, gāte bābūpuravā vāle lai jañjīre lalanā.

I pray and welcome Kherepati and Hanumān.
May mother Jvālā, who is wearing a garland, reside in my throat;
[The goddess] carries a spear and sword with which she destroys enemies.
I pray to Gaurā and Pārvatī, the queen of the mountains;
There have been few donors in this world like King Hariścandra.
I pray to Mother Tapeśvarī to row my boat across;
Only you can row my boat across; At your door, mother, there is a huge crowd.
O mother be kind to Bhairo and keep Mevālāl [composer] in your thoughts;
Lal is enemy of all Muslims, thus sing musicians from Babūpurvā.

(LGT: 16R: 1976, Kanpur, Mixed Men)

३३.

कौन तो फुलवा फूलैं सँझा औ सकारे
कौन फुलवा फूलैं ना आधी रात
बेला तो चमेली फूलैं सँझा औ सकारे
लौंग फुलवा फूलैं ना आधी रात
किनके तौ माथे चढ़िहैं बेला औ चमेला

किनके मथवा चढ़ैं लौंगन वाले हरवा
महादेव के माथे चढ़िहैं बेला औ चमेला
देबिन के मथवा चढ़ैं लौंगन वाले हरवा

kaun to phulavā phūlaiṅ sañjhā au sakāre?
kaun phulavā phūlaiṅ nā ādhī rāt?
belā to camelī phūlaiṅ sañjhā au sakāre;
lauṅg phulavā phūlaiṅ nā ādhī rāt.
kinake tau māthe caṛhihaiṅ belā au camelā?
kinake mathavā caṛhaiṅ lauṅgan vāle haravā?
mahādev ke māthe caṛhihaiṅ belā au camelā;
debin ke mathavā caṛhaiṅ lauṅgan vāle haravā

Which flowers bloom in the evening and in the morning?
Which flowers bloom at midnight?
Belā and jasmine flowers bloom in the evening and in the morning respectively.
Clove's flowers bloom at midnight.
On whose forehead *belā* and jasmine flowers should be offered?
On whose forehead clove-garlands are offered?
Flowers of *belā* and jasmine should be offered to Mahādev:
Clove-garlands are offered to goddesses.

(LGT: 113R: 1972-73, Ganj Muradabad, Dhobī Men)

३४.

नैया मोरी पार हे लगाय दे सबेरे ॥
जब हो गंगा मैया मँशा पुरौबा, भर लुटवा दुधवा चढ़ौउबै सबेरे ॥
जौ हो महादेव बाबा मँशा पुरौबा, भर शिशिया जलवा चढ़ौउबै सबेरे ॥
जौ हो सहजि मैया मँशा पुरौबा, फुलवा और मलवा चढ़ौउबै सबेरे ॥
जौ हो काली मैया मंशा पुरौबा, खासा बोकरवा चढ़ौउबै सबेरे ॥

naiyā morī pār he lagāy de savere.
jab ho gaṅgā maiyā mañśā puraubā, bhar luṭavā dudhavā caṛhauubai savere.
jau ho mahādev bābā mañśā puraubā, bhar śiśiyā jalavā caṛhauubai savere.

jau ho sahaji maiyā mañśā puraubā phulavā, aur malavā caṛhauubai savere.
jau ho kālī maiyā mañśā puraubā, khāsā bokaravā caṛhauubai savere.

Take my boat across in the morning.
I will offer a pot full of milk, O mother Gaṅgā, when you fulfil my wishes.
I will offer a bottle full of water, O Mahādev, when you fulfill my wishes.
I will offer garlands and flowers, O Sahaji mother, when you fulfill my wishes.
I will offer a healthy he-goat, O Goddess Kālī, when you fulfill my wishes.

(LGT:217R: 1972-73, Kanpur, Boat Men)

भजन (आरती)

३५.

आज बनी है छबि न्यारी श्री राघव जी की ॥
सहित जानकी कनक सिंहासन राजत अवधबिहारी ॥
मोर मुकुट पीताम्बर सोहै, गले बनमाल सोहाई ॥
पीताम्बर की कछनी काछे, धनुष बाँण कर धारे ॥
बाँयें अंग जानकी बिराजै, हनुमत आज्ञाकारी ॥
चतुर सखी मिलि करत आरती, कर कँचन की थारी ॥
सुर नर मुनि सब करत आरती, तुलसीदास बलिहारी ॥

āj banī hai chabi nyārī śrī rāghav jī kī.
sahit jānakī kanak siṁhāsan rājat avadhabihārī.
mor mukuṭ pītāmbar sohai, gale banamāl sohāī.
pītāmbar kī kachanī kāche, dhanuṣ bāñṇ kar dhāre.
bāñyeṅ aṅg jānakī birājai, hanumat ājñākārī.
catur sakhī mili karat āratī, kar kañcan kī thārī.
sur nar muni sab karat āratī, tulasīdās balihārī.

Today Rām is wonderfully groomed.
The lord of Avadh is seated on a golden throne with Sītā.

He adorns himself with peacock feather hat, yellow silken clothes and flower garland.
He is wearing a *dhotī* of yellow silk and has a bow and arrow in his hand.
Sītā is sitting on His left side and obedient Hanumān is beside Him.
A lovely woman is performing *āratī* with a golden plate in her hand.
Gods, men, and saints are performing His *āratī*; Tulsīdās sacrifices himself unto his Lord.

(LGT: 71R: 1972-73, Ganj Muradabad, Mixed Women)

अध्याय २
संस्कार गीत

सोहर

३६.

हमें कलमी आम मँगादो हमारा मन मचला ॥
मन ससुरा के आगे मचला मन सासा के आगे मचला ॥
बहू निम्बू नारंगी खाओ, इस ऋतु में आम नहीं हैं हमारा मन मचला ॥
मन जेठा के आगे मचला ॥
छोटी केले की फलियाँ खाओ, इस ऋतु में आम नहीं हैं हमारा मन मचला ॥
मन देवर के आगे मचला ॥
भाभी मटर की फलियाँ खाओ, इस ऋतु में आम नहीं हैं हमारा मन मचला ॥
मन राजा के आगे मचला ॥
राजा एक बन माँगैं दुसर बन, राजा तिज बन आम बगैचा हमारा मन मचला ॥
कुछ कच्चे भी तोड़े कुछ पक्के, कुछ झोला बीच छिपालो हमारा मन मचला ॥
राजा एक बन माँगैं दुसर बन, राजा तीजे बन रनिया के पास हमारा मन मचला ॥
कुछ कच्चे भी खाओ कुछ पक्के, कुछ सखियन बीच लुटादो हमारा मन मचला ॥
जियो जियो रजन के बेटे, तुमने पूरी कराई मेरी साध हमारा मन मचला ॥
जियो जियो रजन की बेटी, तुमने खूब कराया मेरा नाम हमारा मन मचला ॥

hameṅ kalamī ām mañgādo hamārā man macalā.
man sasurā ke āge macalā, man sāsā ke āge macalā.
bahū nimbū nāraṅgī khāo, is ṛtu meṅ ām nahīṅ haiṅ hamārā man macalā.
man jeṭhā ke āge macalā.
choṭī kele kī phaliyāñ khāo, is ṛtu meṅ ām nahīṅ haiṅ hamārā man macalā.
man devar ke āge macalā.
bhābhī maṭar kī phaliyāñ khāo, is ṛtu meṅ ām nahīṅ haiṅ hamārā man macalā.
man rājā ke āge macalā.
rājā ek ban māñgaiṅ dusar ban, rājā tij ban ām bagaicā hamārā man macalā.
kuch kacce bhī toṛe kuch pakke, kuch jholā bīc chipālo hamārā man macalā.
rājā ek ban māñgaiṅ dusar ban, rājā tīje ban raniyā ke pās hamārā man macalā.

kuch kacce bhī khāo kuch pakke, kuch sakhiyan bīc luṭādo hamārā man macalā.
jiyo jiyo rajan ke beṭe, tumane pūrī karāī merī sādh hamārā man macalā.
jiyo jiyo rajan kī beṭī, tumane khūb karāyā merā nām hamārā man macalā.

Bring me *kalamī* mango as I crave for them.
I craved in front of my *sasur* and *sās*.
O *bahū*, eat tangerine; this is not the season for mango.
I craved in front of my *jeṭh*.
O *choṭī*, eat bananas; this is not the season for mango.
I craved in front of my *devar*.
O *bhābhī*, eat peas; this is not the season for mango.
I craved in front of my husband.
My husband went from one garden to the next and at the third garden, he found some mangoes.
He plucked some unripe and some ripe ones and hid some in his bag.
My husband is asking from one garden to the next and at the third garden, he brought them to his wife.
"Eat some unripe and some ripe ones and distribute some among your friends".
"Long live my husband, you satisfied my craving."
"Long live my wife, you added fame to my name."

(LGT: 1R: 1972-73, Dhanabad, Brāhmaṇ Woman)

३७.

एकु साध जिया उपजी है जो बिधि पुरवै हो
लाला दूर खेलन जनि जायो ढूँढन मोरे को जाई
सात भाई की बहिनिया अपने बापा की दुलारी
अपने साहेब सोहगहिली ढूँढन कैसे जइबे
बृन्दाबन की गलियाँ लरिका बहुत ख्यालैं
लरिकौ यहि गलि गे हैं मोरे लाला हाथे मा गेंद लीन्हें
छोटा मोटा बिरवा कदम केरा फरि के लटकि गा है
रानी वहि तरे ख्यालत तोरे लाला हाथे मा गेंद लीन्हें
रानी वहि तरे ख्यालत तोरे लाला मुरलिया धुन बाजै बाँसुरिया धुन बाजै

सात भाई की बहिनिया अपने बापा की दुलारी
माया अपने साहेब सोहगहिली ढूँढन कैसे आइब अकेले कैसे आइब रे
सातो भैया भौज के ददुली मयल के
पूता तुम बिन जग अँधियार कोऊ नहीं आपन रे
जो यहु मंगल गावै अरि गाय के सुनावै रे
तुलसीदास बलि जाइ सुनैया फल पावै
पूतन सुख द्याखै नातिन सुख द्याखै

eku sādh jiyā upajī hai jo bidhi puravai ho.
lālā dūr khelan jani jāyo ḍhūñḍhan more ko jāī.
sāt bhāī kī bahiniyā apane bāpā kī dulārī.
apane sāheb sohagahilī ḍhūñḍhan kaise jaibe.
bṛndāban kī galiyāñ larikā bahut khyālaiṅ.
larikau yahi gali ge haiṅ more lālā hāthe mā geṅd līnheṅ.
choṭā moṭā biravā kadam kerā phari ke laṭaki gā hai.
rānī vahi tare khyālat tore lālā hāthe mā geṅd līnheṅ.
rānī vahi tare khyālat tore lālā muraliyā dhun bājai bāñsuriyā dhun bājai.
Sāt bhāī kī bahiniyā apane bāpā kī dulārī.
māyā apane sāheb sohagahilī ḍhūñḍhan kaise āib akele kaise āib re.
sāto bhaiyā bhauj ke dadulī mayal ke,
pūtā tum bin jag añdhiyār koū nahīn āpan re.
jo yahu maṅgal gāvai ari gāy ke sunāvai re.
tulasīdās bali jāi sunaiyā phal pāvai.
pūtan sukh dyākhai nātin sukh dyākhai.

A desire has sprung in my mind, may god fulfil it.
My dear child, do not go far to play otherwise who will go looking for you.
I am the only sister among seven brothers and my father loves me.
I am my husband's darling and how would I go looking for you?
Many children play in the lanes of Vṛndāvan.
Dear children, my child has gone in this lane carrying a ball in his hands.
There is a small and dense *kadam* tree whose branches are bent with fruits.
Dear queen, your son is playing ball under that tree.
Dear queen, your son is playing his flute under that tree.
I am the only sister among seven brothers and my father loves me.

Oh dear mother, I am dear to my husband; How would I go searching for my child?
All my seven brothers and their wives, father and mother,
O dear son, without you this whole world is dark and no one is mine.
Whoever sings this auspicious song and makes others listen.
Tulsīdās says that I surrender to the singer and the listeners are rewarded.
May they enjoy the happiness of seeing their sons and grandsons!

(LGT: 7R: 1972-73, Dhanabad, Brāhmaṇ Women)

३८.

एक साध जिया उपजी अरि जो बिधि पुरवै हो
राजा अँगने मा बौर लगावव बौर हम द्याखब रे
दुसरी साध जिया उपजी अरि जो बिधि पुरवै हो
रानी कोठरी मा होरिल पजाएव सुनित सुख सोहर रे
महल से उतरी बहुरिया बरोठवा मा ठाढ़ी है रे
द्वारे से आये उनके देवरा तो हिर फिर चितवैं रे
भौजी कस तोरा बदन मलीन केंवल नहीं बिहसैं रे
देवरा न हो मोरे देवरा तुम ही मोरे देवरा हो रे
देवरा हाले बेले डोलिया लै आव नैहर चलि जइबै रे
देवरा तोरे भैया बोले हैं बोल करेजे मोरे सालैं रे
भौजी न हो मोरी भौजी तुमहीं रानी रुकमनि रे
भौजी उवत के सुरिज मनाव ललन तुम्हरे होइ हैं, तुमहीं जुड़वइहैं रे
आठ मास नौ लागत होरिल जलम लीन्हा ललन जलम लीन्हा रे
बाजैं लागी अनन्द बधैया गावैं सखी सोहर रे
ननदी न हो मोरी ननदी तुमहीं मोरी ननदी हो रे
ननदी भैया का लावौ बुलाय सुनैं सुख सोहर रे

ek sādh jiyā upajī ari jo bidhi puravai ho.
rājā an̐gane mā baur lagāvav baur ham dyākhab re.
dusarī sādh jiyā upajī ari jo bidhi puravai ho.
rānī koṭharī mā horil pajāev sunit sukh sohar re.
mahal se utarī bahuriyā baroṭhavā mā ṭhāṛhī hai re.
dvāre se āye unake devarā to hir phir citavaiṅ re.
bhaujī kas torā badan malīn keṅval nahīṅ bihasaiṅ re.

devarā n ho more devarā tum hī more devarā ho re.
devarā hāle bele ḍoliyā lai āv naihar cali jaibai re.
devarā tore bhaiyā bole haiṅ bol kareje more sālaiṅ re.
bhaujī n ho morī bhaujī tumahīṅ rānī rukamani re.
bhaujī uvat ke surij manāv lalan tumhare hoihaiṅ, tumahīṅ juṛavaihaiṅ re.
āṭh mās nau lāgat horil jalam līnhā lalan jalam līnhā re.
bājaiṅ lāgī anand badhaiyā gāvaiṅ sakhī sohar re.
nanadī n ho morī nanadī tumahīṅ morī nanadī ho re.
nanadī bhaiyā kā lāvau bulāy sunaiṅ sukh sohar re.

A desire has sprung in my heart, may god fulfil it.
Dear husband, plant a mango tree in the courtyard so that I could see its flowers.
A second desire has sprung in my heart, may god fulfil it.
Dear wife give birth to a son in the room so that I could hear congratulatory songs.
[Angry] *bahū* came down from the roof and stood on the porch.
From outside came her *devar* and looked at her.
Dear *bhaujī*, how come you look sad without a smile on your face.
O my dear *devar*, you are kind.
Dear *devar*, bring quickly a palanquin so that I could go to my parent's home.
Dear *devar*, your brother has taunted me and his words are paining my heart.
Dear *bhaujī*, you are like queen Rukmanī.
Dear *bhaujī*, worship the rising sun and you will beget a son who will comfort you.
After eight/nine months, a son was born to her.
Auspicious music and congratulatory songs began to be performed.
Dear *nanad*, you are my well wisher.
Dear *nanad*, call your brother so that he can hear congratulatory songs.

(LGT: 8R: 1972-73, Dhanabad, Brāhmaṇ Women)

३९.

चलौ न सखियाँ सहेली मधुबन चलिअइ रे
ए हो जमुना को निरमल नीर चलउ भरि लइयइ रे
कोई सखी हाथ मुख धोवै कोई सखी जल भरै रे
कोई सखी लै लीन्हों नान्ह कन्हैया मेरे रोवइँ मेरे लालन रे
नौवा की हाथा मुख ध्वावइ अरि बरिया की जल भरै रे
जैसे देवकी लै लीहो नान्ह कन्हैया मेरे रोवइँ मेरे लालन रे
घरहिं मा सासु ननदिया अरि देवर जेठनिया रे
घर ही कन्हैया जी के ददुली कन्हैया कैसे र्वावइँ रे
बैरिन सासु ननदिया अरि देवर जेठनिया रे
दुश्मन कन्हैया जी के ददुली कन्हैया मेरे र्वावइँ रे
अड़ुरी तो धरी है दुरौंधी अरि गगरि घनौची रे
झपटि के पलना उघारौ कन्हैया मेरे हरि गे ललैया मेरे
तजिहौं मैं तेल फुलेल आयन बरी काजर नयन बरी
तजिहौं मैं सोलह सिंगार कन्हैया मेरे हरि गै ललन ॥

calau n sakhiyāñ sahelī madhuban caliai re.
e ho jamunā ko niramal nīr calau bhari laiyai re.
koī sakhī hāth mukh dhovai koī sakhī jal bharai re.
koī sakhī lai līnhoṅ nānh kanhaiyā mere rovaiñ mere lālan re.
nauvā kī hāthā mukh dhvāvai ari bariyā kī jal bharai re.
jaise devakī lai līho nānh kanhaiyā mere rovaiñ mere lālan re.
gharahiṅ mā sāsu nanadiyā ari devar jeṭhaniyā re.
ghar hī kanhaiyā jī ke dadulī kanhaiyā kaise rvāvaiñ re.
bairin sāsu nanadiyā ari devar jeṭhaniyā re.
duśman kanhaiyā jī ke dadulī kanhaiyā mere rvāvaiñ re.
aḍurī to dharī hai durauṅdhī ari gagari ghanaucī re.
jhapaṭi ke palanā ughārau kanhaiyā mere hari ge lalaiyā mere.
tajihauṅ maiṅ tel phulel āyan barī kājar nayan barī.
tajihauṅ maiṅ solah siṅgār kanhaiyā mere hari gai lalan.

O dear girlfriends, let's go to Madhuban forest.
Let's go fetch clean water from Jamunā river.
Some girlfriends are washing their hands and face and a few are filling water pots.

A few girlfriends picked up my crying Kṛṣṇa.
Barbers are supposed to clean one's hands and face and *bari* are supposed to fill water.
Take my crying child like Devakī's Kṛṣṇa.
At home, you have *sās, nanad, devar,* and *jeṭhānī.*
At home, child Kṛṣṇa's father is there; then how come Kṛṣṇa is crying.
My *sās, nanad, devar,* and *jeṭhānī,* all are my enemies.
They all are enemies to my dear Kṛṣṇa, who is crying.
My head-rest is lying at the milk place and my pot is lying at the water place.
I rushed to the crib and found my Kṛṣṇa missing.
I will quit using oil, perfume, colour on my feet and mascara in my eyes.
I will quit all sixteen make-ups as my Kṛṣṇa is missing.
(LGT: 61R: 1972-73, Ganj Muradabad, Mixed Women)

४०.

चलौ न सखियाँ सहेली मधुबन चलिअइ रे
ए हो जमुना को निरमल नीर चलउ भरि लइयइ रे
कोई सखी हाथ मुख धोवै कोई सखी जल भरै रे
जैसे देवकी उतरि गईं पार जहाँ न बसैं जसुदा रे
बहिनी न हो मेरी बहिनी तुम मेरी बहिनी रे
बहिनी कौन बिपति तुमपै छा गई तो पार उतरि आइव रे
बहिनी न हो मेरी बहिनी तुम मेरी बहिनी रे
बहिनी आठ पुत्र हम जल्में तो आठौं हरिगै रे
बहिनी अबकी पुत्र जब जलमैं हमार उतरि आइब पार रे
बहिनी न हो मेरी बहिनी तुम मेरी बहिनी रे
बहिनी अबकी पुत्र जब होइहैं बदल तुम लइहउ रे॥

calau n sakhiyāñ sahelī madhuban caliai re.
e ho jamunā ko niramal nīr calau bhari laiyai re.
koī sakhī hāth mukh dhovai koī sakhī jal bharai re.
jaise devakī utari gaīṅ pār jahāñ n basaiṅ jasudā re.
bahinī n ho merī bahinī tum merī bahinī re.
bahinī kaun bipati tumapai chā gaī to pār utari āiv re.

bahinī n ho merī bahinī tum merī bahinī re.
bahinī āṭh putr ham jalmeṅ to āṭhauṅ harigai re.
bahinī abakī putr jab jalamaiṅ hamār utari āib pār re.
bahinī n ho merī bahinī tum merī bahinī re.
bahinī abakī putr jab hoihaiṅ badal tum laihau re.

O girlfriends, let's go to Madhuban forest.
Let's go fetch pure water from Jamunā river.
A few girlfriends are washing their hands and face and a few are filling water.
As Devakī was helped by Yaśodā.
O dear, you are like my sister.
O dear sister, what kind of trouble is upon you? You are almost over that.
O dear, you are like my sister.
O dear sister, I gave birth to eight sons and all were killed.
O dear sister, I will be over [my troubles] when I give birth this time.
O dear, you are like my sister.
O dear sister, this time when I give birth to a son, let's exchange him with your new born.

(LGT: 61R: 1972-73, Ganj Muradabad, Mixed Women)

४१.

केकरे दुवरवा जमिलिया लहर लहर करे हो
ललना केकर बहुआ गरभे से मातल, मने मने हुलसेलि हो
राजा दशरथ के दुवरवा जमिलिया लहर लहर करे हो
ललना रानी कौशल्या गरभे मातल, मने मने हुलसेलि हो
केहि कर जल्में श्री राम केकरे बाबू लछमन हो
ललना केकर भरत भुआल महलिया उठे सोहर हो
कौशल्या के जल्में श्री राम सुमित्रा के लछमन हो
ललना केकई के भरत भुआल महलिया उठे सोहर हो
रामशंकर सोहर गावै गाई के सुनावल हो
ललना जुग जुग जिये बबुआ तोहार, तब खुशी मनावल हो

kekare duvaravā jamiliyā lahar lahar kare ho.
lalanā kekar bahuā garabhe se mātal, mane mane hulaseli ho.
rājā daśarath ke duvaravā jamiliyā lahar lahar kare ho.
lalanā rānī kauśalyā garabhe mātal, mane mane hulaseli ho.
kehi kar jalmeṅ śrī rām kekare bābū lachaman ho?
lalanā kekar bharat bhuāl mahaliyā uṭhe sohar ho?
kauśalyā ke jalmeṅ śrī rām sumitrā ke lachaman ho.
lalanā kekaī ke bharat bhuāl mahaliyā uṭhe sohar ho.
rāmaśaṅkar sohar gāvai gāī ke sunā̃val ho.
lalanā jug jug jiye babuā tohār, tab khuśī manāval ho.

In front of whose house are these decorations fluttering?
Whose *bahū* is pregnant that everyone is excited?
At the gate of King Daśarath, decorations are fluttering.
Queen Kauśalyā is pregnant, that's why everyone is excited.
Who gave birth to Rām and who gave birth to Lakṣmaṇ?
Who gave birth to King Bharat that congratulatory songs are sung in the palace.
Kauśalyā gave birth to Rām and Sumitrā to Lakṣmaṇ.
Kekai gave birth to King Bharat; the congratulatory songs are sung in the palace.
Rāmśaṅkar has sung this congratulatory song for all to listen.
May your child live a long life and may happiness abound.

(LGT: 92CR: 1972-73, Varanasi, Street Blind Musician)

४२.

निहुरि निहुरि बनु ढूढौं मैं बिधि नहीं पायेव रे
ये हो पैयाँ परे बिधि का मनावौं तो बिधि मोरे आवै रे
कऊ घर बिधिया है दस पाँच कऊ घर दुइ चारि रे
ए हो हम घर फेरबो न कोई तौ अपने करम गुन रे
सासू के बिधिया है दुइ चारि ननदी के दस पाँच रे
ए हो हम घर फेरबो न कोई तौ अपने करम गुन रे
धन तौ दीन्हेव सुमिनि कहिआँ बल कनी दुरकहिया रे
ए हो फल तौ दीन्हेव बँबुर कहिआँ सब फल निरफल रे

घिया बिन होम न होय दुधै बिन जाउरि रे
ए हो धिया बिन धर्म न होय पूता के बिन सोहर रे
घिया केरो होम करइबै दुधै केरी जाउरि रे
ए हो धिया केरो धर्म करइबै पुतर केरे सोहर रे

nihuri nihuri banu ḍhūḍhauṅ maiṅ bidhi nahīṅ pāyev re.
ye ho paiyāñ pare bidhi kā manāvauṅ to bidhi more āvai re.
kaū ghar bidhiyā hai das pāñc kaū ghar dui cāri re.
e ho ham ghar pherabo n koī tau apane karam gun re.
sāsū ke bidhiyā hai dui cāri nanadī ke das pāñc re.
e ho ham ghar pherabo n koī tau apane karam gun re.
dhan tau dīnhev sumini kahiāñ bal kanī ṭurakahiyā re.
e ho phal tau dīnhev bañbur kahiāñ sab phal niraphal re.
ghiyā bin hom n hoy dudhai bin jāuri re.
e ho dhiyā bin dharm n hoy pūtā ke bin sohar re.
ghiyā kero hom karaibai dudhai kerī jāuri re.
e ho dhiyā kero dharm karaibai putar kere sohar re.

I looked all around but haven't found a cure for my fate.
I pray at the feet of my fate so that my fate may change.
In some houses there are five-ten children and in some houses there are two-four.
In my home, I do not have any child because of my previous actions.
My *sās* has two-four children and my *nanad* has five-ten.
In my home, I do not have any child because of my previous actions.
You gave wealth to misers and strength to (?).
Like an acacia tree, all fruits are useless. (?)
There is no fire sacrifice without clarified butter and there is no *jāuri* (?) without milk.
Without a wife, one cannot perform religious acts and without a son there are no congratulatory songs.
I will perform a fire sacrifice with clarified butter and *jāuri* (?) with milk.
I will observe all the religious acts with my wife and congratulatory songs in celebration of the birth of my son.

(CYT: 247C: 1975, Sheoli, Brāhmaṇ Women)

४३.

ए हो सँझइन ओनई बटरिया अधिया राति बरसै हो
धरती तो आहीं मोरी माया नेग मोरे कादुल हो
ए हो चारिव नखत मोरे फरिया गरिज जल बरसव रे
ओरियन ओरियन गनि फिरैं रनिया जगावैं हो
रानी खोलि देतिउ झँझरी केंवरिया भीतर चले आई हो
उसिसवा के परी मोरी नाउन पँइतवा के ढकरिन हो
राजा गोदी गजोधर पूता केंवरिया कैसे ख्वालब हो
उठा देव ओसिसवा की नाउन पँइतवा की ढकरिन हो
रानी गोदी ले गजोधर पूता केंवरिया उठि ख्वालउ हो
भोर होत पौ फाटत ललना जलम भे हैं होरिल जलम भे हैं हो
बाजैं लागी आनन्द बधैंयाँ गावैं सखी सोहर हो
अब सात शबद शहनैया ससुर द्वारे बाजै बहुत नीक लागइ हो

e ho sañjhain onaī baṭariyā adhiyā rāti barasai ho.
dharatī to āhīṅ morī māyā neg more kādul ho.
e ho cāriv nakhat more phariyā garij jal barasav re.
oriyan oriyan gani phiraiṅ raniyā jagāvaiṅ ho.
rānī kholi detiu jhañjharī keṅvariyā bhītar cale āī ho.
usisavā ke parī morī nāun pañitavā ke ḍhakarin ho.
rājā godī gajodhar pūtā keṅvariyā kaise khvālab ho.
uṭhā dev osisavā kī nāun pañitavā kī ḍhakarin ho.
rānī godī le gajodhar pūtā keṅvariyā uṭhi khvālau ho.
bhor hot pau phāṭat lalanā jalam bhe haiṅ horil jalam bhe haiṅ ho.
bājaiṅ lāgī ānand badhaiṅyāñ gāvaiṅ sakhī sohar ho.
ab sāt śabad śahanaiyā sasur dvāre bājai bahut nīk lāgai ho.

When the sky is cloudy in the evening, it rains at midnight.
The earth is my mother and (?)
All the four planets are present and it will rain heavy.
The husband (?) is going this and that way to awaken his wife.
"O wife, open these latticed doors so that I can come in."
"The barber's wife is sleeping on my head side and *ḍhakarin* (?) near my feet."

My son is sleeping on my lap, so how could I open the door?"
"Awaken the barber's wife sleeping at your head side and *ḍhakarin* (?) near your feet."
"Carry your child and get up to open the door".
At early dawn, a son was born to her.
Friends began to sing congratualtory songs and music.
The melodious playing of *śahanāī* at the gate of my *sasur* is very pleasing.

(LGT: 192BR: 1972-73, Patti, Brāhmaṇ Women)

४४.

सरग उड़न्ती एक चिरिया सरग मड़रानी रे
चिरिया तुम कौं मोरे हरि देखे जोंधैया ऐसे निरमल रे
देखे तोरी बहुवा देखे मलिन फुलबगिया रे
ठाढ़े कदम केरी छैयाँ तो राधिनी नचावैं रे
केहि आगे एहि दुख कहिबे केहिया आगे सुनिबे
केहि आगे डारौं फरियाद मैं राधिनी छुटावौं
माया आगे यहु दुख कहिबे ददुली आगे सुनिबे
भैया आगे डारौं फरियाद मैं राधिनी छुटावौं

sarag uṛantī ek ciriyā sarag maṛarānī re.
ciriyā tum kauṅ more hari dekhe joṅdhaiyā aise niramal re.
dekhe torī bahuvā dekhe malin phulabagiyā re.
ṭhāṛhe kadam kerī chaiyāñ to rādhinī nacāvaiṅ re.
kehi āge ehi dukh kahibe kehiyā āge sunibe.
kehi āge ḍārauṅ phariyād maiṅ Rādhinī chuṭāvauṅ.
māyā āge yahu dukh kahibe dadulī āge sunibe.
bhaiyā āge ḍārauṅ phariyād maiṅ Rādhinī chuṭāvauṅ.

A bird is hovering very high in the sky.
"O bird, have you seen my child, beautiful as a moonbeam, anywhere?"
I have seen him in the flower garden.
Standing under a *kadam* tree, he is making Rādhā dance.
To whom should I tell my sorrow?

To whom should I complain to get rid of Rādhā?
"I will tell this sadness in front of my mother and father."
"I will complain to my brother to get rid of Rādhā."
(LGT: 146R: 1972-73, Sheoli, Brāhmaṇ Women)

४५.

मेरे पिछवारे पटौना पटौनो मोरो भैया
पटवा रेशम डोरी लै आव बहनोइयै बँधवाऊँ
झपटि के चढ़ि गईं अटरिया झरोखे लागे झाँकैं
भैया राजकुँवर सुकुमार धीरे रस बाँधौ
यह घर घलनी बहिनिया बहुत चक चालिन
अपने रजन बँधवावै तो फेरि छुटावै ॥

mere pichavāre paṭaunā paṭauno moro bhaiyā.
paṭavā reśam ḍorī lai āv bahanoiyai bañdhavāūñ.
jhapaṭi ke caṛhi gaīṅ aṭariyā jharokhe lāge jhāñkaiṅ.
bhaiyā rājakuñvar sukumār dhīre ras bāñdhau.
yah ghar ghalanī bahiniyā bahut cak cālin.
apane rajan bañdhavāvai to pheri chuṭāvai.

Behind my house is *paṭavā* and he is my brother.
I will have *paṭavā* bring silk string to tie his *bahanoi.*
[The woman] climbed to the roof and looked from the window.
"Dear brother, my husband is tender so tie him loosely."
"This my sister is too much trouble;"
"First, she makes me tie her husband and then she requests his release."
(LGT: 146AR: 1972-73, Sheoli, Brāhmaṇ Women)

४६.

पनवन ऐसी धना पतरी कुसुम रंग सुन्दर
पिया की छतिया लगि सोवैं तो नींदा भलि आवै
सोय साय जब जागे महल तन हेरैं
रनिया छतिया को अंग पसीजै तो नींदा नहिं आवै

इतने वचन सुन रनिया नैहर का भागी
राजा अब सुख सोवौ महलिया चलिन हम नैहर
एक बन गईं दुसर बन तिसरे बृन्दाबन
मलहा बेग नवैया लेइ आव पार उतारो
केहकी हो तुम बिटिया कौन की बहुयें
किनकी हौ ब्रजनारि जो पार उतारौं
राजा जनक की बिटिया दशरथ की बहुयें
राजा रामचन्द्र ब्रजनारि तो पार उतारौ
हरी हरी गडरी कटइबै मड़ैया एक छइबै
रनिया आज रैन बसि जाव मैं भोर उतारौं
डाढ़ी में जारौं मल्हाना मछरिया के लोभी
मेरे चन्द्र सुरज ऐसे राजा सुवत घर छोड़े
एक डुब्बी मारी दुसरि डुब्बी मारी तिसरे में पार भई
मलहा ने मीसे दोनों हाथ छिनरिया छल करिगै ॥

panavan aisī dhanā patarī kusum raṅg sundar.
piyā kī chatiyā lagi sovaiṅ to nīṅdā bhali āvai.
soy sāy jab jāge mahal tan heraiṅ.
raniyā chatiyā ko aṅg pasījai to nīṅdā nahiṅ āvai.
itane vacan sun raniyā naihar kā bhāgī.
rājā ab sukh sovau mahaliyā calin ham naihar.
ek ban gaīṅ dusar ban tisare bṛndāban.
malahā beg navaiyā lei āv pār utāro.
kehakī ho tum biṭiyā kaun kī bahuyeṅ?
kinakī hau brajanāri jo pār utārauṅ.
rājā janak kī biṭīyā daśarath kī bahuyeṅ.
rājā rāmacandr brajanāri to pār utārau.
harī harī gaḍarī kaṭaibai maṛaiyā ek chaibai.
raniyā āj rain basi jāv maiṅ bhor utārauṅ.
dāṛhī meṅ jārauṅ malhānā machariyā ke lobhī.
mere candr suraj aise rājā suvat ghar choṛe.
ek ḍubbī mārī dusari ḍubbī mārī tisare meṅ pār bhaī.
malahā ne mīse donoṅ hāth chinariyā chal karigai.

The wife is thin as betel-leaf and beautiful as flowers.
She sleeps well when she is nestled to her husband's chest.
After awaking, her husband looked around his home.
"Dear wife, sleeping nestled, my chest perspires and, therefore, I can't sleep."
Hearing these words, the wife left for her parental home.
"Dear husband, now you sleep in peace at your home as I am off to my parental home."
She travelled many forests and finally reached Vṛndāvan.
"O boatman bring your boat quickly and row me across."
"Whose daughter and whose *bahu* are you?"
"Whose wife are you that I row you across?"
"I am the daughter of King Janak and *bahu* of Daśarath."
"I am the wife of King Rām so row me across."
"I will cut green branches and will build a cottage."
"Dear woman stay one night here and in the morning I wili row you across."
"I will burn such a boatman, greedy of fish."
"I left my sun- and moon-like husband sleeping at home."
She swam underwater one breath, two breath, and by the third breath, she reached the other shore.
The boatman sadly cursed his loss that the woman tricked him.

(LGT: 147R: 1972-73, Sheoli, Brāhmaṇ Women)

४७.

छापा का पेड़ छिउलिया तो ओहि तरे सीता बैठीं हो
ए हो को मोरी खरतिन काटी को बँगला छवाई
ए हो को मोरी जागी रैनिया बिपति मोरी काटै
बन से निकरे हैं ऋषि मुनि सीता समुझावैं
सीता हम तुम्हरी जगिबै रयनिया बिपति तुम्हरी काटब
भोर होत पौ फाटत लव कुश जल्में
ए हो धाऊ रे नगर के नउवा अवध रोचना जाई हो
पहिला रोचना राजा दशरथ दुसरा कौशल्या रानी
ए हो तिसरा रोचना लछमन देवर रामा से न बताएव
दशरथ दिहिन पाँचिव कपड़ा कौशल्या रानी अभरन

लछिमन दिहिन सर की पगड़ी रामा से न बताएव
छापा का पेड़ छिउलिया ओहि तरे रामा बैठे करैं दतीवन
भैया महर महर माथा होय रोचना कहाँ पाएव हो
हमरी तो भौजी शितल देई लव कुश जल्में हैं हो
ए हो उनही के लव कुश जल्में रोचना हम पावा
दशरथ दिहिन पाँचिव कपड़ा कौशल्या रानी अभरन हो
ए हो लछिमन दिहिन सर की पगड़ी हम से न बताएव हो
अब ओहि रे पपिनिया के नौवा हमैं न बताइस बहुत कुछ देइत हो

chāpā kā peṛ chiuliyā to ohi tare sītā baiṭhīṅ ho.
e ho ko morī kharatin kāṭī ko bañgalā chavāī.
e ho ko morī jāgī rainiyā bipati morī kāṭai.
ban se nikare haiṅ ṛṣi muni sītā samujhāvaiṅ.
sītā ham tumharī jagibai rayaniyā bipati tumharī kāṭab.
bhor hot pau phāṭat lav kuś jalmeṅ.
e ho dhāū re nagar ke nauvā avadh rocanā jāī ho.
pahilā rocanā rājā daśarath dusarā kauśalyā rānī.
e ho tisarā rocanā lachaman devar rāmā se n batāev.
daśarath dihin pāñciv kapaṛā kauśalyā rānī abharan.
lachiman dihin sar kī pagaṛī rāmā se n batāev.
chāpā kā peṛ chiuliyā ohi tare rāmā baiṭhe karaiṅ datīvan.
bhaiyā mahar mahar māthā hoy rocanā kahāñ pāev ho.
hamarī to bhaujī śital deī lav kuś jalmeṅ haiṅ ho.
e ho unahī ke lav kuś jalmeṅ rocanā ham pāvā.
daśarath dihin pāñciv kapaṛā kauśalyā rānī abharan ho.
e ho lachiman dihin sar kī pagaṛī ham se n batāev ho.
ab ohi re papiniyā ke nauvā hamaiṅ n batāis bahut kuch deit ho.

Under a fully blooming tree sat Sītā.
Who will cut my branches and who will make my cottage?
Who will keep watch on me at night and help me with this trouble?
The sages came out of the forest and consoled Sītā.
"Sītā, we would keep night vigil and take care of your trouble."
At dawn, just before the sun's rays, Lav and Kuś were born.
Come quickly, O city's barber, and take this *rocanā* to Ayodhyā.

Give first *rocanā* to king Daśarath and second to queen Kauśalyā.
Give third *rocanā* to my *devar*, Lakṣmaṇ but do not tell Rām.
Daśarath gave five traditional clothes and Kauśalyā gave ornaments.
Lakṣmaṇ gave a turban and Rām was not told at all.
Under a fully blooming tree, Ram is sittiing brushing his teeth.
"Dear brother, your forehead is shining with *rocanā*. Where did you get it?"
"My *bhaujī*, Sītā has given birth to Lav and Kuś."
"I got this *rocanā* in celebration of Lav and Kuś's birth."
Daśarath gave five traditional clothes and Kauśalyā gave ornaments.
Lakṣmaṇ gave a turban and no one told me.
"Oh that sinful barber did not tell me; I would have given a lot too."
(LGT: 192CR: 1972-73, Patti, Brāhmaṇ Women)

४८.

एक साध जिया उपजी है जो बिधि पुरवउ हो
राजा हमरे नैहर नौवा पठवव पियरिया लइ आवै हो
तुम्हरा तो नैहर दूरि बसै कोसवन को चलै हो
रानी घर ही मा पियरी रंगाव नितै उठि पहिरउ हो
घर केरी पियरी नितै नित नित उठि पहरिब हो
राजा मैके की पियरी सगुन केरी पहिली चौक केरी हो
भोर होत पौ फाटत ललना जलम भे हैं होरिला जलम भे हैं हो
बाजैं लागी अनन्द बधैयाँ गावैं सखी सोहर हो
सात शबद शहनैया ससुर द्वारे बाजै बहुत नीकी लागै बहुत छबि लागइ हो

ek sādh jiyā upajī hai jo bidhi puravau ho.
rājā hamare naihar nauvā paṭhavav piyariyā lai āvai ho.
tumharā to naihar dūri basai kosavan ko calai ho.
rānī ghar hī mā piyarī raṅgāv nitai uṭhi pahirau ho.
ghar kerī piyarī nitai nit nit uṭhi paharib ho.
rājā maike kī piyarī sagun kerī pahilī cauk kerī ho
bhor hot pau phāṭat lalanā jalam bhe haiṅ horilā jalam bhe haiṅ ho.
bājaiṅ lāgī anand badhaiyāñ gāvaiṅ sakhī sohar ho.
sāt śabad śahanaiyā sasur dvāre bājai bahut nīkī lāgai bahut chabi lāgai ho.

"A desire has sprung in my heart, may God fulfil it."
O husband dear, send the barber to my parents' home to bring my *piyari*"
"Your home is too far! Who will walk those miles?"
O dear wife, have a *piyarī* dyed here and wear it everyday."
"But I wear such a *piyarī* day after day!"
Dear husband, the *piyarī* coming from my home is traditional for such occasions will be a lucky omen — and this is our first child!
At dawn, just before the light breaks, the woman gives birth to a male child.
Auspicious music was aired and women sang congratulatory birth songs.
The playing of the *śahanāī* at the *sasur*'s gate is very pleasing.
(LGT: 193R: 1972-73, Patti, Brāhmaṇ Women)

४९.

लीपिहो पोतिहो ओबरिया झकल मकल होय, महर महर होय रे
वह पर बैठी जच्चारानी बिधना बहुत हैं
अरि अरि लहुरि ननदिया मैं पैंयाँ तोरे लागौं रे
ननदी यह रंगरचनी पलकिया बिछावौ गजओबर
न तेरी नाउन बारिन न तेरी हेलिन न तेरी
भाभी न तेरे बापा केरी चेरिया बलैयाँ तेरी डासँव
न मेरी नाउन बारिन न मेरी हेलिन न मेरी
ननदी अपने हो भैया की बहिनिया भतीजे मिस डासँव
हँस के लीन्हेंन पलकिया बिछाई गजओबर
भाभी करउ पलकिया की लाज होरिलवा जलमियो
बोलिया न बोलौ बोलुवा अरि बोलुवा न बोलौ
ननदी सरगु निहारे घर दूर तो बोलवा न बोलौ
भोरि होति पौ फाटत होरिल अवतरे लालन अवतरे
जैसे बाजैं लागी आनन्द बधैया गावैं सखी सोहर रे
आँगन बाजत बधैया भीतर सखी गावैं रे
ए हो सात शबध शहनैया ससुर द्वारे बाजै सकल जगु जानय बहुत नीको लागइ रे
गैया का गोबर मँगाओ अरे अगँना लिपाओ अरे चौक पुराओ
अरे कलिश धराओ अरे पटुली डराओ अरे दीपक जलाओ रे
भाभी अब बिधि पुरई है राम चउक लइ बइठव रे
फूटी सी अँखियाँ अभरि गईं लाला को जलम भयो
मेरे कमल उठो हरसाय तो सरिया शबध सुनौ रे

सात सिकन केरो डेरवा नवरंग बीनो रे
घर घर फिरत बयनवा हमारे घर लाल भये रे

līpiho potiho obariyā jhakal makal hoy mahar mahar hoy re.
vah par baiṭhī jaccārānī bidhanā bahut haiṅ.
ari ari lahuri nanadiyā maiṅ paiṅyāñ tore lāgauṅ re.
nanadī yah raṅgaracanī palakiyā bichāvau gajaobar.
n terī nāun bārin n terī helin n terī.
bhābhī n tere bāpā kerī ceriyā balaiyāñ terī ḍāsañv.
n merī nāun bārin n merī helin n merī.
nanadī apane ho bhaiyā kī bahiniyā bhatīje mis ḍāsañv.
hañs ke līnheṅn palakiyā bichāī gajaobar.
bhābhī karau palakiyā kī lāj horilavā jalamiyo.
boliyā n bolau boluvā ari boluvā n bolau.
nanadī saragu nihāre ghar dūr to bolavā n bolau.
bhori hoti pau phāṭat horil avatare lālan avatare.
jaise bājaiṅ lāgī ānand badhaiṅyā gāvaiṅ sakhī sohar re
āñgan bājat badhaiyā bhītar sakhī gāvaiṅ re.
e ho sāt śabadh śahanaiyā sasur dvāre bājai sakal jagu jānay bahut nīko lāgai re.
gaiyā kā gobar mañgāo are añganā lipāo are cauk purāo.
are kaliś dharāo are paṭulī ḍarāo are dīpak jalāo re.
bhābhī ab bidhi puraī hai rām cauk lai baiṭhav re.
phūṭī sī añkhiyāñ abhari gaīṅ lālā ko jalam bhayo.
mere kamal uṭho harasāy to sariyā śabadh sunau re.
sāt sikan kero ḍeravā navaraṅg bīno re.
ghar ghar phirat bayanavā hamāre ghar lāl bhaye re.

Freshly plastered room is very bright.
Jaccā is sitting in that room in great pain.
O dear young *nanad*, I touch your feet.
Dear *nanad*, spread this colourful carpet on the bed in the room.
"I am not your barber's wife, nor barin, nor your midwife."
O *bhābhī*, I am not your father's servant that I obey your commands.
"You are not my barber's wife, barin, nor my midwife."

"*Nanad*, you are your brother's sister and for the sake of your nephew, do it.
Happily, she spread the carpet on the bed in the room.
"O *bhābhī*, make sure to give birth to a son to keep the honour of the bed."
"Do not taunt me at this hour!"
"*Nanad*, my home is far away, so do not taunt."
At dawn, just before the sun's rays, a son was born to her.
Joyous music was played and girl-friends began singing congratulatory songs.
In the courtyard joyous music is played and inside girl-friends are singing.
Musical tunes played on *śahanāī* are very pleasing at the *sasur*'s gate and the whole neighbourhood knows the news.
Bring the cowdung and plaster the courtyard and make an altar.
Put the waterfilled pots, wooden sitting boards, and light the lamp.
O *bhābhī*, all preparations are complete, come and take your seat with the baby.
Giving birth to a son has made my blind eyes [world] open.
Hearing congratulatory songs, my heart is blossoming like a lotus.
A basket is woven with seven colourful wickers.
Traditional gifts are sent from house to house in celebration of the birth of a son.

(LGT: 60R: 1972-73, Ganj Muradabad, Mixed Women)

५०.

कौन लोक से नी आएव कौन लोक जइहौ हो
ललुआ केहि घर लेहौ अवतार कहिया जुड़वइहौ हो
इन्द्रलोक से नी आवा मृत्यु लोक जइबै हो
कोऊ राजा घरै लेबै अवतार रानिया जुड़वइबै हो
आवा न तुम मोरे ललुआ हमारे घर आवा हो
ललुआ उजड़ी अजोध्या बसावौ हमैं जुड़वावौ हो
कैसे के आऊँ मोरी रनिया अरे मोरी रनिया हो
रनिया टूटे सुपन पहुड़इहौ तौ फटहा ओढ़इहौ हो
रानी दूरि खेलन हम जइबै घरै कै बुलइहौ थपड़ा दुइ मरिहौ हो

आओ न तुम मोरे पूता कोंखिया जुड़वावौ हो
ललुआ नये नये सुपन पहुड़इबै पीताम्बर ओढ़इबे हो
ललुआ दूरि खेलन तुम जइहौ अजिया ढूँढि लइहैं
बाबा ढूँढि लइहैं मैं हिरदे लगइहौं हो

kaun lok se nī āev kaun lok jaihau ho?
laluā kehi ghar lehau avatār kahiyā juṛavaihau ho.
indralok se nī āvā mṛtyu lok jaibai ho.
koū rājā gharai lebai avatār rāniyā juṛavaibai ho.
āvā n tum more laluā hamāre ghar āvā ho.
laluā ujaṛī ajodhyā basāvau hamaiṅ juṛavāvau ho.
kaise ke āūñ morī raniyā are morī raniyā ho.
raniyā ṭūṭe supan pahuṛaihau tau phaṭahā oṛhaihau ho.
rānī dūri khelan ham jaibai gharai kai bulaihau thapaṛā dui marihau ho.
āo n tum more pūtā koṅkhiyā juṛavāvau ho.
laluā naye naye supan pahuṛaibai pītāmbar oṛhaibe ho.
laluā dūri khelan tum jaihau ajiyā ḍhūñḍhi laihaiṅ.
bābā ḍhūñḍhi laihaiṅ maiṅ hirade lagaihauṅ ho.

From which world do you come and to which world would you go?
Dear child, whose house would you take birth in and who will you make happy?
"I have come from the land of Indra and would go to the land of death."
"I would take birth in some king's home and would make the queen happy."
Come dear child to my home.
Dear child, make this desolate Ayodhyā habitable and make me happy.
How could I come, oh dear queen?
Dear queen, you would make me sleep in a broken winnowing basket and would cover me with rags.
Dear queen, when I would go far to play then you would call me home and would spank me!
Come dear son and let me enjoy the pleasure of motherhood.
Dear child, I would have a new winnowing basket for you to sleep in and would cover you with a silken yellow cloth.

Dear child, if you would go far to play, your grandmother would search and bring you back.
Your grandfather would bring you back and I would embrace you.
(LGT: 192AR: 1972-73, Patti, Brāhmaṇ Women)

५१.

कवना के उपजे कन्हैया कवन बन सोहर
कहना बजत बधैया कौन बन गउवैं चरैं हो
मथुरा मा उपजे कन्हैया बृन्दाबन सोहर हो
गोकुल बजति बधैया बृन्दाबन गउवैं चरैं हो
छिन एक बेलमौं ननदिया तो जल भरि लावउँ हो
ननदी छिन एक पलना झुलावौ मैं जल भरि लावउँ हो
पाँच महीना के कन्हैया तो पलना न जानैं हो
पाँच महीना के कन्हैया तो बँशी बजावैं

kavanā ke upaje kanhaiyā kavan ban sohar.
kahanā bajat badhaiyā kaun ban gauvaiṅ caraiṅ ho.
mathurā mā upaje kanhaiyā bṛndāban sohar ho.
gokul bajati badhaiyā bṛndāban gauvaiṅ caraiṅ ho.
chin ek belamauṅ nanadiyā to jal bhari lāvauñ ho.
nanadī chin ek palanā jhulāvau maiṅ jal bhari lāvauñ ho.
pāñc mahīnā ke kanhaiyā to palanā n jānaiṅ ho.
pāñc mahīnā ke kanhaiyā to bañśī bajāvaiṅ

Where was Kṛṣṇa born and in which locality are congratulatory songs sung?
Where is this congratulatory music played and in which area are cows grazing?
Kṛṣṇa was born in Mathurā and congratulatory songs were sung in Vṛndāvan.
The congratulatory music was played at Gokul and cows are grazing in Vṛndāvan.
Wait for a minute, my *nanad*, so that I can fetch some water.
Nanad, swing the cradle for a minute while I go fetch water.

My Kṛṣṇa is five months old and does not know the cradle.
My five months old Kṛṣṇa is playing flute.

(LGT: 194R: 1972-73, Patti, Brāhmaṇ Women)

५२.

जसोदा आज अलसानी रे॥
अँधेरिया रात है भादौं की, रोहिणी आज लगि जइहैं रे॥
चाँदनी रैन है भादौं की, कृष्ण अवतार लै लीन्हा रे॥
कृष्ण अवतार लिया देवकी के, बधैयाँ गोकुलै बाजी रे॥
खजाना खुल गया राजों का, लुटावैं नन्द औ रानी रे॥
नगाड़े इन्द्र के बाजे, शँख दुनिया में लग जइहैं रे॥

jasodā āj alasānī re.
añdheriyā rāt hai bhādauṅ kī, rohiṇī āj lagi jaihaiṅ re.
cāñdanī rain hai bhādauṅ kī, kṛṣṇ avatār lai līnhā re.
kṛṣṇ avatār liyā devakī ke, badhaiyāñ gokulai bājī re.
khajānā khul gayā rājoṅ kā luṭāvaiṅ nand au rānī re.
nagāṛe indr ke bāje, śañkh duniyā meṅ lag jaihaiṅ re.

Yośodā is slacken today.
It is a dark night in the month of *Bhādauṅ*; the reign of planet Rohiṇī begins today.
It is a moon lit night in the month of *Bhadauṅ* and Kṛṣṇa has taken birth.
Kṛṣṇa was born to Devakī and congratulatory music was played at Gokul.
The treasury of the Kings is open and Nand and his queen are freely distributing riches.
Indra's kettledrums are played and all around the world conch shells are played.

(LGT: 4R: 1972-73, Dhanabad, Brāhmaṇ Women)

५३.

महरि कुछ अनमनि कैसी आज॥
छिन आँगन छिन भीतर डोलय, छिन चढ़ि जात अटारि॥

चोली चीर अरगनी टाँगेंव, केश दिये छिटुकाय ॥
भोर होत पौ फाटन लागे, होरिल रोय सुनायो ॥
सोने के छुरवा नार कटावौं, रूपे खपड़ नहवाये ॥
सिरकी के सूप लाल पौढ़ाये, मोतियन आखत डारे ॥
पियरे पीताम्बर लाल पहिराये, सिंहासन पौढ़ाये ॥

mahari kuch anamani kaisī āj.
chin āñgan chin bhītar ḍolay chin caṛhi jāt aṭāri.
colī cīr araganī ṭāñgeṅv keś diye chiṭukāy.
bhor hot pau phāṭan lāge horil roy sunāyo.
sone ke churavā nār kaṭāvauṅ rūpe khapaṛ nahavāye.
sirakī ke sūp lāl pauṛhāye motiyan ākhat ḍāre.
piyare pītāmbar lāl pahirāye siṅhāsan pauṛhāye.

The mistress of the household is somewhat moody today.
For a moment, she is in the courtyard, the next moment she comes inside, and the next moment, she climbs to the roof.
She took off her bodice and scarf and hung them on a rope and unbraided her hair.
At dawn, just before the breaking of sun's rays, her newborn's crying was heard.
His umbilical cord was cut with a golden razor and he was bathed in a silver bowl.
The son was laid on a winnowing basket and pearls were offered during the ceremony.
The son was clothed in a yellow silken robe and laid on a throne.

(LGT: 98R: 1972-73, Ganj Muradabad, Mixed Women)

५४.

बिरली कोई मात ऐसा अनोखा सुत जाया ॥
अरे जैसे कौशिल्या ने जाया, चारिउ सुकुमार ऐसा अनोखा सुत जाया ॥
अरे जैसे देवकी ने जाया, श्री कृष्ण अवतार ऐसा अनोखा सुत जाया ॥
अरे जैसे कुन्ती ने जाया, अर्जुन अवतार ऐसा अनोखा सुत जाया ॥
अरे जैसे सुभद्रा ने जाया, अभिमन अवतार ऐसा अनोखा सुत जाया ॥

अरे जैसे अंजनी ने जाया, हनुमत अवतार ऐसा अनोखा सुत जाया ॥
अरे जैसे भारत माता ने जाया, महात्मा गाँधी अवतार ऐसा अनोखा सुत जाया ॥

biralī koī māt aisā anokhā sut jāyā.
are jaise kauśilyā ne jāyā, cāriu sukumār aisā anokhā sut jāyā.
are jaise devakī ne jāyā śrī kr̥ṣṇ avatār aisā anokhā sut jāyā.
are jaise kuntī ne jāyā arjun avatār aisā anokhā sut jāyā.
are jaise subhadrā ne jāyā abhiman avatār aisā anokhā sut jāyā.
are jaise añjanī ne jāyā hanumat avatār aisā anokhā sut jāyā.
are jaise bhārat mātā ne jāyā mahātmā gāñdhī avatār aisā anokhā sut jāyā.

Only rare mothers give birth to such a novel son!
When Kauśalyā gave birth; all four children were novel.
When Devakī gave birth to a novel son like Kr̥ṣṇa.
Similarly Kuntī gave birth to a novel son like Arjun.
And Subhadrā gave brith to a novel son like Abhimanyu.
Likewise Añjanī gave birth to a novel son like Hanumān.
And still Mother India gave birth to a novel son like Mahatma Gandhi.
(CYT: 241C: 1975, Sheoli, Brāhmaṇ Woman)

सोहर (बँदनवारी)

५५.

कहाँ लिये जाती बँदनवारी ॥
कौन रजन के लाल भये हैं, केहिके भये हैं नाती ॥
राजा नंद के लाल भये हैं, उग्रसेन के नाती, हुवाँ लिये जाती बँदनवारी ॥
सुघर बँदनवारी लाई मलिनिया, बाँधव रजन के द्वारे ॥
सेर भरि मोती लाईं जसोदा रानी, लेउ लाला की नेछावर ॥
सेर भरि मोती मालिन लेतइ नाहीं, दरश देउ जदुराई ॥
रानी जसोदा की कोंख जुड़ानी, हमरी तुम्हरी शितल भई छाती ॥

kahāñ liye jātī bañdanavārī.
kaun rajan ke lāl bhaye haiṅ, kehike bhaye haiṅ nātī.
rājā nand ke lāl bhaye haiṅ, ugrasen ke nātī huvāñ liye jātī bañdanavārī.
sughar bañdanavārī lāī maliniyā, bāñdhav rajan ke dvāre.
ser bhari motī lāīṅ jasodā rānī leu lālā kī nechāvar.
ser bhari motī mālin letai nāhīṅ daraś deu jadurāī.
rānī jasodā kī koṅkh juṛānī hamarī tumharī śital bhaī chātī.

Where are you taking this festoon of flowers and green leaves?
Which king has been blessed with the birth of a son and which king with a grandson?
King Nand has been blessed with a son and King Ugrasen with a grandson and that's where I am taking this festoon of flowers and green leaves.
Gardener's wife has brought a beautiful festoon of flowers and green leaves; tie them at the king's gate.
Queen Yaśodā brought two pounds of pearls as a propitiatory offering for the gardener's wife.
The gardener's wife does not accept these two pounds of pearls instead she wants to see Kṛṣṇa.
Queen Yaśodā is happy with motherhood and all the rest of us are blessed.

(LGT: 64R: 1972-73, Ganj Muradabad, Mixed Women)

सोहर (बधाई)

५६.

जसुदा रानी जाये हैं लाल बधाई रघुनन्दन की ॥
बोलि लेव नाउन की बिटिया नगर बुलौवा देव
सब सखियन से ऐसी कहियो चलत बिलम्ब ना होय ॥
परदा भीतर जसुदा बोलीं सब सखियन के पैंयाँ लागौं
सब सखियन के पैंयाँ लागौं बैठो गलीचा डारि ॥
बाबा नन्द बजारे जइहैं सुवा सारी लै अइहैं
जो जेहिके मन जैसी भावै सोई पहिर घर जाव ॥

सुरभि गऊ को गोबरु मंगाओ झुकधरि अंगन लिपाओ
भाँति भाँति बम्हन बैठारे चौकहिं दईं हैं पुराय ॥
पहिर ओढ़ि जब सखियाँ चलि भई मुख भरि देत अशीष
जुग जुग जियो नन्द के लाला जिन पहिनाये अम्बर चीर ॥

jasudā rānī jāye haiṅ lāl badhāī raghunandan kī.
boli lev nāun kī biṭiyā nagar bulauvā dev;
sab sakhiyan se aisī kahiyo calat bilamb nā hoy.
paradā bhītar jasudā bolīṅ sab sakhiyan ke paiṅyāñ lāgauṅ;
sab sakhiyan ke paiṅyāñ lāgauṅ baiṭho galīcā ḍāri.
bābā nand bajāre jaihaiṅ suvā sārī lai aihaiṅ;
jo jehike man jaisī bhāvai soī pahir ghar jāv;
surabhi gaū ko gobaru maṅgāo jhukadhari aṅgan lipāo;
bhāñti bhāñti bamhan baiṭhāre caukahiṅ daīṅ haiṅ purāy.
pahir oṛhi jab sakhiyāñ cali bhaī mukh bhari det aśīṣ;
jug jug jiyo nand ke lālā jin pahināye ambar cīr.

Queen Yaśodā has given birth to a boy. Congratulations.
"Go barber's wife's daughter and invite the whole town."
"Tell all the girl-friends to come without delay."
From inside the curtain, Yaśodā respectfully greeted all the invited girlfriends;
Greetings, please take a seat on the carpet.
"Nand will go to the market and bring colourful *sārīs*."
"Out of those, select whichever you like and return home wearing it;"
Smear the interior courtyard with cow-dung;
The invited brāhmaṇs were seated on platforms.
After receiving such lavish gifts, the girlfriends spoke many blessings as they left;
"May Nand's son live long, who gave us beautiful sārīs to wear."
(LGT: 62R: 1972-73, Ganj Muradabad, Mixed women)

सोहर (चरुआ)

५७.

राति भये नन्दलाल अनन्द भये जियरा ॥
सासू जो आवैं चरुआ चढ़ावैं, उनका कँगना गढ़इबै ॥
जीजी जो आवैं पिपरी पिसिहैं, उनका जेहर गढ़इबै ॥
ननदी जो अइहैं छठिया धरिहैं, ननदी जो अइहैं काजर लगइहैं, उनका कुँडल गढ़इबै ॥
देवर जो आवैं वँशी बजावैं, उनका घड़ियाँ पहिरइबो ॥
सखियाँ अइहैं मँगल गइहैं, उनका लेड्डू देवइबे ॥

rāti bhaye nandalāl anand bhaye jiyarā
sāsū jo āvaiṅ caruā caṛhāvaiṅ unakā kaṅganā gaṛhaibai.
jījī jo āvaiṅ piparī pisihaiṅ unakā jehar gaṛhaibai.
nanadī jo aihaiṅ chaṭhiyā dharihaiṅ, nanadī jo aihaiṅ kājar lagaihaiṅ unakā kuñḍal gaṛhaibai.
devar jo āvaiṅ vañśī bajāvaiṅ unakā ghaṛiyāñ pahiraibo.
sakhiyāñ aihaiṅ mañgal gaihaiṅ unakā leḍḍū devaibe.

Nand's son was born at night and everyone has hearty happiness.
My *sās* would come and prepare *caruā*; I would offer her a bracelet.
My *jījī* would come and grind *piparī*; I would offer her an ornament.
My *nanad* would come to prepare *chaṭhī*; My *nanad* would come to apply mascara; I would offer her earrings.
My *devar* would come and play flute; I would offer him a wrist watch.
My friends would come to sing auspicious songs; I would offer them sweetmeat.

(LGT: 67R: 1972-73, Ganj Muradabad, Mixed Women)

५८.

आजु जसुदा के लाल होइहैं ॥
सासू जो अइहैं चरुआ चढ़इहैं, आजु कंगनन के नेग होइहैं ॥
जीजी जो अइहैं पिपरी पिसइहैं, आजु बेसरिन के नेग होइहैं ॥

ननदी जो अइहैं कजरा लगइहैं, आजु बालन के नेग होइहैं ॥
देवर जो अइहैं बंशी बजइहैं, आजु घड़ियन के नेग होइहैं ॥
सखियाँ जो अइहैं मंगल गइहैं, आजु लेड्डुन के नेग होइहैं ॥

āju jasudā ke lāl hoihaiṅ.
sāsū jo aihaiṅ caruā caṛhaihaiṅ āju kaṅganan ke neg hoihaiṅ.
jījī jo aihaiṅ piparī pisaihaiṅ āju besarin ke neg hoihaiṅ.
nanadī jo aihaiṅ kajarā lagaihaiṅ āju bālan ke neg hoihaiṅ.
devar jo aihaiṅ baṅśī bajaihaiṅ āju ghaṛiyan ke neg hoihaiṅ.
sakhiyāñ jo aihaiṅ maṅgal gaihaiṅ āju leḍḍun ke neg hoihaiṅ.

Yaśodā would give birth to a son today.
My *sās* would come to prepare *caruā*; she would receive a bracelet out of gratitude.
My *jījī* would come to grind *piparī*; she would receive a nose ring out of gratitude.
My *nanad* would come to apply mascara; she would receive earrings out of gratitude.
My *devar* would come to play flute; he would receive a wrist watch in gratitude.
My friends would come to sing auspicious songs; they would receive sweets in gratitude.

(LGT: 40R: 1972-73, Dhanabad, Brāhmaṇ Women)

५९.

जच्चा ने नन्दलाल जाये कृष्ण कन्हैया ॥
दाई आवैं होरन जनावैं सासुल आवैं बिंदुला जुड़ावैं
बिंदुले का नेग वे तो माँगैं दे दो मोरे सैयाँ
कँगन का नेग वे तो माँगैं दे दो मोरे सैयाँ ॥
जिठानी आवैं चरुआ चढ़ावैं, देवरानी आवैं डिबिला बिछावैं
पलके का नेग वे तो माँगैं साड़ी दे दो सैयाँ
चरुआ का नेग वे तो माँगैं बेसर दे दो सैयाँ ॥
नन्दुल आवैं सतिया धरावैं, देवर आवैं अचरा धरावैं
अचरे का नेग वे तो माँगैं मुदड़ी दे दो सैयाँ

सतिये का नेग वे तो माँगें पायल दे दो सैयाँ
पंडित आवें नाम धरावें, सखियाँ आवें मंगल गवावें
मंगल का नेग वे तो माँगें मोहरें दे दो सैयाँ

jaccā ne nandalāl jāye kr̥ṣṇ kanhaiyā.
dāī āvaiṅ horan janāvaiṅ sāsul āvaiṅ biṅdulā juṛāvaiṅ.
biṅdule kā neg ve to māñgaiṅ de do more saiyāñ.
kañgan kā neg ve to māñgaiṅ de do more saiyāñ.
jiṭhānī āvaiṅ caruā caṛhāvaiṅ, devarānī āvaiṅ ḍibilā bichāvaiṅ.
palake kā neg ve to māñgaiṅ sāṛī de do saiyāñ.
caruā kā neg ve to māñgaiṅ besar de do saiyāñ.
nandul āvaiṅ satiyā dharāvaiṅ, devar āvaiṅ acarā dharāvaiṅ.
acare kā neg ve to māñgaiṅ mudaṛī de do saiyāñ.
satiye kā neg ve to māñgaiṅ pāyal de do saiyāñ.
paṅḍit āvaiṅ nām dharāvaiṅ sakhiyāñ āvaiṅ maṅgal gavāvaiṅ.
maṅgal kā neg ve to māñgaiṅ mohareṅ de do saiyāñ.

Jaccā has given birth to Nand's son, Kr̥ṣṇa.
Midwife would come to take care of the son; *sās* would come to apply my forehead ornament.
O dear husband, they are asking for presents, please give them.
O dear husband, she is asking for a bracelet, please give it.
My *jeṭhānī* would come to prepare *caruā*; my *devarānī* would come to prepare bed.
O dear husband, she is asking for a present for preparing the bed, please give her *sārīs*.
O dear husband, she is asking for a present for *caruā*, please give her a nose-ring.
My *nanad* would come to prepare *satiyā*; my *devar* would come prepare *acarā* (?)
O dear husband, he is asking for a present for preparing *acara*, please give him a ring.
O dear husband, she is asking for a present for prearing *satiyā*, give her an ankle ornament.
A priest would come to decide a name [for the child]; girlfriends would come to sing auspicious songs.

O dear husband, they are asking for a present for singing auspicious songs, give them gold coins.

(LGT: 188R: 1972-73, Vṛndāvan, Brāhmaṇ Women)

६०.

चलो री आज नन्दराय जी की खोरी ॥
नाइन बायन देत बुलायो, डोलत दौरी दौरी ॥
अपने अपने घर से निकरी आय भईं हैं एक ठौरी ॥
कोई बालक कोई तरुन अवस्था कोई सखी लरकौरी ॥
रानी जसोदा ने बेटा जायो जिनकी है ऊँची खोरी ॥
बँदनवार बँधे दरवाजे बाजत आज बधाई ॥
भर भर मोती लाईं जसोदा पूजन चली हैं शंकर गौरी ॥

calo rī āj nandarāy jī kī khorī.
nāin bāyan det bulāyo ḍolat daurī daurī.
apane apane ghar se nikarī āy bhaīṅ haiṅ ek ṭhaurī.
koī bālak koī tarun avasthā koī sakhī larakaurī.
rānī jasodā ne beṭā jāyo jinakī hai uñcī khorī.
bañdanavār bañdhe daravāje bājat āj badhāī.
bhar bhar motī lāīṅ jasodā pūjan calī haiṅ śaṅkar gaurī.

Let's go today to Nand's home.
The barber's wife is going here and there inviting people to come.
All women came out of their houses and assembled at one place.
Some women are of tender age, some are youths, and some pregnant.
Queen Yaśodā, whose house is high, has given birth to a son.
Festoon of flowers and green leaves are suspended at the door.
With plates full of pearls, Yaśodā is on her way to worship Śiva and Gaurī.

(LGT: 177R: 1972-73, Vṛndāvan, Brāhmaṇ Women)

सोहर (काजर)

६१.

कै लख को तेरो मानिक मदिरा, कै लख को खगवार काजर करुये तेल को
नौ लख को मेरो मानिक मदिरा, दस लख को खगवार काजर करुये तेल को
ठाढ़े ननद रानी काजरु पारैं, वही कटोरा की कोर काजर करुये तेल को
काजर दै जब चली ननद रानी, देव भौज मेरो नेग काजर करुये तेल को
दूध खान को भैंसी लीबो, सैंयाँ चढ़न को घोड़ काजर करुये तेल को
अपने तन की हम सारी लेबौ, सैंयाँ के शीश पगड़िया काजर करुये तेल को
इतनो लै जब चलीं हैं ननद रानी, लोग पूँछैं कहँ पाओ काजर करुये तेल को
हमरे बिरन भैया लालन जाये, उन राखो मेरो मान काजर करुये तेल को
जुग जुग जियो मेरो भाई भतीजा, भौजी के सोरहो सिंगार काजर करुये तेल को

kai lakh ko tero mānik madirā, kai lakh ko khagavār kājar karuye tel ko.
nau lakh ko mero mānik madirā, das lakh ko khagavār kājar karuye tel ko.
ṭhāṛhe nanad rānī kājaru pāraiṅ, vahī kaṭorā kī kor kājar karuye tel ko.
kājar dai jab calī nanad rānī, dev bhauj mero neg kājar karuye tel ko.
dūdh khān ko bhaiṅsī lībo, saiṅyāñ caṛhan ko ghoṛ kājar karuye tel ko.
apane tan kī ham sārī lebau, saiṅyāñ ke śīś pagaṛīyā kājar karuye tel ko.
itano lai jab calīṅ haiṅ nanad rānī log pūñchaiṅ kahañ pāo kājar karuye tel ko.
hamare biran bhaiyā lālan jāye, un rākho mero mān kājar karuye tel ko.
jug jug jiyo mero bhāī bhatījā, bhaujī ke soraho siṅgār kājar karuye tel ko.

What's the value of your jewels and dress? The mascara is made from mustard oil.
My jewels cost nine lakh and my dress costs ten lakh.
Standing, the *nanad* is collecting soot in a bowl.
The *nanad* asked for her gift from *bhaujī* after performing the mascara ceremony.
"I would take a water buffalo to enjoy milk and horse for my husband's riding."
"I would take *sārī* for myself and a turban for my husband."

When *nanad* left with all these gifts, people asked her where she received all this.
My brother is blessed with a son and he has kept my honour.
"May my brother and nephew live long, and may my *bhaujī* enjoy her sixteen traditional ornaments."
(LGT: 105R: 1972-73, Ganj Muradabad, Mixed Women)

६२.

काहे की कजरौटी काहे केरा काजर रे
ए हो को यह देत है काजर अँगुरि नहीं डोलइ रे
सोने की कजरौटी लाऊँगा तेरा काजर रे
देत बुआ उनकी काजर अँगुरि नहीं डोलइ रे
हुवना से आये हैं ससुरा तो बहुआ से अरज करैं हो
बहुआ कंगना की अरझी है बेटी कंगन दइ डारउ रे
न तुम्हरे बेटा के गढ़ाये न तुम्हरेनि मोल कीन्हें रे
ए हो मइके के आहीं कंगनवा भतीजे भये पावा कंगन नहीं देबै रे
इतना वचन सुनि राजा का जियरा दुखित भयो रे
बहिनी लाओ न छड़िया हमारि कंगन लै आई हो
इतना वचन सुनि रानी का जियरा दुखित भयो रे
ए हो लइ लियो कंगना तुम आपनि सवति बनि के राखो रे

kāhe kī kajarauṭī kāhe kerā kājar re.
e ho ko yah det hai kājar aṅguri nahīṅ ḍolai re.
sone kī kajarauṭī lāūṅgā terā kājar re.
det buā unakī kājar aṅguri nahīṅ ḍolai re.
huvanā se āye haiṅ sasurā to bahuā se araj karaiṅ ho.
bahuā kaṅganā kī arajhī hai beṭī kaṅgan dai ḍārau re.
n tumhare beṭā ke gaṛhāye n tumhareni mol kīnheṅ re.
e ho maike ke āhīṅ kaṅganavā bhatīje bhaye pāvā kaṅgan nahīṅ debai re.
itanā vacan suni rājā kā jiyarā dukhit bhayo re.
bahinī lāo n chaṛiyā hamāri kaṅgan lai āī ho.
itanā vacan suni rānī kā jiyarā dukhita bhayo re.
e ho lai liyo kaṅganā tum āpani savati bani ke rākho re.

O what is your mascara container and mascara made of?
Who is hesitating in applying the mascara?
The mascara is brought in a gold mascara container.
Newborn's *bua* is ready to apply mascara without moving finger.
Her *sasur* came and requested his *bahū.*
"Dear *bahū,* my daughter is adamant for the bracelet, please give that to her."
"Your son did not make them for me neither did you purchase them."
"I received these bracelets at my parents' home as a gift for my nephew's birth and I would not give these bracelets."
Hearing these words, the husband became sad.
Dear sister, give me my walking stick so that I could go purchase a bracelet.
Hearing these words, the wife became sad.
"Give her the bracelet and keep her as your co-wife."
(LGT: 43R: 1972-73, Dhanabad, Brāhmaṇ Women)

६३.

अब न ननदिया बोलइबै हो राजा ॥
माया बुलाय के चरुआ चढ़वइबे, सासू का जिया तरसइबै हो राजा ॥
भाभी बुलाय के पीपर पिसइबै, जीजी का जिया तरसइबै हो राजा ॥
बहिनै बुलाय के कजरा लगवइबै, ननदी का जिया तरसइबै हो राजा ॥
भैया बुलाय के बंशी बजवइबै, देवर का जिया तरसइबै हो राजा ॥
सखियाँ बुलाय के मंगल गवइबै, गोइओं का जिया तरसइबै हो राजा ॥

ab n nanadiyā bolaibai ho rājā.
māyā bulāy ke caruā caṛhavaibe, sāsū kā jiyā tarasaibai ho rājā.
bhābhī bulāy ke pīpar pisaibai, jījī kā jiyā tarasaibai ho rājā.
bahinai bulāy ke kajarā lagavaibai, nanadī kā jiyā tarasaibai ho rājā.
bhaiyā bulāy ke baṅśī bajavaibai, devar kā jiyā tarasaibai ho rājā.
sakhiyāñ bulāy ke maṅgal gavaibai, goioṅ kā jiyā tarasaibai ho rājā.

Dear husband, I will not call my *nanad* anymore.
I will invite my mother to prepare *caruā,* and will make my *sās* suffer.

I will invite my *bhābhī* to grind *pīpar* and will make my *jījī* suffer.
I will invite my sisters for mascara ceremony and will make my *nanad* suffer.
I will invite my brother to play flute and will make my *devar* suffer.
I will invite my girlfriends to sing congratulatory songs and will make my friends at in-law's place suffer.

(LGT: 41R: 9172-73, Dhanabad, Brāhmaṇ Women)

सोहर (बधाई)

६४.

भैया की सौं हम तो नथुनिया लीबो ॥
जो तुम ननदी नथुनिया लेहौ, भैया की सौं हम तो नैहर चलि जइबो ॥
जो तुम भाभी नैहर चलि जइहौ, भैया की सौं हम तो हुआँ चलि अइबो ॥
जो तुम ननदी हुवन चलि अइहौ, भैया की सौं हम तो कुलुफ दै लीबो ॥
जो तुम भाभी कुलुफ दै लेहौ, भैया की सौं हम तो दिवाल फाँदि अइबो ॥
जो तुम ननदी दिवाल फाँदि अइहो, भैया की सौं काह बधावा लै अइहौ ॥
दस के खँडुवा दस के पौटा, भैया की सौं दस के खगवार लै अइबो ॥
जो तुम ननदी इतनो लै अइहौ, भैया की सौं हम तो नथुनिया देबो ॥

bhaiyā kī sauṅ[1] *ham to nathuniyā lībo.*
jo tum nanadī nathuniyā lehau, bhaiyā kī sauṅ ham to naihar cali jaibo.
jo tum bhābhī naihar cali jaihau, bhaiyā kī sauṅ ham to huāñ cali aibo.
jo tum nanadī huvan cali aihau bhaiyā kī sauṅ ham to kuluph dai lībo.
jo tum bhābhī kuluph dai lehau bhaiyā kī sauṅ ham to divāl phāñdi aibo.
jo tum nanadī divāl phāñdi aihau, bhaiyā kī sauṅ kāh badhāvā lai aihau.
das ke khañḍuvā das ke pauṭā, bhaiyā kī sauṅ das ke khagavār lai aibo.
jo tum nanadī itano lai aihau, bhaiyā kī sauṅ ham to nathuniyā debo.

---

1. *Bhaiyā kī sauṅ* (literally, "I take an oath on my brother") and other phrases such as *teī sauṅ* (I take an oath on you) are idioms meaning that I am serious and/or am telling the truth.

I take an oath on my brother that I will take a nose ring.
If you insist on taking a nose ring *nanad,* I take an oath on my brother that I will leave for my parents' home.
If you leave for your parents' home *bhābhī,* I take an oath on my brother that I would come there.
If you would come there *nanad,* I take an oath on my brother that I would lock the gate.
If you would lock the gate *bhābhī,* I take an oath on my brother that I would climb the wall.
If you would climb the wall *nanad,* what congratulatory gifts would you bring?
I will bring sweets in tens; I take an oath on my brother that I would bring clothes.
If you would bring this much *nanad,* I take an oath on my brother that I would give you a nose ring.

(LGT:63R: 1972-73, Ganj Muradabad, Mixed Women)

६५.

जच्चा के नैना गर्व से कोऊ देखौ ना ॥
सास ननद से लड्डू बनवइबे, ताला लगवइबे बलम से ॥
सास ननद से खिचड़ी बनवइबे, घी परसइबे बलम से ॥
सास ननद से खटिया बिछवइबे, हुकुम चलइबे बलम से ॥
लड़िका पजानी पलँग चढ़ि बइठीं, हुकुम चलावैं सब घर पे ॥
बिटिया पजानी देहरी चढ़ि बइठीं, उतरि गईं सब मन से ॥

jaccā ke nainā garv se koū dekhau nā.
sās nanad se laḍḍū banavaibe, tālā lagavaibe balam se.
sās nanad se khicaṛī banavaibe, ghī parasaibe balam se.
sās nanad se khaṭiyā bichavaibe, hukum calaibe balam se.
laṛikā pajānī palañg caṛhi baiṭhīṅ, hukum calāvaiṅ sab ghar pe.
biṭiyā pajānī deharī caṛhi baiṭhīṅ, utari gaīṅ sab man se.

Jaccā's eyes are full of pride, somebody should look.
sās and *nanad* will make *laḍḍū* for me; I will make my husband take care of the house.

Sās and *nanad* will make *khicaṛī* for me; my husband will pour *ghī* on it.
Sās and *nanad* will make my bed; I will order my husband.
She gave birth to a male child — that's why she is sitting on the bed; she is giving orders to everyone in the house.
If she had given birth to a female child, she would be sitting on the doorsill; She would have fallen from everyone's eyes.

(LGT: 236: 1972-73, Brāhmaṇ Women)

सोहर (हरदी)

६६.

मेरो अवसर बीतो जाय हरदी चाहिये ॥
लाला कहाँ लग हरदी ऊपजी, अब को यहु लादन जाय ॥
लाला कनउज हरदी ऊपजी, राजन लादन जाँय ॥
लाला को यह हरदी पीसिये, को यह थापन देय ॥
नाउनिया हरदी पीसिये, नानदिया थापैं देय ॥
थापैं दइ जब चली ननद रानी, देउ भौज मेरो नेगु ॥

mero avasar bīto jāy haradī cāhiye.
lālā kahāñ lag haradī ūpajī, ab ko yahu lādan jāy.
lālā kanauj haradī ūpajī, rājan lādan jāñy.
lālā ko yah haradī pīsiye, ko yah thāpan dey.
nāuniyā haradī pīsiye, nānadiyā thāpaiṅ dey.
thāpaiṅ dai jab calī nanad rānī, deu bhauj mero negu.

My time is passing, I need turmeric.[2]
How far away is turmeric grown and who is going to load it?
The turmeric was grown at Kannauj and my husband is going to load it.

---

2. It is customary to put turmeric hand-prints on the gate of a house during auspicious occasions. At the occasion of child's birth, the *nanad* usually performs this ceremony and is given a present.

Who is grinding the turmeric and who is applying the turmeric hand prints?
The barber's wife is grinding the turmeric and *nanad* is applying the turmeric hand prints.
After applying the turmeric hand prints when *nanad* was about to leave, she asked for her customary present.

(LGT: 99R: 1972-73, Ganj Muradabad, Mixed Women)

सोहर (अजवाइन)

६७.

अजवाइन बोय देव मोरे पिया ॥
काहे की खुरपी काहे को बेंट, को यह बैठो निकावै खेत ॥
सोने की खुरपी रूपे को बेंट, भैया औ बहिनी निकावैं खेत ॥
खेत निकावति लगी बड़ी देर, बहिनी के रहि गयो भैया को पेट ॥
कहउ तो भैया जहर बिष खाँउ, भैया को पेट कहाँ लइ के जाँव ॥
काहे को बहिनी जहर बिष खाउ, दाबि दूब ससुरे लइ जाव ॥
जो बहिनी तेरे बिटिया होइहै, भरी सभा मा फजियत होय ॥
जो बहिनी तेरे लड़िका होइहै, मामा के माथे मा रोचना होय ॥
सूप चलनिया खटकति जाय, गौने को ललना ठुनकति जाय ॥

ajavāin boy dev more piyā.
kāhe kī khurapī kāhe ko beṅṭ, ko yah baiṭho nikāvai khet?
sone kī khurapī rūpe ko beṅṭ, bhaiyā au bahinī nikāvaiṅ khet.
khet nikāvati lagī baṛī der, bahinī ke rahi gayo bhaiyā ko peṭ.
kahau to bhaiyā jahar biṣ khāñu, bhaiyā ko peṭ kahāñ lai ke jāñv.
kāhe ko bahinī jahar biṣ khāu, dābi dūb sasure lai jāv.
jo bahinī tere biṭiyā hoihai, bharī sabhā mā phajiyat hoy.
jo bahinī tere laṛikā hoihai, māmā ke māthe mā rocanā hoy.
sūp calaniyā khaṭakati jāy, gaune ko lalanā ṭhunakati jāy.

Dear husband, sow *ajvāin*.
What is a scraping instrument made of? What kind of handle does it have?
The scraping instrument is made of gold, the handle is made of silver and brother and sister are weeding the field.
It took a long time weeding the field and sister became pregnant by her brother.
Tell me brother, should I eat poison? Where could I go pregnant with your child?
Why should you eat poison? Tighten your stomach and go to your in-laws' home.
If you sister, will give birth to a daughter that would bring disgrace to me in front of the full assembly [during the wedding].
If you sister, will give birth to a son that would grace the *māmā's* forehead wiht a *rocanā*.
The winnowing basket and sieve are making noise as the child conceived during the time of *gaunā* is going merrily!
(LGT: 101R: 1972-73, Ganj Muradabad, Mixed Women)

सोहर (धतूरा)

६८.

एक डेल डेलारो खेतु धतूरा मस्तानो है
जामो दुइ दुइ पात धतूरा मस्तानो है
मेरो लहुरो देवरवा ढीठ धतूरा मस्तानो है
मेरे आँगन दियो लगाय धतूरा मस्तानो है
सींचो भरि भरि गडुवा धतूरा मस्तानो है
उइ तो जामों दुइ दुइ पात धतूरा मस्तानो है
मोतियन ऐसे फल लागे धतूरा मस्तानो है
मेरी लहुरी ननदिया ढीठ धतूरा मस्तानो है
उइ तो खूँटो भरि भरि सूप धतूरा मस्तानो है
बाँटो है भरि भरि सील धतूरा मस्तानो है

छानो है पगड़ी के पेंच धतूरा मस्तानो है
बाहुरिया को दियो है पियाय धतूरा मस्तानो है
वै तो घुमरि रहीं दस मास धतूरा मस्तानो है
भोर होत पौ फाटै धतूरा मस्तानो है
लालन रोय सुनावौ धतूरा मस्तानो है
पिया बोलौ अपनी अम्मा धतूरा मस्तानो है
मेरो चरुवा चढ़ावैं आय धतूरा मस्तानो है
वै चरुवा चढ़ाय जब चलीं धतूरा मस्तानो है
वै माँगैं अपनो नेग धतूरा मस्तानो है
लै दउरी बहुरिया बाँसु धतूरा मस्तानो है
पिया बोलौ अपनी भाभी धतूरा मस्तानो है
मेरी पीपरि पीसैं आय धतूरा मस्तानो है
वै पीपरि पीस जब चलीं धतूरा मस्तानो है
वै माँगैं पायन की जेहरी धतूरा मस्तानो है
लै दउरी बहुरिया मुँगरी धतूरा मस्तानो है
पिया बोलौ अपनी बहिनी धतूरा मस्तानो है
मेरी छटिया धरावैं आय धतूरा मस्तानो है
वै छटिया धराय जब चलीं धतूरा मस्तानो है
वै माँगै कानन के कुँडल धतूरा मस्तानो है
लै दउरी बहुरिया डँडा धतूरा मस्तानो है
पिया बोलउ अपनो भैया धतूरा मस्तानो है
मेरी बंशी बजावैं आय धतूरा मस्तानो है
वै बंशी बजाय जब चलैं धतूरा मस्तानो है
वै माँगैं हाथन की घड़ियाँ धतूरा मस्तानो है
लै दउरी बहुरिया डँडा धतूरा मस्तानो है
पड़ोसिन माँगै हींग धतूरा मस्तानो है
लै दउरी बहुरिया ईंट धतूरा मस्तानो है

ek ḍel ḍelāro khetu dhatūrā mastāno hai.
jāmo dui dui pāt dhatūrā mastāno hai.
mero lahuro devaravā ḍhīṭh dhatūrā mastāno hai.
mere āñgan diyo lagāy dhatūrā mastāno hai.
sīṅco bhari bhari gaḍuvā dhatūrā mastāno hai.
ui to jāmoṅ dui dui pāt dhatūrā mastāno hai.
motiyan aise phal lāge dhatūrā mastāno hai.
merī lahurī nanadiyā ḍhīṭh dhatūrā mastāno hai.

ui to khūñṭo bhari bhari sūp dhatūrā mastāno hai.
bāñṭo hai bhari bhari sīl dhatūrā mastāno hai.
chāno hai pagaṛī ke peṅc dhatūrā mastāno hai.
bāhuriyā ko diyo hai piyāy dhatūrā mastāno hai.
vai to ghumari rahīṅ das mās dhatūrā mastāno hai.
bhor hot pau phāṭai dhatūrā mastāno hai.
lālan roy sunāvau dhatūrā mastāno hai.
piyā bolau apanī ammā dhatūrā mastāno hai.
mero caruvā caṛhāvaiṅ āy dhatūrā mastāno hai.
vai caruā caṛhāy jab calīṅ dhatūrā mastāno hai.
vai māñgaiṅ apano neg dhatūrā mastāno hai.
lai daurī bahuriyā bāñsu dhatūrā mastāno hai.
piyā bolau apanī bhābhī dhatūrā mastāno hai.
merī pīpari pīsaiṅ āy dhatūrā mastāno hai.
vai pīpari pīs jab calīṅ dhatūrā mastāno hai.
vai māñgaiṅ pāyan kī jeharī dhatūrā mastāno hai.
lai daurī bahuriyā muñgarī dhatūrā mastāno hai.
piyā bolau apanī bahinī dhatūrā mastāno hai.
merī chaṭiyā dharāvaiṅ āy dhatūrā mastāno hai.
vai chaṭiyā dharāy jab calīṅ dhatūrā mastāno hai.
vai māñgaiṅ kānan ke kuñḍal dhatūrā mastāno hai.
lai daurī bahuriyā ḍañḍā dhatūrā mastāno hai.
piyā bolau apano bhaiyā dhatūrā mastāno hai.
merī baṅśī bajāvaiṅ āy dhatūrā mastāno hai.
vai baṅśī bajāy jab calaiṅ dhatūrā mastāno hai.
vai māñgaiṅ hāthan kī ghaṛiyāñ dhatūrā mastāno hai.
lai daurī bahuriyā ḍañḍā dhatūrā mastāno hai.
paṛosin māñgaiṅ hīṅg dhatūrā mastāno hai.
lai daurī bahuriyā īṅṭ dhatūrā mastānohai.

A thorn-apple bush is thriving on uneven areas.
It grew two leaves at a time.
My younger *devar* is jolly.
He planted it in my courtyard.
He watered it with a bucket full.

It sprouted two leaves at a time.
The pearl-like fruit grew on it.
My younger *nanad* is jolly.
She plucked winnowing basket full of leaves.
She ground it by mortar full.
She strained it with a corner of the turban.
She made the *bahū* drink it.
She [*bahū*] was intoxicated with it for ten months.
At dawn, just before the sun's rays,
A son's cry was heard.
Dear husband, call your mother.
She should prepare my *caruā*.
When she was leaving, after preparing the *caruā*,
She is asking for her present.
Bahū ran towards her witth a bamboo stick [to strike her].
Dear husband, call your *bhābhī*.
She should come to grind my *pīpar*.
When she was leaving, after grinding the pipar,
She is asking for an ankle ornament.
Bahū ran with a mallet [to strike].
Dear husband, call your sister,
She should come to arrange *chaṭhī*.
When she was leaving, after arranging *chaṭhī*,
She is asking ear rings as present.
Bahū ran to strike her with a stick.
Dear husband, call your [younger] brother.
He should come to play flute.
When he was leaving, after playing the flute,
He is asking for a wrist watch.
Bahū ran to strike him with a stick.
The neighbour is asking some asafoetida.
Bahū ran to stirke her with a brick.

(LGT: 102R: 1972-73, Ganj Muradabad, Mixed Women)

सोहर (पीपर)

६९.

पीपरिया झकझालरी अलबेली जच्चा
अलँग बिलँग वइकी डार री अलबेली जच्चा
बोलौ मालिया के छोकड़ा अलबेली जच्चा
गूँदि लावौ बँदनवार अलबेली जच्चा
पहिले तौ बाँधौ गजओबरी अलबेली जच्चा
फिर बाँधौ घुड़सार री अलबेली जच्चा
बाँधौ बाबा की ओबरी अलबेली जच्चा
जिन घर पोता को चाव री अलबेली जच्चा
बाँधि बूँधि जब चली गई मालिन, देउ बहुआ मेरो नेगु री अलबेली जच्चा
ताला सन्दुकिया मा परि गओ अलबेली जच्चा
कुँजी ससुइया के हाथ री अलबेली जच्चा
बटुआ को मुहँ साँकरो अलबेली जच्चा
रेशम परि गई गाँठ री अलबेली जच्चा
बोलौ लोहार के छोकड़ा अलबेली जच्चा
खोलइ सन्दुकिया को तालु री अलबेली जच्चा
बोलौ पटउना के छोकड़ा अलबेली जच्चा
काटौ रेशम गाँठ री अलबेली जच्चा
खोलि सन्दुकिया को झारा जो लीन्हों, मैके की कउड़ी तीन री अलबेली जच्चा
खोलि बटुआ को झारा जो लीन्हों, ससुरे की मोहरैं पचास री अलबेली जच्चा

pīpariyā jhakajhālarī alabelī jaccā.
alañg bilañg vaikī ḍār rī alabelī jaccā.
bolau māliyā ke chokaṛā alabelī jaccā.
gūñdi lāvau bañdanavār alabelī jaccā.
pahile tau bāñdhau gajaobarī alabelī jaccā.
phir bāñdhau ghuḍasār rī alabelī jaccā.
bāñdhau bābā kī obarī alabelī jaccā.
jin ghar potā ko cāv rī alabelī jaccā.
bāñdhi būñdhi jab calī gaī mālin, deu bahuā mero negu rī alabelī jaccā.
tālā sandukiyā mā pari gao alabelī jaccā.
kuñjī sasuiyā ke hāth rī alabelī jaccā.

baṭuā ko muñh sāñkaro alabelī jaccā.
reśam pari gaī gāñṭh rī alabelī jaccā.
bolau lohār ke chokaṛā alabelī jaccā.
kholai sandukiyā ko tālu rī alabelī jaccā.
bolau paṭaunā ke chokaṛā alabelī jaccā.
kāṭau reśam gāñṭh rī alabelī jaccā.
kholi sandukiyā ko jhārā jo līnhoṅ, maike kī kauṛī tīn rī alabelī jaccā.
kholi baṭuā ko jhārā jo līnhoṅ, sasure kī moharaiṅ pacās rī alabelī jaccā.

The *pīpar* tree is like a frill, O beautiful *jaccā.*
Its branches are all over, O beautiful *jaccā.*
Call the gardener's son, O beautiful *jaccā.*
Have him bring frills of flowers, O beautiful *jaccā.*
Tie that frill first at the delivery room, O beautiful *jaccā.*
Then tie the frill at the stable, O beautiful *jaccā.*
Tie the frill at grandfather's room, O beautiful *jaccā.*
In whose house, grandchild is admired, O beautiful *jaccā.*
After typing the frill, when the gardener's wife was leaving, she asked for her present, O beautiful *jaccā.*
[At the name of present], the *jaccā* finds lock on the chest, O beautiful *jaccā.*
My *sās* has the key, O beautiful *jaccā.*
The opening of my purse is narrow, O beautiful *jaccā.*
The silken string of my purse is tangled, O beautiful *jaccā.*
Call the son of a blacksmith, O beautiful *jaccā.*
Have him open the lock of the chest, O beautiful *jaccā.*
Call the son of *paṭavā*, O beautiful *jaccā.*
Have him cut the silken string, O beautiful *jaccā.*
She looked thoroughly at the chest and found only three pennies, O beautiful *jaccā.*
She looked thoroughly in the purse and found fifty gold coins from her in-laws, O beautiful *jaccā.*

(LGT: 103R: 1972-73, Ganj Muradabad, Mixed Women)

सोहर (सोंठ)

७०.

लाला को यह हाट लगाई मन जियरा लाल
को यह सोंठ बेसाई मन जियरा लाल
सासुर लाला हाट लगाई मन जियरा लाल
मोरे राजा सोंठ बेसाई मन जियरा लाल
अब को यह कूटै पीसै मन जियरा लाल
अब को यह बैठो कढ़ैया मन जियरा लाल
नाउनिया कूटै पीसै मन जियरा लाल
सासुरिया बैठी कढ़ैया मन जियरा लाल
ननदिया भरि भरि देवै मन जियरा लाल
जच्चारानी भरि भरि पीवैं मन जियरा लाल
अब कौरे पे राजा ठुनकैं मन जियरा लाल
रानी तनिक हरीरा पावौं मन जियरा लाल
तबसे कहाँ गये थे मन जियरा लाल
मेरो ठाढ़े बबुआ खेलउते मन जियरा लाल
मेरे ठाढ़े बेनिया डोलउते मन जियरा लाल
मेरे मैके की खबर ले अउते मन जियरा लाल

lālā ko yah hāṭ lagāī man jiyarā lāl.
ko yah soṅṭh besāī man jiyarā lāl.
sāsur lālā hāṭ lagāī man jiyarā lāl.
more rājā soṅṭh besāī man jiyarā lāl.
ab ko yah kūṭai pīsai man jiyarā lāl.
ab ko yah baiṭho Kaṛhaiyā man jiyarā lāl.
nāuniyā kūṭai pīsai man jiyarā lāl.
sāsuriyā baiṭhī kaṛhaiyā man jiyarā lāl.
nānadiyā bhari bhari devai man jiyarā lāl.
jaccārānī bhari bhari pīvai man jiyarā lāl.
ab kaure pe rājā ṭhunakaiṅ man jiyarā lāl.
rānī tanik harīrā pāvauṅ man jiyarā lāl.
tabase kahāñ gaye the man jiyarā lāl.
mero ṭhāṛhe babuā khelaute man jiyarā lāl.

mere ṭhāṛhe beniyā ḍolaute man jiyarā lāl.
mere maike kī khabar le aute man jiyarā lāl.

Who has set-up this market? My heart and mind glow with joy.
Who has purchased this dry ginger? My heart and mind glow with joy.
My *sasur* has set-up this market; my heart and mind glow with joy.
My husband has purchased this dry ginger; my heart and mind glow with joy.
Who is grinding and sifting? My heart and mind glow with joy.
Who is tending the frying pan? My heart and mind glow with joy.
The barber's wife is grinding and sifting. My heart and mind glow with joy.
My *sās* is tending the frying pan. My heart and mind glow with joy.
My *nanad* is giving me a dish full [of *harīrā*]; my heart and mind glow with joy.
Jaccā is drinking it bowl full; my heart and mind glow with joy.
Now my husband is sneaking around the corner; my heart and mind glow with joy.
"O dear queen, let me have some *harīrā*;" my heart and mind glow with joy.
"Where have you been, my husband, all this time?" My heart and mind glow with joy.
"You could have taken care of the child for a while." My heart and mind glow with joy.
"You could have fanned me." My heart and mind glow with joy.
"You could have gone to my parent's home with the good news;" my heart and mind glow with joy.

(LGT: 100R: 1972-73, Ganj Muradabad, Mixed Women)

सोहर (जीरा)

७१.

आँगन बोई मैं पीपरिया बहु जीरा लेव
पिछवारे पिपरामूढ़ बहुअर जीरा लेव

आँगन सींची मैं पीपरिया, पिछवारे पिपरामूढ़ बहुअर जीरा लेव
आँगन लागी है पीपरिया, पिछवारे पिपरामूढ़ बहुअर जीरा लेव
सो फूल तोरन चली हैं जच्चा रानी
माली ने पकरो है हाथ बहुअर जीरा लेव
हाथ न पकरौ मेरे मलिया राजा
हमरे तो होइहैं नन्दलाल बहुअर जीरा लेव
कौन ससुर की कुला बधू बहु जीरा लेव
को भँड़ये केरी धीय बहुअर जीरा लेव
ससुरा अपने की कुला बहू बहु जीरा लेव
अपने बाप की धीय बहुअर जीरा लेव
जच्चा नाम लेवायो भँड़ये बाप को
कुल तारो ससुर घर वँश बहुअर जीरा लेव

āñgan boī maiṅ pīpariyā bahu jīrā lev
pichavāre piparāmūṛh bahuar jīrā lev
āñgan sīṅcī maiṅ pīpariyā, pichavāre piparāmūṛh bahuar jīrā lev
āñgan lāgī hai pīpariyā, pichavāre piparāmūṛh bahuar jīrā lev
so phūl toran calī haiṅ jaccā rānī.
mālī nai parako hai hāth bahuar jīrā lev.
hāth n pakarau mere maliyā rājā.
hamare to hoihaiṅ nandalāl bahuar jīrā lev.
kaun sasur kī kulā badhū bahu jīrā lev.
ko bhañṛaye kerī dhīy bahuar jīrā lev.
sasurā apane kī kulā bahū bahu jīrā lev.
apane bāp kī dhīy bahuar jīrā lev.
jaccā nām levāyo bhañṛaye bāp ko.
kul tāro sasur ghar vañś bahuar jīrā lev.

I planted *pīpar* seeds in the courtyard; dear *bahū* take this cumin drink.
In the back, is planted some *pīparmūṛh;*
I watered *pīpar* in the courtyard and *pīparmūṛh* in the back.
Pīpar grew in the courtyard and *pīparmūṛh* in the back.
Dear *jaccā* went out to pluck some flowers.
The gardener grabbed her hand.
Don't grab my hand, dear gardener.
I am going to give birth to a son.

Who is your *sasur* and whose *bahū* are you?
Which pimp's daughter are you?
I am a darling *bahū* of my *sasur.*
I am a darling daughter of my father.
O *jaccā,* you glorified your pimp father's name.
You delivered in-laws' family [by giving birth to a son].
(LGT: 104R: 1972-73, Ganj Muradabad, Mixed Women)

सोहर (पालना)

७२.

झुलावै माई श्याम सुन्दर पलना ॥
काहे का तेरा बना है पालना, श्री राम जानै काहे के लागे फुँदना ॥
अगर चँदन का बनो है पालना, श्री राम जानै रेशम लागे फुँदना ॥
जो मेरे लाल को पलना झुलावै, श्री राम जानै वहिका मैं देहूँ कँगना ॥
कोई गुजरिया की नजर लगी है, श्री राम जानै रोइ रहे ललना ॥
राई लोन जसोदा उतारे, श्री राम जानै चुपकि रहे ललना ॥
सूरदास स्वामी तुम्हरे दरश को, श्री राम जानै जुग जुग जियै ललना ॥

jhulāvai māī śyām sundar palanā.
kāhe kā terā banā hai pālanā śrī rām jānai kāhe ke lāge phuñdanā.
agar cañdan kā bano hai pālanā śrī rām jānai reśam lāge phuñdanā.
jo mere lāl ko palanā jhulāvai śrī rām jānai vahikā maiṅ dehūñ kañganā.
koī gujariyā kī najar lagī hai, śrī rām jānai roi rahe lalanā.
rāī lon jasodā utāre śrī rām jānai cupaki rahe lalanā.
sūradās svāmī tumhare daraś ko śrī rām jānai jug jug jiyai lalanā.

Mother is rocking Kṛṣṇa on a beautiful cradle.
O what is your cradle made and what are tassels made of?
The cradle is made of sandalwood and tassels are made of silk.
I will give a bracelet to whoever would rock the cradle of my child.
Some milkmaid has cast an evil eye because my child is crying.

Jaśodā is throwing mustard and salt into the fire to exorcise an evil eye and child has stopped crying.
Sūrdās says, "It is all for your grace. May the child live a thousand years".

(LGT: 66R: 1972-73, Ganj Muradabad, Mixed Women)

सोहर (झुनझुना)

७३.

मेरे लाले का झुझुना बाजना बबुआ का झुझुना बाजना ॥
कै लख सोनरा मोल कियो है, कै लख बाबा दें रे ॥
नौ लख सोनरा मोल कियो है, दस लख बाबा दें रे ॥
काहे का तेरा बना झुनझुना, काहे के कंकड़ डारे रे ॥
सर्व सोने का बना झुनझुना, हीरों के कंकड़ डारे रे ॥
कमर करधनी पैर पैंजनी, ठुमुक ठुमुक चलि आव रे ॥
रतन जड़े की टोपी सोंहै घूँघर वाले बाल रे ॥
ठुमुक ठुमुक चलि आव रे, खेलौ अपनी दादी की गोद रे ॥
जबहिं झुनझुना बाजन लागो, वइकी दादी बलैयाँ ले रे ॥

mere lāle kā jhujhunā bājanā babuā kā jhujhunā bājanā.
kai lakh sonarā mol kiyo hai, kai lakh bābā deṅ re.
nau lakh sonarā mol kiyo hai, das lakh bābā deṅ re.
kāhe kā terā banā jhunajhunā, kāhe ke kaṅkaṛ ḍāre re.
sarv sone kā banā jhunajhunā, hīroṅ ke kaṅkaṛ ḍāre re.
kamar karadhanī pair paiṅjanī ṭhumuk ṭhumuk cali āv re.
ratan jaṛe kī ṭopī sohai ghūñghar vāle bāl re.
ṭhumuk ṭhumuk cali āv re, khelau apanī dādī kī god re.
jabahiṅ jhunajhunā bājan lāgo, vaikī dādī balaiyāñ le re.

My child is playing with his rattle.
How many thousands a goldsmith asked for and how much grandfather paid for it?

The goldsmith asked for nine hundred thousand and grandfather gave ten hundred thousand.
O what is your rattle made of and what kind of pebbles are inside?
The rattle is made of gold and pieces of diamonds are inside.
With a waist chain and ankle ornament, my child is walking gracefully.
He has a gem-studded cap on his curly hair.
Come dear child and play on your grandmother's lap.
When the child played his rattle, his grandmother fondled him.
(LGT: 65R: 1972-73, Ganj Muradabad, Mixed Women)

मुँडन

७४.

जो मैं जनतिँव बंटी मुड़नो तुम्हार सोने का छुरवा गढ़ावैं तो बाबा तुम्हार
को मोरे झलरी मुड़ावै जँघ बैठावै, को मोरे खरचै दाम झलरिया मोरी पाहुनी
बाबा मोरे झलरी मुड़ावैं जँघ बैठावैं, आजी मोरी खरचै दाम झलरिया मोरी पाहुनी
लाल पेर नहीं पहिनै तौ माया तुम्हार
साग पलकिया न खावइँ तौ माया तुम्हार
माछ मछरिया न खावइँ तौ माया तुम्हार

jo maiṅ janatiñv baṅṭī muṛano tumhār sone kā churavā gaṛhāvaiṅ to bābā tumhār.
ko more jhalarī muṛāvai jañgh baiṭhāvai, ko more kharacai dām jhalariyā morī pāhunī.
bābā more jhalarī muṛāvaiṅ jañgh baiṭhāvaiṅ, ājī morī kharacai dām jhalariyā morī pāhunī.
lāl per nahīṅ pahinai tau māyā tumhār.
sāg palakiyā n khāvaiñ tau māyā tumhār.
māch machariyā n khāvaiñ tau māyā tumhār.

Knowing that it is Baṇṭī's sacred thread ceremony, your father is ordering a razor made of gold.

Who is getting the head-shaving performed by holding on the lap and who is spending money and providing hospitality?
My grandfather is getting the head-shaving performed by holding me on his lap and my grandmother is spending money and providing hospitality.
Your mother is not wearing a yellow *piyarī*.
Your mother does not eat spinach vegetable.
Your mother does not eat fish and meat.

(LGT: 207R: 1972-73, Patti, Brāhmaṇ Women)

७५.

झलरो है आम अमिलिया झलरो जवन केरो खेत झलरि मोरी पाहुनी
मैं तुमसे पूँछउँ दुलहिना देई कैसे कैसे जोगये हैं केश झलरि मोरी पाहुनी
अंबा न खाये हैं भँटवा ऐसे कर जोगये हैं केश झलरि मोरी पाहुनी
खिरिया न खाई महेरिया ऐसे कर जोगये हैं केश झलरि मोरी पाहुनी
अमवा न खाई अमिलिया ऐसे कर जोगये हैं केश झलरि मोरी पाहुनी
पियरी न पहरी हरदि की अरे चुनरी कुसुम की
ऐसे कर जोगये हैं केश झलरि मोरी पाहुनी
काहे के पोखे ललन राजा काहे के पोखे हैं केश झलरि मोरी पाहुनी
घिय गुड़ पोखे हैं लाल तेल फुलेल पोखे हैं केश झलरि मोरी पाहुनी
नौवा चलो अपने घर पंडित चले हैं बनारस झलरि मोरी पाहुनी
ननद चली घर अपने को मेरे परचै केश झलरि मोरी पाहुनी
घोड़िला पढ़ानों राजन लाला बहिनी का लावौ बुलाय झलरि मोरी पाहुनी
बहुरव बहुरव पंडित लाला देहौं बछड़ा सन गाय झलरि मोरी पाहुनी
अहुरव बहुरव नौवा देहौं मैं टोडरा गढ़ाय झलरि मोरी पाहुनी
अहुरव बहुरव ननद रानी देहौं मैं ककना गढ़ाय झलरि मोरी पाहुनी
को मोरी झलरि मुड़ावै जंघ बैठारे को मेरे खरचै दाम झलरि मोरी पाहुनी
दादी मोरी झलरि मुड़ावै औ जंघ बैठारे बाबा मेरो खरचै दाम झलरि मोरी पाहुनी

jhalaro hai ām amiliyā jhalaro javan kero khet jhalari morī pāhunī.
maiṅ tumase pūñchauñ dulahinā deī kaise kaise jogaye haiṅ keś jhalari morī pāhunī.
ambā n khāye haiṅ bhañṭavā aise kar jogaye haiṅ keś jhalari morī pāhunī.
khiriyā n khāī maheriyā aise kar jogaye haiṅ keś jhalari morī pāhunī.
amavā n khāī amiliyā aise kar jogaye haiṅ keś jhalari morī pāhunī.

piyarī n paharī haradi kī are cunarī kusum kī.
aise kar jogaye haiṅ keś jhalari morī pāhunī.
kāhe ke pokhe lalan rājā kāhe ke pokhe haiṅ keś jhalari morī pāhunī.
ghiy guṛ pokhe haiṅ lāl tel phulel pokhe haiṅ keś jhalari morī pāhunī.
nauvā calo apane ghar paṇḍit cale haiṅ banāras jhalari morī pāhunī.
nanad calī ghar apane ko mere paracai keś jhalari morī pāhunī
ghoṛilā paṛhānoṅ rājan lālā bahinī kā lāvau bulāy jhalari morī pāhunī.
bahurav bahurav paṇḍit lālā dehauṅ bachaṛā san gāy jhalari morī pāhunī.
ahurav bahurav nauvā dehauṅ maiṅ ṭoḍarā gaṛhāy jhalari morī pāhunī.
ahurav bahurav nanad rānī dehauṅ maiṅ kakanā gaṛhāy jhalari morī pāhunī.
ko morī jhalari muṛāvai jaṅgh baiṭhāre ko mere kharacai dām jhalari morī pāhunī.
dādī morī jhalari muṛāvai au jaṅgh baiṭhāre bābā mero kharacai dām jhalari morī pāhunī.

The mango tree is blooming, the barley fields are maturing, and this head-shaving ceremony would give a chance for hospitality.
I ask you dear *dulahin,* what did you do that your child has such wonderful hair?
"I did not eat mango and eggplant and therefore my child has such wonderful hair?
"I did not eat rice-pudding and *maheriyā* and therefore my child has such wonderful hair?"
"I did not eat mango and tamarind and therefore my child has such wonderful hair?"
"I did not wear *piyarī* nor scarf dyed yellow."
"Because of all these restrictions my child has such wonderful hair?"
How have you raised this dear child and how did you take care of his hair?
I raised my child with *ghī* and raw sugar and applied oil on the hair.
The barber left his house and the priest has left for Banāras.
My *nanad* has gone to her home. Who would take care of hair during head-shaving?
Go on horseback my husband and bring back your sister for the head-shaving.

Come, son of *paṇḍit*, I would give you a cow with a calf at the hair-shaving ceremony.
Come, barber, I would give an ankle bracelet at the hair-shaving ceremony.
Come, dear *nanad*, I would give a gold bracelet at the hair-shaving ceremony.
Who is taking the baby on her lap and who is spending money at the hair-shaving ceremony?
My grandmother would put me on her lap and my grandfather is spending money at the hair-shaving ceremony.

(LGT: 68R: 1972-73, Ganj Muradabad, Mixed Women)

७६.

जल भरि लेव हिलोर हिलोर रसरिया रेशम की ॥
रेशम रसरिया जब नीकी लागै, सोने का घइला होय ॥
सोने का घइला जब नीको लागै, सुन्दर सी रनिया होय ॥
सुन्दर सी रनिया जब नीकी लागै, गोदी होरिलवा होय ॥
गोदी मा ललना जब नीको लागै, गंगा पै मुड़नो होय ॥
गंगा पै मुड़नो जब नीको लागै, छोटी ननदिया होय ॥
छोटी ननदिया जब नीकी लागै, मुड़ने मा झगड़ा होय ॥

jal bhari lev hilor hilor rasariyā reśam kī.
reśam rasariyā jab nīkī lāgai, sone kā ghailā hoy.
sone kā ghailā jab nīko lāgai, sundar sī raniyā hoy.
sundar sī raniyā jab nīkī lāgai, godī horilavā hoy.
godī mā lalanā jab nīko lāgai, gaṅgā pai muṛano hoy.
gaṅgā pai muṛano jab nīko lāgai, choṭī nanadiyā hoy.
choṭī nanadiyā jab nīkī lāgai, muṛane mā jhagaṛā hoy.

Fill the pot after clearing the surface of the well water.
The silken rope looks charming when it is tied to a golden pot.
The golden pot looks charming when it is handled by a beautiful bride.
The beautiful bride looks charming when she has a baby on her lap.
The charm of the baby on her lap is when the baby's tonsure ceremony takes place at the Ganges.

The tonsure ceremony at the Ganges is charming only when there is a younger *nanad*.
The younger *nanad* is charming only when she fights at the tonsure ceremony.
(LGT: 70R: 1972-73, Ganj Muradabad, Mixed Women)

जनेऊ

७७.

मथुरा मा ठाढ़े कन्हैया बरुआ जनौ जनौ करैं
है कोऊ अजोध्या को पंडित जनेऊ दिवाइये
अथैयें बइठे हैं जशरथ वहि हँसि बोले
हमहीं अजोध्या के पंडित जनौ दिवाइये
मड़ये मा ठाढ़े हैं बरुआ तो भिक्षा भिक्षा करैं
है कोऊ दादी हमार तो भिक्षा दै डारिये
मचियै बइठीं हैं दादी उइ उठि बोलीं
हम हैं दादी तुम्हारी तो भिक्षा लै डारिये
कर लेंव मैं सोलहो सिंगार भिक्षा लै डारिहैं
सोने को सूप सँजोये भिक्षा लै डारिये

mathurā mā ṭhāṛhe kanhaiyā baruā janau janau karaiṅ.
hai koū ajodhyā ko paṅḍit janeū divāiye.
athaiyaiṅ baiṭhe haiṅ jaśarath vahi hañsi bole.
hamahīṅ ajodhyā ke paṅḍit janau divāiye.
maṛaye mā ṭhāṛhe haiṅ baruā to bhikṣā bhikṣā karaiṅ.
hai koū dādī hamār to bhikṣā dai ḍāriye.
maciyai baiṭhīṅ haiṅ dādī ui uṭhi bolīṅ.
ham haiṅ dādī tumhārī to bhikṣā lai ḍāriye.
kar leṅv maiṅ solaho siṅgār bhikṣā lai ḍārihaiṅ.
sone ko sūp sañjoye bhikṣā lai ḍāriye.

My dear child is standing at Mathurā and requesting his sacred-thread ceremony.

Is there any priest from Ayodhyā who can perform the sacred-thread ceremony?
Daśarath, who was seated there, said smiling.
I am a priest from Ayodhyā and will perform the sacred-thread ceremony.
The *baruā* is standing under the ceremonial canopy and requesting alms.
Where is my grandmother who would give me alms?
Sitting on a stool, grandmother responded;
I am your grandmother and will give you alms.
Let me complete my make-up and then I will give you alms.
Decorating her winnowing basket of gold, she gives him alms.
(LGT: 72R: 1972-73, Ganj Muradabad, Mixed Women)

७८.

पाँच पेड़ अंबवा केरे पाँचिव खम्भा गड़इबे हो
तेइ उढ़कइली दुलहिन देई सुनो पिया पंडित हो
बारा बरिस के बरुवा मोरे जनेऊ कइ माँगइं हो
चुप रहो दुलहिन चुप रहो बरुआ कुछ चाहिय हो
चाही तो माठ मठुलिया औ लेड़ुआ पिराकैं हो
पाँच बम्हन मुख भोजन पाँचिव दछिना चाही हो
पाँच पदारथ पचरँग पचरतनी औ चाही हो
आपन मान्य बुलाइ के उनके चरन पखारेव

pāñc peṛ ambavā kere pāñciv khambhā gaṛaibe ho.
tei uṛhakailī dulahin deī suno piyā paṇḍit ho.
Bārā baris ke baruvā more janeū kai māñgaiṅ ho.
cup raho dulahin cup raho baruā kuch cāhiy ho.
cāhī to māṭh maṭhuliyā au leḍuā pirākaiṅ ho.
pāñc bamham mukh bhojan pāñciv dachinā cāhī ho.
pāñc padārath pacarañg pacaratanī au cāhī ho.
āpan māny bulāi ke unake caran pakhārev.

From the five mango trees, I will have five posts to be posted.
From behind them (posts), the wife called her priest husband.
Our child is twelve years old and is requesting his sacred-thread ceremony.

"Keep quiet my wife, we would need a lot for the ceremony."
"Of course, we would need many kinds of sweets;"
We would need dinner and some gift for five Brāhmaṇs.
We would need five material things, five colourful *sārīs*, and a gold ornament with five jewels."
"Invite our respected relations and wash their feet as well."
(LGT: 205R: 1972-73, Patti, Brāhmaṇ Women)

७९.

को मोरे गैया मँगावै अरि दूध दुहावै
को मोरे खीरि बनावै तौ बरुआ जेंवावै
बाबा मोरे गैया मँगावै और दूध दुहावै
आजी मोरी खीरि बनावै तौ बरुआ जेंवावै ॥

ko more gaiyā mañgāvai ari dūdh duhāvai.
ko more khīri banāvai tau baruā jeṅvāvai.
bābā more gaiyā mañgāvai aur dūdh duhāvai.
ājī morī khīri banāvai tau baruā jeṅvāvai.

Who will purchase a cow and milk her?
Who will make rice-pudding and feed my *baruā*?
My grandfather would purchase a cow and would have the cow milked.
My grandmother would make rice-pudding and would feed *baruā.*
(LGT: 73R: 1972-73, Ganj Muradabad, Mixed Women)

८०.

लिल्ला से घोड़ मुँहातोली पुँछिया चितकाबर हो
तई घोड़े चढ़ले बाबा उनके चढ़ि हिरना का मारैं हो
हाथ जोरि हरिनी बिनती करै मोरे हिरनै न मारेव हो
तुमका न मरिबे हरिनिया तोरे हरना का मारब हो
मोरे घर बरुआ ललउनू रामा पहिरैं मृगछाला हो ॥

lillā se ghoṛ muñhātolī puñchiyā citakābar ho.
taī ghoṛe caṛhale bābā unake caṛhi hiranā kā māraiṅ ho.

hāth jori harinī binatī karai more hiranai na mārev ho.
tumakā n maribe hariniyā tore haranā kā mārab ho.
more ghar baruā lalaunū rāmā pahiraiṅ mṛgachālā ho.

The blue horse with the spotted tail is mounted with a bridle.
Riding on such a horse, his *Bābā* is hunting for a deer.
"Don't kill my buck," requested the doe with folded hands.
"I will not kill you doe, but I will kill your buck."
"It is the custom in our family for the *baruā* to wear the deerskin."
(LGT: 16R: 1972-73, Dhanabad, Brāhmaṇ Women)

८१.

ऊँचव चारु नेवल घरु ओके खम्भा ओढ़ाकन हो
तई ओढ़कइली आजी उनकी अपने पिया से अरज करैं हो
बारा बरिस के दुलरुवा बेटा उनका जनेऊ देवावउ हो
चाही तौ धना चाही जनये कछु चाही हो
आपन लाखों लुटाई के बाम्हन करि देइइ हो
तई ओढ़कइली चाची उनकी अपने पिया से अरज करैं हो
सुनौ पिया सुनौ पिया पंडित जनेऊ कब करिहौउ हो
सुनौ धना सुनौ धना सुन्दरि का चाही तोरे जनए मा हो
चाही तो लेडुवा मठोलिया दस लेडुवा पेराकई हो
चाही तो धोती औ पन्ना दस बाम्हन भोजन हो
नये नये सार नया घर नये खम्भा झलावनि हो

ūñcav cāru neval gharu oke khambhā oṛhākan ho.
taī oṛhakailī ājī unakī apane piyā se araj karaiṅ ho.
bārā baris ke dularuvā beṭā unakā janeū devāvau ho.
cāhī tau dhanā cāhī janaye kachu cāhī ho.
āpan lākhoṅ luṭāī ke bāmhan kari deii ho.
taī oṛhakailī cācī unakī apane piyā se araj karaiṅ ho.
sunau piyā sunau piyā paṅḍit janeū kab karihauu ho.
sunau dhanā sunau dhanā sundari kā cāhī tore janae mā ho.
Cāhī to leḍuvā maṭholiyā das leḍuvā perākaī ho.
cāhī to dhotī au pannā das bāmhan bhojan ho.
naye naye sār nayā ghar naye khambhā jhalāvani ho.

The white washed house is on top with posts.
From behind the post, the grandmother is requesting her husband.
Our grandson is twelve years old and we need to perform his sacred-thread ceremony.
"We would need many things for the ceremony."
"We will spend our millions and will make him a Brāhmaṇ."
From behind that post, my *cācī* is requesting her husband.
"Listen my dear priest husband, when would you celebrate his sacred-thread?"
"Listen my beautiful wife, what would we need for the ceremony?"
"We would need a variety of sweets."
"We would need new clothes and some jewels and dinner for the priests."
"We would need to decorate the whole house and the ceremonial canopy."
(LGT: 17R: 1972-73, Dhanabad, Kanyakubja Women)

८२.

चैत से बरुआ चले बैसाख पहूँचे आय
भिक्षा दे माता अशीष दे मैं तो बरुआ बराम्हन हूँ
यहि भिक्षा के कारने मैं तो चले हैं बनारस देश
काहे का जइहौ पूता काशी काहे बनारस
जिनके बाबा सबै जनै होंय ॥

cait se baruā cale baisākh pahūñce āy.[1]
bhikṣā de mātā aśīṣ de maiṅ to baruā barāmhan hūñ.
yahi bhikṣā ke kārane maiṅ to cale haiṅ banāras deś.
kāhe kā jaihau pūtā kaśī kāhe banāras;
jinake bābā sabai janai hoṅy.

1. The months of *Cait* and *Baiśākh* are the two months of the spring season prescribed for the sacred thread ceremony of a *brāhmaṇ* boy. "A boy whose *upanayana* is performed in the month of *Cait* becomes talented and well-versed in the Vedas, in *Baiśākh* provided with all kinds of enjoyment" (Pandey 1966 : 127-28).

The *baruā* set out in the month *Cait,* he arrived in the month of *Baisākh.*
"O mother, give me alms and blessings, as I am a *baruā* Brāhmaṇ."
With these alms, I am proceeding to the city of Banāras.
"O dear son, why are you going to Kāśī, why are you going to Banāras?"
"Your *bābā* is capable of teaching you everything."

(LGT: 74R: 1972-73, Ganj Muradabad, Mixed Women)

विवाह (लड़की)

८३.

मैं तुमसे पूँछूँ गंगा गोसाईं कौने गुन ढबइल जलु है ना
की गंगा तुम मछरी हिलोरा तीरे ढये हैं कगारा ना
ना गोड़िये हम मछरी हिलोरा नारे ढये हैं कगारा ना
बेटी के बाबा वर ढूढैं निकले हाथिन की हिलकोरैं ना

maiṅ tumase pūñchūñ gaṅgā gosāīṅ kaune gun ḍhabail jalu hai nā.
kī gaṅgā tum macharī hilorā tīre ḍhaye haiṅ kagārā nā.
nā goṛiye ham macharī hilorā nāre ḍhaye haiṅ kagārā nā.
beṭī ke bābā var ḍhūḍhaiṇ nikale hāthin kī hilakoraiṅ nā.

"O Ganges priest, I ask you, why is the water dirty?"
"Is it because of fishing nets or because the banks have fallen in?"
"It is not because of fishing nets nor because the banks have fallen in;"
The *bābā* of a girl has set out on an elephant to look for a groom and the elephant's crossing has made the water dirty."[1]

(LGT: 44R: 1972-73, Dhanabad, Brāhmaṇ Women)

---

1. The gist of the song is that the whole family is searching for a groom. They travel from one place to another, never ceasing their search until they have found a suitable groom. The dirtiness of the water suggests that the family has made so many trips back and forth across the river that the water has become dirty.

द्वारचार

८४.

कोई गलियाँ गुलाब से झरइहौ बन्ना मेरा आवति है ॥
जब हरियाले बन्ना बागन आये, राजदुलारे बन्ना बागन आये, कोइलिन शब्द सुनावै ॥
जब हरियाले बन्ना गलियन आये, राजदुलारे बन्ना सड़कन आये, सारे भये अगवानी ॥
जब हरियाले बन्ना द्वारे पर आये, राजदुलारे बन्ना द्वारे पर आये, महरी कलश लिये ठाढ़ी ॥
जब हरियाले बन्ना मड़ये आये, राजदुलारे बन्ना मड़ये आये, पंडित पोथी लिये ठाढ़े ॥
जब हरियाले बन्ना चौकहिं आये, राजदुलारे बन्ना चौकहिं आये,
कन्या सेंधौरा लिये ठाढ़ी ॥
जब हरियाले बन्ना भीतर आये राजदुलारे बन्ना भीतर आये, सरहज खेलैं पंसासारी ॥

koī galiyāñ gulāb se jharaihau bannā merā āvati hai.
jab hariyāle bannā bāgan āye, rājadulāre bannā bāgan āye, koilin śabd sunāvai.
jab hariyāle bannā galiyan āye, rājadulāre bannā saṛakan āye, sāre bhaye agavānī.
jab hariyāle bannā dvāre par āye, rājadulāre bannā dvāre par āye, maharī kalaś liye ṭhāṛhī.
Jab hariyāle bannā maṛaye āye, rājadulāre bannā maṛaye āye, paṅḍit pothī liye ṭhāṛhe.
jab hariyāle bannā caukahiṅ āye, rājadulāre bannā caukahiṅ āye,
kanyā seṅdhaurā liye ṭhāṛhī.
jab hariyāle bannā bhītar āye, rājadulāre bannā bhītar āye, sarahaj khelaiṅ paṅsāsārī.

Someone should have the lanes swept with roses, the groom is coming.
When the charming groom came near the garden the cuckoo greeted him with her songs.
When the charming groom came to the bride's lane, everyone [from the bride's side] came forward to welcome the party.
When the charming groom came to the door, *maharī* stood with her water pot at the door.

When the charming groom came to the canopy, the priest stood with his book.
When the charming groom came to the platform,
The bride stood with her box of *sindūr*.
When the charming groom came insise the house, his *Sarahaj* played the game of *pansāsārī* with him.[2]

(LGT: 81R: 1972-73, Ganj Muradabad, Mixed Women)

बन्ना

८५.

बाजे अंग्रेजी बीन बाजना बन्ना ब्याहन आया ॥
ब्याहन आया जी माया का प्यारा ब्याहन आया
निम्बू लगे चारिउ ओर रे बन्ना ब्याहन आया ॥
ब्याहन आया जी माया का प्यारा गोइड़े आया
सारे ने गलियाँ झराई रे बन्ना ब्याहन आया ॥
ब्याहन आया जी माया का प्यारा द्वारे आया
ससुरा ने आरती उतारी रे बन्ना ब्याहन आया ॥
ब्याहन आया जी माया का प्यारा मड़ये आया
कन्या कलश लिये ठाढ़ी रे बन्ना ब्याहन आया ॥
ब्याहन आया जी माया का प्यारा चौके आया
कन्या सेंधौरा लिये ठाढ़ी रे बन्ना ब्याहन आया ॥

---

2. The Indian cuckoo is considered an auspicious bird by the Hindus. Hearing a cuckoo at the beginning of any occasion is a good omen. Folk songs thus mention the cuckoo's sound as the marriage procession passes through the mango groves. In Song No. 109, the groom, upon hearing the cuckoo's sound, promises that he will decorate her beak and feathers with gold after the marriage, in this way honouring the dignity of the cuckoo. Indian mythology tells that Pārvatī burned herself in the sacrificial fire, due to the disrespect shown towards her husband Śiva by her father; she was later reborn as a cuckoo. See Gupta 1919: 101-11.

ब्याहन आया जी माया का प्यारा ज्योती आया
सरहज खेलै पंसासारी रे बन्ना ब्याहन आया ॥

bāje aṅgrejī bīn bājanā bannā byāhan āyā.
byāhan āyā jī māyā kā pyārā byāhan āyā;
nimbū lage cāriu or re bannā byāhan āyā.
byāhan āyā jī māyā kā pyārā goiṛe āyā;
sāre ne galiyāñ jharāī re bannā byāhan āyā.
byāhan āyā jī māyā kā pyārā dvāre āyā;
sasurā ne āratī utārī re bannā byāhan āyā.
byāhan āyā jī māyā kā pyārā maṛaye āyā;
kanyā kalaś liye ṭhāṛhī re bannā byāhan āyā.
byāhan āyā jī māyā kā pyārā cauke āyā;
kanyā seṅdhaurā liye ṭhāṛhī re bannā byāhan āyā.
byāhan āyā jī māyā kā pyārā jyotī āyā;
sarahaj khelai paṅsāsārī re bannā byāhan āyā.

With a band of English bagpipers, the groom has come for the wedding.
Dear to his mother, the groom has come for the wedding.
The lemons are blooming all over, the groom has come for the wedding.
Dear to his mother, the groom has arrived at the outskirts of the village;
The *sālā* has cleaned all the lanes to welcome the party.
Dear to his mother, the groom has arrived at the door;
Sasur has performed the *āratī*, the groom has arrived.
Dear to his mother, the groom has arrived at the wedding canopy;
The maidens are standing at the entrance with auspicious waterpots.
Dear to his mother, the groom has arrived at the marriage platform;
The bride is standing ready with the *sendhaura*.
Dear to his mother, the groom has come to join the wicks of the lamp;[3]
The *sarahaj* is playing the game of *paṅsāsārī*.

(LGT: 42R: 1972-73, Dhanabad, Brāhmaṇ Women)

---

3. A ceremony in which the bride and groom join the wicks of a lamp, symbolizing the union of bride and groom. See, also Song No. 102.

८६.

गढ़ लंका से खम्भ मँगाइये, अब हरे हरे बाँस छवाइये
अब गैया का गोबर मँगाइये, अब झुकधर अंगना लिपाइये
अब मोतियन चौक पुराइये, अब सोने के कलश धराइये
अब मानिक दियना जलाइये, अब बँदनवार बँधाइये
जब श्री वर गोइड़े मा आइये, तब बाबा ने गलियाँ झराइये
जब श्री वर द्वारे पे आइये, तब ससुरा ने अरति उतारिये
जब श्री वर बरोठवा मा आइये, तब कन्या सेंधौरा लिये ठाढ़ि हो
जब श्री वर मड़ये मा आइये, तब पंडित व्याह रचाइये
जब श्री वर कोहबर आइये, तब सरहज खेलै पंसासारि रे ॥

garh laṅkā se khambh mañgāiye, ab hare hare bāñs chavāiye.
ab gaiyā kā gobar mañgāiye, ab jhukadhar aṅganā lipāiye.
ab motiyan cauk purāiye, ab sone ke kalaś dharāiye.
ab mānik diyanā jalāiye, ab bañdanvār bañdhāiye.
jab śrī var goiṛe mā āiye, tab bābā ne galiyāñ jharāiye.
jab śrī var dvāre pe āiye, tab sasurā ne arati utāriye.
jab śrī var baroṭhavā mā āiye, tab kanyā seṅdhaurā liye ṭhāṛhi ho.
jab śrī var maṛaye mā āiye, tab paṇḍit vyāh racāiye.
jab śrī var kohabaṛ āiye, tab sarahaj khelai paṅsāsāri re.

Summon pillars from Laṅkā and cover the area with green bamboos.
Bring cowdung and plaster the courtyard.
Adorn the ceremonial square with pearls and put golden water pots.
Light bright lamps and hang fastoons of flowers and green leaves.
At the time of the groom's arrival at the marriage canopy, grandfather had the lane swept.
At the time of the groom's arrival at the gate, *sasur* performed *āratī.*
At the time of the groom's arrival at the porch, the bride stood there with *sendhaura.*
At the time of the groom's arrival at the marriage canopy, the priest performed the marriage ceremony.
At the time of the groom's arrival at the *kohabar, sarahaj* played *paṅsāsārī* with him.

(LGT: 225R: 1972-73, Kanpur, Brāhmaṇ Women)

८७.

कोरे कटहरे मा चिरई पाला, को रे दूध पियावा ना ॥
बाबा कटहरे मा चिरई पाला, दादी ने दूध पियावा ना ॥
श्रीवर आये लगाय के लासा, लै गये चिरई उड़ाई ना ॥

kore kaṭahare mā ciraī pālā, ko re dūdh piyāvā nā.
bābā kaṭahare mā ciraī pālā, dādī ne dūdh piyāvā nā.
śrīvar āye lagāy ke lāsā, lai gaye ciraī uṛāī nā.

Who raised this bird (daughter) in a fresh cage and who gave her milk?
Grandfather raised the granddaughter and the grandmother nourished her with milk.
The groom came, limed the bird and carried her.

(LGT: 224R: 1972-73, Kanpur, Brāhmaṇ Women)

८८.

बृन्दाबन एक कुइयाँ सुघर धना पानी भरैं
धनिया बूँद एक पनिया पियाव तो एही राजा बन मा
कैसे के पनिया पियाऊँ तोहे राजा बन मा
राजा जतिया न जानौ तुम्हार तो एही राजा बन मइहाँ
जतिया तो हमरी बम्हन केरी और पंडित केरी
रानी तुम्हरे लेखे भयेन गँवार तो एही राजा बन मइहाँ
जो तुम्हरी जतिया बम्हन केरी और पंडित केरी
राजा बाँचौ न पोथिया पुरान तो एही राजा बन मइहाँ
पोथिया तो भूल्यों बबन घर और बाबुन घर
रानी लिखिनी मैं भूल्यों चौपार तो एही राजा बन मइहाँ

bṛndāban ek Kuiyāñ sughar dhanā pānī bharaiṅ.
dhaniyā būñd ek paniyā piyāv to ehī rājā ban mā.
kaise ke paniyā piyāūñ tohe rājā ban mā?
rājā jatiyā n jānau tumhār to ehī rājā ban maihāñ.
jatiyā to hamarī bamhan kerī aur paṇḍit kerī.
rānī tumhare lekhe bhayen gañvār to ehī rājā ban maihāñ.

jo tumharī jatiyā bamhan kerī aur paṇḍit kerī.
rājā bāñcau n pothiyā purān to ehī rājā ban maihāñ.
pothiyā to bhūlyoṅ baban ghar aur bābun ghar.
rānī likhinī maiṅ bhūlyoṅ caupār to ehī rājā ban maihāñ.

At a well in Vṛndāvan, a beautiful woman is filling water.
O beautiful woman, give me some water to drink in this garden.
Sir, how could I offer you water in this garden?
O dear Sir, I do not know your caste in this garden!
My caste is brāhmaṇ and I am a priest.
Dear queen, for your sake I have become a simpleton.
If you are a brāhmaṇ and a priest,
Then, dear Sir, why don't you recite some sacred books.
"I forgot my books at my grandfather and father's home."
"Dear queen, I forgot my pen on my porch."
(LGT: 199R: 1972-73, Pattı, Brāhmaṇ Women)

८९.

फुलगेंदवा तुम काहे न लै आइये फुलगेंदवा की अरझी दुलारी बेटी
ससुरू एक अरज मेरी मानिये अपने बहुआ का हार लै आइये
ससुरू एक अरज मेरी मानिये सोनरवा दुकनिया होइके आइये
अपनी बहुआ का हार लै आइये ॥
जेठा एक अरज मेरी मानिये बजजवा दुकनिया होइके आइये
अपनी लहुरी का चुँदरी लै आइये ॥
देवरा एक अरज मेरी मानिये चूरीहरवा दुकनिया होइके आइये
सुन्दर चूड़ी चढ़ाये मा लाइये अपनी भाभी का चूड़ी लै आइये
स्वमिया एक अरज मेरी मानिये अपनी रानी का सेंदुर लै आइये ॥

phulageṅdavā tum kāhe n lai āiye phulageṅdavā kī arajhī dulārī beṭī.
sasurū ek araj merī māniye apane bahuā kā hār lai āiye.
sasurū ek araj merī māniye sonaravā dukaniyā hoike āiye.
apanī bahuā kā hār lai āiye.
jeṭhā ek araj merī māniye bajajavā dukaniyā hoike āiye.
apanī lahurī kā cuñdarī lai āiye.

devarā ek araj merī māniye cūrīharavā dukaniyā hoike āiye.
sundar cūṛī caṛhāye mā lāiye apanī bhābhī kā cūṛī lai āiye.
svamiyā ek araj merī māniye apanī rānī kā seṅdur lai āiye.

Why did you purchase *phūlageṅdevā* necklace as our dear daugher insists for it.
I request you, dear *sasur*, to purchase a necklace for your *bahū.*
I request you, dear *sasur*, to go to the goldsmith's shop.
And purchase a necklace for your *bahū.*
I request you, dear *jeṭh*, to go to the cloth merchant's shop,
And purchase a scarf for your younger brother's wife.
I request you, dear *devar*, to go to the bangle seller's shop.
Bring something beautiful bangles for your *bhābhī* at the *carhava.*
I request you, dear husband, to bring *sindūr* for your wife.

(LGT: 206R: 1972-73, Patti, Brāhmaṇ Women)

९०.

को यह पाला रतन चिरैया को एक दाना चुनावै न ॥
अरि बाबा उनके पाला रतन चिरैया आजी उनकी दाना चुनावै न ॥

ko yah pālā ratan ciraiyā ko ek dānā cunāvai n.
ari bābā unake pālā ratan ciraiyā ājī unakī dānā cunāvai n.

Who has raised this wonderful granddaughter and who has fed her?
Her grandfather has raised this wonderful granddaughter and grandmother has fed her.

(LGT: 46/120R: 1972-73, Dhanabad, Brāhmaṇ Women)

९१.

बिनती करौं मैं तुम्हरी बबा जी सोहगवा की बगिया लगाओ न
सोहगवा सोहगवा जनि करि नातिन सोहगवा आजी जी की मँगिया न

binatī karauṅ maiṅ tumharī babā jī sohagavā kī bagiyā lagāo n.
sohagavā sohagavā jani kari nātin sohagavā ājī ji kī mañgiyā n.

I request you, dear grandfather, to arrange for my *sohāg*.
Don't worry for *sohāg* as your grandmother has *sindūr* in her part.[4]
(LGT: 45R: 1972-73, Dhanabad, Brāhmaṇ Women)

विवाह (सोहाग)

१२.

सूहाग बन्नी की डबिया में ॥
आजी रानी ने सुहाग दियो डबिया में
भरि दियो बन्नी की मँगिया में ॥

sūhāg bannī kī ḍabiyā meṅ.
ājī rānī ne suhāg diyo ḍabiyā meṅ.
bhari diyo bannī kī mañgiyā meṅ.

The *suhāg* is inside the bride's box.
Dear grandmother has given *suhāg* in the box.
She has applied it on the part of the bride also.
(LGT: 82R: 1972-73, Ganj Muradabad, Brāhmaṇ Women)

---

4. This particular song describes a ceremony during which the bride ceremoniously begs for *sohāg* from seven married women, including her grandmother, mother, *jeṭhānī*, and *nanad*. In return, one by one each of the seven women puts some *siṅdūr* on her part and then on the bride's part. The expression *suhagavatī raho* (or *saubhāgyavatī raho*) — meaning "May you live a blissful life of union with your husband" — refers to the status of a woman being able to apply *siṅdūr* on her part.

९३.

जैसे उलहति आवे सुहाग बिरुला ॥
मेरे बाबा के आँगन सुहाग बिरुला, मेरे चाचा के आँगन सुहाग बिरुला
दादी रानी जो सींचैं भरि गडुआ, ताई चाची जो सींचैं भरि गडुआ ॥

jaise ulahati āve suhāg birulā.
mere bābā ke āñgan suhāg birulā, mere cācā ke āñgan suhāg birulā;
dādī rānī jo sīñcaiṅ bhari gaḍuā tāī cācī jo sīñcaiṅ bhari gaḍuā.

The climax of *suhāg* ceremony has arrived.
The *suhāg* ceremony would take place in the courtyard of my grandfather and uncle.
My grandmother, *tāī,* and aunt are watering it.
(LGT: 83R: 1972-73, Ganj Muradabad, Mixed Women)

९४.

बेटी गया के गजोधर साँवले, बेटी जन कियो मन पछताइये ॥
बेटी आजी गोरी बाबा साँवले, बेटी माया गोरी बाबू साँवले ॥

beṭī Gayā ke Gajodhar sāñvale, beṭī jan kiyo man pachatāiye.
beṭī ājī gorī bābā sāñvale, beṭī māyā gorī bābū sāñvale.

O dear daughter, Gajodhar of Gayā is black, but don't be upset for this reason.
O dear daughter, your *ājī* is white but your *bābā* is black; your mother is white but your father is black.
(LGT: 195R: 1972-73, Patti, Brāhmaṇ Women)

९५.

चलो न सखियाँ सहेलरी जनकपुर जाई
सखियाँ जनक दुवारे हुये चार चार देखि आई

हाथिन के हलका मा घोड़े न कोभन
देश देश के नरेश तौ रथ चढ़ि आये
सखियाँ तो पूँछैं सीता से सुनौ मोरी सीता
सीता कौनि तपस्या तुम कीन्हेव रामन वरु पायो
बप्पा तो पूजे महादेव माया पारबती
हमरे कन्हैया जी का ध्यान रामन वरु पायो
धन्य भाग राजा दशरथ धन्य कौशिल्या रानी
धन्य भागि सीता तुम्हरी रामन वरु पायो

calo n sakhiyāñ sahelarī janakapur jāī
sakhiyāñ janak duvāre huye cār cār dekhi āī.
hāthin ke halakā mā ghoṛe n kobhan (?)
deś deś ke nareś tau rath caṛhi āye.
sakhiyāñ to pūñchaiṅ sītā se sunau morī sītā.
sītā kauni tapasyā tum kīnhev rāman varu pāyo.
bappā to pūje mahādev māyā pārabatī.
hamare kanhaiyā jī kā dhyān rāman varu pāyo.
dhany bhāg rājā daśarath dhany kauśilyā rānī.
dhany bhāgi sītā tumharī rāman varu pāyo.

Dear girlfriends, let's go to Janakpur.
Dear girlfriends, marriage ceremony is taking place at Janak's gate.
In the dense crowd of elephants, horses are not finding any place (?)
Kings of many countries came riding on their chariots.
The girlfriends are asking Sītā,
What penance did you perform Sītā, that you begot Rām as your husband?
My father worshippepd Śiva and my mother worshipped Pārvatī.
I meditated on Kṛṣṇa and thus begot Rām as my husband.
Blessed are King Daśarath and Queen Kauśalyā.
Blessed are you, Sītā, that you begot Rām as your husband.

(LGT: 14R: 1972-73, Dhanabad, Brāhmaṇ Women)

विवाह (गारी)

९६.

अब एक सुहावन ताल फूलहिं चम्पा कली
अब बेला के नव दस फूल चमेली की एक कली
अब कौनी राधा पनिया का जाँय सिर पर धरे गगरी
अब किन छैल लीन पछुआय तो हाथे गुलाब छड़ी
राधा रानी पनिया का जाँय सिर पर धरे गगरी
श्री कृष्ण लिहेन पछुआय तो हाथे गुलाब छड़ी
बृन्दाबन केरी गलियाँ तो राधा का धर पकरी॥

ab ek suhāvan tāl phūlahiṅ campā kalī.
ab belā ke nav das phūl camelī kī ek kalī.
ab kaunī rādhā paniyā kā jāñy sir par dhare gagarī.
ab kin chail līn pachuāy to hāthe gulāb chaṛī.
Rādhā rānī paniyā kā jāñy sir par dhare gagarī.
Śrī kṛṣṇ lihen pachuāy to hāthe gulāb chaṛī.
Bṛndāban kerī galiyāñ to rādhā kā dhar pakarī.

There is one pleasing pond where *campā* flower blossoms.
Camelī's one flower is as fragrant as nine-ten jasmine flowers.
Which Rādhā [woman] is going for water carrying an earthen pot on her head?
Which dandy followed her, carrying a rose stick in his hand?
Dear Rādhā is going for water carrying an earthen pot on her head.
Kṛṣṇa followed her, carrying a rose stick in his hand.
In the lanes of Vṛndāvan, he grabbed Rādhā.

(LGT: 200R: 1972-73, Patti, Brāhmaṇ Women)

९७.

जसोदा तेरो लालरी बँशी मा देवै गारी॥
कोउ सखी ठाढ़ी कोउ सखी बैठी कोउ सखी चढ़ी अटारी॥

हाथे मा लोटा बगल मा धोती सब सखि गंग नहाई ॥
लै के चीर कदम चढ़ि बैठे सब सखि माँझ उघारी ॥
हमरा चीर दै डारो कन्हैया नहिं देबै लाखन गारी ॥
तुम्हरा चीर जब द्याबै राधिका होइहौ जल से न्यारी ॥
जल से न्यारी होइबे कन्हैया जइहै लाज तुम्हारी ॥
हमरी लाज कहे जइहै राधिका हम पुरुष तुम नारी ॥
तुम तो ढोटा नन्द बबा के हम बृषभान दुलारी ॥
सूरश्याम बलि जाऊँ चरन की तुम जीते हम हारी ॥

jasodā tero lālarī bañśī mā devai gārī.
kou sakhī ṭhāṛhī kou sakhī baiṭhī kou sakhī caṛhī aṭārī.
hāthe mā loṭā bagal mā dhotī sab sakhi gaṅg nahāī.
lai ke cīr kadam caṛhi baiṭhe sab sakhi māñjh ughārī.
hamarā cīr dai ḍāro kanhaiyā nahiṅ debai lākhan gārī.
tumharā cīr jab dyābai rādhikā hoihau jal se nyārī.
jal se nyārī hoibe kanhaiyā jaihai lāj tumhārī.
hamarī lāj kahe jaihai rādhikā ham puruṣ tum nārī.
tum to ḍhoṭā nand babā ke ham bṛṣabhān dulārī.
sūraśyām bali jāūñ caran kī tum jīte ham hārī.

O Jasodā, your son is abusing us with his flute.
A few girlfriends are standing, a few are sitting, and a few are up on the roof.
Carrying metal pots in their hands and *sārī*s tucked under their arms, all the girlfriends went to bathe in the Ganges river.
He [Kṛṣṇa] took their clothes and climbed the *kadam* tree while they bathed naked in the river.
"O Kṛṣṇa, give us back our clothes; otherwise, we will abuse you a million times over"
"I will give you your clothes, of Rādhikā, only upon your coming out of the water."
"If we come out of the water, O Kṛṣṇa, it will be shameful to you."
"Why should I be ashamed? After all, I am a man and you are a woman!"
"You are the son of Nand and I am the daughter of Bṛṣabhān."
Sūrdās says: "I sacrifice to your feet; you won and I lost."
(LGT: 202R: 1972-73, Patti, Brāhmaṇ Women)

९८.

दही वाली जरा सा दही बेंच जाव फेर मथुरा जी का जाव
भैया मेरे पास न आना हाथों मेरे हाथ न लाना
मेरे कँगन का मोल चुकाये जाव फेर मथुरा जी का जाव ॥
भैया मेरे पास न आना गले मेरे हाथ न लाना
मेरे हारन का मोल चुकाये जाव फेर मथुरा जी का जाव ॥
भैया मेरे पास न आना माथे मेरे हाथ न लाना
मेरी बेंदी का मोल चुकाये जाव फेर मथुरा जी का जाव ॥
भैया मेरे पास न आना पैरों मेरे हाथ न लाना
मेरे पायल का मोल चुकाये जाव फेर मथुरा जी का जाव ॥

dahī vālī jarā sā dahī beṅc jāv pher mathurā jī kā jāv.
bhaiyā mere pās n ānā hāthoṅ mere hāth n lānā;
mere kañgan kā mol cukāye jāv pher mathurā jī kā jāv.
bhaiyā mere pās n ānā gale mere hāth n lānā.
mere hāran kā mol cukāye jāv pher mathurā jī kā jāv.
bhaiyā mere pās n ānā māthe mere hāth n lānā;
merī beṅdī kā mol cukāye jāv pher mathurā jī kā jāv.
bhaiyā mere pās n ānā pairoṅ mere hāth n lānā.
mere pāyal kā mol cukāye jāv pher mathurā jī kā jāv.

O yoghurt seller, sell me some yoghurt and then go to Mathurā.
Don't come near me and don't touch my hands;
First, pay for my bracelets and then go to Mathurā.
Don't come near me and don't touch my neck;
First, pay for my necklace and then go to Mathurā.
Don't come near me and don't touch my forehead;
First, pay for my forehead ornament and then go to Mathurā.
Don't come near me and don't touch my feet;
First, pay for my ankle ornament and then go to Mathurā.

(LGT: 201R: 1972-73, Patti, Brāhmaṇ Women)

९९.

सुनो जी अरि हाथ जोड़ि बिनती करौं प्रभु से जोड़ी न बिगड़ै हमार
सुनो जी अरि जोड़ी न बिगड़ै माई बाप की जिन बिन जलम न होय ॥
सुनो जी अरि जोड़ी न बिगड़ै सास ससुर की जिन बिन राज न होय ॥
सुनो जी अरि जोड़ी न बिगड़ै जेठ जेठानी की रहनि बरोबरि होय ॥
सुनो जी अरि जोड़ी न बिगड़ै वारे सुमिया की जलम अकारथ होय ॥

suno jī ari hāth joṛi binatī karauṅ prabhu se joṛī n bigaṛai hamār.
suno jī ari joṛī n bigaṛai māī bāp kī jin bin jalam n hoy.
suno jī ari joṛī n bigaṛai sās sasur kī jin bin rāj n hoy.
Suno jī ari joṛī n bigaṛai jeṭh jeṭhānī kī rahani barobari hoy.
suno jī ari joṛī n bigaṛai vāre sumiyā kī jalam akārath hoy.

I pray to god with folded hands that my pair should not break.
I pray for my mother and father to remain together as without them this life is not possible.
I pray for my *sās* and *sasur* to remain together as without them there is no happiness.
I pray for my *jeṭh* and *jeṭhānī* to remain together so as to live together with them.
I pray for my husband without whom this life would be useless.

(LGT: 24R: 1972-73, Dhanabad, Brāhmaṇ Women)

१००.

राम लक्ष्मण भरत शत्रुघन आये हैं ससुरारी जी
करन कलेवा लगे जनक ग्रह गावैं सखियाँ गारी जी
एक सखी कहै सुनहु लला जी पूँछूँ मैं बात तुम्हारी जी
दूसर सखी कहत मुसकाई सुनौ अब बात हमारी जी
सुन्दर रूप कहाँ तुम पायेव कहाँ गई महतारी जी
खीर खाय पैदा सुत करती अवधपुरी की नारी जी ॥

rām lakṣmaṇ bharat śatrughan āye haiṅ sasurārī jī.
karan kalevā lage Janak grah gāvaiṅ sakhiyāñ gārī jī.

ek sakhī kahai sunahu lalā jī pūñchūñ maiṅ bāt tumhārī jī.
dūsar sakhī kahat musakāī sunau ab bāt hamārī jī.
sunder rūp kahāñ tum pāyev kahāñ gaī mahatārī jī.
khīr khāy paidā sut karatī avadhapurī kī nārī jī.

Rām, Lakṣmaṇ, Bharat, and Śatrughan have come to their in-laws' house.
As they come for a traditional dinner at Janak's palace, the women start singing abusive songs.
One woman is addressing them and asking them a question.
Another woman is saying jokingly: "Listen to me:"
"Where did your mother go that you are all so handsome?"
By eating rice pudding, the women of Avadh give birth to beautiful children."

(LGT: 23R: 1972-73, Dhanabad, Brāhmaṇ Women)

१०१.

कि ए जी आजु सुफल सुख सोने का दिनु है बाजति अनन्द बधाई
कि ए जी जौने दिना पूता तुम्हरा जलम भा पूजैं का मानेव बधाई
कि ए जी जिनका बुलाएँव पूता ओऊ नहीं आये बिनरे बुलाये बहुतेरे
कि ए जी उनका अदरु माता अस कुछ कीन्हेंव ओलियन बाँटेव मिठाई
कि ए जी उनके भवन लागे पठवन जायो हिरि फिरि शीश झुकाई

ki e jī āju suphal sukh sone kā dinu hai bājati anand badhāī.
ki e jī jaune dinā pūtā tumharā jalam bhā pūjaiṅ kā mānev badhāī.
ki e jī jinakā bulāeñv pūtā oū nahīṅ āye benare bulāye bahutere.
ki e jī unakā adaru mātā as kuch kīnheṅv oliyan bāñṭev miṭhāī.
ki e jī unake bhavan lāge paṭhavan jāyo hiri phiri śīś jhukāī.

Today is a blessed day as the auspicious music is being played.
Dear son, on the day of your birth, I had vowed to worship.
Dear son, those I invited did not come but many uninvited came.
Dear mother, honour them and distribute to them plenty of sweets.
Honour them by taking them back home and bowing to them.

(LGT: 25R: 1972-73, Dhanabad, Brāhmaṇ Women)

विवाह (बाती)

१०२.

बैठे बीती जाति सारी राति लाल तुम काहे न टारत बाती ॥
की जननी भगनी सिख दीन्हीं की बाती लग ताती
की तुम जइहौ नगर अजोध्या माता कौशिल्या के खातिर ॥
बाती टारउ नेग चुकावहु लै लीन्हेंव गज हाथी, भूँखे बैठे बराती ॥
ना जननी भगनी सिख दीन्हीं ना बाती लग ताती
ना जइबे हम नगर अजोध्या माता कौशिल्या के खातिर ॥
हमरे कुल की याही रीति है जदुवंशिन की जाती
यह बाती चारौ मिल कातैं जे हमरे संग जाती ॥
बाती टारेन नेग चुकायेन लइ लीन्हें गज हाथी
तुलसीदास भजौ भगवाना जेवन लागे बराती ॥

baiṭhe bītī jāti sārī rāti lāl tum kāhe n ṭārat bātī.
kī jananī bhaganī sikh dīnhīṅ kī bātī lag tātī.
kī tum jaihau nagar ajodhyā mātā kauśilyā ke khātir.
bātī ṭārau neg cukāvahu lai līnheṅv gaj hāthī bhūñkhe baiṭhe barātī.
nā jananī bhaganī sikh dīnhīṅ na bātī lag tātī.
nā jaibe ham nagar ajodhyā mātā kauśilyā ke khātir.
hamare kul kī yāhī rīti hai jaduvaṅśin kī jātī.
yah bātī cārau mil kātaiṅ je hamare saṅg jātī.
bātī ṭāren neg cukāyen lai līṅheṅ gaj hāthī.
tulasīdās bhajau bhagavānā jevan lāge barātī.

The whole night is about to pass, dear groom why aren't you joining the lamp's wick.
Has your mother advised you or is the wick too hot for you?
Would you go to Ayodhyā for the sake of your mother Kauśalyā?
Join the wick and take your ceremonial presents of elephants; members of your wedding party are hungrily waiting.
My mother has not advised me nor is the wick hot for me.
I would not go to Ayodhyā for the sake of my mother Kauśalyā.

This is the custom of our family belonging to the race of Yadu.
All four who are going with us should spin this wick together.
Then they joined the wick and accepted ceremonial presents of elephants.
Tulsīdās recites the name of god; members of the wedding party began their dinner.

(LGT: 86R: 1972-73, Ganj Muradabad, Mixed Women)

कलेवा (गारी)

१०३.

गारी देत सबै मिलि ग्वालिनी ॥
लाला अम्मा तुम्हारी को जानती, वे तो खीर खाय सुत पैदा किये ॥
लाला भाभी तुम्हारी को जानती, वे तो पाँच पुरुष एक नारि हैं ॥
लाला बुआ कुन्ती को जानती, वै तो क्वँवारे कर्ण पजावती ॥
लाला बहिनी सुभद्रा को जानती, वै तो अर्जुन संग सिधारती ॥

gārī det sabai mili gvālinī.
lālā ammā tumhārī ko jānatī, ve to khīr khāy sut paidā kiye.
lālā bhābhī tumhārī ko jānatī, ve to pāñc puruṣ ek nāri haiṅ.
lālā buā kuntī ko jānatī, vai to kvañre karṇ pajāvatī.
lālā bahinī subhadrā ko jānatī, vai to arjun saṅg sidhāratī.

The milkmaids are abusing all of them [in the groom's party].
Dear groom, I know your mother as she gave birth by eating rice-pudding.
Dear groom, I know your *bhābhī*, she is alone woman among five men.
Dear groom, I know your *buā* Kuntī, she gave birth to Karṇ out of wedlock.
Dear groom, I know your sister Subhadrā, she ran away with Arjun.

(LGT: 85R: 1972-73, Ganj Muradabad, Mixed Women)

विवाह (जेउनार)

१०४.

जन जन प्रति कंचन के थारे गनि गनि कनक कटोरा जी
अब व्यंजन चारि प्रकार सुधारस खटरस अति मन भाये जी
अब पूड़ी कचौड़ी और जलेबी मालपुआ बनवाये जी
पूड़ी कचौड़ी और सुहारी भाँति भाँति तरकारी जी
खोया खाँड़ खरोचन खाझा सब रस अति मन भाये जी
भाँति भाँति की बनी मिठाई सब रस व्यंजन आये जी
सुरभि गैया का गोबर मँगाओ झुकधरि अँगना लिपाओ जी
गजमोतिन की चौक पुराई चँदन पटुली डारी जी
भाँति भाँति की पतरी बनवाई सोने के टोब दिवाये जी
राम लक्ष्मन भरत शत्रुघन जाँघ जोरि बैठारे जी
परसत जनक बहुत रुचि लाये सब समाज हरसाई जी
बरजत जनक तनिक नहीं रुकते सब समाज उठि धाये जी
सोने के गेड़ुआ सरजू को जल लै लैके राम अचवाये जी
पान पचीसी की बिरिया लगाई लौंग इलायची डारी जी
मुख भरि बीरा रचौ रामजी तुलसीदास बलिहारी जी

jan jan prati kañcan ke thāre gani gani kanak kaṭorā jī.
ab vyañjan cāri prakār sudhāras khaṭaras ati man bhāye jī.
ab pūṛī kacauṛī aur jalebī mālapuā banavāye jī.[5]
Pūṛī kacauṛī aur suhārī bhāñti bhāñti tarakārī jī.
khoyā khāñṛ kharocan khājhā sab ras ati man bhāye jī.
bhāñti bhāñti kī banī miṭhāī sab ras vyañjan āye jī.
surabhi gaiyā kā gobar mañgāo jhukadhari añganā lipāo jī.
gajamotin kī cauk purāī cañdan paṭulī ḍārī jī.
bhāñti bhāñti kī patarī banavāī sone ke ṭob divāye jī.
rām lakṣmaṇ bharat śatrughan jāñgh jori baiṭhāre jī.
parasat janak bahut ruci lāye sab samāj harasāī jī.

---

5. *Pūrī, kacaurī, jalebī, mālapuā, suhārī, khaṇḍ, kharocana, khājhā* are various foods, desserts, and ingredients.

barajat janak tanik nahīṅ rukate sab samāj uṭhi dhāye jī.
sone ke geḍuā sarajū ko jal lai laike rām acavāye jī.
pān pacīsī kī biriyā lagāī lauṅg ilāyacī ḍārī jī.
mukh bhari bīrā racau rāmajī tulasīdās balihārī jī.

The plates and bowls are of shining gold.
The four varieties of food, sweets and sours are very tasty.
Pūrī, kacaurī, jalebī, and *malapuā* have been made.
Pūrī, kacaurī, and *suhārī* with many kinds of vegetables are made.
Khoyā, khāṇḍ, kharocan, and *khājhā,* all are pleasing.
Many different sweets are being prepared and many other tasty dishes have been set out.
Get the cowdung and smear the whole courtyard.
The dining area has been decorated with pearls and sandalwood boards have been set out for sitting.
Leaf plates of various kinds are being prepared, with golden pins used to join the leaves together.
Rām, Lakṣmaṇ, Bharat, and Śatrughan all sat close to each other.
Janak served the food with pleasure; seeing this, the whole assembled party became very pleased.
After finishing the feast, the whole party got up, even though Janak wanted them to eat more.
With a gold mug filled with water from the Sarayū River, he asked Rām to rinse his mouth.
The betel leaves were made with cloves and cardamom in them.
Tulsīdās says: "I sacrifice myself to Rām, eat a mouthful of betel leaves."
(LGT: 84R: 1972-73, Ganj Muradabad, Mixed Women)

विवाह (गारी)

१०५.

ए जी राम बिना भगवान बिना अब हरि बिन अपना ना कोई ॥

ए जी ई बेटवा अपने सुख का मैं सेएँव अतर सुगंध लगाई
ए जी ई बेटवा मोरे काम न अइहैं जाहि बसे ससुरारि॥
ए जी ई बिटिया मैं अस कै सेएँव अतर सुगंध लगाई
ए जी ई बिटिया मैं अस कै सेएँव खाँड़ चिरौंजी खवाई
ए जी ई बिटिया मोरे काम न अइहैं जइसे कोयल उड़ि जाई॥
ए जी ई देहियाँ मैं मल मल धोएँव अतर सुगंध लगाई
ए जी ई देहियाँ मोरे काम न अइहैं माटी मा माटी मिल जाई॥

e jī rām binā bhagavān binā ab hari bin apanā nā koī.
e jī ī beṭavā apane sukh kā maiṅ seeñv atar sugaṅdh lagāī;
e jī ī beṭavā more kām n aihaiṅ jāhi base sasurāri.
e jī ī biṭiyā maiṅ as kai seeñv atar sugaṅdh lagāī.
e jī ī biṭiyā maiṅ as kai seeñv khāñṛ cirauṅjī khavāī;
e jī ī biṭiyā more kām n aihaiṅ jaise koyal uṛi jāī.
e jī ī dehiyāñ maiṅ mal mal dhoeñv atar sugaṅdh lagāī;
e jī ī dehiyāñ more kām n aihaiṅ māṭī mā māṭī mil jāī.

Oh dear, nobody is mine except Hari.
This son, I raised with all comforts for my own happiness;
This son would not come to help me as he would go and live in his in-laws place.
This daughter, I raised with all comforts;
This daughter, I raised with nourishing food;
This daughter would not come to help me as she would fly away like a cuckoo.
This body, I rubbed and cleaned and applied all kind of perfumes to;
This body would not come to my help as the dirt would mix in dirt.

(LGT: 34R: 1972-73, Dhanabad, Camār Women)

१०६.

ए जी सीता का ब्याह रचालो राम जी धरती के शीश नवाई॥
ए जी सीता पूँछैं अपनी सखिन से कौनि आहीं ससुरा हमार
ए जी महल के नीरे तीरे हथिनी चुगावैं वई आहीं ससुरा तुम्हारे॥
ए जी सीता पूँछैं अपनी सखिन से कौनि आहीं जेठा हमारे

ए जी महल के नीरे तीरे घोड़वा कुँदावैं वई आहीं जेठा तुम्हारे ॥
ए जी सीता पूँछैं अपनी सखिन से कौनि आहीं देवरा हमारे
ए जी सीता पूँछैं अपनी सखिन से कौनि आहीं सँवलिया हमारे
ए जी महल के नीरे तीरे डोलिया सजावैं वई आहीं सँवलिया तुम्हारे ॥

e jī sītā kā byāh racālo rām jī dharatī ke śīś navāī.
e jī sītā pūñchaiṅ apanī sakhin se kauni āhīṅ sasurā hamār;
e jī mahal ke nīre tīre hathinī cugāvaiṅ vaī āhīṅ sasurā tumhāre.
e jī sītā pūñchaiṅ apanī sakhin se kauni āhīṅ jeṭhā hamāre;
e jī mahal ke nīre tīre ghoṛavā kuñdāvaiṅ vaī āhīṅ jeṭhā tumhāre.
e jī sītā pūñchaiṅ apanī sakhin se kauni āhīṅ devarā hamāre;
e jī sītā pūñchaiṅ apanī sakhin se kauni āhīṅ sañvaliyā hamāre;
e jī mahal ke nīre tīre ḍoliyā sajāvaiṅ vaī āhīṅ sañvaliyā tumhāre.

Bow to mother earth and wed Sītā, O Ram.
Sītā is asking her friends which one is her *sasur.*
The one who is tending elephants around the palace is your *sasur.*
Sītā is asking her friends which one is her *jeṭh.*
The one who is jumping the horses around the palace is your *jeṭh.*
Sītā is asking her friends which one is her *devar.*
Sītā is asking her friends which one is her husband.
The one who is decorating the palanquin near the palace is your husband.

(LGT: 35R: 1972-73, Dhanabad, Camār Women)

विवाह (बिदाई)

१०७.

पिता घर छोड़के मुझको पती के घर में जाना है
सदा संसार में बेटी यही एक खार खाना है
तुम्हारी धर्म की माता सास ससुराल में होगी
उसी के कहने में चलना तुझे तो सुख उठाना है ॥

जेठानी नन्द देउरानी परोसिन नारियाँ जितनी
उन्हीं से प्रेमकर चलना यही सुख का खजाना है॥

pitā ghar choṛake mujhako patī ke ghar meṅ jānā hai.
sadā saṅsār meṅ beṭī yahī ek khār khānā hai.
tumhārī dharm kī mātā sās sasurāl meṅ hogī.
usī ke kahane meṅ calanā tujhe to sukh uṭhānā hai.
jeṭhānī nand deurānī parosin nāriyāñ jitanī.
unhīṅ se premakar calanā yahī sukh kā khajānā hai.

I have to leave my father's home and go to my husband's home.
Such envy has always been present in this world.
Your mother by custom is your *sās* in your in-law's place.
If you want happiness, obey her commands.
Your *jeṭhānī, nanad, devarānī,* and all the neighbourhood women.
The treasure of happiness is that you love them all.

(CYT: 244C: 1975, Sheoli, Brāhmaṇ Woman)

विवाह (लड़का)

विवाह (पियरी)

१०८.

माँग मोती सिरह सेंदुर बैठी धना देई अनमनी
दरवार से उनके साहब आये काहे धना तुम अनमनी
तुम्हरी विरध राजा हमका न भावै हमरे बिरन नहीं आइये
लावौ न रानी मेरी कलम दवाइत चिठिया लिखौं तेरे बीर को
तुम्हरे देश राजा नदिया बहति है हमरे बिरन कैसे आइये
बुलाइ केवट नैया डरइहौं धना के बिरन बेग आइये
तुम्हरे देश राजा कजरी का बनु है हमरे बिरन कैसे आइये
बोलाय बढ़ई बन जो कटइहौं धना के बिरन बेग आइये

तुम्हरे देश राजा ठगवा लगति हैं हमरे बिरन कैसे आइये
बुलाय मनई ठगवा मरइहौं धना के बिरन बेग आइये
मेरे बीर आये चीर लाये सासु ननद मुख मोड़िये
आवौ न बहिनी मेरी एकु मत करिये केहिका कहा पहिराइये
सासु का पियरी ननद का चुनरी हम लड़बछुरी का पीयरी
सासु का चाँदी ननद का रूपो हम लड़बछुरी का सोनवा
खोलि सन्दुकिया बैठे बिरन भैया मानों शर्राफ के बेटवा
खोलि बटुका बैठे बिरन भैया मानों बजाज के बेटवा
जेहिके न बहिनी मेरी इतनो जो होवै सो कैसे आवै तेरे माड़ये
जेहिके न भैया मेरे इतनो होवै हाथ जोर बिनती करै ॥

māñg motī sirah seṅdur baiṭhī dhanā deī anamanī.
darabār se unake sāhab āye kāhe dhanā tum anamanī.
tumharī viradh rājā hamakā n bhāvai hamare biran nahīṅ āiye.
Lāvau n rānī merī kalam davāit ciṭhiyā likhauṅ tere bīr ko.
tumhare deś rājā nadiyā bahati hai hamare biran kaise āiye.
bulāi kevaṭ naiyā ḍaraihauṅ dhanā ke biran beg āiye.
tumhare deś rājā kajarī kā banu hai hamare biran kaise āiye.
bolāy baṛhaī ban jo kaṭaihauṅ dhanā ke biran beg āiye.
tumhare deś rājā ṭhagavā lagati haiṅ hamare biran kaise āiye.
bulāy manaī ṭhagavā maraihauṅ dhanā ke biran beg āiye.
mere bīr āye cīr lāye sāsu nanad mukh moṛiye.
āvau n bahinī merī eku mat kariye kehikā kahā pahirāiye.
sāsu kā piyarī nanad kā cunarī ham laṛabachurī kā pīyarī.
sāsu kā cāñdī nanad kā rūpo ham laṛabachurī kā sonavā.
kholi sandukiyā baiṭhe biran bhaiyā mānoṅ śarrāph ke beṭavā.
kholi baṭukā baiṭhe biran bhaiyā mānoṅ bajāj ke beṭavā.
jehike n bahinī merī itano jo hovai so kaise āvai tere māṛaye.
jehike n bhaiyā mere itano hovai hāth jor binatī karai.

With pearls in her part and *sindūr* in her hair, the wife sat unhappily.
Her husband came home from his business and enquired about her sadness.
"I do not like your country because my brother has not come."
"Bring my inkpot and pen so that I can write a letter to your brother."

"There is a raging river in your country and how would my brother come?"
"I would call for a boatman to ready a boat so that your brother could come quickly."
"There is a dense forest in your country and how would my brother come?"
"I would call a wood-cutter to cut the forest so that your brother could come quickly."
"There are *ṭhug*s in your country and how would my brother come?"
"I would call my army to kill the *ṭhug*s so that your brother could come quickly."
My brother came and he brought presents but my *sās* and *nanad* turn their faces.
Come dear sister for a consultation as to who should get which present.
Give my *sās* a yellow *sārī*, a scarf to *nanad* and to me yellow *sārī*.
Give my *sās* silver, a silver rupee to *nanad* and to me a gold ornament.
"My brother sat with his box open like the son of a jeweller."
"My brother sat with his purse open like the son of a jeweller"
"If someone does not have this much for presents, how could he come to your marriage ceremony?"
"If someone does not have this much, dear brother, then he should simply pay respect with folded hands."

(LGT: 77R: 1972-73, Ganj Muradabad, Mixed Women)

१०९.

ऊँचो सो नग्र अजोध्या बसत है हुवना पटौना केरी हाट बिना
बारे दुलहू राजा आरि करति हैं लै देव चकई औ डोरि बिना
बाबा मोर लै देव चकई औ डोरि बिना ॥
चकई खेलत कुछु ऐसी रुचि लागी बारे मा रचउ बिवाहु बिना
बाबा मोर बारे मा रचउ बिवाहु बिना ॥
अम्बा लगन देव महुआ चुअन देव लागन देव बैसाखु बिना
दुलरुवा लागन देव बैसाखु बिना ॥
अम्बा चुइय चले महुआ टपकि चले बीत चलो है बैसाख बिना
बाबा मोरे बीत चलो है बैसाख बिना ॥

जेठ बैसाख की खरी दुपहरी हम न बियाहन जाँइ बिना
बाबा मोरे हम न बियाहन जाँइ बिना ॥
बिच बिच सगर खोदइहौं मेरे अति लड़बछुरे बिच बिच कुँअना खोदावौं बिना
अम्बा की डार कोयल एक बोलै छिन एक धूप निवारौ बिना
दुलरुवा छिन एक धूप निवारौ बिना ॥
हम कैसे धूप निवारैं कोयल देई लगन उमहें हम जाँइ बिना
ब्याह बूहि जब लउटैं कोयल देई सोने मा मढ़इहौं तेरी चोंच बिना
कि देखौ पँख मढ़ावौं तेरे सोने बिना ॥
जुग जुग जियो मेरे दुलहे राजा राखो कोयलिया को मान बिना ॥

ūñco so nagr ajodhyā basat hai huvanā paṭaunā kerī hāṭ binā.
bāre dulahū rājā āri karati haiṅ lai dev cakaī au ḍori binā.
bābā mor lai dev cakaī au ḍori binā.
cakaī khelat kuchu aisī ruci lāgī bāre mā racau bivāhu binā.
bābā mor bāre mā racau bivāhu binā.
ambā lagan dev mahuā cuan dev lāgan dev baisākhu binā.
dularuvā lāgan dev baisākhu binā.
ambā cuiy cale mahuā ṭapaki cale bīt calo hai baisākh binā.
bābā more bīt calo hai baisākh binā.
jeṭh baisākh kī kharī dupaharī ham n biyāhan jāñi binā.
bābā more ham n biyāhan jāñi binā.
bic bic sagar khodaihauṅ mere ati laṛabachure bic bic kuñanā khodāvauṅ binā.
ambā kī ḍār koyal ek bolai chin ek dhūp nivārau binā.
dularuvā chin ek dhūp nivārau binā.
ham kaise dhūp nivāraiṅ koyal deī lagan umaheṅ ham jāñi binā.
byāh būhi jab lauṭaiṇ koyal deī sone mā maṛhaihauṅ terī coṅc binā.
ki dekhau pañkh maṛhāvauṅ tere sone binā.
jug jug jiyo mere dulahe rājā rākho koyaliyā ko mān binā.

In the high city of Ayodhyā, there is a market with many shops.
There the groom is repeatedly asking to buy a whirling toy and string.
O dear grandfather, buy a whirling toy and string for me.
He became so interested in playing that whirling toy and string that now he is asking for his marriage at this early age.
O dear grandfather, arrange for my marriage at this early age.

Let the mango bear fruit and *mahuā* tree drop fruit and the month of *Baisākh* come.
O dear child, let the month of *Baisākh* come.
The mango and *mahuā* fruits have begun dropping and the *Baisākh* month is nearly over.
My dear grandfather, the *Baisākh* month is nearly over.
The sun in the month of *jeṭh* and *Baisākh* is intense and I would not go for my wedding then.
O dear grandfather, I would not go for my wedding then.
I would have ponds and wells dug on our way my dear loving child.
A cuckoo is calling from a mango branch to rest a while in the shade.
O dear child, rest a while in the shade from this intense heat.
How could I rest a while O dear cuckoo, I am rushing to make the auspicious time.
On my return after the marriage, I would cover your beak with gold.
I will cover your wings with gold.
May you, dear groom, live a long life as you have honoured a cuckoo.

(LGT: 80R: 1972-73, Ganj Muradabad, Rastogi Woman)

११०.

मोरे पिछवड़वा सुपरिया का बिरवा अलंग बिलंग वइकै डार
तै तरे ठाढ़े हैं दुलहे दुलरुवा टुरईं सुपरिया कै डार
सो बियहे बइठे हैं बाबा जो उनके मालिनि ओरहनु देइ रे
बरजो न साहेब अपने दुलरुवा टुरईं सुपरिया कै डार
बारे होंइ तउ बरजों री मालिनि छैलु गरजि नहीं जाँय
बारा बरिस केरे दुलहे दुलरुवा, मोरे बूते बरजि न जाँय

more pichavaṛavā supariyā kā biravā alaṅg bilaṅg vaikai ḍār.
tai tare ṭhāṛhe haiṅ dulahe dularuvā ṭuraiṅ supariyā kai ḍār.
so biyahe baiṭhe haiṅ bābā jo unake mālini orahanu ḍei re.
barajo n sāheb apane dularuvā ṭuraīṅ supariyā kai ḍār.
bāre hoṅi tau barajoṅ rī mālini chailu garaji nahīṅ jāñy.
bārā baris kere dulahe dularuvā, more būte baraji n jāñy.

In my backyard there is a betelnut tree whose branches are spread all over.
Standing under that betelnut tree, dear groom is breaking the branches.
The gardener's wife complained to the grandfather, about the groom, who was observing the wedding.
Why don't you forbid the groom from breaking the branch of betelnut tree!
If he was young, I would have forbade him but grownups are not to be shouted at.
My dear groom is twelve years old and it is beyond me to forbid him.
(LGT: 47R: 1972-73, Dhanabad, Brāhmaṇ Women)

१११.

बड़े बड़े नैन राम जी के देखे, धनुष जज्ञ मा ठाढ़े हते री
माथे राम जी के तिलक बिराजै, चन्दन खबर लगाये हते री
माथे उनके तिलक चन्द्रमा कुण्डल मा छबि छाये हते री
अंग राम जी के पटुका सोहै, जामा की छबि पाये हते री
राम लखण और सहित जानकी, सखियन संग सिधाये हते री
तौरें धनुष बरन सीता के, परशुराम संघ आये हते री
कौने तोरो है धनुष शम्भु को, सहिय सवाल बताये हते री
शिवशंकर को चाप कठिन है, किन जोधा ने टोरी चलाये हते री
इतने बचन लखन हँसि बोले, परशुराम समझाये हते री
बहु धनुही तोड़ी रघुबर ने, क्रोध अपने मन छाये हते री
तुलसीदास आश रघुबर की, हरि चरनन सिर नाये हते री

baṛe baṛe nain rām jī ke dekhe dhanuṣ jagy mā ṭhāṛe hate rī.
māthe rām jī ke tilak birājai, candan khabar lagāye hate rī.
māthe unake tilak candramā, kuṇḍal mā chabi chāye hate rī.
aṅg rām jī ke paṭukā sohai, jāmā kī chabi pāye hate rī.
rām lakhaṇ aur sahit jānakī, sakhiyan saṅg sidhāye hate rī.
toraiṅ dhanuṣ baran Sītā ke, paraśurām saṅgh āye hate rī.
kaune toro hai dhanuṣ śambhu ko, sahiy savāl batāye hate rī.
śivasaṅkar ko cāp kaṭhin hai, kin jodhā ne ṭorī calāye hate rī.
itane bacan lakhan hañsi bole, paraśurām samajhāye hate rī.

bahu dhanuhī toṛī raghubar ne, krodh apane man chāye hate rī.
tulasīdās āś raghubar kī hari caranan sir nāye hate rī.

I saw the beautiful eyes of Rām while he was standing near the bow's site.
There was a sandalwood mark on Rām's forehead.
His forehead was marked like a moon and he adorned himself with earrings.
Rām wore a beautiful garment.
Rām, along with Lakṣmaṇ and Sītā, was surrounded by women friends.
He broke the bow to wed Sītā and, as a result, Paraśurām had arrived.
He wanted to know the truth as to who had broken Śiva's bow.
Śiva's bow is very difficult and which warrior had broken it.
Hearing these words of Paraśurām, Lakṣmaṇ had said,
Rām has broken many bows but you were never this angry.
Tulsīdās only knows the hope of Rām and had bowed his head.

(CYT: 243C: 1975, Sheoli, Brāhmaṇ Woman)

११२.

बार बार मैं बरजौं सहजादे पूता घर रहियो हो
सहजाती ननदी के लड़िका बहुत हैं मड़ौना मोरा चुनि डरिहैं हो
आधे तलौना मा नाग बैठे आधे मा नागिन हो
तलवा तेहू न रातुल होय अकेली ननद बिन हो
आधे मड़ौना मा गोप बैठे आधे मा गोपिन हो
मड़वा तेहू न रातुल होय एक ननद बिना हो
अरि अरि ननदी गोसाईं मैं पैंयाँ तोरे लागौं
ननदी बैठो न खम्भा ओढ़काय कलश मोरा गोंठव हो

bār bār maiṅ barajauṅ sahajāde pūtā ghar rahiyo ho.
sahajātī nanadī ke laṛikā bahut haiṅ maṛaunā morā cuni ḍarihaiṅ ho.
ādhe talaunā mā nāg baiṭhe ādhe mā nāgin ho;
talavā tehū n rātul hoy akelī nanad bin ho.
ādhe maṛaunā mā gop baiṭhe ādhe mā gopin ho;
maṛavā tehū n rātul hoy ek nanad binā ho.

ari ari nanadī gosāīṅ maiṅ paiṅyāñ tore lāgauṅ;
nanadī baiṭho n khambhā oṛhakāy kalaś morā goṅṭhav ho.

I repeatedly forbid you, dear son, to remain in the house.
My dear *nanad* has many children and they will take care of the marriage canopy
A cobra sits on one half of the pond and a she-cobra sits on the other half;
Even then the pond is not colourful due to the absence of my *nanad.*
On half the marriage canopy sat cowherds and on the other half milkmaids;
Even then the marriage canopy is not colourful due to the absence of my *nanad.*
O dear *nanad*, I touch your feet;
Dear *nanad*, sit next to the pillar and decorate my ceremonial water pot.
(LGT: 208R: 1972-73, Patti, Brāhmaṇ Women)

विवाह (सेहरा)

११३.

मदन मोहन जी को सेहरा लागो मन मेरो
चंद् चकोर से नैना बने मुखहीं पर सोहै
मुखहिं तमोलिन बसि गई सुन दूल्हा प्यारे
धनि माया धनि बाप को जिन बेटा जायो
सोने को मौरु धराई के बन्ना व्याहन आये
धनि माया धनि बाप को जिन बेटी जायी
मोतिन माँग भराय के बेटी व्याहन आई॥
बाजत बाजे बहु बिधी बाजै शहनाई
कोड़री के बाजन बाजि के बन्ना व्याहन आये॥

madan mohan jī ko seharā lāgo man mero.
caṅd cakor se nainā bane mukhahīṅ par sohai.
mukhahiṅ tamolin basi gaī sun dūlhā pyāre.
dhani māyā dhani bāp ko jin beṭā jāyo.

sone ko mauru dharāī ke bannā vyāhan āye.
dhani māyā dhani bāp ko jin beṭī jāyī.
motin māñg bharāy ke beṭī vyāhan āī.
bājat bāje bahu bidhī bājai śahanāī.
koṛarī ke bājan bāji ke bannā vyāhan āye.

I adore the groom's hat on Kṛṣṇa.
His eyes are like the moon and *cakor* and his mouth is beautiful,
As if a betel seller's wife herself is residing upon his mouth; listen dear groom.
Those mothers and fathers are blessed who give birth to a son.
With a golden crown on his head, the groom has come to be wed.
Those mothers and fathers are blessed who give birth to a daughter.
With pearls in her part, the daughter has come to be wed.
All kinds of musical instruments are played including *śahanāī.*
With instruments of Koṛarī (?) ensemble, the groom has come to be wed.
(LGT: 79R: 1972-73, Ganj Muradabad, Mixed Women)

विवाह (बन्ना)

११४

बाजे नगाड़ा प्रेम का बन्ना व्याहन आयो ॥
जबहिं बन्ना गोइड़वैं आयो, सास टेपारा साज कर बन्ना लेकर आयो ॥
जबहिं बन्ना दुवारे आयो, हाथ फुलन का गाजरा बन्ना लेकर आयो ॥
जबहिं बन्ना मड़ये आयो, हाथ सेंदुर की डेबिया बन्ना लेकर आयो ॥
जबहिं बन्ना कोहबरे आयो, हाथ दही की मेटिया बन्ना लेकर आयो ॥
जबहिं बन्ना महलियै आयो, हाथ बेसन के लेड्डुवा बन्ना लेकर आयो ॥
घूँघट के पट खोल बाँदरी, हमहैं मुसाफिर पाहुना जरा हँस के बोलो ॥

bāje nagāṛā prem kā bannā vyāhan āyo.
jabahiṅ bannā goiṛavaiṅ āyo, sās ṭepārā sāj kar bannā lekar āyo.
jabahiṅ bannā duvāre āyo, hāth phulan kā gājarā bannā lekar āyo.

jabahiṅ bannā maṛaye āyo, hāth seṅdur kī ḍebiyā bannā lekar āyo.
jabahiṅ bannā kohabare āyo, hāth dahī kī meṭiyā bannā lekar āyo.
jabahiṅ bannā mahaliyai āyo, hāth besan ke leḍuvā bannā lekar āyo.
ghūñghaṭ ke paṭ khol bāñdarī, hamahaiṅ musāphir pāhunā jarā hañs ke bolo.

Playing the kettle drum of love, the groom has come to wed.
When the groom came to the lane, he brought with him a ceremonial basket for his *sās*.
When the groom came to the gate, he brought with him a garland of flowers.
When the groom came to the marriage canopy, he brought a *sendur* box with him.
When the groom came to the *kohabar*, he brought a pot of yoghurt with him.
When the groom came to his palace, he brought sweets with him.
Unveil yourself and give me a smile as I am your guest.

(LGT: 196R: 1972-73, Patti, Brāhmaṇ Women)

११५.

गोकुल नहीं जाना जमुना चढ़ीं॥
सिर तेरे अँगरेजी चीरा, कान तेरे नौटँके मोती
लड़ियाँ सँवारे सखियाँ खड़ीं, तेरी गेंटा सँवारे सखियाँ खड़ीं॥
नैन तेरे लाहौरी सुरमा, मुख तेरे पानों का बीड़ा
महबट सँवारे सारी सखियाँ खड़ीं, तेरी लाली सँवारे सब सखियाँ खड़ीं॥
जमुना चढ़ीं कालिन्द्री चढ़ीं॥
गल तेरे सोने का तोरा, हाथ तेरे जड़ाऊ ककना
बेंदी सँवारन को सखियाँ खड़ीं, तेरी चूड़ी, सँवारन को सखियाँ खड़ीं॥
जमुना चढ़ीं महरानी चढ़ीं॥
अंग तेरे केसरिया जामा, कमर तेरे गुजराती पटुका
बन्दे सँवारे सब सखियाँ खड़ीं, तेरी चौरें सँवारे सब सखियाँ खड़ीं॥
हेंठ तेरे काबुल का घोड़ा, पैर तेरे जयपुर का जूता
चाबुक सँवारे सखियाँ खड़ीं, तेरे मोजे सँवारे सखियाँ खड़ीं॥
संग तेरे भैयन की जोड़ी, ब्याह लाये हरयाली बन्नी
तौबत सँभारन को सखियाँ खड़ीं, तेरी डोली सँभारन को सखियाँ खड़ीं॥

gokul nahīṅ jānā jamunā caṛhīṅ.
sir tere añgarejī cīrā, kān tere nauṭañke motī;
laṛiyāñ sañvāre sakhiyāñ khaṛīṅ, terī geṅṭā sañvāre sakhiyāñ khaṛīṅ.
nain tere lāhaurī suramā, mukh tere pānoṅ kā bīṛā;
mahabaṭ sañvāre sārī sakhiyāñ khaṛīṅ, terī lālī sañvāre sab sakhiyāñ khaṛīṅ.
jamunā caṛhīṅ kālindrī caṛhīṅ.
gal tere sone kā torā, hāth tere jaṛāū kakanā;
beṅdī sañvāran ko sakhiyāñ khaṛīṅ, terī cūṛī sañvāran ko sakhiyāñ khaṛīṅ.
jamunā caṛhīṅ maharānī caṛhīṅ.
aṅg tere kesariyā jāmā, kamar tere gujarātī paṭukā;
bande sañvāre sab sakhiyāñ khaṛīṅ, terī coraiṅ sañvāre sab sakhiyāñ khaṛīṅ.
heṅṭh tere kābul kā ghoṛā, pair tere jayapur kā jūtā;
cābuk sañvāre sakhiyāñ khaṛīṅ, tere moje sañvāre sakhiyāñ khaṛīṅ.
saṅg tere bhaiyan kī joṛī, byāh lāye harayālī bannī;
taubat sañbhāran ko sakhiyāñ khaṛīṅ, terī ḍolī sañbhāran ko sakhiyāñ khaṛīṅ.

Do not go to Gokul, the Jamuna river is flooded.
On your head you have an English turban and pearl-studded earrings;
Girlfriends are standing to help you with your strands of hair.
In your eyes, you have collyrium from Lahore and a betelleaf in your mouth.
All the girlfriends are standing to take care of your eye make-up and the red colour of the betelleaf.
The Jamunā river is flooded; Kālindrī[1] river is flooded.
You have a golden necklace and a bracelet studded with gems on your wrist;
Girlfriends are standing to take care of the head ornament and bangles.
The Jamunā river is flooded; Queen [Jamunā] is flooded.
You are wearing a saffron colour garment and a scarf from Gujarat on your waist.
All the girlfriends are standing to button your garment and the pleats of the scarf.
You are riding a horse from Kābul and wearing shoes from Jaipur;
Girlfriends are standing holding your whip and socks.

---

1. An epithet of the river Jamunā.

Your brothers are in pair with you and you wed a beautiful bride;
Girlfriends are standing to take care of your *taubat* (?) and the palanquin.
(LGT: 183R: 1972-73, Vṛndāvan, Brāhmaṇ Women)

११६.

बाँके बिहारी की घोड़ी सजी उस घोड़ी को देखन जसोदा चलीं ॥
कान तेरे नौटंके मोती, कमर तेरे सोने का कोहड़ा
लड़ियाँ सँवारन को राधा खड़ी, तेरी जुगिनी सँवारन को राधा खड़ी ॥
नैन तेरे लाहौरी सुरमा, मुख तेरे पानों का बीड़ा
महबट सँवारन को राधा खड़ी, तेरी लाली सँवारन को राधा खड़ी ॥
अंग तेरे केशरिया जामा, कमर तेरे गुजराती पटुका
बन्नो सँवारन को राधा खड़ी, तेरी चौरें सँवारन को राधा खड़ी ॥
पैर तेरे जयपुर का जूता, हेंठ तेरे काबुल का घोड़िला
मोजे सँवारन को राधा खड़ी, तेरी चाबुक सँवारन को राधा खड़ी ॥
संग तेरे भैयन की जोड़ी, व्याह लाये साजन की बेटी
तौबत सँभारन को राधा खड़ी, तेरे डोला सँभारन को सखियाँ खड़ी ॥

bāñke bihārī kī ghoṛī sajī us ghoṛī ko dekhan jasodā calīṅ.
kān tere nauṭaṅke motī, kamar tere sone kā kohaṛā;
laṛiyāñ sañvāran ko rādhā khaṛī, terī juginī sañvāran ko rādhā khaṛī.
nain tere lāhaurī suramā, mukh tere panoṅ kā bīṛā;
mahabaṭ sañvāran ko rādhā khaṛī, terī lālī sañvāran ko rādhā khaṛī.
aṅg tere keśariyā jāmā kamar tere gujarātī paṭukā;
banno sañvāran ko rādhā khaṛī, terī coraiṅ sañvāran ko rādhā khaṛī.
pair tere jayapur kā jūtā, heṅṭh tere kābul kā ghoṛilā;
moje sañvāran ko rādhā khaṛī, terī cābuk sañvāran ko rādhā khaṛī.
saṅg tere bhaiyan kī joṛī, vyāh lāye sājan kī beṭī;
taubat sañbhāran ko rādhā khaṛī, tere ḍolā sañbhāran ko sakhiyāñ khaṛī.

Yaśodā walked to see the decorated mare of Kṛṣṇa.
In your ears you have pearl-studded earrings and a golden belt on your waist.
Rādhā is standing to comb your hair and to fix your belt.

In your eyes, you have collyrium from Lahore and a betelleaf in your mouth;
Rādhā is standing to take care of your eye make-up and the red colour of the betel-leaf.
You are wearing a saffron colour garment and a scarf from Gujarat on your waist;
Rādhā is standing to take care of your buttons and the pleats of your scarf.
You are wearing shoes from Jaipur and are riding a horse from Kābul.
Rādhā is standing with your socks and whip.
Your brothers are in pair with you and you wed a beautiful bride;
Rādhā is standing to take care of your *taubat* (?) and girlfriends are standing to manage the palanquin.

(LGT: 182R: 1972-73, Vr̥ndāvan, Brāhmaṇ Women)

११७.

मेरा बन्ना आज ससुरारि को चला ॥
वाके बाबा बरात को साजि रहे, वाकी दादी ने बन्ना बनाय दिया ॥
वाके ताऊ जो रुपया लुटाइ रहे, ताई रानी ने बन्ना सँवार दिया ॥
वाके बाबू बरात को साजि रहे, वाकी माया ने बन्ना बनाय दिया ॥
वाके फूफा जो पगड़ी बाँधि रहे, वाकी बुआ ने खौर को खींच दिया ॥
वाके जीजा खड़े जो निछावर करैं, वाकी बहिनी जो रइया उतारि रही ॥

merā bannā āj sasurāri ko calā.
vāke bābā barāt ko sāji rahe, vākī dādī ne bannā banāy diyā.
vāke tāū jo rupayā luṭāi rahe, tāī rānī ne bannā sañvār diyā.
vāke bābū barāt ko sāji rahe, vākī māyā ne bannā banāy diyā.
vāke phūphā jo pagaṛī bāñdhi rahe, vākī buā ne khaur ko khīṅc diyā.
vāke jījā khaṛe jo nichāvar karaiṅ, vākī bahinī jo raiyā utāri rahī.

Today, my groom is going to his in-law's place.
His grandfather is arranging the groom's party and his grandmother prepared the groom.
His *tāu* is distributing money and his *tāī* prepared the groom.

His father is arranging the groom's party and his mother prepared the groom.
His *phūphā* tied his turban and his *buā* tied [or applied] the *khaur*.
His *jījā* is performing propitiatory offerings and his sister is warding off evil spirits.

(LGT: 106R: 1972-73, Ganj Muradabad, Mixed Women)

११८.

खेलैं खेलैं कौशिल्या की गोद् रामचन्द्र बनरा बने ॥
सिर सोहै जाली का सीरा, ओकी कलँगी पे नाच रहे मोर ॥
कान सोहै सूरत के मोती, ओकी चुन्नी पे नाच रहे मोर ॥
नैन सोहै साँवलिया सुरमा, ओकी बिरियों पे नाच रहे मोर ॥
गले सोहै नौ लाख का कण्ठा, ओकी गुड़ियन पे नाच रहे मोर ॥
हाथ सोहै हीरों की पहुँची, ओकी मुड़री पे नाच रहे मोर ॥
अंग सोहै केसरिया जामा, ओके पटुका पे नाच रहे मोर ॥
पैर सोहै लखनौवा मोजा, ओकी चालों पे नाच रहे मोर ॥
संग सोहै भैयों की जोड़ी, ओकी महफिल पे नाच रहे मोर ॥
संग सोहै हरि वाला डोला, ओकी कनरी पे नाच रहे मोर ॥

khelaiṅ khelaiṅ kauśilyā kī god rāmacandr banarā bane.
sir sohai jālī kā sīrā okī, kalañgī pe nāc rahe mor.
kān sohai sūrat ke motī, okī cunnī pe nāc rahe mor.
nain sohai sañvaliyā suramā okī biriyoṅ pe nāc rahe mor.
gale sohai nau lākh kā kaṇṭhā, okī guṛiyan pe nāc rahe mor.
hāth sohai hīroṅ kī pahuñcī, okī muṛarī pe nāc rahe mor.
aṅg sohai kesariyā jāmā, oke paṭukā pe nāc rahe mor.
pair sohai lakhanauvā mojā, okī cāloṅ pe nāc rahe mor.
saṅg sohai bhaiyoṅ kī joṛī, okī mahaphil pe nāc rahe mor.
saṅg sohai hari vālā ḍolā, okī kanarī pe nāc rahe mor.

Rām who once played on mother Kauśalyā's lap has now become a groom.
He is wearing a crochet crown with a peacock's plume.
He has adorned himself with pearl earrings; his scarf is fluttering.

He has dark collyrium on his eyes and a betelleaf in his mouth.
A necklace worth nine lakh adorns his neck as if peacocks are dancing on his face.
A diamond bracelet adorns his wrist as if peacocks are dancing on his shoulders.
He is wearing a saffron colour garment as if peacocks are dancing on his scarf.
He is wearing socks from Lucknow on his feet as if peacocks are dancing in his walk.
He is accompanied by his brothers as if peacocks are dancing in his gathering.
A palanquin accompanies him as if peacocks are dancing on the edge of that palanquin.

(LGT: 2R: 1972-73, Dhanabad, Brāhmaṇ Women)

११९.

मिसरी के घोरे नेवल बन्ना॥
बाबन के उनके हथिया सजे, खूँदैं खूँदैं सँवलिया के द्वार मा॥
बाबुन के उनके घोड़िला सजे, खूँदैं खूँदैं सँवलिया के द्वार मा॥
चाचन के उनके ऊँट सजे, खूँदैं खूँदैं सँवलिया के द्वार मा॥
फूफन के उनके गदहा सजे, रेकैं रेकैं सँवलिया के द्वार मा॥
जीजन के उनके कुकुर सजे, भूँकैं भूँकैं सँवलिया के द्वार मा॥
मामन के उनके बन्दर सजे, खीसैं खीसैं सँवलिया के द्वार मा॥

misarī ke ghore neval bannā.
bāban ke unake hathiyā saje, khūñdaiṅ khūñdaiṅ sañvaliyā ke dvār mā.
bābun ke unake ghoṛilā saje, khūñdaiṅ khūñdaiṅ sañvaliyā ke dvār mā.
cācan ke unake ūñṭ saje, khūñdaiṅ khūñdaiṅ sañvaliyā ke dvār mā.
phūphan ke unake gadahā saje, rekaiṅ rekaiṅ sañvaliyā ke dvār mā.
jījan ke unake kukur saje, bhūñkaiṅ bhūñkaiṅ sañvaliyā ke dvār mā.
māman ke unake bandar saje, khīsaiṅ khīsaiṅ sañvaliyā ke dvār mā.

The groom is beautiful as if made of sweets.
His grandfather is decorating his elephants and they are trumpeting at his door.

His father is decorating his horses and they are neighing at his door.
His uncle is decorating his camels and they are grunting at his door.
His *phūphā* is decorating his donkeys and they are braying at his door.
His *jījā* is decorating his dogs and they are barking at his door.
His *māmā* is decorating his monkeys as they are shrieking at his door.
(LGT: 3R: 1972-73, Dhanabad, Brāhmaṇ Women)

१२०.

पाप भये सब दूरि जनक के रघुवर बनरा ब्याहन आये ॥
सिर सोहै जाली का सीरा, कँलगिन अजब बहार राम के ॥
कान सोहै सूरति के मोती, चमकन अजब बहार राम के ॥
नैन सोहै साँवलिया सुरमा, बिरिया अजब बहार राम के ॥
अंग सोहै काँसे का जामा, जमधर अजब बहार राम के ॥
पैर सोहै लखनौवा मोजा, मेंहदी अजब बहार राम के ॥
संग सोहै हरि वाला डोला, बनरी अजब बहार राम के ॥
संग सोहै भैयों की जोड़ी, महफिल अजब बहार राम के ॥

pāp bhaye sab dūri janak ke raghuvar banarā byāhan āye.
sir sohai jālī kā sīrā, kaṅlagin ajab bahār rām ke.
kān sohai sūrati ke motī, camakan ajab bahār rām ke.
nain sohai sāṅvaliyā suramā, biriyā ajab bahār rām ke.
aṅg sohai kāṅse kā jāmā, jamadhar ajab bahār rām ke.
pair sohai lakhanauvā mojā, meṅhadī ajab bahār rām ke.
saṅg sohai hari vālā ḍolā, banarī ajab bahār rām ke.
saṅg sohai bhaiyoṅ kī joṛī, mahaphil ajab bahār rām ke.

All sins of Janak have been washed as groom Rām has come to wed.
He is wearing a crochet crown and the plume is wonderful.
He is wearing pearl earrings from Sūrat and their brightness is wonderful.
He has black collyrium on his eyes and the betelleaf in his mouth is wonderful.
He is wearing a delicate garment and the dagger [at his waist] is wonderful.

He is wearing socks from Lucknow on his feet and the henna on his feet is wonderful.
He is accompanied by a palanquin and the bride is wonderful.
He is accompanied by his brothers and the gathering is wonderful.
(LGT: 38R: 1972-73, Dhanabad, Brāhmaṇ Women)

विवाह (बनरा)

१२१.

नीका लागै हो सिया प्यारी का बनरा ॥
सिर सोहै जाली का सीरा, नीका लागै हो कलँगी वाला हो बनरा ॥
कान सोहै सूरति के मोती, नीका लागै हो झुमकन वाला हो बनरा ॥
नैन सोहै साँवलिया सुरमा, नीका लागै हो बिरिया वाला हो बनरा ॥
अंग सोहै काँसे का जामा, नीका लागै हो बंदन वाला हो बनरा ॥
संग सोहै हरि वाला डोला, नीका लागै हो परदा वाला हो बनरा ॥

nīkā lāgai ho siyā pyārī kā banarā.
sir sohai jālī kā sīrā, nīkā lāgai ho kalañgī vālā ho banarā.
kān sohai sūrati ke motī, nīkā lāgai ho jhumakan vālā ho banarā.
nain sohai sāñvaliyā suramā, nīkā lāgai ho biriyā vālā ho banarā.
aṅg sohai kāñse kā jāmā, nīkā lāgai ho baṅdan vālā ho banarā.
saṅg sohai hari vālā ḍolā, nīkā lāgai ho paradā vālā ho banarā.

I adore dear Sītā's groom.
He is wearing a crochet crown and I adore that groom with a plume.
He is wearing pearl earrings from Sūrat and I adore that groom with a pendant.
He is wearing dark collyrium on his eyes and I adore that groom with a betelleaf in his mouth.
He is wearing a delicate garment and I adore that groom with ties.
He is riding on a palanquin and I adore that groom behind the curtain.
(LGT: 39R: 1972-73, Dhanabad, Brāhmaṇ Women)

विवाह (बन्ना)

१२२.

बाँकी रानी ने जाया बनरा ॥
सिर सोहै जाली का चीरा, बाँकी कलँगी वाला बनरा ॥
कान सोहै सूरत के मोती, बाँकी चुन्नी वाला बनरा ॥
नैन सोहै साँवलिया सुरमा, मुख सोहै नरवल का बीरा ॥
बाँकी रेखों वाला बनरा, बाँकी लाली वाला बनरा ॥
अँग सोहै मुसरू का जामा, कमर सोहै गुजराती पटुका
बाँकी लरियन वाला बनरा, बाँके फेंटे वाला बनरा ॥
पैर सोहै नखलौवा मोजा, बाँकी बन्दे वाला बनरा ॥
संग सोहै भैयन की जोड़ी, संग सोहै हरिवाला डोला
बाँकी परदे वाला बनरा, बाँकी रानी को जाया ॥

Bāñkī rānī ne jāyā banarā.
sir sohai jālī kā cīrā, bāñkī kalañgī vālā banarā.
kan sohai sūrat ke motī, bāñkī cunnī vālā banarā.
nain sohai sāñvaliyā suramā, mukh sohai naraval kā bīrā.
bāñkī rekhoṅ vālā banarā, bāñkī lālī vālā banarā.
añg sohai musarū kā jāmā, kamar sohai gujarātī paṭukā.
bāñkī lariyan vālā banarā, bāñke pheṅṭe vālā banarā.
pair sohai nakhalauvā mojā, bāñkī bande vālā banarā.
saṅg sohai bhaiyan kī joṛī, saṅg sohai harivālā ḍolā.
bāñkī parade vālā banarā, bāñkī rānī ko jāyā.

That beautiful queen gave birth to this groom.
He is wearing a crochet crown with a plume.
He is wearing pearl earrings from Sūrat and a beautiful scarf.
He is wearing dark collyrium on his eyes and a betelleaf from Naraval.
O, the groom has wonderful dark eyes and red lips.
He is wearing a garment from Musarū (?) and a scarf from Gujarat around his waist.
O, the groom's garment has wonderful pleats and his scarf is tied nicely.
He is wearing socks from Lucknow and his shoes are wonderful.

He is accompanied by his brothers and a decorated palanquin.
O, the groom with a wonderful curtain on his palanquin has married a wonderful queen.

(LGT: 75R: 1972-73, Ganj Muradabad, Mixed women)

१२३.

सोंधौली लच्छेदार बन्ना किन्ने सजाया॥
बाबा सजाया बन्ना ताऊ सजाया,
दादी का ताबेदार बन्ना किन्ने सजाया॥

soṅdhaulī lacchedār bannā kinne sajājā.
bābā sajāyā bannā tāū sajāyā;
dādī kā tābedār bannā kinne sajāyā.

Who has decorated this delicate groom?
His grandfather and his *tāū* have decorated the groom;
Who has decorated this delicate groom who is obedient to his grandmother.

(LGT: 76R: 1972-73, Ganj Muradabad, Mixed Women)

विवाह (घुड़चढ़ी)

१२४.

घोड़ी तो राजकुँवर जी को सोहै॥
बाबा सबै जन सजउ बरायत, ताऊ सबै जन सजउ बरायत
एक लख घोड़ सवा लख हाथी॥
सज घोड़ी बन्ना चले हैं सजन ग्रह
पहुँचे ससुर दरवार॥

ghoṛī to rājakuñvar jī ko sohai.
bābā sabai jan sajau barāyat, tāū sabai jan sajau barāyat.

ek lakh ghoṛa savā lakh hāthī.
saj ghoṛī bannā cale haiṅ sajan grah.
pahuñce sasur daravār.

Riding on a mare, the groom is adorable.
Dear grandfather and *tāū*, all of you should get ready for the marriage party.
There were one lakh horses and one and a one quarter lakh elephants.
Thus, decorated, the groom proceeded on his mare towards his in-law's home.
And arrived at the in-law's gate.

(LGT: 78R: 1972-73, Ganj Muradabad, Mixed Women)

विवाह

१२५.

मायन पूता बुलावै अरि जँघ बैठावय
लालन कैसी तुम्हारी ससुरारि तो कौनि जुगुति केरी
जबहीं गएन ओहिके गोइड़े सुनहु मोरी माया
अम्बवा लगे चारिव ओर तौ बहुत सुहावन
जबहीं गएन ओहिके गोइड़े सुनहु मोरी माया
माया सारिन कीन्ह अगवानी तौ बड़े हे धूम सेनी
जबहीं गएन ओहिके द्वारे सुनहु मोरी माया
माया ससुरा ने अरति उतारी तौ बड़े हे हुलस सेनी
माया तिरिया कलसु लीन्हें ठाढ़ि तौ बड़े हे सगुन सेनी
जबहीं गएन ओहिके मड़ये सुनहु मोरी माया
पंडित वेद धुनि लागि तौ बड़े हे वेद सेनी
जबहीं गएन ओहिके चौके सुनहु मोरी माया
कन्या सेन्धौरा लीन्हें ठाढ़ि तौ बड़े हे सगुन सेनी
जबहीं गएन ओहिके कोहबर सुनहु मोरी माया
सरहज खेलैं पंसासार तौ बड़े हे हुलस सेनी

जबहीं गएन ओहिके महले सुनहु मोरी माया
बनरी बिरिया लीन्हें ठाढ़ि तौ बड़े हे हुलस सेनी

māyan pūtā bulāvai ari jañgh baiṭhāvay.
lālan kaisī tumhārī sasurāri to kauni juguti kerī.
jabahīṅ gaen ohike goiṛe sunahu morī māyā.
ambavā lage cāriv or tau bahut suhāvan.
jabahīṅ gaen ohike goiṛe sunahu morī māyā.
māyā sārin kīnh agavānī tau baṛe he dhūm senī,
jabahīṅ gaen ohike dvāre sunahu morī māyā.
māyā sasurā ne arati utārī tau baṛe he hulas senī,
māyā tiriyā kalasu līnheṅ ṭhāṛhi tau baṛe he sagun senī.
jabahīṅ gaen ohike maṛaye sunahu morī māyā.
paṇḍit ved dhuni lāgi tau baṛe he ved senī,
jabahīṅ gaen ohike cauke sunahu morī māyā,
kanyā sendhaurā līnheṅ ṭhāṛhi tau baṛe he sagun senī,
jabahīṅ gaen ohike kohabar sunahu morī māyā,
sarahaj khelaiṅ paṅsāsār tau baṛe he hulas senī.
jabahīṅ gaen ohike mahale sunahu morī māyā,
banarī biriyā līnheṅ ṭhāṛhi tau baṛe he hulas senī.

The mother is calling her son and is making him sit on her lap.
"Dear son, tell me how is your in-law's place?"
"When I reached their yard, listen my mother,"
There were pleasing mangoes all around,
When I reached their yard, listen my mother,
Dear mother, *Salis* welcomed us with great fanfare.
When I arrived at their door, listen my mother,
Dear mother, my *sasur* performed *āratī* with great happiness.
Dear mother, women were standing with auspicious water-pots [on their head],
When I reached their wedding canopy, listen my mother,
The priests recited vedic hymns with great ceremony,
When I reached their ceremonial square, listen my mother,
The bride was standing with auspicious *sendhaurā* box.
When I reached their *kohabar*, listen my mother,

Sarahaj played the game of *pañsāsār* with great enthusiasm.
When I arrived at their palace, listen my mother,
The bride was standing with betelleaf in great delight.
(LGT: 15R: 1972-73, Dhanabad, Brāhmaṇ Women)

विवाह (नकटा)

१२६.

बिन बोले रहा ना जाय बलम अनबोलना ॥
सुन सासू री बेटा तेरा अनबोलना और हमसे रहा ना जाय ॥
सुन बहुवा री कर ले चने की रोटियाँ और कर ले अलोना साग ॥
सुन सासू री खागै चने की रोटियाँ और खागै अलोना साग ॥
सुन बेटा रे बड़े घरन की बेटिया इन्हें रखियो जतन से लाल ॥
सुन माया री माई बाप की लाज है इस बहुवा से प्यारा कौन ॥

bin bole rahā nā jāy balam anabolanā.
sun sāsū rī beṭā terā anabolanā aur hamase rahā nā jāy.
sun bahuvā rī kar le cane kī roṭiyāñ aur kar le alonā sāg.
sun sāsū rī khāgai cane kī roṭiyāñ aur khāgai alonā sāg.
sun beṭā re baṛe gharan kī beṭiyā inheṅ rakhiyo jatan se lāl.
sun māyā rī māī bāp kī lāj hai is bahuvā se pyārā kaun.

I cannot keep myself from talking and my husband is not talking.
Listen my *sās*, your son is not talking and I cannot keep myself from talking.
Listen *bahū*, make bread from chickpea flour and vegetable greens.
Listen my *sās*, he ate the bread made from chickpea flour and the vegetable greens.
Listen dear son, your wife is from a rich family and therefore take good care of her.
Listen my mother, my wife is very dear to me and I would keep my parent's honor.
(LGT: 226R: 1972-73, Kanpur, Brāhmaṇ Women)

१२७.

दिल को तसल्ली दिये जाना सजन जब जाना बिदेशवा ॥
सास ससुर मोरे जनम के बैरी
उनसे अलग किये जाना, सजन जब जाना बिदेशवा ॥
देवर जेठानी मेरी संग सहेली
उनसे मेल किये जाना, सजन जब जाना बिदेशवा ॥
छोटी ननदिया बड़ी चँचलिया
उसकी बिदा किये जाना, सजन जब जाना बिदेशवा ॥
छोटा देवरवा बड़ा छलबलिया
उसको साथ लिये जाना, सजन जब जाना बिदेशवा ॥

dil ko tasallī diye jānā sajan jab jānā bideśavā.
sās sasur more janam ke bairī;
unase alag kiye jānā, sajan jab jānā bideśavā.
devar jeṭhānī merī saṅg sahelī;
unase mel kiye jānā, sajan jab jānā bideśavā.
choṭī nanadiyā baṛī cañcaliyā;
usakī bidā kiye jānā, sajan jab jānā bideśavā.
choṭā devaravā baṛā chalabaliyā;
usako sāth liye jānā, sajan jab jānā bideśavā.

Dear husband, make sure to satisfy my heart before you go abroad.
My *sās* and *sasur* are my enemies from birth;
Make sure that I live separate from them, before you go abroad.
My *devar* and *jeṭhānī* are my dear friends;
Make sure I befriend them, before you go abroad.
My younger *nanad* is very energetic;
Make sure to send her off to her in-laws, before you go abroad.
My younger *devar* is very mischievous;
Make sure to take him abroad with you.

(LGT: 148RL: 1972-73, Sheoli, Brāhmaṇ Women)

१२८.

कहाँ लग जागूँ रे मेरी अँखियाँ लाल गुलाल ॥

बागों जात बहुत डर लागै, मलिया देख डेरनि अम्मा झपको ॥
ताला जात बहुत नीको लागै, धुबिया देख डेरनि अम्मा लउको ॥
कुँवना जात बहुत नीको लागै, घैला देख डेरनि अम्मा फूटो ॥
कमरा जात बहुत नीको लागै, खिड़की देख डेरनि अम्मा दौरो ॥
गलियाँ जात बहुत नीको लागै, कुत्ता देख डेरनि अम्मा भौंको ॥
सेजा जात बहुत डर लागै, दुलहा देख डेरनि अम्मा पकरो ॥

kahāñ lag jāgūñ re merī añkhiyāñ lāl gulāl.
bāgoṅ jāt bahut ḍar lāgai, maliyā dekh ḍerani ammā jhapako.
tālā jāt bahut nīko lāgai, dhubiyā dekh ḍerani ammā lauko.
kuñvanā jāt babut nīko lāgai, ghailā dekh ḍerani ammā phūṭo.
kamarā jāt bahut nīko lāgai, khiṛakī dekh ḍerani ammā dauro.
galiyāñ jāt bahut nīko lāgai, kuttā dekh ḍerani ammā bhauṅko.
sejā jāt bahut ḍar lāgai, dulahā dekh ḍerani ammā pakaro.

How long can I stay awake, my eyes are blood shot?
I was scared going to the garden; Seeing the gardener approach scared me, my mother.
It was pleasing going to the pond; Seeing the washerman approach scared me, my mother.
It was pleasing going to the well; The pot broke as I was scared, my mother.
It was pleasing gõing to the room; Seeing the window scared me, run my mother.
It was pleasing going in the lane; Seeing the dog bark scared me, my mother.
I was scared going to bed; Seeing the groom scared me, help, my mother.
(CYT: 245C: 1975, Sheoli, Brāhmaṇ Woman)

१२९.

आजि राजा परदेसिया से आय गये ॥
गगरी का मोरा हमैं नथुनी लै आये ॥
मोती का मोरा हमैं हरवा लै आये ॥
बोकरी की लेड़ी हमें रेउड़ी ले आये ॥

कुत्ता के पिल्ला हमें लरिका ले आये ॥
पीपा के मोरा हमें कननी लै आये ॥

āji rājā paradesiyā se āy gaye.
gagarī kā morā hamaiṅ nathunī lai āye.
motī kā morā hamaiṅ haravā lai āye.
bokarī kī leṛī hameṅ reuṛī le āye.
kuttā ke pillā hameṅ larikā le āye.
pīpā ke morā hameṅ kananī lai āye.

My husband returned from abroad today.
He brought me a nose-ring as big as the mouth of the earthen pot.
He brought me a pearl necklace.
Like goat droppings, he brought me *reuṛī* sweetmeat.
Like a puppy, he brought me a son.
(?), he brought me a comb.

(CYT: 246C: 1975, Sheoli, Brāhmaṇ Woman)

१३०.

कजरवा ने मारे बिदेशी जवान
एक लख मारे दुई लख मारे, लाखों हैं परे हैं उतान

kajaravā ne māre bideśī javān.
ek lakh māre duī lakh māre, lākhoṅ haiṅ pare haiṅ utān.

My eyes killed [made them love sick] many young from abroad.
They killed one lakh and two lakh; many are lying on their back.

(CYT: 246C: 1975, Sheoli, Brāhmaṇ Woman)

१३१.

हम मूत दीन उइ रपट गये घर भाग आइँव रे

ham mūt dīn ui rapaṭ gaye ghar bhāg āiñv re.

I pissed and he slipped and I ran home.

(CYT: 246C: 1975, Sheoli, Brāhmaṇ Woman)

१३२.

बदरिया बरसै श्याम नहीं आये ॥
बागों में बरसै बगीचों में बरसै, मलिनिया तरसै श्याम नहीं आये ॥
कुँवनों में बरसै जगतियों में बरसै कहारिन तरसै श्याम नहीं आये ॥
तालों में बरसै तलैयों में बरसै, धोबिनिया तरसै श्याम नहीं आये ॥
महलों में बरसै दुमहलों में बरसै, ननदिया तरसै श्याम नहीं आये ॥
सेजों में बरसै सेजरियों में बरसै, सवतिया तरसै श्याम नहीं आये ॥

badariyā barasai śyām nahīṅ āye.
bāgoṅ meṅ barasai bagīcoṅ meṅ barasai, maliniyā tarasai śyām nahīṅ āye.
kuñvanoṅ meṅ barasai jagatiyoṅ meṅ barasai, kahārin tarasai śyām nahīṅ āye.
tāloṅ meṅ barasai talaiyoṅ meṅ barasai, dhobiniyā tarasai śyām nahīṅ āye.
mahaloṅ meṅ barasai dumahaloṅ meṅ barasai, nanadiyā tarasai śyām nahīṅ āye.
sejoṅ meṅ barasai sejariyoṅ meṅ barasai, savatiyā tarasai śyām nahīṅ āye.

It's raining, but Kṛṣṇa has not come.
It's raining in the fields and gardens; poor gardener's wife is suffering.
It's raining in the wells and on the platform; poor *kahārin* is suffering.
It's raining in the lakes and tanks; poor washerwoman is suffering.
It is raining on the palace; poor *nanad* is suffering.
It's raining on the bed; poor co-wife is suffering.

(LGT: 13/119R: 1972-73, Dhanabad, Brāhmaṇ Women)

१३३.

कहाँ गई तुम्हारि तबै की ऐसी चितवनि

हम देखन तुम देखत नाहीं, जब देखौ तब भौंहैं सिकोड़ ॥
हम बोलन तुम बोलत नाहीं, जब बोलौ तब बचन कठोर ॥
हम पकड़न तुम पकड़त नाहीं, जब पकड़ौ तब बहियाँ झिंकोर ॥
हम सोवन तुम सोवत नाहीं, जब सोवौ तब पीठी घुमाय ॥

kahāñ gaī tumhāri tabai kī aisī citavani?
ham dekhan tum dekhat nāhīṅ, jab dekhau tab bhauṅhaiṅ sikoṛ.
ham bolan tum bolat nāhīṅ, jab bolau tab bacan kaṭhor.
ham pakaṛan tum pakaṛat nāhīṅ, jab pakaṛau tab bahiyāñ jhiṅkor.
ham sovan tum sovat nāhīṅ, jab sovau tab pīṭhī ghumāy.

What happened to the looks you used to give me?
I look at you, but you don't look at me; whenever you look at me, you frown.
I talk to you, but you don't talk to me; whenever you talk to me, you say harsh words.
I hold you, but you don't hold me; whenever you hold me, you jerk my arms.
I lie down with you, but you don't lie down with me; whenever you sleep with me, you turn your back towards me.

(LGT: 149R: 1972-73, Sheoli, Brāhmaṇ Women)

१३४.

अकेले मा झगड़ा न डार बालमा रे ॥
बरफिन का राजा घर बनवा देव लेड्डुन के दरवाजा
अमिरतिन की खिड़की लगवा दो बालमा रे ॥
सोने की राजा नथ बनवा दो तारन के चार चँदा
जोधैंया की बिंदिया लगवा दो बालमा रे ॥
धरती का राजा लहँगा सिलवा दो बादल की ओढ़निया
पटारदार अँगिया सिलवा दो बालमा रे ॥
बेसन की राजा पूड़ी बनवा दो आलुन की तरकारी
पुदीने की चटनी मँगा दो बालमा रे ॥
कानपूर से कलम मँगा दो मेरठ की चार कापी
बम्बई से मास्टरनी बुलवा दो बालमा रे ॥

akele mā jhagaṛā n ḍār bālamā re.
baraphin kā rājā ghar banavā dev leḍḍun ke daravājā;
amiratin kī khiṛakī lagavā do bālamā re.
sone kī rājā nath banavā do tāran ke cār cañdā;
jodhaiṁyā kī biṁdiyā lagavā do bālamā re.
dharatī kā rājā lahañgā silavā do bādal kī oṛhaniyā;
paṭāradār añgiyā silavā do bālamā re.
besan kī rājā pūṛī banavā do ālun kī tarakārī;
pudīne kī caṭanī mañgā do bālamā re.
kānapūr se kalam mañgā do meraṭh kī cār kāpī;
bambaī se māsṭaranī bulavā do bālamā re.

Don't get the fight started while I am alone.
Make a home made of sweetmeat (*baraphī*) and doors made of sweetmeats (*laḍḍū*)
Put windows made of sweetmeat (*amirti*).
Make me a gold nose-ring decorated with stars and moon;
Make me a forehead ornament made of moonlight.
Make me a skirt made of earth and a scarf made of clouds;
Have a bodice sown with silken cords.
Make me *pūrī* from chickpea flour and potato vegetable;
Get me mint chutney.
Buy me pen from Kānpur and four notebooks from Meerut;
Get me a mistress from Bombay.[2]

(LGT: 26R: 1972-73, Dhanabad, Brāhmaṇ Women)

१३५.

अँगुठिया है सुलेमानी अगर बेंचो तो मैं ले लूँ॥
तुम्हारे बाग के आगे बगैचा हम लगावैंगे
मलिनिया है सुलेमानी अगर बेंचो तो मैं ले लूँ॥
तुम्हारे कुँवन के आगे जगतिया मैं बँधावैंगे

2. *Barphī*, *laḍḍu*, and *imarti* are various Indian sweets; *pūrī* is a deep fried bread.

कहारिन है सुलेमानी अगर बेंचो तो मैं ले लूँ॥
तुम्हारे ताल के आगे तलैया मैं बँधावैंगे
धोबिनिया है सुलेमानी अगर बेंचो तो मैं ले लूँ॥
तुम्हारे सेज के आगे सुफेदी मैं लगावैंगे
रनीवा है सुलेमानी अगर बेंचो तो मैं ले लूँ॥

añguṭhiyā hai sulemānī agar beṅco to maiṅ le lūñ.
tumhāre bāg ke āge bagaicā ham lagāvaiṅge;
maliniyā hai sulemānī agar beṅco to maiṅ le lūñ.
tumhāre kuñvan ke āge jagatiyā maiṅ bañdhāvaiṅge;
kahārin hai sulemānī agar beṅco to maiṅ le lūñ.
tumhāre tāl ke āge talaiyā maiṅ bañdhāvaiṅge;
dhobinyā hai sulemānī agar beṅco to maiṅ le lūñ.
tumhāre sej ke āge suphedī maiṅ lagāvaiṅge;
ranīvā hai sulemānī agar beṅco to maiṅ le lūñ.

If you sell the agate ring, I will buy it.
In front of your garden, I would plant a garden;
The gardener's wife is special, if you sell her, I will buy her.
In front of your well, I would construct a high platform surrounding it;
The *kahārin* is special, if you sell her, I will buy her.
In front of your pond, I would construct a pool;
The washerwoman is special, if you sell her, I will buy her.
On your bed, I would spread a white linen;
The queen is special, if you sell her, I will buy her.

(LGT: 29R: 1972-73, Dhanabad, Camār Women)

विवाह (बधाई)

१३६.

बहू घर ब्याहि कै आई बधाई है बधाई है॥
पालकी साज कर आई देखकर रंज छाई है

सखी हिलमिल लगी रोने मात ने गोद लै लीना
पालकी जा बैठारी है प्रभू दासी तुम्हारी है ॥
आरती सास ने साजी बहू द्वारे उतारी है
पाँवड़े पड़ गये आँगन बहू कमरे बिठाई है ॥
नेगु सब सास करवाये बधाई है बधाई है
चन्द्रमुख खोलि के देखा सुरज चन्द्रा लजाये हैं ॥
मँगाये चार सिंहासन बहू लै सास सोई है
कहें तुलसीदास कर जोरे अवध आनन्द छाई है ॥

bahū ghar byāhi kai āī badhāī hai badhāī hai.
pālakī sāj kar āī dekhakar rañj chāī hai.
sakhī hilamil lagī rone māt ne god lai līnā.
pālakī jā baiṭhārī hai prabhūdāsī tumhārī hai.
āratī sās ne sājī bahū dvāre utārī hai.
pāñvaṛe paṛa gaye āñgan bahū kamare biṭhāī hai.
negu sab sās karavīye badhāī hai badhāī hai.
candramukh kholi ke dekhā suraj candrā lajāye haiṅ.
mañgāye cār siṅhāsan bahū lai sās soī hai.
kaheṅ tulasīdās kar jore avadh ānand chāī hai.

Bahū has come home, congratulations, congratulations.
The decorated palanquin arrived [at the bride's house]; seeing that, everyone became sad.
All the girlfriends started crying and the mother took the bride into her arms.
The bride was taken to the palanquin; "O God," [says the mother to her daughter's husband], "she is your slave."
[Upon arrival at the groom's house] The *sās* did the *āratī* and helped the bride out of the palanquin.
Carpets were spread along the courtyard and the *bahū* was taken inside.
The *sās* observed all gift-giving traditions.
When the bride's moonlike face was revealed, the sun and moon were put to shame.
Four thrones were called for and the *sās* slept with the *bahū*.
Tulsīdās says with folded hands: "Happiness covered Avadh city."

(LGT: 107R: 1972-73, Ganj Muradabad, Mixed Women)

अध्याय ३
ऋतुविशेष गीत

होरी / फाग

१३७.

कौने छयल केरी नारि झमाझम पानी का निकरी॥
अपने ससुर की मैं बहुत दुलारी॥
घर ही मा कुइयाँ खोदावैं बहुआ मोरी पानी ना जइहैं॥
अपने जेठ की मैं बहुत दुलारी
रेशम रसरिया मँगावैं छोटी मोरी पानी ना जइहैं॥
अपने देवर की मैं बहुत दुलारी
सोने घयलवा मँगावैं भाभी मोरी पानी ना जइहैं॥
अपने सजन की मैं बहुत दुलारी
बारे कहरिया लगावैं धना मोरी पानी ना जइहैं॥
सासु ननद मोरी जलम कै बैरिन
बारे कहरिया छोड़ावैं बहुआ मोरी पानी का जइहैं॥

kaune chayal kerī nāri jhamājham pānī kā nikarī.
apane sasur kī maiṅ bahut dulārī!
ghar hī mā kuiyāñ khodāvaiṅ bahuā morī pānī nā jaihaiṅ.
apane jeṭh kī maiṅ bahut dulārī!
reśam rasariyā mañgāvaiṅ choṭī morī pānī nā jaihaiṅ.
apane devar kī maiṅ bahut dulārī!
sone ghayalavā mañgāvaiṅ bhābhī morī pānī nā jaihaiṅ.
apane sajan kī maiṅ bahut dulārī!
bāre kahariyā lagāvaiṅ dhanā morī pānī nā jaihaiṅ.
sāsu nanad morī jalam kai bairin!
bāre kahariyā choṛāvaiṅ bahuā morī pānī kā jaihaiṅ.

Whose wife is it who has come out lustrously to fetch water?
She is very dear to her *sasur*!
He is getting a well dug inside the house; his *bahū* would not go out to fetch water.
She is very dear to her *jeṭh*!
He is getting a silken rope; his *choṭī* would not go out to fetch water.

She is very dear to her *devar*!
He is getting a golden pitcher; his *bhābhī* would not go out to fetch water.
She is very dear to her husband!
He has hired a *kaharin;* his wife would not fetch water from the well.
My *sās* and *nanad* are my life long enemies!
They are firing *kahārin;* my *bahū* would fetch water from the well.

(LGT: 21R: 1972-73, Dhanabad, Brāhmaṇ Women)

१३८.

छूटी अयोध्या कै राज बृन्दाबन नीका ना लागै ॥
राजा दशरथ ऐसे बाप जो छूटे, छूटी कौशल्या महतारी ॥
राम लखन ऐसे भैया जो छूटे, छूटी सितल भौजाई ॥
गंगा नहाने की गंगा जो छूटी, छूटा सखियों केरा साथ ॥

chūṭī ayodhyā kai rāj bṛndāban nīkā nā lāgai.
rājā daśarath aise bāp jo chūṭe, chūṭī kauśalyā mahatārī.
rām lakhan aise bhaiyā jo chūṭe, chūṭī sital bhaujāī.
gaṅgā nahāne kī gaṅgā jo chūṭī, chūṭā sakhiyoṅ kerā sāth.

I am leaving the kingdom of Ayodhyā and I do not like Vṛndāvan.
Father like Daśarath and mother like Kauśalyā are left behind.
Brother like Rām and Lakṣmaṇ and *bhāujī* like Sītā are left behind.
River source like Gaṅgā and girlfriends are all left behind.

(LGT: 22R: 1972-73, Dhanabad, Brāhmaṇ Women)

१३९.

बाऊ नैहरवा कै रीति नैहरवा से कोऊ नहिं आवा ॥
माया जो होती हमरि सुधि लेती, बप्पा हैं बन के भँवरवा ॥
भौजी जो होती हमरि सुधि लेती, भैया है मुरुख गँवारा ॥
बहिनी जो होती हमरि सुधि लेती, जीजा का दूसर नाता ॥

bāū naiharavā kai rīti naiharavā se koū nahiṅ āvā.
māyā jo hotī hamari sudhi letī, bappā haiṅ ban ke bhañvaravā.

bhaujī jo hotī hamari sudhi letī, bhaiyā hai murukh gañvārā.
bahinī jo hotī hamari sudhi letī, jījā kā dūsar nātā.

O dear father, it's a custom but no one came from my parent's home.
If I had my mother, she would have remembered me; my father is like a forest bee.
If I had a *bhaujī*, she would have remembered me; my brother is stupid.
If I had a sister, she would have remembered me; with *jījā*, it's a different story.

(LGT: 37R: 1972-73, Dhanabad, Camār Women)

१४०.

होरी खेलन आयो श्याम आज याये रंग में बोरौं री॥
कोरे कोरे कलश मँगाये केसर घोरौं री
रंग बिरंगो करो जाय कारे से गोरो री॥
पार परोसिन बोल याय आँगन में घेरौं री
पीताम्बर लेऊँ छीन जाय पहनाय देंव चोली री॥
हरे बाँस की बाँसुरी याहे तोर मरोरौं री
राधे जू की करै अस्तुती जब याहे छोड़ौं री
श्यामा जू की करै अस्तुती जब याहे छोड़ौं री॥

horī khelan āyo śyām āj yāye raṅg meṅ borauṅ rī.
kore kore kalaś mañgāye kesar ghorauṅ rī;
raṅg biraṅgo karo jāy kāre se goro rī.
pār parosin bol yāy āñgan meṅ gherauṅ rī;
pītāmbar leūṅ chīn jāy pahanāy deṅv colī rī.
hare bāñs kī bāñsurī yāhe tor marorauṅ rī;
rādhe jū kī karai astutī jab yāhe choṛauṅ rī.
śyāmā jū kī karai astutī jab yāhe choṛauṅ rī

Kṛṣṇa has come to play Holī; today I will dip him in colour.
I will mix saffron colour in new pots;
I will make Kṛṣṇa multi-coloured; I will turn him from black to white.
I will call my neighbours and will surround him in the courtyard;

We will snatch away his yellow silken robe and make him wear a brassiere.
I will break his flute of green bamboo;
I will not leave him until he prays to Rādhājī.
I will not leave him until he prays to Śyāmājī.

(LGT: 179R: 1972-73, Vṛndāvan, Brāhmaṇ Women)

१४१.

आज बिरज में होरी रे रसिया ॥
कौन गाँव के कुँवर कन्हैया लाला, कौन गाँव राधा गोरी रे रसिया ॥
नन्दगाँव के कुँवर कन्हैया लाला, बरसाने की राधा गोरी रे रसिया ॥
कौने के हाथ माट केसर को, कौने के हाथ कमोरी रे रसिया ॥
कान्हा के हाथ माट केसर को लाला, राधे के हाथ कमोरी रे रसिया ॥
उड़त गुलाल लाल भये बादल, मारत भर भर झोरी रे रसिया ॥
बोलत हो हो होरी रे रसिया ॥
चन्द्रसखी भज बालकृष्ण छबि, जुग जुग जियो यह जोरी रे रसिया ॥

āj biraj meṅ horī re rasiyā.
kaun gāñv ke kuñvar kanhaiyā lālā, kaun gāñv rādhā gorī re rasiyā.
nandagāñv ke kuñvar kanhaiyā lālā, barasāne kī rādhā gorī re rasiyā.
kaune ke hāth māṭ kesar ko, kaune ke hāth kamorī re rasiyā.
kānhā ke hāth māṭ kasar ko lālā, rādhe ke hāth kamorī re rasiyā.
uṛat gulāl lāl bhaye bādal, mārat bhar bhar jhorī re rasiyā;
bolat ho ho horī re rasiyā.
candrasakhī bhaj bālakṛṣṇ chabi, jug jug jiyo yah jorī re rasiyā.

O admirer, today is Holī in Braj.
To which village does Kṛṣṇa belong and to which village does Rādhā belong?
Kṛṣṇa comes from Nandagāñv and Rādhā from Barasānā.
Who is carrying the pitcher full of saffron colour and who is carrying this big pitcher?
Kṛṣṇa is carrying the pitcher full of saffron colour and Rādhā is carrying the big bitcher.
Clouds of red powder are all over; they throw it by the handful onto each other;

Shouting: it is Holī.
Candrasakhī says: "Recite the name of the child Kṛṣṇa, May this couple live forever!"

(LGT: 180R: 1972-73, Vṛndāvan, Brāhmaṇ Women)

१४२.

पिया मोरा हो जाई बन के ब्रज मोरा॥
वृन्दाबन के घने बगइचा बैठे पंख मरोरा हो जाई बन के ब्रज मोरा॥
उड़ उड़ पँख गिरे धरनी पै बीनैं नन्द किशोरा हो जाई बन के ब्रज मोरा॥
वै पँखन के मुकुट बनाय लै बाँधे नन्द किशोरा हो जाई बन के ब्रज मोरा॥
बाँधे मुकुट श्याम यों डोलैं नाचैं नन्द किशोरा हो जाई बन के ब्रज मोरा॥

piyā morā ho jāī bana ke braj morā.
vṛndāban ke ghane bagaicā baiṭhe paṅkh marorā ho jāī ban ke braj morā.
uṛa uṛa pañkh gire dharanī pai bīnaiṅ nand kiśorā ho jāī ban ke braj morā
vai pañkhan ke mukuṭ banāy lai bāñdhe nand kiśorā ho jāī ban ke braj morā.
bāñdhe mukuṭ śyām yoṅ ḍolaiṅ nācaiṅ nand kiśorā ho jāī ban ke braj morā.

Dear husband, let's go to the groves of Braj.
In the dense groves of Vṛndāvan, there are many peacocks sitting with their feathers together.
Kṛṣṇa is collecting the feathers which fall to the ground.
From those feathers, Kṛṣṇa makes a crown which he wears.
With that crown on his head, Kṛṣṇa is dancing.

(LGT: 127R: 1972-73, Nandana, Mixed Men)

१४३.

मोहन नन्दलाल बरसाने नहिं आये॥
होरी खेलै साँवरो अपनी ससुराल हाथ लिये पिचकारी
रँग चुवै गुलाल रँगईं अटा अटारी रंगे चौपार रंगई सारी सराजैं
बाहर मैं लाल आध कोस जमुना बहीं॥

बरसाने की गूजरी दधि बेचन जाय बीच मिले कान्हैया
दधि लियो छुड़ाय हुँवाँ कदम की छैयाँ जहँ ग्वालिन झगड़ा डारे
दधि खान न दे मटकी धरकै झटकी बहियाँ झकझोर
टोर बरी के पत्ता बाके दोना बनाय, दोना दोना बाँटो ॥
इन्द्रलोक बरसा भई भर गये पताल डूबत मैं बच आये जसुदा के लाल
बेला फूल चमेली चम्पा बौराय हरवा गुँदे मलिनिया जसुदै पहनाव
रोकौ अपन कन्हैया हमपे अठलाय ॥
गोरी खोलै डेब्बा रे गोरी पान चबाय
हम पै धै मुस्क्यानी हम पै कछू कही ना जाय
आँगू देवर हमारे पाछूँ से जेठ बीच में ननद हमारी
लिलिया असवार केशरिया को जामा बन्द लगे हजार ॥

mohan nandalāl barasāne nahiṅ āye.
horī khelai sañvaro apanī sasurāl hāth liye picakārī;
rañg cuvai gulāl rañgaīṅ aṭā aṭārī raṅge caupār raṅgaī sārī sarājaiṅ;
bāhar maiṅ lāl ādh kos jamunā bahīṅ.
barasāne kī gūjarī dadhi becan jāy bīc mile kānhaiyā;
dadhi liyo churāy huñvāñ kadam kī chaiyāñ jahañ gvālin jhagaṛā ḍāre;
dadhi khān n de maṭakī dharakai jhaṭakī bahiyāñ jhakajhor;
ṭor barī ke pattā bāke donā banāy, donā donā bāñṭo.
indralok barasā bhaī bhar gaye patāl ḍūbat maiṅ bac āye jasudā ke lāl;
belā phūl camelī campā baurāy haravā guñdai maliniyā jasudai pahanāv;
rokau apan kanhaiyā hamape aṭhalāy.
gorī kholai ḍebbā re gorī pān cabāy;
ham pai dhai muskyānī ham pai kachū kahī nā jāy;
āñgū devar hamāre pāchūñ se jeṭh bīc meṅ nanad hamārī;
liliyā asavār keśariyā ko jāmā band lage hajār.

Son of Nand, Kṛṣṇa, did not come to Barasānā.
Kṛṣṇa is playing Holī at his in-law's place with a squirt gun in his hand.
There is so much colour and powder that the rooftop, sitting area and *sari* and *sarahaj* are all coloured;
I am outside, O dear; It looks as though the Jamunā river has flown in half a *kos*.
The milkmaid of Barasānā was on her way to sell yoghurt when midway she ran into Kṛṣṇa.

He snatched her yoghurt under the shade of *kadam* tree and the milkmaid is fighting
Milkmaid was obstructing him from eating the yoghurt; so he twisted her arms and snatched her yoghurt-pot.
Then he plucked leafs from *bari* tree and made bowls and then distributed a bowl full.
At the time when Indra had sent torrential rains that all was submerged then only the son of Yaśodā saved us;
The gardener's wife is making a garland out of *belā, camelī* and *campā* flowers to offer to Yaśodā;
Stop your Kṛṣṇa, he is flirting with me.
The milkmaid opens her betel leaf container and ate a betel leaf;
She smiled at me and I couldn't say a word;
In front of me is my *devar* and behind is my *jeṭh* and in the middle is my *nanad;*
He is riding on horse wearing a saffron colour robe with thousands of buttons.

(LGT: 128R: 1972-73, Nandana, Mixed Men)

१४४.

ब्रज मा हरि होरी मचाई
लपटि झपटि गईं श्यामसुन्दर के, बरबटि पकड़ लै आयीं
लाल को नारि बनाई॥
बेंदी भाल नयन बिच कजरा नकबेसर पहराई
छीन लई मुख मोर मुरलिया, सिर पर चुनरी ओढ़ाई॥
बाजत ताल मृदंग झाँझ ढप और मंजीरा शहनाई
चोया चंदन अतर सुगँधन रंग की कीच मचाई॥
कहाँ गये तेरे नन्द बबा जी कहना जसोदा माई
लाल को लेंय छुड़ाई॥
नन्द बबा घर बजत बधाई, कोई न शबद सुनाई
सूरदास गति कँह लग बरनौ, शोभा बरनि ना जाई॥

braj mā hari horī macāī.
lapaṭi jhapaṭi gaīṅ śyāmasundar ke, barabaṭi pakaṛa lai āyīṅ;

lāl ko nāri banāī.
beṅdī bhāl nayan bic kajarā nakabesar paharāī.
chīn laī mukh mor muraliyā, sir par cunarī oṛhāī.
bājat tāl mr̥daṅg jhāñjh ḍhap aur mañjīrā śahanāī;
coyā caṅdan atar sugañdhan raṅg kī kīc macāī.
kahāñ gaye tere nand babā jī kahanā jasodā māī;
lāl ko leṅy churāī.
nand babā ghar bajat badhāī, koī n śabad sunāī;
sūradās gati kañh lag baranau, śobhā barani nā jāī.

Kr̥ṣṇa is playing Holī in Braj.
The milkmaids grabbed Kr̥ṣṇa and took hold of him;
They dressed Kr̥ṣṇa up as a woman.
They put on *beṅdī* on his forehead, mascara on his eyes and a nose ring.
They snatched his flute and covered his head with a scarf.
Mr̥dañg, jhāñjh, tambourine, cymbals and *śahanāī* are being played.
They made a mess of Kr̥ṣṇa with sandalwood paste, perfume, and colour.
Where have your father Nand and mother Yaśodā gone?
To rescue dear Kr̥ṣṇa.
Congratulatory music is being played at Nand's home and nobody can hear anything.
Surdas (the composer) says, "How much can I recount, this beauty is beyond description"

(LGT: 145R: 1972-73, Sheoli, Brāhmaṇ Woman)

१४५.

मोहन नन्दलाल बरसाने नहिं आये ॥
उहै बरसाने की गुजरिया गुहै फूलौं के हार
चम्पा चमेली के हरवा पहिरैं नन्दलाल बरसाने नहिं आये ॥

mohan nandalāl barasāne nahiṅ āye.
uhai barasāne kī gujariyā guhai phūlauṅ ke hār;
campā camelī ke haravā pahiraiṅ nandalāl barasāne nahiṅ āye.

Son of Nand, Kṛṣṇa did not come to Barasānā.
The milkmaid of Barasānā is stringing a garland of flowers;
Son of Nand is wearing that garland of *campā* and *camelī* flowers.

(LGT: 162R: 1972-73, Varanasi, Mixed Men)

१४६.

ब्रज कइलै बिहार श्याम राधिका दूनो जने॥
केकरे हाथे कँगनवा केकरे गरे हार
केकरे हाथे बँसुरिया केहिके हो किनार॥
राधा के हाथे कँगनवा रुकमिन गले हार
कृष्णा के हाथे बँसुरिया जमुना के किनार॥

braj kailai bihār śyām rādhikā dūno jane.
kekare hāthe kañganavā kekare gare hār;
kekare hāthe bañsuriyā kehike ho kinār.
rādhā ke hāthe kañganavā rukamin gale hār;
kṛṣṇā ke hāthe bañsuriyā jamunā ke kinār.

Kṛṣṇa and Rādhā are amusing themselves in Braj.
Who is wearing a bracelet and who is wearing a necklace?
Who is carrying a flute in his hand and on which bank are they strolling?
Rādhā is wearing a bracelet and Rukmiṇī is wearing a necklace;
Kṛṣṇa is carrying a flute in his hand on the bank of the river Yamuna.

(LGT: 163R: 1972-73, Varanasi, Mixed Men)

१४७.

सुनो सुनो जनक की बतियाँ ए सखियाँ सुनो जनक की बतियाँ॥
राजा जनक परन एक ठाने वही द्वारे मा धइलै पिनकिया॥
देश देश के भूपति आये वही टारे न टारैं पिनकिया॥
बाणासुर रावण चलि आयो ऊहो भगे आधी रतिया॥
मुनि जी के संग दोउ बालक आये वही धर तोरे पिनकिया॥

suno suno janak kī batiyāñ e sakhiyāñ suno Janak kī batiyāñ.
rājā janak paran ek ṭhāne vahī dvāre mā dhailai pinakiyā.
deś deś ke bhūpati āye vahī ṭāre n ṭaraiṅ pinakiyā.
bāṇāsur rāvaṇ cali āyo ūho bhage ādhī ratiyā.
muni jī ke saṅg dou bālak āye vahī dhar tore pinakiyā.

O dear girlfriend, listen to Janak's message.
King Janak has taken a vow by putting that bow at the gate.
Kings of many countries came but could not move that bow.
Bāṇāsur and Rāvaṇ came but they too ran away in the middle of the night.
Two young lads came with a respected sage and they broke the bow.

(LGT: 165R: 1972-73, Karmi, Mixed Men)

१४८.

होरी खेलैं रघुबीरा अवध में ॥
केकरे हाथे कनक पिचकारी, केकरे हाथे अबीरा ॥
राम के हाथे कनक पिचकारी, लछिमन हाथे अबीरा ॥
राम का भीजल जोड़ा जामा, सीता का भीजा लकीरा ॥
राम के काँधे ढोलक भल सोहै, लछिमन हाथे मँजीरा ॥

horī khelaiṅ raghubīrā avadh meṅ.
kekare hāthe kanak picakārī, kekare hāthe abīrā?
rām ke hāthe kanak picakārī lachiman hāthe abīrā.
rām kā bhījal joṛā jāmā, sītā kā bhījā lakīrā.
rām ke kāñdhe ḍholak bhal sohai, lachiman hāthe mañjīrā.

Ram is playing Holī in Avadh.
Who had a golden squirt gun and who is carrying coloured powder?
Rām is carrying a golden squirt gun and Lakṣmaṇ is carrying coloured powder.
Rām's clothes are wet and Sītā is wet from the head down.
Rām, with a drum on his shoulder, is beautiful and so is Lakṣmaṇ with cymbals.

(LGT: 166R: 1972-73, Karmi, Mixed Men)

१४९.

बृन्दाबन की साँकर खोरी भगौती चला हिंडोला झूलि आई॥
काहू काठ का बना हिंडोला, काहू के लागल डोरी॥
के न झूलै के न झुलावै, के न चँवर डुलावै॥
चंदन काठ का बना हिंडोला, रेशम लागल डोरी॥
राम झूलैं लछिमन झुलावैं सीता चँवर डुलावैं॥

bṛndāban kī sāñkar khorī bhagautī calā hiṅḍolā jhūli āī.
kāhū kāṭh kā banā hiṅḍolā, kāhū ke lāgal ḍorī?
ke n jhūlai ke n jhulāvai, ke n cañvar ḍulāvai?
caṅdan kāṭh kā banā hiṅḍolā, reśam lāgal ḍorī.
rām jhūlaiṅ lachiman jhulāvaiṅ, sītā cañvar ḍulāvaiṅ.

Let's go through the narrow lanes of Vṛndāvan to swing.
Of what wood is the swing made and with what kind of rope is it attached?
Who is on the swing, who is making it swing and who is fanning?
The swing is made of sandalwood and is attached with a silken rope.
Rām is swinging, Lakṣmaṇ is pushing the swing and Sītā is fanning.

(LGT: 167R: 1972-73, Karmi, Mixed Men)

१५०.

लहजै जिया मोर बालम मोर गदेलवा॥
कहवाँ बोलै कोयलिया कहवाँ बोलै मोर
कहवाँ बोलै पपिहरा कहवाँ पिया मोर बालम मोर गदेलवा॥
अंबा की डारि कोयलिया बनवा बोलै मोर
नदी किनारे पपिहरा सेजिया पिया मोर बालम मोर गदेलवा॥

lahajai jiyā mor bālam mor gadelavā.
kahavāñ bolai koyaliyā kahavāñ bolai mor?
kahavāñ bolai papiharā kahavāñ piyā mor bālam mor gadelavā?
aṁbā kī ḍāri koyaliyā banavā bolai mor;
nadī kināre papiharā sejiyā piyā mor bālam mor gadelavā.

I am excited and my husband is young.
Where are cuckoos and peacocks calling?
Where is *papīhā* calling and where is my young husband calling from?
The cuckoo is calling from a mango branch and the peacock is calling from the forest.
Papīhā bird is calling from the river bank and my young husband is calling from bed.

(LGT: 169R: 1972-73, Karmi, Mixed Men)

१५१.

होरी खेलैं बनवारी बिरज में ॥
इत से आये श्याम सखा संग, उत से गोप कुमारी ॥
इत से अबीर गुलाल उड़ावैं उत से हैं पिचकारी ॥
पटुका रुमाल श्याम के भीजे, राधा जू की सारी ॥
सो लखि फाग लालचन होरी, बारबार बलिहारी ॥

horī khelaiṅ banavārī biraj meṅ.
it se āye śyām sakhā saṅg, ut se gop kumārī.
it se abīr gulāl uṛāvaiṅ ut se haiṅ picakārī.
paṭukā rumāl śyām ke bhīje, rādhā jū kī sārī.
so lakhi phāg lālacan horī, bārabār balihārī.

Kṛṣṇa is playing Holī in Braj.
Kṛṣṇa, along with his friends, came from this side and milkmaids came from that side.
Abīr and *gulāl* were thrown from this side and squirt guns from that side.
Kṛṣṇa's clothes and scarf and Rādhā's *sārī* are wet.
Lālcan (the composer) says, "I sacrifice myself having observed such a Holī."

(LGT: 172R: 1972-73, Vāranasi, Mixed Men)

१५२.

ऐसी चतुर ब्रजनारि हाँ रे लाला रंग में हो रही होरी ॥
हाँ रे लाला कै मन उड़त गुलाल, कै मन केसर घोरी ॥

हाँ रे लाला दस मन उड़त गुलाल, सवा मन केसर घोरी ॥
हाँ रे लाला राधे पै छिड़कत श्याम, श्याम पर राधा गोरी ॥
हाँ रे लाला राधे को फाटो है चीर, श्याम की पचरंग पागी ॥
हाँ रे लाला राधे चली हैं मुखमोर, श्याम तोसे को खेलै होरी ॥

aisī catur brajanāri hāñ re lālā raṅg meṅ ho rahī horī.
hāñ re lālā kai man uṛat gulāla, kai man kesar ghorī.
hāñ re lālā das man uṛat gulāl, savā man kesar ghorī.
hāñ re lālā rādhe pai chiṛakat śyām, śyām par rādhā gorī.
hāñ re lālā rādhe ko phāṭo hai cīr, śyām kī pacaraṅg pāgī.
hāñ re lālā rādhe calī haiṅ mukhamor, śyām tose ko khelai horī.

Holī is colourfully celebrated by clever women of Braj.
How many "*man*" of red farinaceous powder has been thrown and how much saffron was mixed?
Ten *man* red farinaceous powder was thrown and one and one quarter *man* saffron was mixed.
Kṛṣṇa is sprinkling Rādhā and fair Rādhā is sprinkling Kṛṣṇa.
Rādhā's *sārī* is torn and Kṛṣṇa's multicoloured turban is torn.
Rādhā prepared to leave protesting to Kṛṣṇa *that* who will play Holī with him.

(LGT: 184R: 1972-73, Vṛndavan, Brāhmaṇ Women)

१५३.

अरी ए री मोपे बरजोरी रंग डारो ॥
सुन सजनी वो नन्द महर जी को, पग में कन्हैया ठाढ़ो ॥
भर पिचकारी मेरे सन्मुख मारी, भीज गयो तन सारो ॥
अपनी मौज से बैंयाँ मरोरी, मुख छुवो न बदन उघारी ॥

arī e rī mope barajorī raṅg ḍāro.
sun sajanī vo nand mahar jī ko, pag meṅ kanhaiyā ṭhāṛho.
bhar picakārī mere sanmukh mārī, bhīj gayo tan sāro.
apanī mauj se baiṅyāñ marorī, mukh chuvo n badan ughārī.

O dear, he forcibly threw colour on me.
O dear girlfriend listen that Kṛṣṇa of Nand was standing on the road.
He emptied his full squirt gun on my front and my whole body is wet.
At will, he twisted my arms, kissed and undressed me.
(LGT: 185R:1972-73, Vṛndāvan, Brāhmaṇ Women)

१५४.

साँवरो सलोनो मेरे गोहन पड़ो ॥
याकी आली मेरी आली कहो कित जाय, साँवरे सलोने बिन रहयोउ न जाय ॥
अँगना में ठाढ़ी हूँ अटा चढ़ि जाय, मुकुट की छइयाँ मेरे नैनों में छुवाइ ॥
इत घन उत घन आँड़ो दै दे चीर, सैनन में कहे चलो कुँज कुटीर ॥
साँवरे कमल नयन आगे नेक आ, बाँसुरी में गावै छैला लेले मेरो नाम ॥
इत घन श्याम मिलूँगी धाय, लाजन के मारे मोपे गयउ न जाय ॥

sāñvaro salono mere gohan paṛo.
yākī ālī merī ālī kaho kit jāy, sāñvare salone bin rahayou n jāy.
añganā meṅ ṭhāṛhī hūñ aṭā caṛhi jāy, mukuṭ kī chaiyāñ mere nainoṅ meṅ chuvāi.
it ghan ut ghan āñṛo dai de cīr sainan meṅ kahe calo kuñj kuṭīr.
sāñvare kamal nayan āge nek ā, bāñsurī meṅ gāvai chailā lele mero nām.
it ghan śyām milūñgī dhāy, lājan ke māre mope gayau n jāy.

Beautiful dark one has become my partner.
O dear friend where should I go, for without the dark one I cannot live.
As I was standing in my courtyard, he climbed the roof and put the shadow of his crown on my eyes.
Signalling with his scarf this and that way, he is asking me to go to groves.
O dark one comes in front of my eyes as he plays flute calling my name.
I wish to go and meet Kṛṣṇa right away but due to shyness I couldn't go.
(LGT: 186R: 1972-73, Vṛndāvan, Brāhmaṇ Women)

१५५.

कन्हैया घर चालौ गुइयाँ आज खेलैं होरी ॥
अपने अपने भवन से निकरीं कोई साँवल कोई गोरी
एक से एक जोबन मदमाती वयस दिनन की थोरी ॥
कोई चटकत कोई मटकत आवै कोई नाचत मुख मोरी
भर पिचकारी सन्मुख मारी भीज गयो तन सारो ॥
अबीर गुलाल के बादर छाये कैसो रंग मच्यो री
भर पिचकारी सन्मुख मारी भीज गयो तन सारो
अपने अपने भवन से निकरीं कोई साँवल कोई गोरी
चन्द्रसखी भज बालकृष्ण छबि हरि चरनन चित डोरी ॥

kanhaiyā ghar cālau guiyāñ āj khelaiṅ horī.
apane apane bhavan se nikarīṅ koī sāñval koī gorī;
ek se ek joban madamātī vayas dinan kī thorī.
koī caṭakat koī maṭakat āvai koī nācat mukh morī;
bhar picakārī sanmukh mārī bhīj gayo tan sāro.
abīr gulāl ke bādar chāye kaiso raṅg macyo rī;
bhar picakārī sanmukh mārī bhīj gayo tan sāro.
apane apane bhavan se nikarīṅ koī sāñval koī gorī;
candrasakhī bhaj bālakṛṣṇ chabi hari caranan cit ḍorī.

O dear friends, let's go to Kṛṣṇa's house to play Holī.
A few dark ones and a few fair ones came out of their homes;
They are tender in age and competing amongst each other's intoxicated youth.
Some are colourful, some are coquette, and some are coming hiding their faces.
[Kṛṣṇa] emptied his full squirt gun on them and made them all wet.
Clouds of *abīr* and *gulāl* are hovering; it was such a colourful scene;
[Kṛṣṇa] emptied his full squirt gun on them and made them all wet.
A few dark ones and a few fair ones came out of their homes;
Candrasakhī says to meditate on child Kṛṣṇa and attach yourself to Hari's feet.

(LGT: 189R: 1972-73, Vṛndāvan, Brāhmaṇ Women)

१५६.

आज बिरज में होरी रे रसिया, होरी नहीं तो बरजोरी रे रसिया॥
कौन गाँव के कुँवर कन्हैया लाला, कौन गाँव राधा गोरी रे रसिया॥
नन्दगाँव के कुँवर कन्हैया लाला, बरसाने की राधा गोरी रे रसिया॥
उड़त गुलाल लाल भये बादर, केसर गागर घोरी रे रसिया॥
बाजत ताल मृदंग झाँझ ढप, और नगारे की जोड़ी रे रसिया॥
कौन के हाथ कनक पिचकारी, कौन के हाथ कमोरी रे रसिया॥
श्याम के हाथ कनक पिचकारी, राधे के हाथ कमोरी रे रसिया॥
अबीर गुलाल कुमकुम केसर, फेंकत भर भर झोरी रे रसिया॥
चन्द्रसखी भज बालकृष्ण छबि, हरि के चरणों में चित जोरी रे रसिया॥

āj biraj meṅ horī re rasiyā, horī nahīṅ to barajorī re rasiyā.
kaun gāñv ke kuñvar kanhaiyā lālā, kaun gāñv rādhā gorī re rasiyā.
nandagāñv ke kuñvar kanhaiyā lālā, barasāne kī rādhā gorī re rasiyā.
uṛat gulāl lāl bhaye bādar, kesar gāgar ghorī re rasiyā.
bājat tāl mṛdaṅg jhāñjh ḍhap, aur nagāre kī joṛī re rasiyā.
kaun ke hāth kanak picakārī, kaun ke hāth kamorī re rasiyā.
śyām ke hāth kanak picakārī, rādhe ke hāth kamorī re rasiyā.
abīr gulāl kumakum kesar, pheṅkat bhar bhar jhorī re rasiyā.
candrasakhī bhaj bālakṛṣṇ chabi, hari ke caraṇoṅ meṅ cit jorī re rasiyā.

O lover, today it is Holī in Braj and it is a day of freedom.
Which village does Kṛṣṇa comes from? What village does fair Rādhā come from?
Kṛṣṇa is from Nandgāon and Rādhā is from Barasānā.
The abundance of *gulāl* has made clouds red and pitchers full of saffron water has been readied.
Mṛdaṅg, Jhañjh, tambourine, and *nagārā* are being played.
Who has a golden squirting gun in his hand and who has a pitcher full of colour water in his hand?
Kṛṣṇa has a golden squirting gun in his hand and Rādhā has a pitcher full of colour water in her hand.
They are throwing bags full of *abīr, gulāl, kumkum* and saffron.

Candrasakhī says to meditate on child Kṛṣṇa and attach yourself to Hari's feet.

(LGT: 190R: 1972-73, Vṛndāvan, Brāhmaṇ Women)

१५७.

रसिया को नारि बनावौं री रसिया को ॥
बेंदी भाल नयन बिच कजरा, हाँ रे याये नकबेसर पहिराओ री ॥
कटि लहँगा उर माँहि कंचुकी, हाँ रे याये सिर से चुँदर उढ़ाओ री ॥
लाल गुलाल द्रगन में अँजन, हाँ रे याये नकबेसर पहिराओ री ॥
नारायण तारी बजाय के, हाँ री याये जसुमति निकट नचाओ री ॥
याये बनाओ होरी को भँडुवा, हाँ रे याये अबीर गुलाल लगाओ री ॥
पुरषोत्तम प्रभु की छबि निरखत, हाँ रे याये हरि के चरन चित लगाओ री ॥

rasiyā ko nāri banāvauṅ rī rasiyā ko.
beṅdī bhāl nayan bic kajarā, hāñ re yāye nakabesar pahirāo rī.
kaṭi lahañgā ur māñhi kaṅcukī, hāñ re yāye sir se cuñdar uṛhāo rī.
lāl gulāl dragan meṅ añjan, hāñ re yāye nakabesar pahirāo rī.
nārāyaṇ tārī bajāy ke, hāñ rī yāye jasumati nikaṭ nacāo rī.
yāye banāo horī ko bhañḍuvā hāñ re yāye abīr gulāl lagāo rī.
puraṣottam prabhu kī chabi nirakhat, hāñ re yāye hari ke caran cit lagāo rī.

I will make this lover-boy a woman.
I will put on *beṅdī* on his forehead, mascara in his eyes and a nose ring.
I will make him put on a skirt and a bodice and will make him wear a scarf.
I will smear red *gulāl* on him and put mascara in his eyes and make him wear a nose ring.
Clapping, I will make him dance near Yaśodā.
Make him a pimp of Holī and smear *abīr* and *gulāl* on him.
Puruṣottam (the composer) says, "Looking at this sight, meditate on Hari's feet."

(LGT: 191R: 1972-73, Vṛndāvan, Brāhmaṇ Women)

१५८.

मैं कैसे होरी खेलूँ री या साँवलिया के संग रंग मैं॥
कोरे कोरे कलश भराये जिसमें घोरा रंग
भर पिचकारी सन्मुख मारी चोली हो गई तंग॥
तबला बाज सरंगी बाजे और बाजे मरदंग
साँवलिया की बँशी बाजे राधे जी के संग॥
लटकत लटकत शंकर आये पारबती के संग
लोटा डोरी लुढ़कत आवैं घोटत आवैं भंग॥
सारी भीजै मिसुरी भीजै और भीजो है अंग
साँवलिया को कहाँ भिगोऊँ काली कामर अंग॥
लहँगा मेरा घूम घुमारा चोली मेरी तंग
खसम तुम्हारा बड़ा निखट्टू चलो हमारे संग॥
चन्द्रसखी भज बालकृष्ण छबि हरि के चरन चित संग॥

maiṅ kaise horī khelūñ rī yā sāñvaliyā ke saṅg raṅg maiṅ.
kore kore kalaś bharāye jisameṅ ghorā raṅg;
bhar picakārī sanmukh mārī colī ho gaī taṅg.
tabalā bāj saraṅgī bāje aur bāje maradaṅg;
sāñvaliyā kī bañśī bāje rādhe jī ke saṅg.
laṭakat laṭakat śaṅkar āye pārabatī ke saṅg;
loṭā ḍorī luṛhakat āvaiṅ ghoṭat āvaiṅ bhaṅg.
sārī bhījai misurī bhījai aur bhījo hai aṅg;
sāñvaliyā ko kahāñ bhigoūñ kālī kāmar aṅg.
lahañgā merā ghūm ghumārā colī merī taṅg;
khasam tumhārā baṛā nikhaṭṭū calo hamāre saṅg.
candrasakhī bhaj bālakrar̥ṣṇ chabi hari ke caran cit saṅg.

How could I play Holī with the Dark one?
Colour was mixed in new pitchers filled with water.
He squirted his gun right in front of me and my bodice has become tight.
Tablā, sāraṅgī, and *mr̥daṅg* are played;
Kr̥ṣṇa is playing his flute in the company of Rādhā.
Śaṅkar came staggering along with Pārvatī;
Pitcher and rope are coming along rolling and he is grinding his hemp on the way.

My *sārī,* bodice and whole body is wet;
Where should I throw colour on the Dark one who has a dark blanket around him.
My skirt is wide and my bodice is tight;
"Your husband is lazy so come with me."
Candrasakhī (the composer) says, meditate on this image of child Kṛṣṇa and devote yourself to Him.

(LGT: 192R: 1972-73, Vṛndāvan, Brāhmaṇ Women)

१४९.

सैयाँ हो मोरी बात न मानी ॥
पुरब दिशा मति जायो मोरे स्वामी, पुरब का लागत पानी
पानी लगत सब तुम मरि जइहौ, हम धन होब बिरानी,
बिना दास के जिन्दगानी ॥
उत्तर दिशा मति जायो मोरे स्वामी, उत्तर की नारि सयानी
राति सुतावत लाल पलँग पर, भोर भरावै पानी,
नार हमहूँ से सयानी ॥
दक्षिण दिशा मति जायो मोरे स्वामी, हुवाँ मेवा की खानी
खाई पी के मौज करि अइहौ, लइहौ गजब निशानी,
नारि देखी मुस्क्यानी ॥

saiyāñ ho morī bāt n mānī.
purab diśā mati jāyo more svāmī, purab kā lāgat pānī;
panī lagat sab tum mari jaihau, ham dhan hob birānī,
binā dās ke jindagānī.
uttar diśā mati jāyo more svāmī, uttar kī nāri sayānī;
rāti sutāvat lāl palañg par, bhor bharāvai pānī,
nār hamahūñ se sayānī.
dakṣiṇ diśā mati jāyo more svāmī, huvāñ mevā kī khānī;
khāī pī ke mauj kari aihau, laihau gajab niśānī,
nāri dekhī muskyānī.

O dear husband, you didn't listen to me!
Do not go in an easterly direction as water is bad there;

You will die with that water and I, your wife, would become a widow.
Life would be without any bond.
Do not go in a northern direction, my dear husband, as the women of the north are clever;
At night, she would make you sleep in bed and in the morning would make you fetch water.
A woman more clever than I!
Do not go in a southern direction, my dear husband; there is plenty of dry fruits.
You would eat and drink and enjoy your life and would bring a delightful present,
Woman would look at it and would smile.

(LGT: 197R: 1972-73, Patti, Brāhmaṇ Women)

१६०.

बोरि दई मोरी सारी रंगन मा।
गवन हमरो नकचाना करिबै कौन बहाना॥
सब सखियन मा चुँदर मोरी मैली, दूजे पिया घर जाना
तीजे डर है मोहें सास ननद को चौथे पिया देहैं ताना॥
प्रेम नगर की राह कठिन है हुवाँ रंगरेज सयाना
एक बोर दई मोरी चूँदर तासे पिया से पहिचाना॥

bori daī morī sārī raṅgan mā.
gavan hamaro nakacānā karibai kaun bahānā.
sab sakhiyan mā cuñdar morī mailī, dūje piyā ghar jānā;
tīje ḍar hai moheñ sās nanad ko cauthe piyā dehaiṅ tānā.
prem nagar kī rāh kaṭhin hai huvāñ raṅgarej sayānā;
ek bor daī morī cūñdar tāse piyā se pahicānā.

My *sārī* is soaked in many colours!
My *gaunā* is getting close and what excuse would I give?
Among all my friends, my scarf is dirty and secondly, I am about to go to my husband's home.

Thirdly, I am sacred of my *sās* and *nanad* and fourthly, my husband would taunt me.
The road to the city of love is hard and the dyer is clever there;
He soaked my scarf and thus I recognized my husband.
(LGT: 198R: 1972-73, Patti, Brāhmaṇ Women)

१६१.

चटकीली है सुन्दर नार अँगिया बैंजनी ॥
की अँगिया तोरे मैके से आई, की पठवा तोरा यार ॥
न अँगिया मोरे मैके से आई, न पठवा मोरा यार ॥
अँगिया तो पठवै सास जी के पूता, ननदिया के लगवार ॥

caṭakīlī hai sundar nār añgiyā baiṅjanī.
kī añgiyā tore maike se āī, kī paṭhavā torā yār.
n añgiyā more maike se āī, n paṭhavā morā yār;
añgiyā to paṭhavai sās jī ke pūtā, nanadiyā ke lagavār.

The woman is dazzling and her bodice is purple.
Has this bodice come from your parents' home or has your boyfriend sent it?
This bodice has not come from my parents' home neither my boy-friend sent it!
The bodice has been sent by my *sās's* son who is *nanad's* lover.
(LGT: 203R: 1972-74, Patti, Brāhmaṇ Women)

बारहमासी / चौमासा

१६२.

चैत महीना पाख रामनवमी को जल्म लियो
अवधपुरी सुखधाम सखिन मिल मंगलचार कियो

खबरि जब दशरथ ने पाई दिये दान गजदान गऊ दिन थोरे की ब्याई
सभा सब प्रफुलित से आई
कर्म रेख न मिटै करै कोई लाखों चतुराई॥
लागत ही बैसाख कैकई बवाल करि डार्‌यो
धृत जीवन धिक्कार भरत की ऐसी महतारी
दुख सब नगरी को दीन्हेव
तीन लोक के नाथ राम बनवासी कर दीन्हेव
कुमति या कैसी बनि आई॥
जेठ पंच मिलि कहैं भरत को गद्दी बैठारौ
भरत धरत कानौ पर हाथ नाथ मेरी गरदन मति मारौ
सबै नहीं भाषन काजा
हम तौ उनके दास राम हैं अजोध्या के राजा, बात या सबके मन भाई॥
असाढ़ आसा राम मिलन की मन में लागि रही
रथ डोला गजबाज भीड़ भई भारत सब त्यारी
नदी जैसे सागर को धाई॥
सावन फेरि बेलपुर पहुँचे भीर भई भारी
भील निकट दल जोड़े लड़ने की त्यारी
भरत से पूँछि कै राँधि करौ
राम लखण सिया काज तीर गंगा के जूझि मरौ
भरत जब ऐसी सुनि पाई॥
भादौं भरत भील से भेंटे भक्त जान मन में
कन्द मूल फल तोड़ भरत की भेंट करी बन में
भरत को अगुआ कर दीन्हेव
भारद्वाज प्राग में जाय आनि दरशन दीन्हेव
प्राग की दुनिया सब धाई॥
क्वाँर करि महिमानी मुनि ने पूँछी कुशलाता
दोउ कर जोर कीन्हि पैकरमा कौशिल्या माता
आजु मेरो जीवन सफल भये
इतनी बात सुनी जब मुनि ने आशिरबाद दियो
भरत की मातै समुझावैं॥
कातिक कूच प्राग से कीन्हेव चित्रकोट आये
शीश जटा झटझोट सिया राम लखण पाये
भरत चरणों में जाय गिरे
भरत उठाय राम उर लाये नयनन नीर भरे
भरत तुम भाई सुखदाई॥
अगहन बारम्बार भरत को रघुबर समुझावैं

भरत उलटि घर जाव राज तुम करौ अजोध्या की
लोग सुख तबहीं पावैंगे
चौदा बरस बीति जइहैं जब लौट के हमहू आवैंगे
भरत को ऐसे समुझावैं ॥
पूस मास सिया राम लखण के जुरिगै भीर घनी
जनक बसिष्ठ गुरु समुझावैं कहैं अपनी अपनी
राम ने चरन खड़ाऊँ दै दीन्ही
भरत उलटि घर जाव राज तुम करौ अजोध्या की ॥
माह महीना मानि राम ने सुख पायो मन में
जनक जनकपुर को पहुँचायो भरत अजोध्या को
खड़ाऊँ गद्दी धर दीन्हीं
रामचन्द्र से कठिन तपस्या भारत ने कीन्हीं
बड़ाई याई में पाई ॥
फागुन फेरि हरी सीता जब रावण बधि कर दीन्हेव
रावण मारि कै रामचन्द्र ने राज भभीषण को दीन्हेव
शिव सनकादि आदि ब्रह्मादिक दरशन को आये
राम को गद्दी बैठारौ ॥

cait mahīnā pākh rāmanavamī ko jalm liyo.
avadhapurī sukhadhām sakhin mil maṅgalacār kiyo.
khabari jab daśarath ne pāī, diye dān gajadān gaū din thore kī byāī;
sabhā sab praphulit se āī.
karm rekh n miṭai karai koī lākhoṅ caturāī.
lāgat hī baisākh kaikaī bavāl kari ḍāryo;
dhṛt jīvan dhikkār bharat kī aisī mahatārī;
dukh sab nagarī ko dīnhev;
tīn lok ke nāth rām banavāsī kar dīnhev.
kumati yā kaisī bani āī.
jeṭh pañc mili kahaiṅ bharat ko gaddī baiṭhārau;
barat dharat kānau par hāth nāth merī garadan mati mārau;
sabai nahiṅ bhāṣan kājā;
ham tau unake dās rām haiṅ ajodhyā ke rājā, bāt yā sabake man bhāī.
asāṛh āsā rām milan kī man meṅ lāgi rahī;
rath ḍolā gajabāj bhīṛ bahī bhārat sab tyārī.
nadī jaise sāgar ko dhāī.

sāvan pheri belapur pahuñce bhīr bhaī bhārī;
bhīl nikaṭ dal joṛe laṛane kī tyārī;
bharat se pūñchi kai rāñdhi karau.
rām lakhaṇ siyā kāj tīr gaṅgā ke jūjhi marau.
bharat jab aisī suni pāī.
bhādauṅ bharat bhīl se bheṅṭe bhakt jān man meṅ;
kand mūl phal toṛ bharat kī bheṅṭ karī ban meṅ;
bharat ko aguā kar dīnhev.
bhāradvāj prāg meṅ jāy āni daraśan dīnhev;
prāg kī duniyā sab dhāī.
kvāñr kari mahimānī muni ne pūñchī kuśalātā;
dou kar jor kīnhi paikaramā kauśilyā mātā;
āju mero jīvan saphal bhaye.
itanī bāt sunī jab muni ne āśirabād diyo;
bharat kī mātai samujhāvaiṅ.
kātik kūc prāg se kīnhev citrakoṭ āye;
śīś jaṭā jhaṭajhoṭ siyā rām lakhaṇ pāye;
bharat caraṇoṅ meṅ jāy gire.
bharat uṭhāy rām ur lāye nayanan nīr bhare;
bharat tum bhāī sukhadāī.
agahan bārambār bharat ko raghubar samujhāvaiṅ;
bharat ulaṭi ghar jāv rāj tum karau ajodhyā kī;
log sukh tabahīṅ pāvaiṅge.
caudā baras bīti jaihaiṅ jab lauṭ ke hamahū āvaiṅge.
bharat ko aise samujhāvaiṅ.
pūs mās siyā rām lakhaṇ ke jurigai bhīr ghanī.
janak basiṣṭh guru samujhavaiṅ kahaiṅ apanī apanī.
rām ne caran khaṛāūñ dai dīnhī.
bharat ulaṭi ghar jāv rāj tum karau ajodhyā kī.
māh mahīnā māni rām ne sukh pāyo man meṅ;
janak janakapur ko pahuñcāyo bharat ajodhyā ko;
khaṛāūñ gaddī dhar dīnhīṅ.
rāmacandr se kaṭhin tapasyā bhārat ne kīnhīṅ.
baṛāī yāī meṅ pāī.
phāgun pheri harī sītā jab rāvaṇ badhi kar dīnhev;

rāvaṇ māri kai rāmacandr ne rāj bhabhīṣaṇ ko dīnhev.
śiv sanakādi ādi brahmādik daraśan ko āye.
rām ko gaddī baiṭhārau.

Rām was born on the ninth day of the first half of *Cait* month.
There was happiness all over Avadh and girlfriends sang auspicious songs.
When Daśarath heard the news, he gave elephants, cows with calf, and other gifts.
The whole assembly was full of happiness.
The fate line cannot be erased no matter how clever one is!
In the early month of *Baiśākh,* Kaikeyī staged an uproar;
Curse on her life, such is Bharat's mother.
She gave sorrow to the whole country.
She made Rām, the king of the three worlds, a forest dweller.
How did this bad advice come about?
In the month of *Jeṭh,* five elders decided to place Bharat on the throne;
Bharat does not want to hear of it and begs not to kill him;
There is no need for any further talk;
I am his servant and Rām is the king of Ayodhyā. Everyone appreciated this talk.
There is a desire in the mind to meet Rām in the month of *Āsāṛh.*
Bharat made all arrangements for chariots, palanquins and elephants for the whole crowd.
It was like a river flowing to meet the ocean.
In the month of *Sāvan* there was a great crowd in Belapur.
Tribal Bhīl people assembled their group to fight.
Ask Bharat first before fighting!
[Only then] for the sake of Rām, Lakṣmaṇ, and Sītā die fighting on the bank of the Ganges.
When Bharat heard all this.
In the month of *Bhadau*, Bharat met Bhīl knowing that he is Rām's devotee;
They offered Bharat, tuber roots and fruits.
Bharat was made the leader.
In Prayāg, they all went to see sage Bharadvāj.
The whole population of Prayāg came [to meet them].

In the month of *Kvār* performing all hospitality, the sage asked their well-being.
With folded hands, mother Kauśalyā performed circumambulation;
Today my life has gained merit.
When the sage heard this, he blessed her;
He consoled Bharat's mother.
In the month of *Kārtīk*, they left Prayāg and arrived at Citrakūṭ.
They met Rām, Lakṣmaṇ, and Sītā in their matted hair.
Bharat prostrated at Rām's feet.
With tears in his eyes, Rām picked Bharat up and embraced him.
O Bharat, you are a brother who gives happiness.
In the month of *Agahan*, Rām is advising Bharat repeatedly;
O Bharat, go back home and rule Ayodhyā;
Only then your people will be happy.
At the end of fourteen years, I too will return.
They are advising Bharat thus.
In the month of *Pūṣ* there was a great crowd around Sītā, Rām, and Lakṣmaṇ.
Janak and teacher Vasiṣṭh are advising according to their understanding.
Rām gave his wooden sandals [and advised].
O Bharat, go back home and rule Ayodhyā.
In the month of *Māgh*, Rām was at peace;
Janak returned to Janakpur and Bharat to Ayodhyā;
[Bharat] installed Rām's sandals on the throne.
Bharat performed harder penance than Rām.
He was praised by all.
In the month of *Phāgun*, Rāvaṇ abducted Sītā and was later killed.
After killing Rāvaṇ, Rām gave the kingdom to Vibhīṣaṇ.
Śiva, Brahmā and other gods came to see.
Install Rām on the throne.

(LGT: 1964, Brāhmaṇ Woman)

१६३.

अरे जाऊँगा गढ़ महोबा पिथौरा से लड़िहौं अगारी ॥
क्वाँर में कोपे धनी चौहान फूलमती के चरण मनाय

कि लसिगर में डंका दियो है बजाय
सुनि करिके छत्री हुये तैयार, सैन सब सम्भारी॥ अरे जाऊँगा०
कातिक कुसुमा उठी अकुलाय बोली है पीतम से शीश नवाय
कहाँ को ये लसिगर रहे हौ सजाय
प्राण पियारे देव बतलाय अंदेसा है भारी
अरे जाओ ना गढ़ महोबा पिया बात मानौ हमारी॥
अगहन अंदेसा करे मत नारि ऊदन से हमने किया है करार
लिया घेर महोबा पिथौरा ने आय
जाकर के देखूँ वो कैसा है शूर, सोच तज पियारी॥ अरे जाऊँगा०
पूस मास सुनिये भरतार जो तुम महोबे को होते तैयार
सो काहे को गवना लाएव हमार
नैया को मोरी लगैहे पार, उमरिया है बारी॥ अरे जाओ ना०
माह मास नहिं मानैं मुनीष आये हैं जगनिक आल्हा के तीर
लिया घेर महोबा पिथौरा ने हीर
जाकर के देखूँ वो कैसा है बीर, ना मानो तुम्हारी॥ अरे जाऊँगा०
फागुन में सुनिये भरतार अब तुम छोड़ धरो हथियार कि आई है होली
करौ त्योहार खेलौ फाग पिया रंग को डार, चलै पिचकारी॥ अरे जाओ ना०
चैत मास भुरही कसि तंगु जाकर सागर पार लगाऊँगा जंग
खून छत्रिन का बहाऊँगा, रंग खेलूँगा फाग पिथौरा के सँग
हाथ गहि कटारी॥ अरे जाऊँगा०
बैसाख मास निकरै अति घाम भागैगी भुरही तपै जब चाम
पिथौरा से कैसे करो संग्राम प्राण पियारे होउ बदनाम
पड़ै पग पिछारी॥ अरे जाओ ना०
जेठ जगतपति चरन मनाय तापर देहौं मैं चक्र चलाय
कि शिव ब्रह्मादिक सकैं न बचाय
क्यों तुम पियारी रही घबड़ाय, मैं हूँ छत्रधारी॥ अरे जाऊँगा
असाढ़ महोबे के दरम्यान जब रण कोपै धनी चौहान
पिथौरा से कैसे बीरा है चौड़ा ताहिर शेर
धाँधू मुकाबिल है पीतम न खैर, गई मति क्या मारी॥ अरे जाओ ना०
सावन महोबे मा जइहौं जरूर देखिहौं दिलावर वो कैसा है शेर
पिथौरा को छिन में लचा दूँ गरूर या मार उसको मिला दूँगा धूर
अकिल कहँ तुम्हारी॥ अरे जाऊँगा
भादौं में मत करे अबेर होके खुशी दीजे शमशेर
कि गाँधी के कमलू कहत हैं टेर ऊदन दुवारे रहे बाट हेर, न मानो तुम्हारी॥

are jāūñgā gaṛh mahobā pithaurā se laṛihauṅ agārī.
kvāñr meṅ kope dhanī cauhān phūlamatī ke caraṇ manāy;
ki lasigar meṅ ḍaṅkā diyo hai bajāy.
suni karike chatrī huye taiyār, sain sab sambhārī. are jaūñgā....
kātik kusumā uṭhī akulāy bolī hai pītam se śīś navāy;
kahāñ ko ye lasigar rahe hau sajāy;
prāṇ piyāre dev batalāy aṅdesā hai bhārī.
are jāo nā gaṛh mahobā piyā bāt mānau hamārī.
agahan aṅdesā kare mat nāri ūdan se hamane kiyā hai karār;
liyā gher mahobā pithaurā ne āy;
jākar ke dekhūñ vo kaisā hai śūr, soc taj piyārī. are jaūñgā....
pūs mās suniye bharatār jo tum mahobe ko hote taiyār;
so kāhe ko gavanā lāev hamār;
naiyā ko morī lagaihai pār, umariyā hai bārī. are jāo nā....
māh mās nahiṅ mānaiṅ munīṣ āye haiṅ jaganik ālhā ke tīr;
liyā gher mahobā pithaurā ne hīr.
jākar ke dekhūñ vo kaisā hai bīr, nā māno tumhārī. are jāūñgā....
phāgun meṅ suniye bharatār ab tum choṛ dharo hathiyār ki āī hai holī;
karau tyohār khelau phāg piyā raṅg ko ḍār, calai picakārī. are jāo nā....
cait mās bhurahī kasi taṅgu jākar sāgar pār lagāūñgā jaṅg;
khūn chatrin kā bahāūñgā, raṅg khelūñgā phāg pithaurā ke sañg.
hāth gahi kaṭārī. are jāūñgā....
baisākh mās nikarai ati ghām bhāgaigī bhurahī tapai jab cām;
pithaurā se kaise karo saṅgrām prāṇ piyāre hou badanām,
paṛai pag pichārī. are jāo nā....
jeṭh jagatapati caran manāy tāpar dehauṅ maiṅ cakr calāy;
ki śiv brahmādik sakaiṅ n bacāy;
kyoṅ tum piyārī rahī ghabaṛāy, maiṅ hūñ chatradhārī are jāūñgā....
asāṛh mahobe ke daramyān jab raṇ kopai dhanī cauhān;
pithaurā se kaise bīrā hai cauṛā tāhir śer;
dhāñdhū mukābil hai pītam n khair, gaī mati kyā mārī. are jāuā nā....
sāvan mahobe mā jaihauṅ jarūr dekhihauṅ dilāvar vo kaisā hai śer;
pithaurā ko chin meṅ lacā dūñ garūr yā mār usako milā dūñgā dhūr;
akil kahñ tumhārī. are jāūñgā....
bhādauṅ meṅ mat kare aber hoke khuśī dīje śamaśer;

ki gāñdhī ke kamalū kahat haiṅ ṭer ūdan duvāre rahe bāṭ her, n māno tumhārī.

I will go to fort Mahobā to fight first with Pṛthvīrāj.[1]
In the month of *Kvār,* rich Pṛthvīrāj became angry and worshipped at the feet of goddess, Phūlmatī.
He ordered battle drums played in the army camp.
All the warriors got ready and the army was ready to march.
In the month of *Kārtik,* weary Kusuma got up and bowing her head at her husband enquired.
Where are you going with your army?
O dear to my life, tell me as I have grave anxiety.
O dear husband, listen to me and do not go to fort Mahobā.
In the month of *Agahan,* do not worry my dear wife as I have made a promise with Ūdal.
Pṛthvīrāj has surrounded Mahobā;
I will go and see what kind of warrior he is! Do not worry my dear.
In the month of *Pūṣ,* if you are getting ready for Mahobā then listen my husband;
So, why did you bring me after *gaunā* ceremony.
Who will row my boat across as I am young.
In the month of *Māgh,* Jagnik came to visit Ālhā;
O diamond warrior, Pṛthvīrāj has surrounded Mahobā.
I will go and see what kind of warrior he is! I will not listen to you.
In the month of *Phāgun,* put down your weapons dear as the festival of Holī has come;
Enjoy the festival by throwing and squirting colour dear husband.
In the month of *Cait,* I will tighten seat on my elephant and will cross the river to raze battle;
I will waste the warrior's blood and will play colour [of blood] with Pṛthvīrāj.
Holding a dagger in my hand.

1. The song is referring to Lakhan of Kannauj, preparing to travel to Mahobā to battle with Pṛthvīrāj. Therefore, instead of Dhani Cauhan, it should read Dhani Rāṭhaur.

The month of *Baiśākh* is known for intense sun and your elephant will run away when her skin will burn from that intense heat;
How will you fight with Pṛthvīrāj? Dear to my life, you will become infamous,
If you take a step back.
In the month of *Jeṭh,* after worshipping the feet of the Lord of the universe, I will use my discus;
Even Śiva or Brahmā could not save him from that;
Why are you scared my dear, I am a warrior.
In the month of *Āṣāṛh,* when Pṛthvīrāj will get angry in the middle of battlefield;
Stronger than Pṛthvīrāj are his generals, Caurā and Tāhir
How will you face Dhāñdhu? Have you lost your mind?
In the month of *Sāvan,* I will go to Mahobā to see what kind of warrior is he!
I will put Pṛthvīrāj to shame or will waste his body in the dirt by killing him;
Where are your senses?
In the month of *Bhādau,* do not delay and happily hand me my sword;
As Kamalū [composer] is saying, "Ūdal is waiting at the gate and I will not listen to you".

(LGT: 36R: 1976, Kanpur, Brāhmaṇ Women)

१६४.

आली री उन श्याम सुन्दर बिन कैसे जियब हो ॥
पहिला महीना जो कातिक लाग मोरे पिया लाद् चले बनजार. सो मैं तो बनजारिन
नाचत अइहैं चरावत गाय पिया बिन कातिक हमें न सोहाय. कहौ कैसे करिबै ॥
कातिक उतरत अगहन लाग मैके की बिटियाँ चली ससुरारि
सो पान फूल रस त्यागन कीन बिछुड़े हैं कंथ दइव दुख दीन. कहौ कैसे करिबै ॥
पूस मास ऋतु परत तुषार कम्पत गेड़ुआ औ कल्पत सेज
पिया बिन कल्पत गोरी का करेज. कहौ कैसे करिबै ॥
माह मास स्वामी बरत तुम्हार मैं बरतेरित पाँच एत्वार
न्हाइ धोइ के दीन असीस तुम पिया जीवौ लाख बरीस. कहौ कैसे करिबै ॥
फागुन मा डोलै फगुई बयार परवर पत्र सबै झरि जाँय
झरिगे हैं पतवा खड़े हैं रूख तुम पिया इतनो सहायो दुख. कहौ कैसे करिबै ॥

चैत मास बन फूले हैं टेसु गोरिया ने पठवा पिया का सन्देश
इतना सन्देशवा कहेव समझाय उमरि बरिस मोसे रहिओ न जाय, कहौ कैसे करिबै ॥
बैसाख हरे हरे बँसवा कटाय छावत मड़वा गवावत गीत
पिया बिन लागत सबै अनरीति, कहौ कैसे करिबै ॥

āli rī un śyām sundar bin kaise jiyab ho.
pahilā mahīnā jo kātik lāg more piyā lād cale banajār, so maiṅ to banajārin;
nācat aihaiṅ carāvat gāy piyā bin kātik hameṅ n sohāy, kahau kaise karibai.
kātik utarat agahan lāg maike kī biṭiyāñ calī sasurāri;
so pān phūl ras tyāgan kīn bichuṛe haiṅ kaṅth daiv dukh dīn, kahau kaise karibai.
pūs mās ṛtu parat tuṣār kampat geḍuā au kalpat sej;
piyā bin kalpat gorī kā karej, kahau kaise karibai.
māh mās svāmī barat tumhār maiṅ baraterit pāñc etvār;
nhāi dhoi ke dīn asīs tum piyā jīvau lākh barīs, kahau kaise karibai.
phāgun mā ḍolai phaguī bayār paravar patr sabai jhari jāñy;
jharige haiṅ patavā khaṛe haiṅ rūkh tum piyā itano sahāyo dukh, kahau kaise karibai.
cait mās ban phūle haiṅ ṭesū goriyā ne paṭhavā piyā kā sandeś;
itanā sandeśavā kahev samajhāy umari baris mose rahio n jāy, kahau kaise karibai.
baisākh hare hare bañsavā kaṭāy chāvat maṛavā gavāvat gīt;
piyā bin lāgat sabai anarīti, kahau kaise karibai.

How will I live without Kṛṣṇa?
In the first month of *Kārtik*, my husband left for grain business;
He will come dancing tending his cows! Without my husband I do not like *Kārtik*.
After the month of *Kārtik*, *Agahan* came and daughters [visiting their parents home] began to leave for their in-laws' home.
I gave up betel leaves, flowers, and pleasures in the absence of my husband; God has given me a great sorrow.
The month of *Pūṣ* is cold and my body and bed are shivering;
Without husband, woman's heart is shivering.
In the month of *Māgh*, I kept a fast for your well-being, my husband, and fasted five Sundays.

After bathing, I blessed that, O my husband, may you live hundreds of years.
In the month of *Phāgun*, winds blow and all the leaves fall;
All the leaves have fallen, only tree trunks remain; you, my husband, have given me great sadness.
In the month of *Cait, ṭesū* flowers are blooming in the forest and the woman has sent a message to her husband;
Request him with this message that I am in my youth and it is hard to live without him.
In the month of *Baiśākh*, people cut green bamboos to make a canopy and sing songs [in preparation for marriages];
Without my husband, all these traditions have no meaning.

(LGT: 20R: 1972-73, Dhanabad, Brāhmaṇ Women)

१६५.

लागे मसवा असाढ़ जिनके घर मा सुन्दर नार
पिया ना जाएव परदेश छोड़ बचपन मा रे
लागे मसवा सावन ढेपी यों काढ़े नयन
कब तक मैं करौं तपन्न बारे बालमवा रे
लागे मसवा भदउना पिया छाये कउने गउना
कब तक त्याकौं तोरा नउना बारे बालमवा रे
लागे मसवा कुँवार जिनके देवरा कुँवार
चोली फारत हमार बारे बालमवा रे
लागे मसवा कतिक गोरी होइ गई सतीक
करती ध्यान अपने का बारे बालमवा रे
लागे मसवा अगहन गोरी कगवा भवन
लरिकइयन के यार रवावत खरिकन मा रे
लागे मसवा पूस गोरी आँगन कै गै चूस
जाकी लै गै चोली मूस बारे बालमवा रे
लागे मसवा माघ बोले बड़ेरी मा काग
उड़ी ड्योढ़ी पर ते आग बारे बालमवा रे
लागे मसवा फागुन गोरी यों करै सगुन्न
केहि पर मैं छोड़ौं रगन्न बारे बालमवा रे
लागे मसवा चैत बेला यों फूले कइत

नइना होइ गये डकइत बारे बालमवा रे
लागे मसवा बैसाख रही सैंयाँ जी की आश
बसे कुबरी के पास बारे बालमवा रे
लागे मसवा जेठ होइगै सइयाँ से भेंट
कटे सोरहो कलेश बारे बालमवा रे
गाई मैं बारामासी गीत छोड़ि दियो परदेशी से प्रीत
गइले बारहो महीना बीत कब होइहैं मिलना

lāge masavā asāṛh jinake ghar mā sundar nār;
piyā nā jāev paradeś choṛ bacapan mā re.
lāge masavā sāvan ḍhepī yoṅ kāṛhe nayan;
kab tak maiṅ karauṅ tapann bāre bālamavā re.
lāge masavā bhadaunā piyā chāye kaune gaunā;
kab tak tyākauṅ torā naunā bāre bālamavā re.
lāge masavā kuñvār jinake devarā kuñvār.
colī phārat hamār bāre bālamavā re.
lāge masavā katik gorī hoi gaī satīk;
karatī dhyān apane kā bāre bālamavā re.
lāge masavā agahan gorī kagavā bhavan;
larikaiyan ke yār rvāvat kharikan mā re.
lāge masavā pūs gorī āñgan kai gai cūs;
jākī lai gai colī mūs bāre bālamavā re.
lāge masavā māgh bole baṛerī mā kāg;
uṛī ḍyoṛhī par te āg bāre bālamavā re.
lāge masavā phāgun gorī yoṅ karai sagunn;
kehi par maiṅ choṛauṅ ragann bāre bālamavā re.
lāge masavā cait belā yoṅ phūle kait;
nainā hoi gaye ḍakait bāre bālamavā re.
lāge masavā baisākh rahī saiṅyāñ jī kī āś;
base kubarī ke pās bāre bālamavā re.
lāge masavā jeṭh hoigai saiyāñ se bheṅṭ;
kaṭe soraho kaleś bāre bālamavā re.
gāī maiṅ bārāmāsī gīt choṛi diyo paradeśī se prīt;
gaile bāraho mahīnā bīt kab hoihaiṅ milanā.

At the beginning of the *Āṣāṛh* month, whoever has a beautiful woman in the house;
O dear husband don't go abroad leaving me alone in my youth.
In the month of *Sāvan*, the woman is looking around;
How long should I suffer, O my dear husband?
In the month of *Bhādau*, in which country are you living, my husband?
How long should I wait for you, O my dear husband?
In the month of *Kvār*, unmarried *Devars;*
They are tearing my bodice, O dear husband.
In the month of *Kārtik*, the woman became virtuous;
She meditates on her husband, O dear husband.
In the month of *Agahan*, the woman remained in her house.
Her childhood friends are crying in the barn.
In the month of *Pūṣ*, woman's courtyard became barren;
Her bodice was taken by mice, O dear husband.
In the month of *Māgh*, a crow crowed on her thatched roof;
Fire was burned at the gate, O dear husband.
In the month of *Phāgun*, woman is predicting;
Who should I throw colour at, O dear husband.
In the month of *Cait*, jasmine bloomed everywhere;
My eyes have become dacoit, O dear husband.
In the month of *Baiśākh* there was a hope for my husband;
He is living with Kubarī, O my dear husband.
In the month of *Jeṭh*, I met my husband;
All my sixteen pains disappeared, O my dear husband.
I sang this Bārāhmāsi and abandoned my love for a foreigner;
All twelve months have passed, when will I meet [with my lover].

(LGT: 126R: 1972-73, Akohariyā, Ahīr Man)

१६६.

ऊधो अबके गइल कब अइहौ ॥
सावन में प्रभु आवन कहिगै, भादौं में रैन गँवइहौ
क्वाँर मास में जो न अइहौ, कपटी मित्र कहइहौ ॥
कातिक में नित्य कर्म करतु हैं, अगहन बिलम्ब मति करिहौ

पूस मास मा जाड़ा परत बा, केह करे गले लपटइहौ॥
माघ मास में मकर नहइहौ, फागुन मास खेलइहौ
चैत मास में फुलति चमेली, के करे गले मा पहिनइहौ॥
बैसाख मास में धूप परत बा, जेठ में गरमी सतइहौ
असाढ़ मास में बूँद गिरत बा, काछे में बँगला छवइहौ॥

ūdho abake gail kab aihau.
sāvan meṅ prabhu āvan kahigai, bhādauṅ meṅ rain gañvaihau;
kvāñr mās meṅ jo n aihau, kapaṭī mitr kahaihau.
kātik meṅ nity karm karatu haiṅ, agahan vilaṃb mati karihau.
pūs mās mā jāṛhā parat bā, keh kare gale lapaṭaihau.
māgh mās meṅ makar nahaihau, phāgun mās khelaihau;
cait mās meṅ phulati camelī, ke kare gale mā pahinaihau.
baisākh mās meṅ dhūp parat bā, jeṭh meṅ garamī sataihau;
asāṛh mās meṅ būñd girat bā, kāche meṅ baṅgalā chavaihau.

O Ūdho, now that you are leaving, when will you come back?
You promised to come in the month of *Sāvan* and in the month of *Bhādau,* I will waste my nights.
If you do not come in the month of *kvar*, you will be called a cunning friend.
I will observe my daily routine in the month of *Kārtik* but do not delay in the month of *Agahan.*
During cold month of *Pūṣ,* who will embrace you?
In the month of *Māgh,* you will bathe during the festival of *Makar Sankranti* and in the month of *Phāgun* you will play [Holī];
In the *Cait,* Jasmine will bloom, unto whose neck will you offer your garland?
There is an intense solar heat in the month of *Baiśākh* and heat will be tormenting in the month of *Jeṭh.*
It will rain in the month of *Āṣāṛh* so prepare your quarters nearby.

(LGT: 156R: 1972-73, Varanasi, Blind Street Musician)

१६७.

राम लखन दोनों बन का जात हैं राम लखन दोउ भैया

असाढ़ मास ऋतु लागी सजनी रिमझिम मेघा बरसै
कौन बिरिछ तरे भीजत होइहैं राम लखन दोउ भैया
सावन मास ऋतु लागी सजनी पड़ गये कृष्ण हिंडोला
सब सखियाँ मिल झूला झूलै गावैं बारामासी
भादौं मास ऋतु लागै सजनी दैया जोर जनाई
दैवा गरजै बिजली चमकै मोरे जिया बहुत डेराई
क्वाँर मास ऋतु लागै सजनी घर घर पीतर आये
आई अमावस पिंडा पारैं तीन लोक कुल तारे
कातिक मास ऋतु लागै सजनी सब सखी गंगा नहाई
सब सखियन मिल गंग नहाई दान औ पुन्य कराई
अगहन मास ऋतु लागै सजनी सब सखी गौने जाई
आज हमारे कृष्ण मधुपुर छाये हमरा गवन को लेई
पूस मास ऋतु लागै सजनी जाड़ा जोर जनाई
सेजा सुफेदी उसीसे मा तकिया प्रभु बिन जाड़ न जाई
माघ मास की बसंत पँचमी मालिन बौर लै आई
आज हमारे केशव मधुपुर छाये तुम्हरी बौर को लेई
फागुन मास ऋतु लागो सजनी घर घर रंग अबीरा
आज हमारे कृष्ण मधुपुर छाये केहि संग खेलब होरी
चैत मास ऋतु लागो सजनी बन बन टेसू फूले
आज हमारे कृष्ण मधुपुर छाये केहि संग रंग हिलोरा
बैसाख मास ऋतु लागो सजनी गरमी जोर जनाई
सीता तो चढ़ि गइ रंगमहल मा रस भरी बेनिया डोलाई
जेठ मास ऋतु लागो सजनी लूकै जोर जनाई
राम लखन की कोमल देहियाँ धूप लगत कुम्हलाई

rām lakhan donoṅ ban kā jāt haiṅ rām lakhan dou bhaiyā.
asāṛha mās ṛtu lāgī sajanī rimajhim meghā barasai;
kaun birich tare bhījat hoihaiṅ rām lakhan dou bhaiyā.
sāvan mās ṛtu lāgī sajanī paṛh gaye kṛṣṇ hiṅḍolā;
sab sakhiyāñ mil jhūlā jhūlai gāvaiṅ bārāmāsī.
bhādauṅ mās ṛtu lāgai sajanī daiyā jor janāī;
daivā garajai bijalī camakai more jiyā bahut ḍerāī.
kvāñr mās ṛtu lāgai sajanī ghar ghar pītar āye;
āī amāvas piṅḍā pāraiṅ tīn lok kul tāre.
kātik mās ṛtu lāgai sajanī sab sakhī gaṅgā nahāī;
sab sakhiyan mil gaṅg nahāī dān au puny karāī.

agahan mās ṛtu lāgai sajanī sab sakhī gaune jāī;
āj hamāre kṛṣṇ madhupur chāye hamarā gavan ko leī.
pūs mās ṛtu lāgai sajanī jāṛā jor janāī;
sejā suphedī usīse mā takiyā prabhu bin jāṛ n jāī.
māgh mās kī basaṅt pañcamī mālin baur lai āī;
āj hamāre keśav madhupur chāye tumharī baur ko leī.
phāgun mās ṛtu lāgo sajanī ghar ghar raṅg abīrā;
āj hamāre kṛṣṇ madhupur chāye kehi saṅg khelab horī.
cait mās ṛtu lāgo sajanī ban ban ṭesū phūle;
āj hamāre kṛṣṇ madhupur chāye kehi saṅg raṅg hilorā.
baisākh mās ṛtu lāgo sajanī garamī jor janāī;
sītā to caṛhi gaī raṅgamahal mā ras bharī beniyā ḍolāī.
jeṭh mās ṛtu lāgo sajanī lūkai jor janāī;
rām lakhan kī komal dehiyāñ dhūp lagat kumhalāī.

Brother Rām and Lakṣmaṇ are going to the forest.
O dear friend, the rainy season begins in the month of *Āṣāṛh* and it rains.
Under which tree, are the brothers Rām and Lakṣmaṇ getting wet?
O dear friend, swings are hung in the month of *Sāvan;*
All girlfriends are swinging and singing Barahmāsī.
In the month of *Bhādau*, the clouds become intense;
I am scared when there is thunder and lightning.
In the month of *Kvār*, ancestral worship is performed in every home;
On the last day of the dark half, ancestral worship is performed to free three generations.
In the month of *Kārtik*, a festival of bathing in the Ganges is observed.
All friends took bath in the Ganges and gave charity.
In the month of *Agahan*, all friends are going after *gaunā;*
My Kṛṣṇa is dwelling in Mathurā, who will take my *gaunā*?
In the month of *Pūṣ*, it is very cold, my darling;
Without my lord, cold will not go away as I lie on the white bed and pillow on my head.
For the festival of *Basant Pañcamī* in the month of *Māgh*, the gardener's wife brought mango blossom;
Today my Kṛṣṇa is residing in Mathurā, who will take your mango blossom?
There is colour water and *abīr* in every house in the month of *Phāgun;*

Today my Kṛṣṇa is residing in Mathurā, with whom will I play Holi.
Ṭesū flowers are in bloom in the month of *Cait*.
Today my Kṛṣṇa is residing in Mathurā, with whom will I play colour?
It is hot in the month of *Baiśākh*, O dear friend;
Sītā climbed on the palace and waved her fan.
Hot wind blows in the month of *Jeṭh*, O dear friend;
Rām and Lakṣmaṇ's delicate bodies will wither in sun.

(LGT: 209R: 1972-73, Patti, Brāhmaṇ Women)

चातुरमासा

१६८.

श्याम तुम अइहौ कौन महीना, सूरत लिखी नगीना ॥
जेठ नाहीं अइबै असाढ़ नाहीं अइबै, अइबै सावन महीना
श्याम तुम्हें झुलवा झुलाय घरै रखिबे ॥
भादौं नाहीं अइबे क्वाँर नाहीं अइबे, अइबे कातिक महीना
श्याम तुम्हें सलवा ओढ़ाय घरै रखिबे ॥
पूस नाहीं अइबे माह नाहीं अइबे,अइबे फागुन महीना
श्याम तुम्हें फगुआ खेलाय घरै रखिबे ॥
चैत नाहीं अइबे बैसाख नाहीं अइबे, अइबे असल महीना
श्याम तुम्हें तकिया सोवाय घरै रखिबे ॥

śyām tum aihau kaun mahīnā, sūrat likhī nagīnā.
jeṭh nāhīṅ aibai asāṛh nāhīṅ aibai, aibai sāvan mahīnā,
śyām tumheṅ jhulavā jhulāy gharai rakhibe.
bhādauṅ nāhīṅ aibe kvāñr nāhīṅ aibe, aibe kātik mahīnā,
śyām tumheṅ salavā oṛhāy gharai rakhibe.
pūs nāhīṅ aibe māh nāhīṅ aibe, aibe phāgun mahīnā.
śyām tumheṅ phaguā khelāy gharai rakhibe.
cait nāhīṅ aibe baisākh nāhīṅ aibe, aibe asal mahīnā;
śyām tumheṅ takiyā sovāy gharai rakhibe.

In which month will you come, Kṛṣṇa?
I will not come in the months of *Jeṭh* and *Āṣāṛh* but will come in the month of *Sāvan,*
Kṛṣṇa, I will swing you and keep you home.
I will not come in the month of *Bhādau* and *Kvār*, but will come in the month of *Kārtik.*
O Kṛṣṇa, I will cover you with a hand woven blanket and will keep you home.
I will not come in the month of *Pūṣ*, and *Māgh*, but will come in the month of *Phāgun.*
O Kṛṣṇa, I will play Holī with you and will keep you home.
I will not come in the month of *Cait* and *Baiśākh*, but will come during the real month.
O Kṛṣṇa, I will prepare a bed for you and will keep you home.

(LGT: 91R: 1972-73, Tahirapur, Camār Men)

चौमासा

१६९.

मास असाढ़ कहे मन मोर जवानी की जोर सेज परी खाली
तन बिरह सतावै जोर फिरै मतवारी
कह रैन अँधेरी आई इन्दर ने झड़ी लगाई
चलै सनन सनन पुरवाई कोयल ने कोहक सुनाई
कोयल ने कोहक सुनाई ननद जी के भाई, न लेहु रुठाई चाहने वाले
ना जाएव पिया बैरी बँगाले ॥
सावन में नागर चला रूप के आगर भरे हैं सागर खूब पानी से
मैं जाता हूँ घूमने एक जिन्दगानी से
तुम पहिदो रंगीली चूड़ी तोर खुशी होय दिल प्यारी
तेरे कानों में फँसती बाली, तेरी बाँकी है छबि न्यारी
झुलवा झुलै पिया की प्यारी, चाहे कुसमी रँगाय लेव ॥
भादौं मा इन्दर की गोली करती है ठिठौली सुरति है जारी
जिनके पिया कहने मा ओ सनीनों मनाती

सब सखियाँ जइहैं मइके हो काजर टिकली दइके
हम करब का हियाँ रहिके मरि जान दुख सब सहि के
बारो बारो करि हारेव न मानेव वारे भोले ॥
क्वाँर मा लीन्हों पान लगाय चली दरम्यान महल के अन्दर
हम तुम ख्यालन पँसासारी कि चोरी चोरी
कहीं बोलै मुरइला बन मा मोरा सोच भये हैं तन मा
कहीं मौती बसी मोरे मन मा जो मिलतिव बालेपन मा
कहैं जँघीर सभा दँगल मा चहै सो गुन गाइ लेव ॥

mās asāṛh kahai man mor javānī kī jor sej parī khālī.
tan birah satāvai jor phirai matavārī.
kah rain añdherī āī indar ne jhaṛī lagāī.
calai sanan sanan puravāī koyal ne kohak sunāī.
koyal ne kohak sunāī nanad jī ke bhāī, n lehu ruṭhāī cāhane vāle;
nā jāev piyā bairī bañgāle.
sāvan meṅ nāgar calā rūp ke āgar bhare haiṅ sāgar khūb pānī se;
maiṅ jātā hūñ ghūmane ek jindagānī se.
tum pahido raṅgīlī cūṛī tor khuśī hoy dil pyārī;
tere kānoṅ meṅ phañsatī bālī, terī bāñkī hai chabi nyārī.
jhulavā jhūlai piyā kī pyārī, cāhe kusamī rañgāy lev.
bhādauṅ mā indar kī golī karatī hai ṭhiṭhaulī surati hai jārī,
jinake piyā kahane mā o sanīnoṅ manātī.
sab sakhiyāñ jaihaiṅ maike ho kājar ṭikalī daike;
ham karab kā hiyāñ rahike mari jān dukh sab sahi ke.
bāro bāro kari hārev n mānev vāre bhole.
kvāñr mā līnhoṅ pān lagāy calī daramyān mahal ke andar.
ham tum khyālan pañsāsārī ki corī corī;
kahīṅ bolai murailā ban mā morā soc bhaye haiṅ tan mā;
kahīṅ mautī basī more man mā jo milativ bālepan mā;
kahaiṅ jañghīr sabhā dañgal mā cahai so gun gāi lev.

In the month of *Āṣāṛh*, adolescence begins to push and my bed is empty.
The body begins to suffer in separation and one becomes intoxicated.
It is dark night and Indra has leased rain.
Easterly wind is blowing and one hears cuckoo.

O my *nanad*'s brother, why don't you please me;
O my dear husband, do not go to Bengal.
In the month of *Sāvan,* there is water all around like an ocean;
I am going to take a walk from this life.
Put on colourful bangles pleasing to you;
You are beautiful with earrings in your ear.
Dear to her husband, she is swinging, all in red.
In the month of *Bhādau,* she jokes around (?)
Those women whose husbands are pleasing, perform *Salino.*
All girlfriends will go to their parents' homes dressed with mascara and forehead mark.
Living here, what can I do but die in grief.
You didn't listen although I tried many times and finally gave up.
In the month of *Kvār,* after eating betel leaves, she went inside her palace.
Hiding, we will play a game of *pansāsāri;*
A peacock is making noise in the forest and I think in my mind;
I am full of passion, if only I had met you in your childhood.
Janghir [the composer] openly sings what pleases him.

(LGT: 117R: 1972-73, Ganj Muradabad, Dhobi Men)

१७०.

पिया चलौ पँलग पर आवति हूँ ॥
सासु मोरि स्वावै ननद मोरि जागै
लरिका बाल कहा ना मानैं ताको दूध पियावत हूँ
जब नारि परोसिन कथा कहति है ताके अरथ लगावति हूँ ॥
लँगहा पहिरेन फरिया पहिरेन मोती लरी लगावति हूँ
दुलरी तिलरी कमर करधनी अँगिया मा लाल जड़ावति हूँ ॥
पान खाय मुख परी बतीसी तापर मिसी लगावति हूँ
जब तेल फुलेल अतर कै शीशी माँगै लरी लगावति हूँ ॥
बारि कै दियना चढ़ी अटा पर जय जगदम्ब मनावति हूँ
सूरदास अस कहति राधिका स्वावत छैल जगावति हूँ ॥

piyā calau palañg par āvati hūñ.
sāsu mori svāvai nanad mori jāgai;

larikā bāl kahā nā mānaiṅ tāko dūdh piyāvat hūñ.
jab nāri parosin kathā kahati hai tāke arath lagāvati hūñ.
lañhagā pahiren phariyā pahiren motī larī lagāvati hūñ;
dularī tilarī kamar karadhanī añgiyā mā lāl jaṛāvati hūñ.
pān khāy mukh pari batīsī tāpar misī lagāvati hūñ.
jab tel phulel atar kai śīśī māñgai larī lagāvati hūñ.
bāri kai diyanā caṛhī aṭā par jay jagadamb manāvati hūñ;
sūradās as kahati rādhikā svāvat chail jagāvati hūñ.

O dear husband wait in the bed, I am coming.
My *sāś* is sleeping but my *nanad* is awake;
My child is not listening so I am feeding him milk.
When the neighbour woman tells a story then I try to understand it.
I am dressing in skirt and blouse and pearls.
I am putting two-three layered waist chains and am putting on jewels on my bodice.
After eating betel leaf and on top of that I am adorning myself with *missi.*
After applying perfume and oil, I am applying a layer on my part.
Climbing on the roof with lighted lamp, I am worshipping Jagadambā.
Sūrdās says, "Saying this, Rādhā is making sleeping [Kṛṣṇa] awake."
(LGT: 124R: 1972-73, Akohariya, Ahīr Man)

१७१.

परदेशी न आये नैन तरसैं ॥
असाढ़ नहीं आये सवन नहीं आये, भादौं मा आये मेघ बरसैं ॥
क्वाँर नहीं आये कतिक नहीं आये, अगहन आये गवन लेने ॥
पूस नहीं आये माह नहीं आये, फागुन आये रंग बरसै ॥
चैत नहीं आये बैसाख नहीं आये, जेठ मा आये अगिन बरसै ॥

paradeśī n āye nain tarasaiṅ.
asāṛh nahīṅ āye savan nahīṅ āye, bhādauṅ mā āye megh barasaiṅ.
kvañr nahīṅ āye katik nahīṅ āye, agahan āye gavan lene.
pūs nahīṅ āye māh nahīṅ āye, phāgun āye raṅg barasai.
cait nahīṅ āye baisākh nahīṅ āye, jeṭh mā āye agin barasai.

My husband from abroad did not come and my eyes are longing for him.
He did not come in *Āṣāṛh* and *Sāvan*. He came in the rainy month of *Bhādau*.
He did not come in *Kvār* and *Kārtik*. He came in the month of *Agahan* to take my *gaunā*.
He did not come in *Pūṣ* and *Māgh*. He came in the month of *Phāgun* to play Holi.
He did not come in *Cait* and *Baiśākh*. He came in the hot month of *Jeṭh*.

(LGT: 125R: 1972-73, Akohariya, Ahīr Man)

कजरी

१७२.

अरे रामा कृष्ण बने मनिहार ओढ़ि लई साड़ी रे हारी॥
अरे रामा कानों झुमका बारी माथे मा बेंदी निराली रामा
अरे रामा गले मा सोहै हार नारि मतवाली रे हारी॥
अरे रामा सिर पर धरे डेलैया चूड़िन की जोड़ि निराली रामा
अरे रामा गलिन गलिन श्री कृष्ण पुकारैं कोउ सखी पहिरौ ना॥
अरे रामा अपने महल से बोलीं राधा चूड़ी इधर लै आवौ रामा
अरे रामा ऐसी चुड़ियाँ पहिरावौ पिया का लागैं प्यारी रे हारी॥
अरे रामा बहियाँ पकड़ि पहिरावैं मन ही मन मुसकाने रामा
अरे रामा चौक पड़ी राधा प्यारी हसैं नर नारी रे हारी॥

are rāmā kṛṣṇ bane mahihār oṛhi laī sāṛī re hārī.
are rāmā kānoṅ jhumakā bārī māthe mā beṅdī nirālī rāmā;
are rāmā gale mā sohai hār nāri matavālī re hārī.
are rāmā sir par dhare ḍelaiyā cūṛin kī joṛi nirālī rāmā;
are rāmā galin galin śrī kṛṣṇ pukāraiṅ kou sakhī pahirau nā.
are rāmā apane mahal se bolīṅ rādhā cūṛī idhar lai āvau rāmā;
are rāmā aisī cuṛiyāñ pahirāvau piyā kā lāgaiṅ pyārī re hārī.
are rāmā bahiyāñ pakaṛi pahirāvaiṅ man hī man musakāne rāmā;
are rāmā cauk paṛī rādhā pyārī hasaiṅ nar nārī re hārī.

Kṛṣṇa has become a bangle seller by putting on a *sārī*.
He has earrings in his ears and a forehead ornament;
A necklace adorns his neck and he is acting like an intoxicated woman.
He is carrying beautiful bangles in a basket on his head;
Shouting, "come girlfriends wear these bangles", Kṛṣṇa is hawking in the lanes.
From her palace, Rādhā called him to bring bangles here.
"Put on beautiful bangles which my husband may like," [said Rādhā].
Holding her hand and smiling, Kṛṣṇa began to put bangles on her wrist;
Realizing [Who he was], Rādhā was surprised and all friends laughed at this sight.

(LGT: 18R: 1972-73, Dhanabad, Brāhmaṇ Women)

१७३.

बँसिया बाजि रही मधुबन में ॥
उत से आवति राधा प्यारी, इत से आवत मदन मुरारी
छुम छन ननतन पायल बाजत, राधा के पयरन में ॥
काँधा को निरखत है राधा, राधा को निरखत है काँधा
राधा के मन काँधा औ राधा काँधा मन में ॥
मोर मुकुट काँधा सिर सोहत, राधा की बिंदिया मन मोहत
उत राधा ग्वालिन में सोहति, इत काँधा ग्वालन में ॥
काँधा वँशी मधुर बजावत, राधा गीत मनोहर गावत
लालचंद आनन्द भयो री, बसुधा के आँगन में ॥

bañsiyā bāji rahī madhuban meṅ.
ut se āvati rādhā pyārī, it se āvat madan murārī;
chum chan nananan pāyal bājat, rādhā ke payaran meṅ.
kāñdhā ko nirakhat hai rādhā, rādhā ko nirakhat hai kāñdhā;
rādhā ke man kāñdhā au rādhā kāñdhā man meṅ.
mor mukuṭ kāñdhā sir sohat, rādhā kī biṅdiyā man mohat;
ut rādhā gvālin meṅ sohati, it kāñdhā gvālan meṅ.
kāñdhā vañśī madhur bajāvat, rādhā gīt manohar gāvat;
lālacaṅd ānand bhayo rī, basudhā ke āñgan meṅ.

[Kṛṣṇa's] flute is resounding in the Madhuban forest.
Rādhā is coming from that direction and Kṛṣṇa is coming from this direction.
Ankle ornaments on the feet of Rādhā are making tinkling sounds.
Rādhā is looking at Kṛṣṇa and Kṛṣṇa is looking at Rādhā;
Kṛṣṇa is in Rādhā's heart and Rādhā is in Kṛṣṇa's.
Kṛṣṇa is beautiful with his peacock crown on his forehead; Rādhā's forehead ornament is charming.
Rādhā is beautiful amidst milkmaids and here is Kṛṣṇa amidst cowherds.
Kṛṣṇa is playing a wonderful flute and Rādhā is singing pleasing songs;
Lalcand [the composer] says, "Happiness abounds at the courtyard of the world."

(LGT: 173R: 1972-73, Varanasi, Mixed Men)

१७४.

कन्हैया बड़ा रगरी मोरे बालमवा ॥
मैं जमुना जल भरन चली हो, फोरेला मोरी गगरी मोरे बालमवा ॥
जब दही बेचन जाती बृन्दाबन, रोकेला मोरी डगरी मोरे बालमवा ॥
सब सखियाँ गई जल में नहाये, चोराये भगे चुनरी मोरे बालमवा ॥

kanhaiyā baṛā ragarī more bālamavā.
maiṅ jamunā jal bharan calī ho, phorelā morī gagarī more bālamavā.
jab dahī becan jātī bṛndāban, rokelā morī ḍagarī more bālamavā.
sab sakhiyāñ gaī jal meṅ nahāye, corāye bhage cunarī more bālamavā.

Kṛṣṇa is very quarrelsome, O dear husband.
As I proceeded to Jamunā to fetch water, he broke my pot.
When I go to Vṛndāvan to sell yoghurt, he shackles my way.
All girlfriends went for a bath and he stole their cothes.

(LGT: 211R: 1972-73, Varanasi, Ahīr Men)

१७५.

कहवाँ से आवल कुँवर कन्हैया पड़ेला झीर झीर बुँदिया
सखी कहवाँ से आवैं राधा गोरी पड़ेला झीर झीर बुँदिया

गोकुला से आवल कुँवर कन्हैया पड़ेला झीर झीर बुँदिया
बरिसनवा से आवैं राधा गोरी पड़ेला झीर झीर बुँदिया
केतना बरिसवा के कुँवर कन्हैया पड़ेला झीर झीर बुँदिया
सखी केतना बरिस के राधा गोरी पड़ेला झीर झीर बुँदिया
बारह बरिसवा के कुँवर कन्हैया पड़ेला झीर झीर बुँदिया
सखी तेरह बरिस के राधा गोरी पड़ेला झीर झीर बुँदिया
कहवाँ से आयल चंदन पटरवा पड़ेला झीर झीर बुँदिया
सखी कहवाँ से आवै रेशम डोरी पड़ेला झीर झीर बुँदिया
गोकुला से आवल चंदन पटरवा पड़ेला झीर झीर बुँदिया
बरिसनवा से आवै रेशम डोरी पड़ेला झीर झीर बुँदिया
पड़ल हिंडोलवा वही कदम की डरिया पड़ेला झीर झीर बुँदिया
सखी झूला झूलैं नन्द के किशोर पड़ेला झीर झीर बुँदिया
सखियाँ सहेलियाँ सब गावैंलीं कजरिया पड़ेला झीर झीर बुँदिया
सखी चौका घाट गावै नित होरी पड़ेला झीर झीर बुँदिया

kahavāñ se āval kuñvar kanhaiyā paṛelā jhīr jhīr buñdiyā.
sakhī kahavāñ se āvaiṅ rādhā gorī paṛelā jhīr jhīr buñdiyā.
gokulā se āval kuñvar kanhaiyā paṛelā jhīr jhīr buñdiyā.
barisanavā se āvaiṅ rādhā gorī paṛelā jhīr jhīr buñdiyā.
ketanā barisavā ke kuñvar kanhaiyā paṛelā jhīr jhīr buñdiyā.
sakhī ketanā baris ke rādhā gorī paṛelā jhīr jhīr buñdiyā.
bārah barisavā ke kuñvar kanhaiyā paṛelā jhīr jhīr buñdiyā.
sakhī terah baris ke rādhā gorī paṛelā jhīr jhīr buñdiyā.
kahavāñ se āyal caṅdan paṭaravā paṛelā jhīr jhīr buñdiyā.
sakhī kahavāñ se āvai reśam ḍorī paṛelā jhīr jhīr buñdiyā.
gokulā se āval caṅdan paṭaravā paṛelā jhīr jhīr buñdiyā.
barisanavā se āvai reśam ḍorī paṛelā jhīr jhīr buñdiyā.
pāṛal hinḍolavā vahī kadam kī ḍariyā paṛelā jhīr jhīr buñdiyā.
sakhī jhūlā jhūlaiṅ nand ke kiśor paṛelā jhīr jhīr buñdiyā.
sakhiyāñ saheliyāñ sab gāvaiṅlīṅ kajariyā paṛelā jhīr jhīr buñdiyā.
sakhī caukā ghāṭ gāvai nit horī paṛelā jhīr jhīr buñdiyā.

Where did Kṛṣṇa come from? It is drizzling.
O dear girlfriend, where did Rādhā come from? It is drizzling.
Kṛṣṇa came from Gokul. It is drizzling.

Rādhā came from Barasānā. It is drizzling.
How old is Kṛṣṇa? It is drizzling.
O dear girl-friend, how old is Rādhā? It is drizzling.
Kṛṣṇa is twelve year old. It is drizzling.
O dear girlfriend, Rādhā is thirteen. It is drizzling.
Where did the sandalwood board come from? It is drizzling.
O dear girlfriend, where did the silken rope come from. It is drizzling.
The sandalwood board came from Gokul. It is drizzling.
The silken rope came from Barasānā. It is drizzling.
The swing has been put on a branch of the *kadam* tree. It is drizzling.
O dear girlfriend, Kṛṣṇa is swinging. It is drizzling.
All the girlfriends are singing *kajarī.* It is drizzling.
O dear girlfriend, people from Cauka Ghat sing this with delight. It is drizzling.

(LGT: 216R: 1972-73, Varanasi-Ahīr Men)

झूलन

१७६.

झूलन चलौ हिंडोलना बृषभान नन्दनी ॥
सावन की तीज आई घन घोर घटा छाई
मेघन झड़ी लगाई पड़ै बूँद मन्दनी ॥
पहनो सुरंग साड़ी मानो विनय हमारी
मुख चन्द सी उजारी मृदुहास फन्दनी ॥
मन मान सीख लीजै सुन्दर न देरी कीजै
हूँ तौ बिलोक दीजै मृदुहास फन्दनी ॥
सुन्दर कदम की डारी झूला पड़ा है प्यारी
झूलै कुँवर कन्हाई सब दुख निकन्दनी ॥

jhūlan calau hiṇḍolanā bṛṣabhān nandanī.
sāvan kī tīj āī ghan ghor ghaṭā chāī;
meghan jhaṛī lagāī paṛai būñd mandanī.

pahano suraṅg sāṛī māno vinay hamārī;
mukh cand sī ujārī mṛduhās phandanī.
man mān sīkh lījai sundar n derī kījai;
hūñ tau bilok dījai mṛduhās phandanī.
sundar kadam kī ḍārī jhūlā paṛā hai pyārī;
jhūlai kuñvar kanhāī sab dukh nikandanī.

Let's go for a swing, O daughter of Bṛṣabhān.
The *Tīj* of the month of *Sāvan* has arrived and thick black clouds have gathered;
It has begun to rain slowly.
Listen to my prayer and put on a colourful *sārī;*
O moon face, you are very delicate.
Please listen to my advice and do not delay;
Just look at the sight, O delicate one.
A swing is set on a branch of a beautiful *kadam* tree.
Dear Kṛṣṇa is swinging; the remover of all sorrow.

(LGT: 187R: 1972-73, Vṛndāvan, Brāhmaṇ Women)

सावन

१७७.

हमें नेहाँ नैहरवा की साध भले राजा हम न मयरि लगे जइबै हो
पहली पठउनी नौवा जो आवा,
नौवा का देव लौटार भले राजा हम न मयरि लगे जइबै हो
दुसरी पठउनी बरिया जो आवा,
बारी का देव लौटार भले राजा हम न मयरि लगे जइबै हो
तिसरी पठउनी बिरना जो आये,
साले लौटार नहीं जाँय भले रानी तुम तो मयरि लगे जइहौ हो
धरौ न हमारे सिर हाथ भले राजा हमका अनन कब अइहौ हो
कँवार मा बन मोरिला जो बोलै

कातिक दियना जलवना भले रानी तुमका अनन नहीं अइबे हो
कातिक मा कतकी होइहैं प्यारी धना तुमका अनन नहीं अइबे हो
अगहन मा गउने जइहैं गोरिया तबहीं अनन तुम्हें अइबे हो

hameṅ naihāñ naiharavā kī sādh bhale rājā ham n mayari lage jaibai ho.
pahalī paṭhaunī nauvā jo āvā;
nauvā kā dev lauṭār bhale rājā ham n mayari lage jaibai ho.
dusarī paṭhaunī bariyā jo āvā;
bārī kā dev lauṭār bhale rājā ham n mayari lage jaibai ho.
tisarī paṭhaunī biranā jo āye;
sāle lauṭār nahīṅ jāñy bhale rānī tum to mayari lage jaihau ho.
dharau n hamāre sir hāth bhale rājā hamakā anan kab aihau ho.
kvāñr mā ban morilā jo bolai;
kātik diyanā jalavanā bhale rānī tumakā anan nahīṅ aibe ho.
kātik mā katakī hoihaiṅ pyārī dhanā; tumakā anan nahīṅ aibe ho.
agahan mā gaune jaihaiṅ goriyā tabahīṅ anan tumheṅ aibe ho.

"O, dear husband, I have no yearnings for my parents' house, I will not go to my mother."
On the first trip, when the barber came to take me, I said:
"O, dear husband, send back the barber, I will not go to my mother."
On the second trip, when the *Bari* came to take me, I said:
"O, dear husband send back the *Bari*, I will not go to my mother."
On the third trip, my brother came, [and my husband said:]
"I cannot refuse my *sālā*; now, O dear queen, you have to go to your mother."
"O, dear husband, keep your hand on my head and tell me when you will come to bring me back."
In the month of *Kvār*, peacocks sing in the grove;
In the month of *Kārtik*, my dear, you will enjoy the burning of lamps; so I will not come to bring you back.
Also, in *Kārtik*, you will enjoy festival of *Katakī*; so I will not come to bring you back.
In the moth of *Agahan*, the girls will go on *gaunā*, then I will come to bring you back.

(LGT: 204R: 1972-73, Patti, Brāhmaṇ Women)

१७८.

कृष्णा छिपे रहो गुलशन में जब तक रहे सवनवा ना॥
सोने की थाली मा जेंवना बनायो,
कृष्णा जेंवे रहो गुलशन में जब तक रहे सवनवा ना॥
जँजा न गेडुवा गंगा जल पानी,
कृष्णा घुटे रहो गुलशन में जब तक रहे सवनवा ना॥
पाँच पान का बीरा लगायों॥
कृष्णा रचे रहो गुलशन में जब तक रहे सवनवा ना॥
चुन चुन के कलियों की सेज लगायों,
कृष्णा सुते रहो गुलशन में जब तक रहे सवनवा ना॥

kṛṣṇā chipe raho gulaśan meṅ jab tak rahe savanavā nā.
sone kī thālī mā jeṅvanā banāyo;
kṛṣṇā jeṅve raho gulaśan meṅ jab tak rahe savanavā nā.
jañjā n geḍuvā gaṅgā jal pānī;
kṛṣṇā ghuṭe raho gulaśan meṅ jab tak rahe savanavā nā.
pāñc pān kā bīrā lagāyoṅ;
kṛṣṇā race raho gulaśan meṅ jab tak rahe savanavā nā.
cun cun ke kaliyoṅ kī sej lagāyoṅ;
kṛṣṇā sute raho gulaśana meṅ jab tak rahe savanavā nā.

O Kṛṣṇa, remain hiding in the garden during the *Sāvan* season.
I will serve food on a gold plate.
O Kṛṣṇa, I will feed you thus in the garden during the *Sāvan* season.
In a (?) pot there is Ganges water [for you to drink];
O Kṛṣṇa, drink that water in the garden during the *Sāvan* season.
I prepared a betel leaf with five leaves;
O Kṛṣṇa, relish that in the garden during the *Sāvan* season.
I made a bed with choice flower buds;
O Kṛṣṇa, sleep in the garden during the *Sāvan* season.

(LGT: 19R: 1972-73, Dhanabad, Brāhmaṇ Women)

१७९.

रिमझिम रिमझिम मेंह बरासै बिजुरी चमकै सावन में॥
घटा घूम घन बादर गरजै डरै पियारी सावन में
आये हैं बरखा ऋतु सखियाँ सजी कामिनी सावन में
अपनी अपनी रंगावो चूँदर धानी रंग सब सावन में
चली शिव को मनावन सावन में, सब सजी अनोखी सावन में
गया कलेजा सूख सखी बिन पिया किनी मोरे सावन में॥
पिया गये परदेश सखी मैं पड़ी अकेली सावन में
सूनी सेज पर नींद न आवै बिरह सतावै सावन में
कुछ काम न भावै सावन में, घर पिया न आये मोर सावन में
पिया मदन तन जोर सखी को राखै मन मोर सावन में॥
पड़ा पचैया नागदेव घर घर खुशियाली सावन में
हुआ वक्त जब शाम किनी जल सैन करैं सखी सावन में
मेंहदी लगवावै सावन में, गुड़िया पिटवावै सावन में
डारि हिंडोला प्रेम से नी कजरी ललकारै सावन में॥
पहुँच गये भगवान गुरू जाकर समझाया सावन में
उठो पियारी चेत करो तुम दिया जलाओ सावन में
मत मुझे सताओ सावन में, तन दिल बहलाओ सावन में
पकड़ के पँजा गले लगैं तब खुशी भई वो सावन में॥

rimjhim rimjhim meṅh barāsai bijurī camakai sāvan meṅ.
ghaṭā ghūm ghan bādar garajai ḍarai piyārī sāvan meṅ.
āye haiṅ barakhā ṛtu sakhiyāñ sajī kāminī sāvan meṅ.
apanī apanī raṅgāvo cūñdar dhānī raṅg sab sāvan meṅ.
calī śiva ko manāvan sāvan meṅ, sab sajī anokhī sāvan meṅ.
gayā kalejā sūkh sakhī bin piyā kinī more sāvan meṅ.
piyā gaye parades sakhī maiṅ paṛī akelī sāvan meṅ.
sunī sej par nīṅd n āvai birah satāvai sāvan meṅ.
kuch kām n bhāvai sāvan meṅ, ghar piyā n āye mor sāvan meṅ.
piyā madan tan jor sakhī ko rākhai man mor sāvan meṅ.
paṛā pacaiyā nāgadev ghar ghar khuśiyālī sāvan meṅ.
huā vakt jab śām kinī jal sain karaiṅ sakhī sāvan meṅ.
meṅhadī lagvāvai sāvan meṅ, guṛiyā piṭavāvai sāvan meṅ.
ḍāri hiṅḍolā prem se nī kajarī lalakāraiṅ sāvan meṅ.

pahuñc gaye bhagavān gurū jākar samajhāyā sāvan meṅ.
uṭho piyārī cet karo tum diyā jalāo sāvan meṅ.
mat mujhe satāo sāvan meṅ, tan dil bahalāo sāvan meṅ.
pakaṛ ke pañjā gale lagaiṅ tab khuśī bhaī vo sāvan meṅ.

In the month of *Sāvan*, drizzling rain is falling and lightning is flashing.
The gathered clouds are thundering and the dear woman is frightened in the month of *Sāvan*.
The rainy season has come and lustful women are dressed up in the month of *Sāvan*.
Get your scarves dyed a light green colour for the month of *Sāvan*.
All wonderfully dressed, they go to worship Śhiv, in the month of *Sāvan*.
O dear friend, I am terrified without my husband in the month of *Sāvan*.
O dear friend, my husband has gone abroad and I am lying alone in the month of *Sāvan*.
I cannot sleep in my bed alone; this separation is tormenting me in the month of *Sāvan*.
No work pleases me, for my husband did not come home in the month of *Sāvan*.
Lustful desires are strong in my body; who could satisfy me in the month of *Sāvan*.
The festival of *Nāgapañcamī* has come and every household is full of happiness.
In the evening, friends are enjoying water sports in the month of *Sāvan*.
Women apply hennā, dolls are beaten in the month of *Sāvan*.
Full of love, *kajarī* songs are sung on the swing in the month of *Sāvan*.
God [husband] arrived and consoled the dear one in the month of *Sāvan*.
O dear, get up and light the lamp in the month of *Sāvan*.
Don't tease me but be happy in the month of *Sāvan*.
She grabbed the palm of his hand and embraced him; then she became happy in the month of *Sāvan*.[1]

(LGT: 220R: 1972-73, Kanpur, Boatmen)

---

1. Putting one's hand on another's head is one manner of taking a vow.

१८०.

हरो हरो गोबर पियरी है माटी रानी जी को महल लिपाइये
उस महल ऊपर रूख डँड़िया काग के बचन सुहावने
उस रूख ऊपर कागा बोलै कागा के बचन सुहावने
उड़ि जाउ कागा देउँ धागा मेरे बीर अजहूँ न आइये
कागा बिचारे उड़नउ न पाये मेरे बीर घोड़िला पर आइये
मेरे बीर आये चीरु लाये सासु ननद मुख मोड़िये
जेठानी दोखिल बोल बोलै मेरे बीर घोड़िला पल्हानिये
मेरे हाँथ मेंहदी पाँय मेंहदी कैसे के बिरन मनाइये
छूटो छूटो री रंगरचनी मेंहदी झपटि के बीर मनाइये
डारि कम्मर बैठ धम्मर करउ सजन संग बीनती
पठौ पाठौ साजन बहिनी मेरी सावन के दिन चारि हैं
सावन बेटी गुड़िया जो खेलै भादौं गौर सेराइये
क्वाँर बेटी नेवरता जो खेलै कातिक गंग नहाइये
अगहन बेटी अगर सनेही पूस लौट घर आइये

haro haro gobar piyarī hai māṭī rānī jī ko mahal lipāiye.
us mahal ūpar rūkh ḍañṛiyā kāgā ke bacan suhāvane.
us rūkh ūpar kāgā bolai kāgā ke bacan suhāvane.
uṛi jāu kāgā deuñ dhāgā mere bīr ajahūñ n āiye.
kāgā bicāre uṛanau n pāye mere bīr ghoṛilā par āiye.
mere bīr āye cīru lāye sāsu nanad mukh moṛiye.
jeṭhānī dokhil bol bolai mere bīr ghoṛilā palhāniye.
mere hāñth meṅhadī pañy meṅhadī kaise ke biran manāiye.
chūṭo chūṭo rī raṅgaracanī meṅhadī jhapaṭi ke bīr manāiye.
ḍāri kammar baiṭh dhammar karau sajan saṅg bīnatī.
paṭhau pāṭhau sājan bahinī merī sāvan ke din cāri haiṅ.
sāvan beṭī guṛiyā jo khelai bhādauṅ gaur serāiye.
kvāñr beṭī nevaratā jo khelai kātik gaṅg nahāiye.
agahan beṭī agar sanehī pūs lauṭ ghar āiye.

The palace of the queen is smeared with green cowdung mixed with yellow mud.
On top of the palace there is a pole on which a crow is crowing pleasingly.
On top of that pole a crow is crowing pleasingly.

"Fly, O crow, I will give you a gift, my brother has not come yet."
Before the crow had a chance to fly, my brother came riding on a horse.
My brother came and brought the gifts, but *sāś* and *nanad* turned their faces away.
Jeṭhānī said insulting words to him, so my brother turned his horse to leave.
My hands and feet are covered with *menhadī,* so how could I plead with my brother?
"O *menhadī,* wash away so that I can plead with my brother."
Adamantly, sit and plead with my husband and request him:
"Send my sister for a short time to enjoy the festive time in the month of *Sāvan* at home."
During the month of *Sāvan,* daughters observe the festival of dolls, in the month of *Bhādau,* they observe Gaurī worship;
In the month of *Kvār*, daughters celebrate *Navarātra* and in the month of *Kārtik,* they bathe in the Ganges.
In the month of *Agahan,* if the daughter is affectionate, she comes back to her in-law's house in the month of *Pūṣ.*

(LGT: 95R: 1972-73, Ganj Muradabad, Rastogī Woman)

१८१.

हरो हरो गोबर पियरी है माटी रानी जी को महल लिपाइये
महल ऊपर कागा जो बोले कागा के बचन सुहावने
उड़ि उड़ि कागा जइयो दखिन का बीर भैया खबर ले आइये
कागा बिचारो उड़नौ न पावो बीर भैया खड़े दरवाज ना
बीर आये कछू न लाये सास ननद मुख मोड़िये
जेठानी निगोड़ी मुखऊ न बोली जो बीर भैया मोरे आये हैं
ऊंचन चढ़ि चढ़ि माया जो हेरैं धिया पूता कितनी दूर हैं
खाली है डोलिया छूँछे कहरवा छूँछे बहिन जी के बीर हैं
बेंचौ न माया मोरी ढ़ल तलवरिया बहिनी चलन हम जाब ना
बाँधौ न माया मोरी गरुई गठरिया और दखिन केरा चीर न
करौ न माया मोरी पूरी पचासा बहिनी चलन हम जाब ना
बीर आये सब कुछ लाये सास ननद हँस बोलिहैं
जेठानी निगोड़ी पलँगा बिछावै जो बीर भैया मोरे आये हैं
हाथ मेंहदी पाँव मेंहदी कैसे मिलौं राजा बीर से

धोय डारौ मेंहदी छुटाय डारौ मेंहदी झपट मिलौ राजा बीर से
ऊंचन चढ़ि चढ़ि माया जो हेरैं धिया पूता कितनी दूर हैं
भरी है डोलिया भरे कहरवा भरे बहिन जी के बीर हैं

haro haro gobar piyarī hai māṭī rānī jī ko mahal lipāiye.
mahal ūpar kāgā jo bole kāgā ke bacan suhāvane.
uṛi uṛi kāgā jaiyo dakhin kā bīr bhaiyā khabar le āiye.
kāgā bicāro uṛanau n pāvo bīr bhaiyā khaṛe daravāj nā.
bīr āye kachū n lāye sās nanad mukh moṛiye.
jeṭhānī nigoṛī mukhaū n bolī jo bīr bhaiyā more āye haiṅ.
ūñcan caṛhi caḍhi māyā jo heraiṅ dhiyā pūtā kitanī dūr haiṅ.
khālī hai ḍoliyā chūñche kaharavā chūñche bahin jī ke bīr haiṅ.
beṅcau n māyā morī ḍhal talavariyā bahinī calan ham jāb nā.
bāñdhau n māyā morī garuī gaṭhariyā aur dakhin kerā cīr n.
karau n māyā morī pūrī pacāsā bahinī calan ham jāb nā.
bīr āye sab kuch lāye sāś nanad hañs bolihaiṅ.
jeṭhānī nigoṛī palañgā bichāvai jo bīr bhaiyā more āye haiṅ.
hāth meṅhadī pāñv meṅhadī kaise milauṅ rājā bīr se.
dhoy ḍārau meṅhadī chuṭāy ḍārau meṅhadī jhapat milau rājā bīr se.
ūñcan caṛhi caṛhi māyā jo heraiṅ dhiyā pūtā kitanī dūr haiṅ.
bharī hai ḍoliyā bhare kaharavā bhare bahin jī ke bīr haiṅ.

The palace of the queen is smeared with green cowdung mixed with yellow mud.
The crowing of the crow on top of the palace is pleasing.
"Fly, O crow, towards the south and bring news of my brother."
My brother arrived at the door, before the crow had a chance to fly.
My brother came empty-handed, so *sāś* and *nanad* turned their faces away.
Wicked *jeṭhāni* didn't even speak to my brother who just came.
The mother is anxiously waiting as she looks towards the road from a high place, to see how far away are her daughter and son.
The palanquin and *kahārs* are empty; the brother came without his sister.
"O, mother, sell my sword and shield, so that I can go to bring my sister."
Make a heavy bundle loaded with presents and scarves brought from the south.

Prepare *purīs*; with all this I will go and bring my sister home.
My brother came and brought all the presents; *sās* and *nanad* talked with him happily.
Wicked *jeṭhānī* is preparing the bed for my brother who just came.
"My hands and feet are covered with *meṅhadī*, how can I welcome my brother."
"Wash away the *meṅhadī* and quickly go and meet your dear brother.
Mother is anxiously waiting as she looks toward the road from a high place, to see how far away are her daughter and son.
The palanquin, carried by *kahārs*, is full and sister's brother is full of pride.

(LGT: 228R: 1972-73, Kanpur, Brāhmaṇ Women)

१८२.

अरे रामा लेने मोर गवनवा आये हैं सजनवा रे हारी॥
सुन करके मेरी बिदाई आये देखन लोग लुगाई रामा
अरे रामा बरसत नीर नयनवा आये हैं सजनवा रे हारी॥
मेरा छूटा जगत से नाता छूटे भाई बहन पितु माता रामा
अरे रामा छूटा जाय भवनवा आये हैं सजनवा रे हारी॥
मेरी डोली खूब सजाई मेरो दियो सिंगार बनाई रामा
अरे रामा भये लखि बिकल परनवा आये हैं सजनवा रे हारी॥
गोबिन्द जो जग में आता वह अवश्य एक दिन जाता रामा
अरे रामा फिर नहीं होत मिलनवा आये हैं सजनवा रे हारी॥

are rāmā lene mor gavanavā āye haiṅ sajanavā re hārī.
sun karake merī bidāī āye dekhan log lugāī rāmā;
are rāmā barasat nīr nayanavā āye haiṅ sajanavā re hārī.
merā chūṭā jagat se nātā chūṭe bhāī bahan pitu mātā rāmā;
are rāmā chūṭā jāy bhavanavā āye haiṅ sajanavā re hārī.
merī ḍolī khūb sajāī mero diyo siṅgār banāī rāmā;
are rāmā bhaye lakhi bikal paranavā āye haiṅ sajanavā re hārī.
gobind jo jag meṅ ātā vah avaśy ek din jātā rāmā;
are rāmā phir nahīṅ hot milanavā āye haiṅ sajanavā re hārī.

O, Rāmā! my husband has come to take my gaunā.
With the news of my departure, everyone has come to say goodbye;
Like rain, the tears are coming out of my eyes; my husband has come.
All the relations from my hometown, my brother, sister, and parents must all be left behind;
I must say goodbye to my house; my husband has come.
My palanquin is nicely decorated and people have groomed me beautifully;
Seeing all this happening, my heart feels uneasy; my husband has come.
Gobind says: "Whoever has come into this world must leave one day;
After that, there is no reunion. My husband has come.

(LGT: 230R: 1972-73, Kanpur, Brāhmaṇ Women)

१८३.

बारे बलम परदेशवा री सजनी, सपने मा नहीं सुख चैन रे॥
बाऊ चलै पुरवैया मेरी बैरिन, सुलगै बरसिया मा आगि रे
चिलमा भरत मेरी जरि गई चुटुकिया, सैयाँ निरमोही के काज रे॥
मेरे पिछवारे एक बगिया लगति है, लागे हैं निबुला अनार रे
पहिलो निबुला सुवना खुतरि गयो, पर गयो चुनरिया मा दाग रे॥
मेरे पिछवारे एक धोबिया बसति है, वह है ननदिया को यार रे
पाँच रुपैया मैं तोहें देऊँ धोबिया, चुनरी को दाग छुटाव रे॥
ताल मा चमकै ताल मछरिया, रन चमकै तलवार रे
सेजिया मा चमकै सैयाँ की पगड़िया माथे मा बिंदिया हमार रे॥

bāre balam padeśavā rī sajanī, sapane mā nahīṅ sukh cain re.
bāū calai puravaiyā merī bairin, sulagai barasiyā mā āgi re;
cilamā bharat merī jari gaī cuṭukiyā, saiyāñ niramohī ke kāj re.
mere pichavāre ek bagiyā lagati hai, lāge haiṅ nibulā anār re;
pahilo nibulā suvanā khutari gayo, par gayo cunariyā mā dāg re;
mere pichavāre ek dhobiyā basati hai, vah hai nanadiyā ko yār re;
pāñc rupaiyā maiṅ toheṅ deūñ dhobiyā, cunarī ko dāg chuṭāv re.
tāl mā camakai tāl machariyā, ran camakai talavār re;
sejiyā mā camakai saiyāñ kī pagaṛiyā, māthe mā biṅdiyā hamār re.

O dear friend, my inexperienced husband is abroad and I am restless even in my dreams.
Enemy easterly wind is blowing and a fire is burning in the pot.
In service to my husband, tip of my fingers got burned as I was putting fire in the tobacco pipe.
There is a garden in my backyard which has lemons and pomegranate fruits;
The first lemon was pecked by a parrot, and my scarf has a spot. [from eating the fruit?]
There is a washerman im my backyard who is a lover of my *nanad*;
"I will give you five rupees O washerman to clean that spot from my scarf."
A fish shines in the pond and a sword shines on the battlefield;
Husband's turban shines on the bed and my *bindi* shines on my forehead.

(LGT: 93R: 1972-73, Ganj Muradabad, Rastogī Woman)

१८४.

ऊँची अटरियाँ अरे सासुर जी की, जेहि चढ़ि हेरौं मैं बाट
मैं परदेसिनी के बीरनु भैया, आवति देखे अरि तीनिउ जने तीनिउ घोड़े सवार
अगिले के घोड़वा अरे बाबुल मेरे पीछे चचुली हमार
मझिली पलकिया अरे बीरनु भैया जिनकी हेरऊँ मैं बाट रे
रातों तो लाये अरे बाबुल मेरे औ पियरी चचुली हमार रे
चटक चुनरिया अरे बीरनु भैया जिनकी हेरउँ मैं बाट

ūñcī aṭariyāñ are sāsur jī ki, jehi caṛhi herauṅ maiṅ bāṭ.
maiṅ paradesinī ke bīranu bhaiyā, āvati dekhe ari tīniu jane, tīniu ghoṛe savār.
agile ke ghoṛavā are bābul mere pīche caculī hamār;
majhilī palakiyā are bīranu bhaiyā jinakī herauñ maiṅ bāṭ re.
rātoṅ to lāye are bābul mere au piyarī caculī hamār re;
caṭaka cunariyā are bīranu bhaiyā jinakī herauñ maiṅ bāṭ.

Climbing on my in-laws' high roof, I am longingly looking at the road.
In this foreign land, I am waiting for my brother's arrival; I saw three people coming, riding on horses.

My father was riding on the first horse and my uncle on the rear horse;
My brother is in the middle palanquin, for whom I have been waiting.
My father brought many things and my uncle brought a yellow *sārī*;
My brother, for whom I have been waiting, brought a colorful scarf.

(LGT: 94R: 1972-73, Ganj Muradabad, Restogi Woman)

१८५.

निबुला तरे डोला रखि दे मुसाफिर सावन की आई बहार रे॥
अपने महल में मैं भोजन जेंवति थी सैयाँ के आये कहार रे
ए री सखी भोजना जेंवनउ न पाई सावन की आई बहार रे॥
अपने महल में मैं गेडुआ पियत थी सैयाँ के आये कहार रे
ए री सखी गेडुआ पियनउ न पाई सावन की आई बहार रे॥
अपने महल में मैं बिरिया रचति थी सैयाँ के आये कहार रे
ए री सखी बिरिया जेंवनउ न पाई सावन की आई बहार रे॥
अपने महल में मैं सेजिया सोवति थी सैयाँ के आये कहार रे
ए री सखी सेजिया सोवनउ न पाई सावन की आई बहार रे॥

nibulā tare ḍolā rakhi de musāphir sāvan kī āī bahār re.
apane mahal meṅ maiṅ bhojan jeṅvati thī saiyāñ ke āye kahār re;
e rī sakhī bhojanā jeṅvanau n pāī sāvan kī āī bahār re.
apane mahal meṅ maiṅ geḍuā piyat thī saiyāñ ke āye kahār re;
e rī sakhī geḍuā piyanau n pāī sāvan kī āī bahār re.
apane mahal meṅ maiṅ biriyā racati thī saiyāñ ke āye kahār re;
e rī sakhī biriyā jeṅvanau n pāī sāvan kī āī bahār re.
apane mahal meṅ maiṅ sejiyā sovati thī saiyāñ ke āye kahār re;
e rī sakhī sejiyā sovanau n pāī sāvan kī āī bahār re.

Put the palanquin under a lemon tree, O traveller, the season of *sāvan* has come.
In my home, I was eating my food when my husband's *kahār* arrived;
O dear friend, I couldn't eat properly; the season of *Sāvan* has come.
In my home, I was drinking water when my husband's *kahār* arrived;
O dear friend, I couldn't drink properly; the season of *Sāvan* has come.

In my home, I was preparing a betelleaf when my husband's *kahār* arrived;
O dear friend I couldn't relish my betelleaf; the season of *Sāvan* has come.
In my home, I was getting ready to go to sleep when my husband's *kahār* arrived;
O dear friend, I could sleep properly; the season of *Sāvan* has come.
(LGT: 96R: 1972-73, Ganj Muradabad, Rastogī Woman)

१८६.

काहे को दीन्हों बिदेश रे लखि बाबुल मोरे ॥
भैया को दीन्हों है महल दुमहला, हम काहे दीन्हों बिदेश रे ॥
हम तो बाबुल तेरे खूँटे की गैया, जित हाँकौ हँकि जाँव रे ॥
हम तो बाबुल तोरे अँगने की चिड़िया, भोर होत उड़ि जाँई रे ॥
महलों के नीचे नीचे आया री डोला, भाभी खड़ी मुसकाई रे ॥
बागों के नीचे नीचे आया री डोला, कोयल बोलति बोल रे ॥
अब का बोलत कोयल बैना, छूटा बाबुल जी का देश रे ॥

kāhe ko dīnhoṅ bideś re lakhi bābul more.
bhaiyā ko dīnhoṅ hai mahal dumahalā, ham kāhe dīnhoṅ bideś re;
ham to bābul tere khūñṭe kī gaiyā, jit hāñkau hañki jāñv re.
ham to bābul tore añgane kī ciṛīyā, bhor hot uṛī jāñi re;
mahaloṅ ke nīce nīce āyā rī ḍolā, bhābhī khaṛī musakāī re.
bāgoṅ ke nīce nīce āyā rī ḍolā, koyal bolati bol re.
ab kā bolat koyal bainā, chūṭā bābul jī kā deś re.

Why did you give me a foreign land, O dear father?
My brother received a home, etc, so why did you give me a foreign land?
O dear father, I am like your cow; you can drive me wherever way you want.
O dear father, I am like birds in your courtyard; we fly away at dawn;
When my palanquin came under my house, my *bhābhī* stood there smiling.
When my palanquin came near the garden, the cuckoo called.
Cuckoo, why are you calling when I am leaving my father's land.
(LGT: 223R: 1972-73, Kanpur, Brāhmaṇ Women)

१८७.

ए री सखी मोरी बाली उमरिया बूढ़े हैं सजन हमार रे॥
काह कहौं उन मात पिता को कीन्हों न सोच विचार रे
बिचवानी को बिषहा काटै पंडित नीर गँवार रे॥
हमरे संग केरी सखियाँ सहेलरी करती हैं सोलौ सिंगार रे
रंग बिरंगी पहन कर साड़ी गावत कजरी मल्हार रे॥

e rī sakhī morī bālī umariyā būṛhe haiṅ sajan hamār re.
kāh kahauṅ un māt pitā ko kīnhoṅ n soc vicār re;
bicavānī ko biṣahā kāṭai paṇḍit nīr gañvār re.
hamare saṅg kerī sakhiyāñ sahelarī karatī haiṅ solau siṅgār re.
raṅg biraṅgī pahan kar sāṛī gāvat kajarī malhār re.

O dear friend, I am young and my husband is old.
What can I say to such a father and mother who consented to this!;
May a poisonous snake bite the gobetween and the priest is stupid.
Girlfriends of mine are enjoying all kinds of make up.
They are wearing colourful *sārīs* and are singing *kajarī malhār* songs.
(LGT: 227R: 1972-73, Kanpur, Brāhmaṇ Women)

१८८.

जात नगरिया मैं भूली रे डगरिया, अब सुधि लीन्हों मोरे नाथ रे॥
अम्मा ने दीन्ही है पचरंग साड़ी, बाबुल दीन्हा दहेज रे
भैया ने दीन्हो है चढ़िबे को घोड़िला, भाभी सेन्दुर भरी माँग रे॥
अम्मा कहैं बेटी नित उठि अइयो, बाबुल कहैं छै मास रे
भैया कहैं बहना कामे औ काजे तो भाभी कहैं क्या काम रे॥
माया के रोये नदी नारे बहत हैं, बाबुल रोये तालाब रे
भैया के रोये से धोतिया भींजति है, तो भाभी खड़े मुसकाय रे॥

jāt nagariyā maiṅ bhūlī re ḍagariyā, ab sudhi līnhoṅ more nāth re.
ammā ne dīnhī hai pacaraṅg sāṛī, bābul dīnhā dahej re;
bhaiyā ne dīnho hai caṛhibe ko ghoṛilā, bhābhī sendur bharī māñg re.
ammā kahaiṅ beṭī nit uṭhi aiyo, bābul kahaiṅ chai mās re;

bhaiyā kahaiṅ bahanā kāme au kāje to bhābhī kahaiṅ kyā kām re.
māyā ke roye nadī nāre bahat haiṅ, bābul roye tālāb re;
bhaiyā ke roye se dhotiyā bhīñjati hai, to bhābhī khaṛe musakāy re.

On my way to my husband's country, I lost my way. O husband, I am soley dependent on you now.
Mother gave me a *sārī* of five colours, father gave the dowry;
Brother gave a horse to ride on, and *bhābhī* put *sendur* in my part.
Mother says to come back everyday, father says to come every six months or so;
Brother says come when there is some occasion, but *bhābhī* says there is no need to come at all.
[When I left,] mother cried like a flowing river, and father cried as far as the outskirts of the village pond;
Brother cried so much that his *dhotī* got wet, but *bhābhī* was laughing.

(LGT: 229R: 1972-73, Kanpur, Brāhmaṇ Women)

पूर्वी

१८९.

कैसे काटी रे सहेली तूने रात सो बात बताइ देव गउने की॥
व्याह भई गवने मा आई मैं मन में शरमाई रे
सास ननद मोरी हँसी खुशी मा भीतर खाट बिछाई रे
आधी रात के बीच बलम मैं आइ गई हरसाई रे
सैयाँ धरि दौ धरि दौ रे जूबन पर दूनौ हाथ॥
साया की मोरी सरका फूँदी झट बालम ने खोली रे
हाथ डाल अँगिया बिच बालम मसकन लागे चोली रे
हाय रे दैया धरि दौ धरि दौ कम्मर पै दूनउ हाथ॥
आगे आगे चले बलम मैं पाछे मैं मुसक्यानी रे
हाय रे दैया थर्रानों सहेली मेरो गात॥

kaise kāṭī re sahelī tūne rāt so bāt batāi dev gaune kī.
vyāh bhaī gavane mā āī maiṅ man meṅ śaramāī re;
sās nanad morī hañsī khuśī mā bhītar khāṭ bichāī re;
ādhī rāt ke bīc balam maiṅ āi gaī harasāī re;
saiyāñ dhari dau dhari dau re jūban par dūnau hāth.
sāyā kī morī sarakā phūñdī jhaṭ bālam ne kholī re;
hāṭh ḍāl añgiyā bic bālam masakan lāge colī re;
hāy re daiyā dhari dau dhari dau kammar pai dūnau hāth.
āge āge cale balam maiṅ pāche maiṅ musakyānī re;
hāy re daiyā tharrānoṅ sahelī mero gāt.

O dear friend, tell me how you passed your night after *gaunā.*
After marriage and later *gaunā,* I came to my home and I was a little shy.
Happily, my *sās* and *nanad* arranged my bed inside;
At midnight my husband came full of excitement;
My husband put his hands on my breasts.
In great rush, my husband undid the tie of my skirt;
By putting his hand inside my bodice, my husband began to massage my breasts;
O dear, he put both his hands on my waist.
My husband led the way while I, behind, smiled [thinking of our last encounter];
O dear friend [think about it], my whole body quivered.

(LGT: 89R: 1972-73, Tahirapur, Camar Men)

१९० .

खोल न बजर किवाड़ी बारी धनिया ॥
एक समै मा इन्द्र बबा के कामदेव कइलें जारी
इन्द्र जी पूँछैं चन्दरमा जी से जगवा में केकर सुन्दर नारी ॥
हाथ जोर के बोले चन्दरमा सुन मुनि अरज हमारी
गौतम ऋषि के नारि अहिल्या जगवा में हुआँ सुन्दर नारी ॥
कपट के मिरिगा बने चन्दरमा ऋषि मुनि के द्वारी
कपट के मिरिगा बने चन्दरमा गौतम ऋषि के द्वारी

मुनि जी जाने भोर हो गइले खूँटी से कमँडल उतारी ॥
हाथ जोरि के बोले गंगा जी सुन मुनि अरज हमारी
तोहरे घरवा चोरवा घुसत बा इन्द्र जी करें ब्यभिचारी ॥
करि असनान घरि का लौटलैं गौतम जी अपना दुवारी
अइसन शराप देहिलनि अहिल्या के नारि से पत्थर बनाई ॥

khol n bajar kivāṛī bārī dhaniyā.
ek samai mā indra babā ke kāmadev kaileṅ jārī
indr jī pūñchaiṅ candaramā jī se jagavā meṅ kekar sundar nārī.
hāth jor ke bole candaramā sun muni araj hamārī;
gautam ṛṣi ke nāri ahilyā jagavā meṅ huāñ sundar nārī.
kapaṭ ke mirigā bane candaramā ṛṣi muni ke dvāri
kapaṭ ke mirigā bane candaramā gautam ṛṣi ke dvārī;
muni jī jāne bhor ho gaile khūñṭī se kamñḍal utārī.
hāth jori ke bole gaṅgā jī sun muni araj hamārī;
tohare gharavā coravā ghusat bā indr jī kareṅ byabhicārī.
kari asanān ghari kā lauṭalaiṅ gautam jī apanā duvārī;
aisan śarāp dehilani ahilyā ke nāri se patthar banāī.

O dear wife open the door.
One time, King Indra was tormented by the god of desire;
Indra asked the moon whose wife is the most beautiful in this world.
With folded hands the moon told him to listen to his suggestion;
Sage Gautam's wife, Ahilyā, is the most beautiful woman in this world.
The moon became the deceitful dawn at the gate of the sage's abode;
The moon became the deceitful dawn at the gate of sage Gautam;
The respected sage thought that it is dawn and thus took his wooden spout from a hanger.
With folded hands, Gaṅgā said to the sage;
There is a thief in your house; Indra is committing adultery.
After bathing, the sage Gautam returned to his home;
He gave Ahilyā such a curse that she became a stone.

(LGT: 92BR: 1972-73, Varanasi, Street Blind Musician)

१९१.

गोकुला नगरिया में तरसै ली गुजरिया,
काँधा दइके गइलैं कलेश निरमोहिया॥
कवने कसूर मोरी सुधिया बिसारी गइलैं
बिरहा के गोलिया करेजवा मा मारि गइलैं
छइलैं सवतिया के देश निरमोहिया॥
जमुना किनरवा कदमिया के तरवा
खोजली बेइलिया के ओहिरे अतरवा
नाहीं मिलैं गोकुला नरेश निरमोहिया॥
अपने ना आये न पठाये एकौ पतिया
हरि की सुरतिया न भूलै दिन रतिया
बारे ला बदनिया मा गैस निरमोहिया॥
कुबरी सवतिया के सँगवाँ भुलइलैं
अपने तो मुँहवाँ देखावैं नाहीं अइलैं
ऊधो से पठइलैं संदेश निरमोहिया॥
हे हो लालचन अब धीर नाहीं धरिहैं
मथुरा नगरिया में जाई सब लड़िहैं
कुबरी सवतिया के केश निरमोहिया॥

gokulā nagariyā meṅ tarasai lī gujariyā,
kāñdhā daike gailaiṅ kaleś niramohiyā;
kavane kasūr morī sudhiyā bisārī gailaiṅ;
birahā ke goliyā karejavā mā māri gailaiṅ;
chailaiṅ savatiyā ke deś niramohiyā.
jamunā kinaravā kadamiyā ke taravā;
khojalī beiliyā ke ohire ataravā;
nāhīṅ milaiṅ gokulā nareś niramohiyā.
apane nā āye n paṭhāye ekau patiyā;
hari kī suratiyā n bhūlai din ratiyā;
bāre lā badaniyā mā gais niramohiyā.
kubarī savatiyā ke saṅgavāñ bhulailaiṅ;
apane to muñhavāñ dekhāvaiṅ nāhīṅ ailaiṅ;
ūdho se paṭhailaiṅ saṅdeś niramohiyā.
he ho lālacan ab dhīr nāhīṅ dharihaiṅ;

mathurā nagariyā meṅ jāī sab laṛihaiṅ;
kubarī savatiyā ke keś niramohiyā.

In the village of Gokul, milkmaids are longing,
Cruel Kṛṣṇa has left us in great pain.
For what fault has he forgotten to remember us;
He has shot our heart with the bullet of separation;
He is staying with co-wife.
Around the banks of the Yamunā and under the *kadam* tree;
I searched for him all around the fragrant groves;
I can't find the cruel king of Gokul.
He has not come nor has he sent any letter;
Day and night, I can't forget Kṛṣṇa's face;
All my body is burning like a gas O cruel one.
He has lost himself in the company of his hunchback co-wife;
He did not come to show his face;
Cruel one has sent a message through Ūdho.
O Lalacan [composer], now they will not be patient;
They will go to the city of Mathurā to fight;
They will [pull] the hunchback co-wife's hair.

(LGT: 170R: 1972-73, Varanasi, Mixed Men)

१९२.

जहवाँ किसानन की बसली नगरिया, नगरिया हो गोइयाँ बड़ा मजा दे ला॥
दुनियाँ में सबसे बड़ी हौ किसानी, जवने से सबकर रहे इज्जत पानी
जहवाँ चले हरवा फरसा कुदरिया, कुदरिया हो गोइयाँ बड़ा मजा दे ला॥
बाढ़ै किसानन कै अइसन कमाई, खाके रहे जवन सबही मोटाई
खीरा तौ खीरा ककरिया जोन्हरिया, जोन्हरिया हो गोइयाँ बड़ा मजा दे ला॥
ओनके कमइया से सबही जियत बा, खाना तौ खातै बा दूधौ पियत बा
गेहूँ चना जौ केसारी मठरिया, मठरिया हो गोइयाँ बड़ा मजा दे ला॥
ए लालचन ओनकर मेवा मिठाई, दुनियाँ में ऊ भला के के न भाई
पूड़ी कचौड़ी औ हलुआ सोहरिया, सोहरिया हो गोइयाँ बड़ा मजा दे ला॥

jahavāñ kisānan kī basalī nagariyā, nagariyā ho goiyāñ baṛā majā de lā.
duniyāñ meṅ sabase baṛī hau kisānī, javane se sabakar rahe ijjat pānī;
jahavāñ cale haravā pharasā kudariyā, kudariyā ho goiyāñ baṛā majā de lā.
bāṛhai kisānan kai aisan kamāī, khāke rahe javan sabahī motāī;
khīrā tau khīrā kakariyā jonhariyā, jonhariyā ho goiyāñ baḍā majā de lā.
onake kamaiyā se sabahī jiyat bā, khānā tau khātai bā dūdhau piyat bā;
gehūñ canā jau kesārī maṭhariyā, maṭhariyā ho goiyāñ baṛā majā de lā.
e lālacan onakar mevā miṭhāī, duniyāñ meṅ ū bhalā ke ke n bhāī;
pūṛī kacauṛī au haluā sohariyā, sohariyā ho goiyāñ baṛā majā de lā.

The village where farmers live, that area, dear friend, is very pleasant.
Farming is the best of all professions in this world; thus everyone's respect is maintained;
Where plough, axe, and hoe are used; O dear friend, the hoe is very pleasant.
By eating farmer's product everyone becomes fat [healthy].
Cucumber, *kakarī,* and millet all grow, O dear friend; millet is very pleasant.
Because of their produce everyone is living; they eat as well as drink milk;
Wheat, chickpea, barley, pea and bread [all are grown by them], bread is very tasty.
O Lalacan [composer] who will not like their nuts and sweets in this world.
Puri, kacauṛī and haluā and soharī, soharī are very delicious, O dear friend.[1]

(LGT: 171R: 1972-73, Varanasi, Mixed Men)

१९३.

मुनि के गोहनवा कौनो राजा के ललनवा सिय के जोग सँवरिया ना
अइलैं मिथिला की नगरिया सिय के जोग सँवरिया ना ॥
श्यामली सूरत रूप मनोहर बिधना दियो बनाय
पोर पोर में भरी मोहिनी मनवा लेत लुभाय
अबहीं बारी उमरिया ना, जदुवा भरल बा हो नजरिया ॥
ई की धौं राजा के बालक की धौं देवकुमार
कामदेव से बढ़कर सुन्दर लै लीन्हेन अवतार

---

1. *Pūrī, kacaurī, haluā,* and *sohārī,* are different Indian breads and dishes.

हँसि के फेरैं पुतरिया ना, मारैं बिरहा की हो कटरिया ॥
एक सखी बोली हो आली आय जुटा संजोग
आजु बिधाता भेजि दिहेन ई वर सीता के जोग
बाटैं लागी खबरिया ना, वरिहैं राजा की हो कुमरिया ॥
बोली एक सखी मनवाँ इहै कहत बा मोर
धनुषाई तौ शंकर जी कै जरूर देइहैं तोर
हँसि के गाँवैं खबरिया ना, बहि हैं सुखवा की हो बयरिया ॥

muni ke gohanavā kauno rājā ke lalanavā siy ke jog sañvariyā nā.
ailaiṅ mithilā kī nagariyā siy ke jog sañvariyā nā.
śyāmalī sūrat rūp manohar bidhanā diyo banāy.
por por meṅ bharī mohinī manavā let lubhāy.
abahīṅ bārī umariyā nā, jaduvā bharal bā ho najariyā.
ī kī dhauṅ rājā ke bālak kī dhauṅ devakumār.
kāmadev se baṛhakar sundar lai līnhen avatār.
hañsi ke pheraiṅ putariyā nā, māraiṅ birahā kī ho kaṭariyā.
ek sakhī bolī ho ālī āy juṭā sañjog.
āju bidhātā bheji dihen ī var sītā ke jog;
bāṭaiṅ lāgī khabariyā nā, varihaiṅ rājā kī ho kumariyā.
bolī ek sakhī manavāñ ihai kahat bā mor;
dhanuṣāī tau śaṅkar jī kai jarūr deihaiṅ tor;
hañsi ke gāñvaiṅ khabariyā nā, bahi haiṅ sukhavā kī ho bayariyā.

The young boys accompanying the sage are a perfect match for Sītā.
The perfect match for Sītā has come to the city of Mithilā.
He is brown complexioned and god has given him a beautiful face.
Each part of him is full of charm and is captivating.
He is very young and there is magic in his eyes.
Either he is a king's son or god's child.
For more beautiful than the God of Love has incarnated.
Smiling, he moves his pupils and that look strikes like a dagger.
One girlfriend said that a chance has arrived.
Today, God has sent this suitable groom for Sītā;
He will wed the king's daughter, such news began to spread.

One girlfriend said that my mind is thinking of only one thing;
I am sure that he will break Śankar's bow.
The wind of happiness will flow, thus they sing this news.

(LGT: 174R: 1972-93, Varanasi, Mixed Men)

पूर्वी (पाटा पर की)

१९४.

ये जोबना मोरे बजुर हैं किँवारा, दै दै साँकर मैं हारिवँ न पिया
बैरी बलम जोबनवा नाहीं मानै पिया ॥
ये जोबना मोरे मस्ता हैं हाथी, दै दै आँकुस मैं हारिवँ न पिया ॥
ये जोबना मोरे कोतल हैं घोड़िला, धरि कै काठी औ फेरै न पिया ॥
ये जोबना मोरे रस के हैं रसीले, दूनौ हाथ से हरे निचोवौ न पिया ॥

ye jobanā more bajur haiṅ kiñvārā dai dai sāñkar maiṅ hārivañ n piyā.
bairī balam jobanavā nāhīṅ mānai piyā.
ye jobanā more mastā haiṅ hāthī, dai dai āñkus maiṅ hārivañ n piyā.
ye jobanā more kotal haiṅ ghoṛilā, dhari kai kāṭhī au pherai n piyā
ye jobanā more ras ke haiṅ rasīle, dūnau hāth se hare nicovau n piyā.

My youthful breasts are like strong doors, I constantly keep them in check but am losing O dear husband.
O dear husband, my youthful breasts are wild.
My breasts are like intoxicated elephants and I am weary of prodding.
My breasts are like a sumpter-horse, O dear husband put a saddle and train them.
My breasts are very juicy, O dear husband, squeeze them with both your hands.

(LGT: 115R: 1972-73, Ganj Muradabad, Dhobī Men)

पूर्वी (बधावा)

१९५.

बाँके डोमवा मदिया पीके तजिले परान ॥
मोरी जाति ठकुराइन डोमवा तोरे संग डोमिन होबै ना
नदी किनारे बाँसिया बजावै हमरा जिव तरसावै ॥
रात मा डोमवा सूप बनावै दिन मा फेरी लगावै ना
सबसे अच्छा सूप बनावै हमका बैठ खवावै ॥
तीन महीना प्रीत लगे भई चौथे मा परदेश ना
बारा महीना बितैं न पावैं आवा मरे का सन्देश ॥
छोड़ फिकर डोमवा की गोरिया कर मेवा से प्रीत ना
माई बाप कै लाज करौं नहिं लइके सरग उड़ जाऊँ ॥

bāñke ḍomavā madiyā pīke tajile parān.
morī jāti thakurāin ḍomavā tore saṅg ḍomin hobai nā;
nadī kināre bañsiyā bajāvai hamarā jiv tarasāvai.
rāt mā ḍomavā sūp banāvai din mā pherī lagāvai nā
sabse acchā sūp banāvai hamakā baiṭh khavāvai.
tīn mahīnā prīt lage bhaī cauthe mā paradeś nā;
bārā mahīnā bitain n pāvaiṅ āvā mare kā sandeś.
choṛ phikar ḍomavā kī goriyā kar mevā se prīt nā;
māī bāp kai lāj karauṅ nahiṅ laike sarag uṛ jāūñ.

Dandy *ḍom* you lost your life from drinking.
My caste is warrior and I will not become your wife;
He plays a flute at the river bank and makes my heart long for him.
At night my *ḍom* makes winnowing baskets and by morning he peddles his wares.
He makes the best of all winnowing baskets and takes care of me.
Our love was only three months old when, in the fourth month, he went away;
Before twelve months had passed, news came of his death.

O beautiful woman, don't brood on *ḍom*'s death, come and love Mewā
[the composer]
I care for my parent's honour; otherwise I would take you to heaven.
(LGT: 17R: 1976, Kanpur, Mixed Men)

अध्याय ४
झोंझी-टेसू त्योहार

टेसू गीत (बच्चों के)[1]

१९६.

टेसू आये बावन वीर हाथ लिये सोने का तीर
एक तीर मार दिया गंगा जी को पार किया
गंगा जी ने दिया असीस भर भर बेला खाई खीर
ल्याव नाज

ṭesū āye bāvan vīr hāth liye sone kā tīr.
ek tīr mār diyā gaṅgā jī ko pār kiyā.
gaṅgā jī ne diyā asīs bhar bhar belā khāī khīr.
lyāv nāj.

Powerful Tesu came, carrying a gold arrow in his hand.
He shot an arrow which crossed the River Gaṅgā.
The River Gaṅgā gave him the boon of eating a bow of rice pudding.
Give me grain![2]

(LGT: 1989, Nandana)

१९७.

मुनमुन बोकरिया अस्सी डला भुस खाय
सात समुन्दर पानी पियै हगन बटेसुर जाय

munamun bokariyā assī ḍalā bhus khāy.
sāt samundar pānī piyai hagan baṭesur jāy.

---

1. For details of the Jhoñjhī-Ṭesū festival, see Tewari 1982.
2. टेसू आये बावन वीर हाथ लिये सोने का तीर
एक तीर मार दिया धर दिल्ली फटकार दिया
दिल्ली मेरा भाई सास लगे भौजाई
भौजाई के भई बिटिया नाम धरो सरसुतिया
सरसुत सरसुत (LGT : 1989)

The Munmun goat eats eighty baskets of chaff.
She drinks the water of seven oceans and goes to Baṭesur to defecate.

(LGT: 1989, Nandana)

१९८.

इमली की जड़ से उड़ी पतंग नौ सौ मोती नौ सौ रंग
(इमली के तरे तरे निकली पतंग नौ सै बगुला एकई रंग)
एक रंग की बनी कमान उसमें निकरे टेसूराम
टेसूराम की चार मेहरियाँ दो नाचैं दो चढ़ी अटरियाँ
एक अटरिया फूट गई टेसू की अम्मा रूठ गई
कौन बात पै रूठ गई कढ़ी भात पै रूठ गई

imalī kī jaṛ se uṛī pataṅg nau sau motī nau sau raṅg.
(imalī ke tare tare nikalī pataṅg nau sai bagulā ekaī raṅg.)
ek raṅg kī banī kamān usameṅ nikare ṭesūrām.
ṭesūrām kī cār mehariyāñ do nācaiṅ do caṛhī aṭariyāñ.
ek aṭariyā phūṭ gaī ṭesū kī ammā rūṭh gaī.
kaun bāt pai rūṭh gaī kaṛhī bhāt pai rūṭh gaī.

From the root of a tamarind tree flew a kite with nine hundred pearls of nine hundred colours.
A row of nine hundred herons of one colour walked underneath a tamarind tree.
Out of that row appeared Mr. Ṭesu.
Mr. Ṭesu has four wives: two of them were dancing and two climbed upto the roof.
One roof got broken, and Ṭesu's mother was displeased.
For what was she displeased? For *kaṛhī* and rice.[3]

(LGT: 1989, Nandana)

3. Author's version of this song:
एक चवन्नी चाँदी की उसमें निकले गांधी जी
गांधी जी ने खोदा गड्ढा उसमें निकले टेसूराम
टेसूराम की चार बहुरियाँ दो नाचें दो चढ़ी अटरियाँ
एक अटारी फूट गई टेसू की अम्मा रूठ गई
कौन बात पै रूठ गई कढ़ी भात पै रूठ गई (LGT : 1989)

१९९.

बगुली के बगधौरे अण्डा, सोऊ खेलैं सातौ खण्डा
सात खण्ड की धौर बियानी, उई धौरी को का करिहौ
खैहैं पीहैं राज करिहैं, त्रगदास की बड़ी सलाय
ते पै बैठे टेसूराम, टेसूराम बड़ी बात कहैं
अपनी उन्डी गाँव बसाव, बरसन देव भई रसन देव

bagulī ke bagadhaure aṇḍā, soū khelaiṅ sātau khaṇḍā.
sāt khaṇḍ kī dhaur biyānī, uī dhaurī ko kā karihau.
khaihaiṅ pīhaiṅ rāj karihaiṅ, tragadās kī baṛī salāy.
te pai baiṭhe ṭesūrām, ṭesūrām baṛī bāt kahaiṅ.
apanī unḍī gāñv basāv, barasan dev bhaī barasan dev.

The heron has calico eggs; they are found in all seven continents.
A white cow gave birth. What would you do with that cow?
We will eat, drink and be merry; that's the advice of Tragadās (?)
Mr. Ṭesu took that advice; Mr. Ṭesu made a big comment:
Populate your own village and let it rain [prosper].

(LGT: 1976, Nandana)

२००.

हिन्नकुरी भई हिन्नकुरी
हिन्ना माँगै चार कुरी

hinnakurī bhaī hinnakurī.
hinnā māñgai cār kurī.

[Children] Run around like a deer.
The deer [children] ask for only four handfuls [of grain].

(LGT: 1976, Nandana)

टेसूगीत (पुरुष वर्ग)

२०१.

धार धरीता हो अरे नदिये बाढ़े, आल्हा वामा हनाय।
रानी तौ पूँछै रे जयचांद की, कहाँ कै ठाकुर जाय॥

dhār dharītā ho are nadiye bāṛhe, ālhā vāmā hanāy.
rānī tau pūñchai re jayacāṁd kī, kahāñ kai ṭhākur jāy.

The flooded river has a strong current and Ālhā is bathing there.
The queen of Jaicand is asking: "Where is this warrior going?"
(LGT: 1989, Sandalpur)

२०२.

सँकरी तो गलियाँ अरे गढ़ कनवज की, पैर धरे धानाय।
धीरे से फेरौ रे रस बेन्दुला, पाँय मुरक न जाय॥

sañkarī to galiyāñ are gaṛh kanavaj kī, pair dhare dhānāy.
dhīre se pherau re ras bendulā, pāñy murak n jāy.

The lanes of Fort Kannauj are narrow, and one can hear the echo of footsteps.
Ride the horse Bendulā carefully, lest its feet get twisted.
(LGT: 1989, Sandalpur)

२०३.

किनकी अटरिया दियना जले, किनकी सेज कुम्हलाय।
कौन सी तिरिया रनबन भई, कीन्हैं दुःख दये भगवान॥ १॥
आल्हा अटरिया दियना जले, ऊदल सेज कुम्हलाय॥
लाखन की तिरिया रनबन भई, मल्हैं दुःख दये भगवान॥ २॥

kinakī aṭariyā diyanā jale, kinakī sej kumhalāy?
kaun sī tiriyā ranaban bhaī, kīnhaiṅ duḥkh daye bhagavān?
ālhā aṭariyā diyanā jale, ūdal sej kumhalāy.
lākhan kī tiriyā ranaban bhaī, malhanai duḥkh daye bhagavān.

On whose roof is the lamp burning? Whose bed has lost its lustre?
Which woman became a widow? To whom did God give sorrow?
The lamp burns at Ālha's roof. Ūdal's bed has lost its luster.
Lakhan's wife became a widow. God gave sorrow to Malhanā.

(LGT: 1989, Sandalpur)

२०४.

सरग चमंका हो अरे रन चमकै, रन चमकै तरवार।
शेला चमंका रे पृथ्वीराज को, गढ़ सिरसा के मैदान॥

sarag camaṅkā ho are ran camakai, ran camakai taravār.
śelā camaṅkā re pṛthvīrāj ko, gaṛh sirasā ke maidān.

Lightning lights the sky, and the sword shines in the battlefield.
Pṛthvīrāj's spear shone at the battlefield of Fort Sirasā.

(LGT: 1989, Sandalpur)

२०५.

राम से भइया अरे बैफय चले, लछिमन गही मरजाद।
सीता सी तिरिया बन को गई, उनके कुलै न लागे दाग॥

rām se bhaiyā are baiphay cale, lachiman gahī marajād.
sītā sī tiriyā ban ko gaī, unake kulai n lāge dāg.

A brother like Rām left without argument, while Lakṣmaṇ maintained the propriety.
A woman like Sītā went to the forest, so as to avoid criticism of their race.

(LGT: 1989, Sandalpur)

२०६.

सावन मेंदी अरे जिन धारो, लइ दुइ दुइ पात।
दसौ अँगुरियाँ मेंहदी रची, उनके आय गये चालनहार॥

sāvan meṅdī are jin dhāro, lai dui dui pāt.
dasau añguriyāñ meṅhadī racī, unake āy gaye cālanhār.

Do not pluck myrtle leaves in the month of *Sāvan*.
All ten fingers were stained with red colour; people [from her husband's home] came to take her away.

(LGT: 1989, Sandalpur)

२०७.

सरगा नसेनी हो अरे को चाढ़ै, को बिष गाँडर खाय।
ब्यानी बघिनिया रे भला को दुहै, को आल्हा मनावन जाय॥ १ ॥
सरगा नसेनी हो अरे जगनिक चाढ़ै, ओही बिष गाँडर खाय।
ब्यानी बघिनिया रे जगनिक दुहै, जगनिक आल्हा मनावन जाय॥ २ ॥
पाँय पनहियाँ रे अरे हम पर नाहीं, नाहीं ढाल तरवार।
अपने जोत को रे घोड़िला नहीं, कैसे आल्हा मनावन जोय॥ ३ ॥
पाँय पनहियाँ रे अरे हम तुमकै देबै, अरे देबै ढाल तलवार।
ब्रह्मा चढ़त को रे घोड़िला दिहैं, जगनिक आल्हा मनावन जाव॥ ४ ॥
तुम्हरे मनाये आल्हा न माने, या कहियो समझाय।
महोबो घेरो पृथ्वीराज ने, चौड़ा ने किले पै तोप लड़ाई आय॥ ५॥
एहू कहे ते अरे जब आल्हा न मानैं, तब या कहियो समुझाय।
जहाँ रसोइयाँ रानी देवैं की, भूरा मुगल पछाड़ै गाय॥६॥
एहू कहे ते अरे जब आल्हा न मानैं, तब या कहियो समुझाय।
जहाँ अखाड़ो थो नुनि आल्हा को, चौड़ा जोत बवाये धान॥ ७ ॥

saragā nasenī ho are ko cāṛhai, ko biṣ gāñḍar khāy.
byānī baghiniyā re bhalā ko duhai, ko ālhā manāvan jāy?
saragā nasenī ho are jaganik cāṛhai, ohī biṣ gāñḍar khāy.
byānī baghiniyā re jaganik duhai, jaganik ālhā manāvan jāy.
pāñy panahiyāñ re are ham par nāhīṅ, nāhīṅ ḍhāl taravār.

apane jot ko re ghoṛilā nahīṅ, kaise ālhā manāvan joy.
pāñy panahiyāñ re are ham tumakai debai, are debai ḍhāl talavār.
brahmā caṛhat ko re ghoṛilā dihaiṅ, jaganik ālhā manāvan jāv.
tumhare manāye ālhā n māne, yā kahiyo samajhāy.
mahobo gheṛo pr̥thvīrāj ne, cauṛā ne kile pai top laṛāī āy.
ehū kahe te are jab ālhā n mānaiṅ, tab yā kahiyo samujhāy.
jahāñ rasoiyāñ rānī devaiṅ kī, bhūrā mugal pachāṛai gāy.
ehū kahe te are jab ālhā n mānaiṅ, tab yā kahiyo samujhāy.
jahāñ akhāṛo tho nuni ālhā ko, cauṛā jot bavāye dhān.

Who would climb the ladder to heaven, and who would eat poisonous grass?
Who would milk a lioness with a cub, and who would go to persuade Ālhā?
Jaganik would climb the ladder to heaven, and he would eat poisonous grass.
Jaganik would milk a lioness with a cub, and he would go to persuade Ālhā.
I do not have shoes on my feet and do not have a shield and sword.
I do not have my own horse, so how could I go to persuade Ālhā?
I will give you shoes for your feet and a shield and sword.
I give you Brahmā's horse, so, Jaganik, go to persuade Ālhā.
If Ālhā does not accept your persuasion, then reason with him thus:
That Pr̥thviraj has surrounded Mahobā and Caurā has aimed his cannon at the fort.
If Ālhā still does not agree, then reason with him thus:
Bhūrā, the Muslim, is butchering cows where once Queen Devai had her kitchen.
If Ālhā still does not agree, then reason with him once again:
Where Ālhā had his wrestling place, there Caurā has sown rice.

(LGT: 24R: 1976/1989, Nandana, Mixed Men)

२०८.

कौने घरीता हो अरे लंका रावण के, कौन घरी राजाराम।

कौन घरीता रे महादेवता, अरि हो कौने घरी नन्द के लो ॥ १ ॥
साँझ घरीता हो अरे लंका रावण के, अधरतिया राजाराम।
बड़े भोर ही रे महादेवता, अरि हो दिन चढ़े नन्द के लो ॥ २ ॥
का वर माँगैं हो अरे लंका रावण के, काय अवध के राम।
का वर माँगैं रे महादेवता, अरि हो कहा माँगैं नन्द के लो ॥ ३ ॥
माँगैं मदोवर हो अरे लंका रावण के, सीता अवध के राम।
गौरा वर माँगैं रे महादेवता, अरि हो राधा माँगैं नन्द के लो ॥ ४ ॥
का चढ़ ब्याहैं हो अरे लंका रावण के, कहा अवध के राम।
का चढ़ ब्याहैं रे महादेवता, अरि हो का चढ़े नन्द के लो ॥ ५ ॥
हाथी चढ़ ब्याहैं हो अरे लंका रावण के, घुड़ला अवध के राम।
ढूँडो नादिया रे महादेवता, अरि हो रथ चढ़े नन्द के लो ॥ ६ ॥
कहा बजावैं हो अरे लंका रावण के, कहा अवध के राम।
कहा बजावैं रे महादेवता, अरि हो कहा बजे नन्द के लो ॥७॥
बजे नगाड़े हो अरे लंका रावण के, डंका अवध के राम।
डमरू बजावैं रे महादेवता, अरि हो डफ बजे नन्द के लो ॥८॥

kaune gharītā ho are laṅkā rāvaṇ ke, kaun gharī rājārām;
kaun gharītā re mahādevatā, ari ho kaune gharī nand ke lo ॥1 ॥
sāñjh gharītā ho are laṅkā rāvaṇ ke, adharatiyā rājārām;
baṛe bhor hī re mahādevatā, ari ho din caṛhe nand ke lo ॥2 ॥
kā var māñgaiṅ ho are laṅkā rāvaṇ ke, kāy avadh ke rām;
kā var māñgaiṅ re mahādevatā, ari ho kahā mañgaiṅ nand ke lo ॥3 ॥
māṅgaiṅ madovar ho are laṅkā rāvaṇ ke, sītā avadh ke rām;
gaurā var māñgaiṅ re mahādevatā, ari ho rādhā māṅgaiṅ nand ke lo ॥4 ॥
kā caṛh byāhaiṅ ho are laṅkā rāvaṇ ke, kahā avadh ke rām;
kā caṛh byāhaiṅ re mahādevatā, ari ho kā caṛhe nand ke lo ॥5 ॥
hāthī caṛh byāhaiṅ ho are laṅkā rāvaṇ ke, ghuṛalā avadh ke rām;
ḍūñḍo nādiyā re mahādevatā, ari ho rath caṛhe nand ke lo ॥6 ॥
kahā bajāvaiṅ ho are laṅkā rāvaṇ ke, kahā avadh ke rām;
kahā bajāvaiṅ re mahādevatā, ari ho kahā baje nand ke lo ॥7 ॥
baje nagāṛe ho are laṅkā rāvaṇ ke, ḍaṅkā avadh ke rām;
ḍamarū bajāvaiṅ re mahādevatā, ari ho ḍaph baje nand ke lo ॥8 ॥

At what time was Rāvaṇ of Laṅkā born? At what time was King Rām born?
At what time was Mahādev born? At what time was the darling of Nand born?

Rāvaṇ of Laṅkā was born in the evening; King Rām was born at midnight.
Mahādev was born early in the morning; the darling of Nand was born late in the day.
What boon did Rāvaṇ of Laṅkā ask? What boon did King Rām ask?
What boon did Mahādev ask? What favour did the darling of Nand ask?
Rāvaṇ of Laṅkā asked for Mandodarī's hand; Rām asked for Sītā's hand.
Mahādev asked for Gaurī's hand; the darling of Nand asked for Rādhā's hand.
What did Rāvaṇ of Laṅkā ride in his marriage procession? What did Rām of Avadh ride in his marriage procession?
What did Mahādev ride in his marriage procession? What did the darling of Nand ride in his marriage procession?
Rāvaṇ of Laṅkā rode an elephant in his marriage procession; Rām rode a horse in his marriage procession.
Mahādev rode a one-horned bull; the darling of Nand rode chariot in his marriage procession.
What instruments were played at Rāvaṇ of Laṅkā's wedding? What instruments were played at Rām's wedding?
What instruments were played at Mahādev's wedding? What instruments were played at the darling of Nand's wedding?
Big kettledrums were played at Rāvaṇ of Laṅkā's wedding; drums were played at Rām's wedding.
Hour glass drums were played at Mahādev's wedding; tambourines were played at the darling of Nand's wedding.

(LGT: 23R/1976, Nandana, Mixed Men)

२०९.

ऊँचे चहुतरा हो अरे मलखानन के, झुकुवन आवै बयार।
रानी गजमोतिन रे पँखा ढुरै, अरी हो सुख सोवै मरद मलखान॥१॥
रनिया जगावै हो अरे मलखानन को, उठौ पिया बलवान।
फौज तो आय गईं रे पृथ्वीराज की, अरी हो गढ़ सिरसा के मैदोन॥२॥
फौज हो आईं हो अरे रनिया आवन दे, बडे करौ सन्मान।
तोप रहकला रे घर में धरीं, अरी हो तरवारन करत जुहोर॥३॥

ūñce cahutarā ho are malakhānan ke, jhukuvan āvai bayār;
rānī gajamotin re pañkhā ḍhurai, arī ho sukh sovai marad malakhān ॥1॥
raniyā jagāvai ho are malakhānan ko, uṭhau piyā balavān;
fauj to āy gaīṅ re pr̥thvīrāj kī, arī ho gaṛh sirasā ke maidon ॥2॥
fauj ho āīṅ ho are raniyā āvan de, baṛe karau sanmān;
top rahakalā re ghar meṅ dharīṅ, arī ho taravāran karat juhor ॥3॥

The platform of Malakhān is on high ground; much wind blows there.
Queen Gajamotin is fanning brave Malakhān as he sleeps sweetly.
"Arise, dear brave one," thus the queen awakens Malakhān.
The forces of Pr̥thvīrāj have arrived at the grounds of Fort Sirasā.
O dear queen, let the forces come; give them a proper welcome.
The cannons and their carriages are at home; we will salute them with swords.

(LGT: 25R: 1976, Nandana, Mixed Men)

२१०.

काहे तो बाढ़ी हो अरे शर औरैया, काहे तो बाढ़ी है फफूँद।
काहे तो बाढ़ी रे घाटमपुरा, अरि हो काहे बढ़ो खानपुर गाँव ॥१॥
बनियन बाढ़ी हो शर औरैया, तुरकन बढ़ी है फफूँद।
घटियन बाढ़ो रे घाटमपुरा, अरि हो ठकुरन बढ़ो खानपुर गाँव ॥२॥

kāhe to bāṛhī ho are śar auraiyā, kāhe to bāṛhī hai fafūñd;
kāhe to bāṛhī re ghāṭamapurā, ari ho kāhe baṛho khānapur gāñv ॥1॥
baniyan bāṛhī ho śar auraiyā, turakan baṛhī hai fafūñd.
ghaṭiyan bāṛho re ghāṭamapurā, ari ho ṭhakuran baṛho khānpur gāñv ॥2॥

Why is the city of Auraiyā so populated, and why is the city of Fafūnd so populated?
Why is the city of Ghātampur so populated, and why is the village Khānpur so populated?
The city of Auraiyā has a big population of business caste, and the city of Fafūnd has a big population of Turkish people.

The city of Ghātampur has a big population of Ghaṭiās (?), and Khānpur village has a big population of warrior caste people.

(LGT: 32R 1976, Sandalpur, Mixed Men)

२११.

क्वाँरा जुन्हैया हो अरे निरबल उइयो, निरबल उवत न कोय।
बिटियाँ खेलैं रे संसार की, अरि हो मेरो जियरा लहरियाँ ले ॥१॥
काहे लौ मारैं हो बारी जोंधइयो, काहे लौ मारैं सास।
काहे लौ मारैं रे बारी नन्द की, अरि हो मेरो जियरा लहरियाँ ले ॥२॥
बाना लौ मारै हो अरी बारी जोंधइयो, बिष दै मारौ सास।
धर फटकारौ रे बारी नन्द की, अरि हो मेरो जियरा सुफल होइ जाय ॥३॥
जो तुम बहुअर झोंझी खेलौ, बिरना का लेबौ मनाय।
चनन पालकी सजवाइ कै, बहुअर नैहर खेलन जाउ ॥४॥

kvāñrā junhaiyā ho are nirabal uiyo, nirabal uvat n koy;
biṭiyāñ khelaiṅ re saṅsār kī, ari ho mero jiyarā lahariyāñ le ॥1॥
kāhe lau māraiṅ ho bārī joṅdhaiyo, kāhe lau māraiṅ sāṣ;
kāhe lau māraiṅ re bārī nand kī, ari ho mero jiyarā lahariyāñ le ॥2॥
bānā lau mārai ho arī bārī joṅdhaiyo, biṣ dai mārau sās;
dhar phaṭakārau re bārī nand kī, ari ho mero jiyarā suphal hoi jāy ॥3॥
jo tum bahuar jhoṅjhī khelau, biranā kā lebau manāy;
canan pālakī sajavāi kai, bahuar naihar khelan jāu ॥4॥

O moon of *Kvār*, come out clear, because no one in this world is as clear as you are.
May the girls of the whole world enjoy themselves, so that my mind will feel pleasure.
How can I turn off this moonlight, and how can I get rid of my *sāś*?
How can I get away from my *Nand*; my heart is nervous.
Shoot an arrow at the moonlight, and kill your *sās* with poison.
Confront your Nand so that my heart feels happy.
If you *bahū*, want to play *jhoṅjhī*, go plead with your brother.
Then go to your parents' home in a decorated sandalwood palanquin.

(LGT: 129: 1972, Nandana)

झोंभी गीत (स्त्री वर्ग)

२१२.

ऊँचे चौतरा चाकले नर सुवना, जहँ बेटी खेलन जाँय रे सुवना
खेल मेल बेटी घर चलीं नर सुवना, दादुल के दरवाजे रे सुवना
भौजी ने डारो पीसनो नर सुवना, चिरई चुन चुन जाँय रे सुवना
भैया ने घाली साटुली नर सुवना, भौजी ने बोले हैं बोल रे सुवना
काहे भैया घाली साटुली नर सुवना, काहे भौजी बोले हैं बोल रे सुवना
जितनी बंबुर भर की चीरई नर सुवना, उतनो हैं सखियन झूँड़ रे सुवना
जितनी घनौची भर की गागरी नर सुवना, उतनो है सखियन झूँड़ रे सुवना
जितनी बढ़ैयाँ भर की सीकरी नर सुवना, उतनो है सखियन झूँड़ रे सुवना
छूटी बढ़ैयाँ भर की सीकरी नर सुवना, बिछड़ो है सखियन झूँड़ रे सुवना
फूटी घनौची पर की गागरी नर सुवना, बिछड़ो है सखियन झूँड़ रे सुवना
उड़ गईं बंबुर भर की चीरई नर सुवना, बिछड़ो है सखियन झूँड़ रे सुवना
गंग बड़ी जमुना बड़ी नर सुवना सबसे बड़ी प्रयाग
तिरियन में सीता बड़ी नर सुवना मरदन में श्री राम
माई बाप की लाड़ली नर सुवना घर घर देत अशीष

ūñce cautarā cākale nar suvanā, jahñ beṭī khelan jāñy re suvanā.
khel mel beṭī ghar calīṅ nar suvanā, dādul ke daravāje re suvanā.
bhaujī ne ḍāro pīsano nar suvanā, ciraī cun cun jāñy re suvanā.
bhaiyā ne ghālī sāṭulī nar suvanā, bhaujī ne bole haiṅ bol re suvanā.
kāhe bhaiyā ghālī sāṭulī nar suvanā, kāhe bhaujī bole haiṅ bol re suvanā.
jitanī baṅbur bhar kī cīraī nar suvanā, utano hai sakhiyan jhūñṛ re suvanā.
jitanī ghanaucī bhar kī gāgarī nar suvanā, utano hai sakhiyan jhūñṛ re suvanā.
jitanī baṛhaiyāñ bhar kī sīkarī nar suvanā, utano hai sakhiyan jhūñṛ re suvanā.
chūṭī baṛhaiyāñ bhar kī sīkarī nar suvanā, bichaṛo hai sakhiyan jhūñṛ re suvanā.
fūṭī ghanaucī par kī gāgarī nar suvanā, bichaṛo hai sakhiyan jhūñṛ re suvanā.
uṛ gaīṅ baṅbur bhar kī cīraī nar suvanā, bichaṛo hai sakhiyan jhūñṛ re suvanā.

gaṅg baṛī jamunā baṛī nar suvanā sabase baṛī prayāg.
tiriyan meṅ sītā baṛī nar suvanā maradan meṅ śrī rām.
māī bāp kī lāṛalī nar suvanā ghar ghar det aśīṣ.

The porches are high where the daughter goes to play.
After playing, the daughter came to her father's house.
My *bhauji* gave grain for grinding but the birds ate the grain.
The brother made her bed, but her *bhauji* taunted her.
Why did brother make her bed and why did *bhaujī* say harsh words?
She has as many friends as there are birds on an acacia tree.
As many pots as are on the platform for water containers, she has that many friends.
As many wickers as there are on a broom, she has that many friends.
All the wickers of the broom became scattered; she got separated from her friends.
All the pots on the platform for water containers got broken; she got separated from her friends.
All the birds of the acacia tree flew away; she got separated from her friends.
River Gaṅgā is big, River Jamunā is big, but biggest of all is Prayāg.
Sītā is the most respected woman among women, and Rām among men.
Dear to her mother and father, the loving daughter blesses each household.

(LGT: 1972: 133R; 1976, 10R, Nandana)

२१३.

पाटी फूल नौ पंख रे सुवना, किनके हाथे बिराजे रे सुवना
रनियन के जाये कोई बिरन भैया, उनहिन के हाथे बिराजे रे सुवना
घोड़ी बेंची बछेड़ी रे बेंची, बेंचे हैं मोहन माला रे सुवना
इतनो खरच बउवा बेंदी गढ़ाई, तेऊना बहुरिया के मनए न भाई
बेंदी चमक बउवा पनिया का निकरी, फाँसो है घाट घएलना रे सुवना
मेरे नैन कजर की लाली, लोग कहैं मतवारो रे सुवना
मेरे भड़ुवा तेरे पैयाँ लागौं, बेंदी देव ढुंढाय रे सुवना
बेंदी पाई धर धमकाई, सास ननदिया ने ठुनका दिखाओ

pāṭī fūl nau paṅkh re suvanā, kinake hāthe birāje re suvanā.
raniyan ke jāye koī biran bhaiyā, unahin ke hāthe birāje re suvanā.
ghoṛī beñcī bacheṛī re beñcī, beṅce haiṅ mohan mālā re suvanā.
itano kharac bauvā beṅdī gaṛhāī, teūnā bahuriyā ke manae n bhāī.
beṅdī camak bauvā paniyā kā nikarī, fāñso hai ghāṭ ghaelanā re suvanā.
mere nain kajar kī lālī, log kahaiṅ matavāro re suvanā.
mere bhaḍuvā tere paiyāñ lāgauṅ, beṅdī dev ḍhuṅḍhāy re suvanā.
beṅdī pāī dhar dhamakāī, sās nanadiyā ne ṭhunakā dikhāo.

Who is carrying flowers and fans on a wooden board?
Being born of a queen, my brother is carrying these things in his hand.
He sold his horse, calf, and garland of gold beads.
Spending this much money, he had a head ornament made and the *bahū* appreciates it.
Wearing that sparkling head ornament, she went out to fetch water and tighten the pot.
My eyes are red with mascara, but people say that I am intoxicated!
O my pimp, I beg at your feet, help me find my head ornament.
She proudly displayed her head ornament, but her *sās* and *nanad* showed no response.

(LGT: 11R: 1976, Nandana)

२१४.

राहुल सुवना राहुल सुवना, सिड्ढी लगी सौ साठ सुवना
सिड्ढिन सिड्ढिन चढ़ि गये बिरन भैया, चढ़ि गये बिरन भैया
पीछे से चढ़ि गई उनकी दुलैया, लै बेला भर तेल सुवना
मलत मलत मोरी बैयाँ पिरानी, तेउ न जगे दोउ नैन सुवना
सोनवा मढ़ैबे गोरी गोरी बैयाँ, कजरा मढ़े दोउ नैन सुवना

rāhul suvanā rāhul suvanā, siḍḍhī lagī sau sāṭh suvanā.
siḍḍhin siḍḍhin caṛhi gaye biran bhaiyā, caṛhi gaye biran bhaiyā.
pīche se caḍhi gaī unakī dulaiyā, lai belā bhar tel suvanā.
malat malat morī baiyāñ pirānī, teu n jage dou nain suvanā.
sonavā maṛhaibe gorī gorī baiyāñ, kajarā maṛhe dou nain sovanā.

O dear {Rāhul}, there is a ladder with one hundred and sixty steps.
Step by step, my brother climbed that ladder.
Following him, his wife also climbed, carrying a bowl full of oil.
My hands got tired from massaging him, but even then he did not awake.
I will cover your fair hands with gold and put mascara on both of your eyes.

(LGT: 12R: 1976, Nandana)

२१५.

बिन उड़री की गागर सुवना, डगमग डगमग होय सुवना
बिन बछुवा की गैया रे सुवना, राँभत दिन और रात सुवना
बिन पुत्र की मैया रे सुवना, बिलखत दिन और रात सुवना
सत भैयन की बहिनी रे सुवना, डोला चमकत जाय सुवना

bin uṛarī kī gāgar suvanā, ḍagamag ḍagamag hoy suvanā.
bin bachuvā kī gaiyā re suvanā, rāñbhat din aur rāt suvanā.
bin putr kī maiyā re suvanā, bilakhat din aur rāt suvanā.
sat bhaiyan kī bahinī re suvanā, ḍolā camakat jāy suvanā.

A water pot without the headrest quivers {on the head}.
A cow without a calf bellows day and night.
A mother without a son laments day and night.
When a sister has seven brothers, her palanquin goes with pomp and ceremonial gifts.

(LGT: 13R: 1976, Nandana)

२१६.

हमरे अँगन एक तुलसी को बिरवा, जुगिया भँवर धरे जाय रे सुवना
जुगिया जुगिया जिन करो बहिनी, जुगिया हैं बिरने तुम्हारे रे सुवना
लावौ न सासु मोरे कपड़े औ लत्ते, हम जोगिया होइ जाय रे सुवना
काहे का बहू मोरी जोग जोगैहो, करहो अजोध्या को राज रे सुवना
आगि लगै ऐसे राज पाठ को, हम जोगिया होय जाँय रे सुवना

hamare añgan ek tulasī kā biravā, jugiyā bhañvar dhare jāy re suvanā.
jugiyā jugiyā jin karo bahinī, jugiyā haiṅ birane tumhāre re suvanā.
lāvau n sāsu more kapaṛe au latte, ham jogiyā hoi jāy re suvanā
kāhe kā bahū morī jog jogaiho, karaho ajodhyā ko rāj re suvanā.
āgi lagai aise rāj pāṭh ko, ham jogiyā hoy jāñy re suvanā.

There is a basil bush in my courtyard; an ascetic goes around it.
O dear sister, do not call him an ascetic; that ascetic is your brother.
Give me my clothes, dear *sās*, I too will become an ascetic.
Why would you, my *bāhū*, become an ascetic, but rule the kingdom of Ayodhyā?
Let this kingdom burn to ashes; I will become an ascetic.

(LGT: 14R: 1976, Nandana)

२१७.

आटोले पाटोले साटोले नर सुवना, सटुली के चारो पाँय रे सुवना
सटुली के लम्बे लम्बे केश रे सुवना
काहे की मोरी बनी रे पटुलिया, काहे के चारो पाँय रे सुवना
चंदन की मोरी बनी रे पटुलिया, रूपे के चारो पाँय रे सुवना
आधी पटुलिया में फूल कटे हैं, आधे में रतन जड़ाओ रे सुवना
काहे में सिरैबे चंदन पटुलिया, काहे में चारो पाँय रे सुवना
गंगा सिरैबे चंदन पटुलिया, जमुना सिरैबे चारो पाँय रे सुवना

āṭole pāṭole sāṭole nar suvanā, saṭulī ke cāro pāñy re suvanā.
saṭulī ke lambe lambe keś re suvanā.
kāhe kī morī banī re paṭuliyā, kāhe ke cāro pāñy re suvanā.
caṅdan kī morī banī re paṭuliyā, rūpe ke cāro pāñy re suvanā.
ādhī paṭuliyā meṅ fūl kaṭe haiṅ, ādhe meṅ ratan jaṛāo re suvanā.
kāhe meṅ siraibe caṅdan paṭuliyā, kāhe meṅ cāro pāñy re suvanā.
gaṅgā siraibe caṅdan paṭuliyā, jamunā siraibe cāro pāñy re suvanā.

My loving wooden board has four legs.
That wooden board has long hair.
Of what material is this wooden board and its four feet made of?

The wooden board is made of sandalwood, and the four feet are made of silver.
Half of the board is decorated with flowers, and the other half is set with jewels.
Where would you dispose of the sandalwood board and the four feet?
I will dispose of the sandalwood board in the Gaṅgā, and the four feet in the Jamunā.

(LGT: 15R: 1976, Nandana)

२१८.

पाटुल पाटुले पाटुली अरे पटुली के लम्बे लम्बे पाट सुवना
को तोरे मुतिया बीन है और को तोरी भरिहै माँग सुवना
भैया मेरे मोतिया बीन है और भाभी भरैं मेरी माँग सुवना

pāṭul pāṭule pāṭulī are paṭulī ke lambe lambe pāṭ suvanā.
ko tore mutiyā bīn hai aur ko torī bharihai māṅg suvanā.
bhaiyā mere motiyā bīn hai aur bhābhī bharaiṅ merī māṅg suvanā.

A darling daughter has a long part [in her hair].
Who will make a strand of pearls and who will fill that part [with *siṅdūr*]?
My brother will make a strand of pearls and my *bhābhī* will fill my part.

(LGT: 26R : 1976, Sandalpur)

२१९.

मेरे अंगन में सेहुड़ा को पेड़ो, फूले फूल झर जाय सुअना
बहुआ जो बोली अपने ससुर से, ससुरा से चुनरी रँगैहैं रे सुअना
कल करौ बहुआ ऐसी मैं चुनरी रँगैहैं रे सुअना
द्वारे बसै रंगरेज सुअना, द्वारे पै लपझक होय सुअना ॥टेक॥
बहुआ जो बोली अपने जेठ से, जेठा से चुनरी रँगैहैं रे सुअना
कल करौ बहुआ ऐसी मैं चुनरी रँगैहैं रे सुअना
द्वारे बसै रंगरेज सुअना, द्वारे पै लपझक होय सुअना ॥टेक॥
बहुआ जो बोली अपने देवर से, देवरा से चुनरी रँगैहैं रे सुअना
कल करौ भौजी ऐसी मैं चुनरी रँगैहैं रे सुअना

द्वारे बसै रंगरेज सुअना, द्वारे पै लपझक होय सुअना ॥टेक ॥
धनिया जो बोली अपने सहब से, सहबा से चुनरी रँगैहैं रे सुअना
कल करौ रानी ऐसी मैं चुनरी रँगैहैं रे सुअना
द्वारे बसै रंगरेज सुअना, द्वारे पै लपझक होय सुअना ॥टेक ॥

mere aṅgan meṅ sehuṛā ko peṛo, fūle fūl jhar jāy suanā.
bahūā jo bolī apane sasur se, sasurā se cunarī raṅgaihaiṅ re suanā.
kal karau bahuā aisī maiṅ cunarī raṅgaihaiṅ re suanā.
dvāre basai raṅgarej suanā, dvāre pai lapajhak hoy suanā.
bahūā jo bolī apane jeṭh se, jeṭhā se cunarī raṅgaihaiṅ re suanā.
kal karau bahuā aisī maiṅ cunarī raṅgaihaiṅ re suanā.
dvāre basai raṅgarej suanā, dvāre pai lapajhak hoy suanā.
bahūā jo bolī apane devar se, devarā se cunarī raṅgaihaiṅ re suanā.
kal karau bhaujī aisī maiṅ cunarī raṅgaihaiṅ re suanā.
dvāre basai raṅgarej suanā, dvāre pai lapajhak hoy suanā.
dhaniyā jo bolī apane sahab se, sahabā se cunarī raṅgaihaiṅ re suanā.
kal karau rānī aisī maiṅ cunarī raṅgaihaiṅ re suanā.
dvāre basai raṅgarej suanā, dvāre pai lapajhak hoy suanā.

There is a Sehurā (?) tree in my courtyard full of flowers.
Bahū asked her *sasur* to colour her scarf.
Have patience, dear *bahū*, I will get your scarf coloured well.
There is a dyer living outside our house who will dye [your scarf] in front of our gate.
Bahū asked her *jeṭh* to colour her scarf.
Have patience, dear *bahū*, I will get your scarf coloured well.
There is a dyer living outside our house who will dye [your scarf] in front of our gate.
Bahū asked her *devar* to colour her scarf.
Have patience, dear *bhaujī*, I will get your scarf coloured well.
There is a dyer living outside our house who will dye [your scarf] in front of our gate.
Bahū asked her husband to colour her scarf.
Have patience, my dear wife, I will get your scarf coloured well.
There is a dyer living outside our house who will dye [your scarf] in front of our gate.

(LGT: 27R: 1976, Sandalpur)

२२०.

आठ फूल नौ पंखा रे सुअना, केखे हाथ बिराजैं रे सुअना
रंनिया के जाये राजू लाला, उनहीं के हाथ बिराजैं रे सुअना
उनकी दुलैया उदक लड़ैती, आधो फुल बटावै रे सुअना
फुल के बटैइया गाँव में गये हैं, रह गये रतनघर छाये रे सुअना

āṭh fūl nau paṅkhā re suanā, kekhe hāth birājaiṅ re suanā.
raniyā ke jāye rājū lālā, unahīṅ ke hāth birājaiṅ re suanā.
unakī dulaiyā udak laṛaitī, ādho ful baṭāvai re suanā.
ful ke bataiyā gāñv meṅ gaye haiṅ, rah gaye ratanaghar chāye re suanā.

In whose hand is this coloured fan?
Born of a queen, dear Rājū is carrying that fan.
His wife instigates fights. She wants to divide the house in half.
The one who is authorised for the division has gone to the village, where he remains with his mistress.

(LGT: 28R: 1976, Sandalpur)

२२१.

हम बिचारी भुला गई थीं, ता तथा ता थेई थेई
ससुरा घरई में रखिओ, ता तथा ता थेई थेई
ससुरा खटिया में बाँधे, ता तथा ता थेई थेई
जेठा घरई में रखिओ, ता तथा ता थेई थेई
जेठा खुटिया में बाँधे, ता तथा ता थेई थेई
देवर घरई में रखिओ, ता तथा ता थेई थेई
देवर खुटिया में बाँधे, ता तथा ता थेई थेई
सहबा घरई में रखिओ, ता तथा ता थेई थेई
सहबा नरा में बाँधे, ता तथा ता थेई थेई

ham bicārī bhulā gaī thīṅ, tā tathā tā theī theī.
sasurā gharaī meṅ rakhio, tā tathā tā theī theī.
sasurā khaṭiyā meṅ bañdhe, tā tathā tā theī theī.
jeṭhā gharaī meṅ rakhio, tā tathā tā theī theī.

jeṭhā khuṭiyā meṅ bāñdhe, tā tathā tā theī theī.
devar gharaī meṅ rakhio, tā tathā tā theī theī.
devar khuṭiyā meṅ bāñdhe, tā tathā tā theī theī.
sahabā gharaī meṅ rakhio, tā tathā tā theī theī.
sahabā narā meṅ bāñdhe, tā tathā tā theī theī.

I had forgotten how to dance.
Keep *sasur* in the house; let's dance.
Tie *sasur* to a cot; let's dance.
Keep *jeṭh* in the house; let's dance.
Tie *jeṭh* to a peg; let's dance.
Keep *devar* in the house; let's dance.
Tie *devar* to a peg; let's dance.
Keep the husband in the house; let's dance.
Tie the husband to the drain; let's dance.

(LGT: 29R: 1976, Sandalpur)

२२२.

सरकत नहियाँ बटुआ डोरी बिना
सोने की थाली में भोजन बनाये
जेवत नहियाँ राजा रानी बिना
सोने के गडुआ गंगा जल पानी
पीवत नहियाँ राजा रानी बिना
पान पचासी के बीरा लगाये
राचत नहियाँ राजा रानी बिना
फूलन निवारी की सेजा बिछाई
सोवत नहियाँ राजा रानी बिना

sarakat nahiyāñ baṭuā ḍorī binā.
sone kī thālī meṅ bhojan banāye.
jevat nahiyāñ rājā rānī binā.
sone ke gaḍuā gaṅgā jal pānī.
pīvat nahiyāñ rājā rānī binā.
pān pacāsī ke bīrā lagāye.

rācat nahiyāñ rājā rānī binā.
fūlan nivārī kī sejā bichāī.
sovat nahiyāñ rājā rānī binā.

I am unable to open my purse because the cord is broken.
I served food on a golden plate.
My husband will not eat without his wife.
There is Gaṅgā water in a golden water pot.
My husband will not drink without his wife.
I prepared a special betel leaf.
My husband will not eat without his wife.
I made a bed of cotton strips and flowers.
My husband will not sleep without his wife.

(LGT: 30R: Sandalpur, Mixed Women)

२२३.

किन्ने ये निबुला लगाये रे नर सुवना, कौन बेटी सींचन जाँय
बीरा भैया निबुला लगाये रे नर सुवना, मुन्नी बेटी सींचन जाँय
जब बेटी ढुरि गई ससुरे रे नर सुवना, निबुला रहे कुम्हलाय
जब बेटी ढुरि आई मइके रे नर सुवना, निबुला रहे फलफूल

kinne ye nibulā lagāye re nar suvanā, kaun beṭī sīṅcan jāñy.
bīrā bhaiyā nibulā lagāye re nar suvanā, munnī beṭī sīṅcan jāñy.
jab beṭī ḍhuri gaī sasure re nar suvanā, nibulā rahe kumhalāy.
jab beṭī ḍhuri āī maike re nar suvanā, nibulā rahe falafūl.

Who planted this lemon, and which daughter waters it?
My brave brother planted the lemon, and daughter Munnī waters it.
When the daughter was at her in-law's house, the lemon withered.
When the daughter returned to her parents' home, the lemon began to bloom.

(LGT: 130R:1972, Nandana

२२४.

मेरी झुँझिया आउर माँगे चाउर माँगे
बेला भर तिलचउरी माँगे, ऊपर गुड़ की बट्टी माँगे
एड़िया महाउर माँगे, माँग भरत को सेन्दुर माँगे
हाथ भरे की चुड़िया माँगे, माथे की जो बिन्दी माँगे
पायन की जो बिछिया माँगे
रे नर सुवना मोरी झोंझिया को रचो है बिहाव
टेसू तो गये हैं बराते रे नर सुवना मोरी झोंझी रही गुर खेत

merī jhuñjhiyā āur māñge cāur māñge;
belā bhar tilacaurī māñge, ūpar guṛ kī baṭṭī māñge;
eṛiyā mahāur māñge, māñg bharat ko sendur māñge;
hāth bhare kī cuṛiyā māñge, māthe kī jo bindī māñge;
pāyan kī jo bichiyā māñge;
re nar suvanā morī jhoñjhiyā ko raco hai bihāv.
ṭesū to gaye haiṅ barāte re nar suvanā morī jhoñjhī rahī gur khet.

My Jhuñjhiyā asks for rice;
She asks for a bowl full of sesame seeds with a lump of raw sugar on top;
She asks for red dye for her heels and red powder for the part of her hair;
She asks for bangles for her wrists and a red dot for her forehead;
She asks for toe-rings for her feet;
My Jhuñjhiyā is getting ready for her wedding.
Ṭesu has gone with wedding procession and my *jhuñjhiyā* is alone in the field.

(LGT: 131R:1972, Nandana)

२२५.

हाय मोरी नार की सिया बन छोड़ चले हैं निरमोही
हाय मोरी नार की बागा लगाये बगैचा लगाये
हाय मोरी नार की छोड़ि चले निबुलन की जोड़ी
हाय मोरी नार की कुँवना खोदाये जगतिया बँधाई
हाय मोरी नार की छाड़ि चले मरुवन की जोड़ी

हाय मोरी नार की ताला खोदाये तलैया बँधाई
हाय मोरी नार की छाड़ि चले पाटन की जोड़ी
हाय मोरी नार की महला उठाये दुमहला उठाये
हाय मोरी नार की छाड़ि चले खिरकिन की जोड़ी
हाय मोरी नार की सड़कैं खुदाई सड़किया बँधाई
हाय मोरी नार की छाड़ि चले मोटर की जोड़ी
हाय मोरी नार की सिया बन छोड़ि चले हैं निरमोही

hāy morī nār kī siyā ban choṛ cale haiṅ niramohī.
hāy morī nār kī bāgā lagāye bagaicā lagāye.
hāy morī nār kī choṛi cale nibulan kī joṛī.
hāy morī nār kī kuñvanā khodāye jagatiyā bañdhāī.
hāy morī nār kī chāṛi cale maruvan kī joṛī.
hāy morī nār kī tālā khodāye talaiyā bañdhāī.
hāy morī nār kī chāṛi cale pāṭan kī joṛī.
hāy morī nār kī mahalā uṭhāye dumahalā uṭhāye.
hāy morī nār kī chāṛi cale khirakin kī joṛī.
hāy morī nār kī saṛakaiṅ khudāī saṛakiyā bañdhāī.
hāy morī nār kī chāṛi cale moṭar kī joḍī.
hāy morī nār kī siyā ban choṛi cale haiṅ niramohī.

The cruel husband has left for the forest, leaving Sītā behind.
I planted a garden.
He left a pair of lemons behind.
I constructed a well with a platform.
He left a pair of bullocks behind.
I constructed a pool.
He left a pair of bathing places.
I constructed a two-storey palace.
He left the palace with windows behind.
I had roads and lanes constructed.
He left his cars behind.
The cruel husband has left for the forest, leaving Sītā behind.

(LGT: 132R:1972, Nandana)

२२६.

हाय मोरी नार की तेरी अँगनैया में मेरा क्या काम है
हाय मोरी नार की जिसकी औरत छोटी उसी का बड़ा नाम है
हाय मोरी नार की गोदी में रख लो बच्चे का क्या काम है
हाय मोरी नार की जिसकी औरत लम्बी उसी का बड़ा नाम है
हाय मोरी नार की छप्पर में रख लो बल्ली का क्या काम है
हाय मोरी नार की जिसकी औरत गोरी उसी का बड़ा नाम है
हाय मोरी नार की कमरे में रख लो बिजली का क्या काम है
हाय मोरी नार की जिसकी औरत मोटी उसी का बड़ा नाम है
हाय मोरी नार की पलँगे पे रख दो गद्‌दे का क्या काम है
हाय मोरी नार की तेरी अँगनैया में मेरा क्या काम है

hāy morī nār kī terī añganaiyā meṅ merā kyā kām hai.
hāy morī nār kī jisakī aurat choṭī usī kā baṛā nām hai.
hāy morī nār kī godī meṅ rakh lo bacce kā kyā kām hai.
hāy morī nār kī jisakī aurat lambī usī kā baṛā nām hai.
hāya morī nār kī chappar meṅ rakh lo ballī kā kyā kām hai.
hāy morī nār kī jisakī aurat gorī usī kā baṛā nām hai.
hāy morī nār kī kamare meṅ rakh lo bijalī kā kyā kām hai.
hāy morī nār kī jisakī aurat moṭī usī kā baṛā nām hai.
hāy morī nār kī palañge pe rakh do gadde kā kyā kām hai.
hāy morī nār kī terī añganaiyā meṅ merā kyā kām hai.

O dear, why do you need me in your courtyard?
O dear, one whose wife is small is well-known;
O dear, keep her on your lap and there is no need of a child.
O dear, one whose wife is tall is well-known;
O dear, stick her on a thatched roof and there is no need of a pole.
O dear, one whose wife is of fair complexion is well-known;
O dear, keep her in a room and there is no need for electricity.
O dear, one whose wife is fat is well-known.
O dear, put her on the bed and there is no need for a mattress.
O dear, why do you need me in your courtyard?

(LGT: 134R:1972, Nandana)

२२७.

डुड़ी पिपरिया झलरी बनजरिया लोग
झलरी चारो ओर प्यारे खरगोले बनजरिया लोग
उतरी के मोढ़ा उइ चाढ़ैं बनजरिया लोग
हेरैं चारो ओर प्यारे खरगोले बनजरिया लोग
पहर के हेरैं मइको बनजरिया लोग
घर घर बसैं सुनार प्यारे खरगोले बनजरिया लोग
नौ मन सोना उइ गाढ़ै बनजरिया लोग
पहरैं माया हमार प्यारे खरगोले बनजरिया लोग
पहर ओढ़ जब निकरी बनजरिया लोग
कौन सुहागिल जाये प्यारे खरगोले बनजरिया लोग
डुड़ी पिपरिया झलरी बनजरिया लोग
झलरी चारो ओर प्यारे खरगोले बनजरिया लोग
दूज तो हेरैं ससुरो बनजरिया लोग
घर घर बसैं लुहार प्यारे खरगोले बनजरिया लोग
नौ मन लोहो उइ गाढ़ैं बनजरिया लोग
पहरैं सास हमार प्यारे खरगोले बनजरिया लोग
पहर ओढ़ जब निकरी बनजरिया लोग
कौन छछूँदर जाय प्यारे खरगोले बनजरिया लोग
डुड़ी पिपरिया झलरी बनजरिया लोग
झलरी चारो ओर प्यारे खरगोले बनजरिया लोग

ḍuṛī pipariyā jhalarī banajariyā log.
jhalarī cāro or pyāre kharagole banajariyā log.
utarī ke moḍhā ui cāṛhaiṅ banajariyā log.
heraiṅ cāro or pyāre kharagole banajariyā log.
pahar ke heraiṅ maiko banajariyā log.
ghar ghar basaiṅ sunār pyāre kharagole banajariyā log.
nau man sonā ui gāṛhai banajariyā log.
paharaiṅ māyā hamār pyāre kharagole banajariyā log.
pahar oṛh jab nikarī banajariyā log.
kaun suhāgil jāy pyāre kharagole banajariyā log.
ḍuṛī pipariyā jhalarī banajariyā log.
jhalari cāro or pyāre kharagole banajariyā log.
dūj to heraiṅ sasuro banajariyā log.

ghar ghar basaiṅ luhār pyāre kharagole banajariyā log.
nau man loho ui gāṛhaiṅ banajariyā log.
paharaiṅ sās hamār pyāre kharagole banajariyā log.
pahar oṛh jab nikarī banajariyā log.
kaun chachūñdar jāy pyāre kharagole banajariyā log.
ḍuṛī pipariyā jhalari banajariyā log.
jhalarī cāro or pyāre kharagole banajariyā log.

The dried bush in lush.
O dear, it is green all around.
She is excitingly getting up and down on a stool.
O dear, she looks all around.
Wearing [her ornaments], she looks towards her parents' home.
A goldsmith lives in each house.
[Those goldsmiths] make ornaments of nine pounds of gold.
My mother wears it.
Wearing [all that gold] when she came out,
Everyone asks, "Which married woman is she?"
The dried bush in lush.
O dear, it is green all around.
Then she looks towards her in-laws' home.
A blacksmith lives in each house.
[Those blacksmiths] make ornaments of nine pounds of iron.
My *sās* wears it.
Wearing [all that iron] when she came out.
Everyone asks, "Who is this muskrat?"
The dried bush in lush.
O dear, it is green all around.

(LGT: 140R:1972, Nandana)

२२८.

अनगढ़ लइयो गोकुल के कन्हैया पहचानत नैयाँ भौजी बेंदुल देव
काहे पै हम खेती करिहैं काहे पै ख़रिहाना हो
काहे के हम बैल बनइहैं को यह करै किसाना हो ॥

सूरज पै हम खेती करिहैं चन्द्रा पै खरिहाना हो
सुरा गऊ के बैल बनइहैं सैंयाँ करैं किसाना हो ॥
बाली बाली सुवना लै गओ घिटिया लै गई चमरदो हो
हाथ मोड़ कै चलो किसाना ठुमकिन नचै चमरदो हो ॥
आमदनी को लगो बुलउवा सैंयाँ घुसे भुसौरा हो ॥
पीस लाईं कूट लाईं भर लाईं टोकनिया हो
चूल्हे पै जब चालन बैठीं भड़ुवन आग लगाई हो ॥
सवा लाख की भैंस बिकानी औ जोड़ू को गहनो हो
चूल्हे पर को तवा बिकानो अँगिया लै गओ सुवना हो ॥
सास हमारी पूजा करति है ससुर करत अगियारी हो
देवरा हमारे बारे के मुहरा मूत भरी अगियारी हो ॥
काँहाँ के हैं लेंदी पेंदा काँहाँ के बड़पेटा हो
काँहाँ के हैं छैल चिकनिया डारे लम्बे तुर्रा हो ॥
निन्हौरा के हैं लेंदी पेंदा सिकन्द्रा के बड़पेटा हो
नन्दना के हैं छैल चिकनिया डारे लम्बे तुर्रा हो ॥

anagaṛh laiyo gokul ke kanhaiyā pahacānat naiyāñ bhaujī beṅdul dev.
kāhe pai ham khetī karihaiṅ kāhe pai kharihānā ho.
kāhe ke ham bail banaihaiṅ ko yah karai kisānā ho.
sūraj pai ham khetī karihaiṅ candrā pai kharihānā ho.
surā gaū ke bail banaihaiṅ saiṅyāñ karaiṅ kisānā ho.
bālī bālī suvanā lai gao ghiṭiyā lai gaī camarado ho.
hāth moṛ kai calo kisānā ṭhumakin nacai camarado ho.
āmadanī ko lago bulauvā saiṅyāñ ghuse bhusaurā ho.
pīs lāīṅ kūṭ lāīṅ bhar lāīṅ ṭokaniyā ho.
cūlhe pai jab cālan baiṭhīṅ bhaḍuvan āg lagāī ho.
savā lākh kī bhaiṅs bikānī au joḍū ko gahano ho.
cūlhe par ko tavā bikāno añgiyā lai gao suvaā ho.
sās hamārī pūjā karati hai sasur karat agiyārī ho.
devarā hamāre bāre ke muharā mūt bharī agiyārī ho.
kāñhāñ ke haiṅ leṅdī peṅdā kāñhāñ ke baṛapeṭā ho.
kāñhāñ ke haiṅ chail cikaniyā ḍāre lambe turrā ho.
ninhaurā ke haiṅ leṅdī peṅdā sikandrā ke baṛapeṭā ho.
ṇandanā ke haiṅ chail cikaniyā ḍāre lambe turrā ho.

You are rude, O Kṛṣṇa of Gokul, you don't recognize me; O bhaujī, give me a *beṅdul* ornament.
Where will I do the farming? Where will I have my threshing place?
From where will I get my bullock team? Who will do the farming?
I will do farming on the sun and make my threshing place on the moon.
I will make a bullock team and my husband will do the farming.
The parrots picked all the corn and the stalks were taken by the *camār*'s wife.
The farmer came out with empty hands, but the *camār*'s wife was dancing.
At the time of accounting, my husband hid himself in the straw house.
She ground and pounded and brought back a basket [of flour].
When she sat winnowing next to the stove, the pimp lit the stove.
The she-buffalo was sold for one hundred and twenty-five thousand rupees; all the wife's ornaments were sold.
The baking plate was also sold, and the bodice was taken by the parrot.
My *sās* is worshipping and my *sasur* is burning the incense.
My *devar* is very mischievous; he pisses on the incense burner.
Where have these funny-looking ones come from and where have these big-bellied ones come from?
Where have these fashionable ones with curly hair come from?
The funny ones are from Ninhaurā village and the big-bellied ones are from Sikandrā village.
The fashionable ones with curly hair are from Nandana village.

(LGT: 141R:1972, Nandana)

२२९.

हाथ मा लुटिया बगल मा धुतिया गहि लई मईके की राय सखीरी
बीच मा मिल गये स्वामी हमारे कहाँ धना कहाँ का जाव सखीरी
सास ने मारो ननद नें गारी दीन्हीं देवर दये हैं बनवास सखीरी
माया हमारी बन की लकड़िया आज मरै की काल सखीरी
बहनी हमारी धना बन की चिरैया आज उड़े की काल सखीरी
भैया हमारे धना हींसा के बटैया आज बटै की काल सखीरी

hāth mā luṭiyā bagal mā dhutiyā gahi laī maīke kī rāy sakhīrī.
bīc mā mil gaye svāmī hamāre kahāñ dhanā kahāñ kā jāv sakhīrī.

sās ne māro nanad neṅ gārī dīnhīṅ devar daye haiṅ banavās sakhīrī.
māyā hamārī ban kī lakaṛiyā āj marai kī kāl sakhīrī.
bahanī hamārī dhanā ban kī ciraiyā āj uṛai kī kāl sakhīrī.
bhaiyā hamāre dhanā hīṅsā ke baṭaiyā āj baṭai kī kāl sakhīrī.

Carrying a jar in my hand and a *dhoti* under my arm, I took the road to my parents' home.
On the way, I met my husband, who asked: "O, wife, where are you off to?"
My *sās* has hit me, my *nanad* has abused me and my *devar* has asked me to leave the house.
My mother is like a stick in the forest, she might die today or tomorrow.
My sister is like a bird in the forest, she might fly away today or tomorrow.
My brother will share the property, the share may be divided today or tomorrow.

(LGT: 143R:1972, Nandana)

२३०.

छिटकी चन्दरमा चुरवा डाटै मोरो ककना
ससुरा जगावौं ससुइया दुःख मानै, कौन का जगावौं बच जाय मोरो ककना ॥
जेठ जगावौं जेठनिया दुःख मानै, कौन का जगावौं बच जाय मोरो ककना ॥
देवर जगावौं देवरनिया दुःख मानै, कौन का जगावौं बच जाय मोरो ककना ॥
साहबै जगावौं सौतिनिया दुःख मानै, कौन का जगावौं बच जाय मोरो ककना ॥

chiṭakī candaramā curavā ḍāṭai moro kakanā.
sasurā jagāvauṅ sasuiyā duḥkh mānai, kaun kā jagāvauṅ bac jāy moro kakanā.
jeṭh jagāvauṅ jeṭhaniyā duḥkh mānai, kaun kā jagāvauṅ bac jāy moro kakanā.
devar jagāvauṅ devaraniyā duḥkh mānai, kaun kā jagāvauṅ bac jāy moro kakanā.
sāhabai jagāvauṅ sautiniyā duḥkh mānai, kaun kā jagāvauṅ bac jāy moro kakanā.

In the bright moonlight, a thief is removing my bracelet.

If I awaken my *sasur*, my *sās* will be upset.
If I awaken my *jeṭh*, my *jeṭhānī* will be upset.
If I awaken my *devar*, my *devāranī* will be upset.
If I awaken my husband, my co-wife will be upset.

(LGT: 144R:1972, Nandana)

२३१.

हाय मोरी नार की छज्जे वाली ईंट कलकत्ते वाली ननदी
हाय मोरी नार की बागा गई थी संग में गई ननदी
हाय मोरी नार की मलिया देख मचल गई ननदी
हाय मोरी नार की हाथ जोड़ूँ पैर पड़ूँ घर चलो ननदी ॥
हाय मोरी नार की ताला गई थी संग में गई ननदी
हाय मोरी नार की धोबी देख मचल गई ननदी
हाय मोरी नार की हाथ जोड़ूँ पैर पड़ूँ घर चलो ननदी ॥
हाय मोरी नार की कुआँ गई थी संग में गई ननदी
हाय मोरी नार की कहरा देख मचल गई ननदी
हाय मोरी नार की हाथ जोड़ूँ पैर पड़ूँ घर चलो ननदी ॥
हाय मोरी नार की सड़का गई थी संग में गई ननदी
हाय मोरी नार की बाबू देख मचल गई ननदी
हाय मोरी नार की हाथ जोड़ूँ पैर पड़ूँ घर चलो ननदी ॥

hāy morī nār kī chajje vālī īṅṭ kalakatte vālī nanadī.
hāy morī nār kī bāgā gaī thī saṅg meṅ gaī nanadī.
hāy morī nār kī maliyā dekh macal gaī nanadī.
hāy morī nār kī hāth joḍūñ pair paḍūñ ghar calo nanadī.
hāy morī nār kī tālā gaī thī saṅg meṅ gaī nanadī.
hāy morī nār kī dhobī dekh macal gaī nanadī.
hāy morī nār kī hāth joḍūñ pair paḍūñ ghar calo nanadī.
hāy morī nār kī kuāñ gaī thī saṅg meṅ gaī nanadī.
hāy morī nār kī kaharā dekh macal gaī nanadī.
hāy morī nār kī hāth joḍūñ pair paḍūñ ghar calo nanadī.
hāy morī nār kī saṛakā gaī thī saṅg meṅ gaī nanadī.
hāy morī nār kī bābū dekh macal gaī nanadī.
hāy morī nār kī hāth joḍūñ pair paḍūñ ghar calo nanadī.

O dear, the brick balcony and my *nanad* from Calcutta.
O dear, I went to the garden and my *nanad* came with me.
O dear, my *nanad* fell in love with the gardener.
O dear, *nanad*, with folded hands and touching your feet, I beg you to return home.
O dear, I went to the pond and my *nanad* came with me.
O dear, my *nanad* fell in love with the washerman.
O dear *nanad*, with folded hands and touching your feet, I beg you to return home.
O dear, I went to the well and my *nanad* came with me.
O dear, my *nanad* fell in love with the *kahār*.
O dear *nanad*, with folded hands and touching your feet, I beg you to return home.
O dear, I went to the road and my *nanad* came with me.
O dear, my *nanad* fell in love with a gentleman.
O dear *nanad*, with folded hands and touching your feet, I beg you to return home.

(LGT: 1989, Nandana)

२३२.

हाय मोरी नार की सलमा सितारे जड़ी मेरी साड़ी
हाय मोरी नार की साड़ी पहिन मैं तो बागा गई थी
हाय मोरी नार की मलिया के मन में बसी मेरी साड़ी ॥
हाय मोरी नार की साड़ी पहिन मैं तो ताला गई थी
हाय मोरी नार की धोबी के मन में बसी मेरी साड़ी ॥
हाय मोरी नार की साड़ी पहिन मैं तो कुअँना गई थी
हाय मोरी नार की कहरा के मन में बसी मेरी साड़ी ॥
हाय मोरी नार की साड़ी पहिन मैं तो सड़का गई थी
हाय मोरी नार की बाबू के मन में बसी मेरी साड़ी ॥

hāy morī nār kī salamā sitāre jaṛī merī sāṛī.
hāy morī nār kī sāṛī pahin maiṅ to bāgā gaī thī
hāy morī nār kī maliyā ke man meṅ basī merī sāṛī.
hāy morī nār kī sāṛī pahin maiṅ to tālā gaī thī.

hāy morī nār kī dhobī ke man meṅ basī merī sāṛī.
hāy morī nār kī sāṛī pahin maiṅ to kuañnā gaī thī.
hāy morī nār kī kaharā ke man meṅ basī merī sāṛī.
hāy morī nār kī sāṛī pahin maiṅ to saḍakā gaī thī.
hāy morī nār kī bābū ke man meṅ basī merī sāṛī.

O dear, my *sārī* is all sparkling with colour and stars.
O dear, I went to the garden wearing this *sārī*.
O dear, the gardener fell in love with my *sārī*.
O dear, I went to the pond wearing this *sārī*.
O dear, the washerman fell in love with my *sārī*.
O dear, I went to the well wearing this *sārī*.
O dear, the *kahār* fell in love with my *sārī*.
O dear, I went to the road wearing this *sārī*.
O dear, a gentleman fell in love with my *sārī*.

(LGT: 1989, Nandana)

२३३.

हाय मोरी नार की गगरी में चूर धरी है पिया तुमका
हाय मोरी नार की एक बताशा में हम मेरो लड़का
हाय मोरी नार की ओहू मे चूर धरी है पिया तुमका ॥
हाय मोरी नार की एक रोटी में हम मेरो लड़का
हाय मोरी नार की ओहू में टुकड़ा धरो है पिया तुमका ॥
हाय मोरी नार की एक चदरिया में हम मेरो लड़का
हाय मोरी नार की ओहू में कोना पड़ो है पिया तुमका ॥

hāy morī nār kī gagarī meṅ cūr dharī hai piyā tumakā.
hāy morī nār kī ek batāśā meṅ ham mero laṛakā.
hāy morī nār kī ohū meṅ cūr dharī hai piyā tumakā.
hāy morī nār kī ek roṭī meṅ ham mero laṛakā.
hāy morī nār kī ohū meṅ ṭukaṛā dharo hai piyā tumakā.
hāy morī nār kī ek cadariyā meṅ ham mero laṛakā.
hāy morī nār kī ohū meṅ konā paṛo hai piyā tumakā.

O dear, there are crumbs for you in the earthen pot, dear husband.
O dear, my son and I shared a sugar cake.
O dear, I have saved some crumbs for you, dear husband.
O dear, my son and I shared a bread.
O dear, I have saved a piece for you, dear husband.
O dear, my son and I shared a bed sheet.
O dear, I have saved one corner for you, dear husband.

(LGT: 1989, Nandana)

२३४.

तेरे मुख पे है चँदा चाँदनी मैं बन जाऊँगी
अगर बाग लगाओगे बगीचा मैं लगवाऊँगी
जरा सी देर के लिये मलिनिया मैं बन जाऊँगी॥
अगर ताला खुदाओगे तलैया मैं खुदवाऊँगी
जरा सी देर के लिये धोबिनिया मैं बन जाऊँगी॥
अगर कुअँना खुदाओगे जगतिया मैं बँधवाऊँगी
जरा सी देर के लिये कहरिया मैं बन जाऊँगी

tere mukh pe hai cañdā cāñdanī maiṅ ban jāūñgī.
agar bāg lagāoge bagīcā maiṅ lagavāūñgī.
jarā sī der ke liye maliniyā maiṅ ban jāūñgī.
agar tālā khudāoge talaiyā maiṅ khudavāūñgī.
jarā sī der ke liye dhobiniyā maiṅ ban jāūñgī.
agar kuañnā khudāoge jagatiyā maiṅ bañdhavāūñgī.
jarā sī der liye kahariyā maiṅ ban jāūñgī.

Your face is the moon and I will become a moonbeam.
If you plant a garden, then I will also plant a grove.
For the time being, I will become a gardener's wife.
If you dig a pond, then I will also dig a small pond.
For the time being, I will be a washerwoman.
If you construct a well, then I will construct a platform.
For the time being, I will become a *kahārin*.

(LGT: 1989, Nandana)

२३५.

मेरी पसुरी में मारी हन के कील कमर में मेरे दर्द भई
बारह बरस बम्बइया कमायो पैसा न जानो एक
तेरे झालों पे भई बदनामी कमर में मेरे दर्द भई ॥
बारह बरस बम्बइया कमायो पैसा न जानो एक
तेरी लड़ियों पे भई बदनामी कमर में मेरे दर्द भई ॥
बारह बरस बम्बइया कमायो पैसा न जानो एक
तेरी पायल पे भई बदनामी कमर में मेरे दर्द भई ॥

merī pasurī meṅ mārī han ke kīl kamar meṅ mere dard bhaī.
bārah baras bambaiyā kamāyo paisā n jāno ek.
tere jhāloṅ pe bhaī badanāmī kamar meṅ mere dard bhaī.
bārah baras bambaiyā kamāyo paisā n jāno ek.
terī laḍiyoṅ pe bhaī badanāmī kamar meṅ mere dard bhaī.
bārah baras bambaiyā kamāyo paisā n jāno ek.
terī pāyal pe bhaī badanāmī kamar meṅ mere dard bhaī.

You hit me so hard on my ribs that my back hurts.
You worked for twelve years in Bombay, but I haven't seen a penny.
I am blamed for bringing earrings for you; my back hurts.
You worked for twelve years in Bombay, but I haven't seen a penny.
I am blamed for bringing a necklace for you; my back hurts.
You worked for twelve years in Bombay, but I haven't seen a penny.
I am blamed for bringing ankle ornaments for you; my back hurts.
(LGT: 1989, Nandana)

२३६.

हाय मोरी नार की रातैं डोकर डोकरन ते लड़ी थीं
हाय मोरी नार की डुको कहैं हमें नथुनी बनवाय देव
हाय मोरी नार की डुकरा कहै याकी नाक कटवाय देव ॥
हाय मोरी नार की डुको कहैं हमें झुमकी बनवाय देव
हाय मोरी नार की डुकरा कहैं याके कान कटवाय देव
हाय मोरी नार की डुको कहैं हमें कँगन बनवाय देव

हाय मोरी नार की डुकरा कहै याके हाथ कटवाय देव ॥
हाय मोरी नार की डुको कहैं हमें अँगुठी बनवाय देव
हाय मोरी नार की डुकरा कहै याकी उँगली कटवाय देव ॥

hāy morī nār kī rātaiṅ ḍokar ḍokaran te laṛī thīṅ.
hāy morī nār kī ḍuko kahaiṅ hameṅ nathunī banavāy dev.
hāy morī nār kī ḍukarā khai yākī nāk kaṭavāy dev.
hāy morī nār kī ḍuko kahaiṅ hameṅ jhumakī banavāy dev.
hāy morī nār kī ḍukarā kahaiṅyāke yake kan kaṭavāy dev.
hāy morī nār kī ḍuko kahaiṅ hameṅ kañgan banavāy dev.
hāy morī nār kī ḍukarā kahai yāke hāth kaṭavāy dev.
hāy morī nār kī ḍuko kahaiṅ hameṅ añguṭhī banavāy dev.
hāy morī nār kī ḍukarā kahai yākī uñgalī kaṭavāy dev.

O dear, there was a fight between and old man and his wife at night.
O dear, the old woman asks her husband for a nose ring.
O dear, the old man wants to cutoff her nose.
O dear, the old woman asks her husband for a pair of earrings.
O dear, the old man wants to cutoff her ears.
O dear, the old woman asks her husband for a bracelet.
O dear, the old man wants to cutoff her hands.
O dear, the old woman asks her husband for a ring.
O dear, the old man wants to cutoff her finger.

(LGT: 1989, Nandana)

२३७.

मोहब्बत दूर की अच्छी
अँगूठी सोने की बनवाओ अँगूठी सोने की
नगीना जरा ग्यान का धरवाओ अँगूठी सोने की ॥
हिंडोला बाग में डरवाओ सखी मेरे देश की बुलवाओ ॥
हिंडोला बाग के टूटे सखी मेरे देश की छूटी ॥
मड़ैया हार में डरवाओ यार मेरे देश के बुलवाओ
मड़ैया हार की टूटी यार मेरे देश के छुटे ॥

mohabbat dūr kī acchī.
añgūṭhī sone kī banavāo añgūṭhī sone kī.
nagīnā jarā gyān kā dharavāo añgūṭhī sone kī.
hiṅḍolā bāg meṅ ḍaravāo sakhī mere deś kī bulavāo.
hiṅḍolā bāg ke ṭūṭe sakhī mere deś kī chūṭī.
maṛaiyā hār meṅ ḍaravāo yār mere deś ke bulavāo.
maṛaiyā hār kī ṭūṭī yār mere deś ke chuṭe.

A love affair is good from a distance.
Make me a ring of gold.
Set a jewel of knowledge on this gold ring.
Put a swing in the garden and call my girlfriends from my hometown.
The swing in the garden is broken and the girlfriends from my hometown have been left behind.
Build a cottage in a pasture and invite my boyfriend from my hometown.
The cottage in the pasture is broken and the boyfriend from my hometown has been left behind.

(LGT: 1989, Nandana)

२३८

हाय मोरी नार की आँगन घाट में छैली करिलिया
हाय मोरी नार की ससुरा कहैं बहू तोड़ौ करिलिया
हाय मोरी नार की कैसे के ससुरा मैं तोड़ौ करिलिया
हाय मोरी नार की घूँघटा मार बहू तोड़ौ करिलिया ॥
हाय मोरी नार की जेठा कहैं बहू तोड़ौ करिलिया ॥
हाय मोरी नार की कैसे के जेठा मैं तोड़ौ करिलिया
हाय मोरी नार की घूँघटा मार बहू तोड़ौ करिलिया ॥
हाय मोरी नार की देवरा कहैं भाभी तोड़ौ करिलिया
हाय मोरी नार की कैसे के देवरा मैं तोड़ौ करिलिया
हाय मोरी नार की हँसत खेलत भाभी तोड़ौ करिलिया ॥
हाय मोरी नार की स्वामी कहैं धना तोड़ौ करिलिया
हाय मोरी नार की कैसे के स्वामी मैं तोड़ौ करिलिया
हाय मोरी नार की बहियाँ पकड़ धना तोड़ै करिलिया

hāy morī nār kī āñgan ghāṭ meṅ chailī kariliyā.
hāy morī nār kī sasurā kahaiṅ bahū toṛau kariliyā.
hāy morī nār kī kaise ke sasurā maiṅ toṛau kariliyā.
hāy morī nār kī ghūñghaṭā mār bahū toṛau kariliyā.
hāy morī nār kī jeṭhā kahaiṅ bahū toṛau kariliyā.
hāy morī nār kī kaise jeṭhā maiṅ toṛau kariliyā.
hāy morī nār kī ghūñghaṭā mār bahū toṛau kariliyā.
hāy morī nār kī devarā kahaiṅ bhābhī toṛau kariliyā.
hāy morī nār kī kaise ke devarā maiṅ toṛau kariliyā.
hāy morī nār kī hañsat khelat bhābhī toṛau kariliyā.
hāy morī nār kī svāmī kahaiṅ dhanā toṛau kariliyā.
hāy morī nār kī kaise ke svāmī maiṅ toṛau kariliyā.
hāy morī nār kī bahiyāñ pakaṛ dhanā toṛau kariliyā.

O dear, the bittermelon plant is bearing fruit in the courtyard.
O dear, my *sasur* asks me to pluck bittermelons.
O dear, *sasur* how should I pluck bittermelons?
O dear *bahū*, cover your head and pluck the bittermelons.
O dear, my *jeṭh* asks me to pluck bittermelons.
O dear, *jeṭh*, how should I pluck bittermelons?
O dear *bahū*, cover your head and pluck the bittermelons.
O dear, my *devara* asks me to pluck bittermelons?
O dear *devar*, how should I pluck bittermelons.
O dear *bhābhī*, playfully and happily pluck the bittermelons.
O dear, my husband asks me to pluck bittermelons.
O dear husband, how should I pluck bittermelons?
O dear, wife, hold on to my hands and pluck bittermelons.

(LGT: 1989, Nandana)

२३९.

नेबुला के दोय दोय पात मकनपुर गेंडुवा हो
बरहीं बरस पिया बनज से लौटे बर तरे लये हैं मिलान मकनपुर गेंडुवा हो
बुड्ढी डोकरिया एक कंडा बिनत है मेरे घर कहियो संदेश मकनपुर गेंडुवा हो
निहुर निहुर धना अँगना बटोरैं तेरे पिया मरत पियास मकनपुर गेंडुवा हो

धोय माँज गेंडुवा भरे हो लेव पिया जल नीर मकनपुर गेंडुवा हो
गेंडुवा उतारौ धना भुवैं धरौ कर लेव दुःख सुख बात मकनपुर गेंडुवा हो
माया तुम्हारी पिया बहुत बुरी हैं तुल तुल पिसनो देंय मकनपुर गेंडुवा हो
भाभी तुम्हारी पिया बहुत बुरी हैं गिन गिन लोई देंय मकनपुर गेंडुवा हो ॥
बहिनी तुम्हारी पिया बहुत बुरी हैं गिन गिन टोना देंय मकनपुर गेंडुवा हो ॥
माया निकारे धना न बनै हो घर को बुढ़ापा चलो जाय मकनपुर गेंडुवा हो
भाभी निकारे धना न बनै हो घर को जेठापो चलो जाय मकनपुर गेंडुवा हो
बहिनी निकारे धना न बनै हो आये सजन फिर जाँय मकनपुर गेंडुवा हो
तुमहीं निकारे धना सबै बनै हो घर को शनीचर चलो जाय मकनपुर गेंडुवा हो
हमहीं निकारे पिया न बनै हो तुम रँडुवा होय जाव मकनपुर गेंडुवा हो
लइ कंडा पिया डोलिया हो कोई अगनी दइ देव मकनपुर गेंडुवा हो
लइ पिसनो पिया डोलिया हो कोई पिसनो पीस देव मकनपुर गेंडुवा हो
लइ ललना पिया डोलिया हो कोई कउरा दइ देव मकनपुर गेडुवा

nebulā ke doy doy pāt makanapur geṅḍuvā ho.
barahīṅ baras piyā banaj se lauṭe bar tare laye haiṅ milān makanapur geṅḍuvā ho.
buḍḍhī ḍokariyā ek kaṅḍā binat hai mere ghar kahiyo saṅdeś makanapur geṅḍuvā ho.
nihur nihur dhanā aṅganā baṭoraiñ tere piyā marat piyās makanapur geṅḍuvā ho.
dhoy māñj geṅḍuvā bhare ho lev piyā jal nīr makanapur geṅḍuvā ho.
geṅḍuvā utārau dhanā bhuvaiṅ dharau kar lev duḥkh sukh bāt makanapur geṅḍuvā ho.
māyā tumhārī piyā bahut burī haiṅ tul tul pisano deṅy makanapur geṅḍuvā ho.
bhābhī tumhārī piyā bahut burī haiṅ gin gin loī deṅy makanapur geṅḍuvā ho.
bahinī tumhārī piyā bahut burī haiṅ gin gin ṭonā deṅy makanapur geṅḍuvā ho.
māyā nikāre dhanā n banai ho ghar ko buṛhāpā calo jāy makanapur geṅḍuvā ho.
bhābhī nikāre dhanā n banai ho ghar ko jeṭhāpo calo jāy makanapur geṅḍuvā ho.
bahinī nikāre dhanā n banai ho āye sajan fir jāñy makanapur geṅḍuvā ho.

tumahīṅ nikāre dhanā sabai banai ho ghar ko śanīcar calo jāy makanapur geṅḍuvā ho.
hamahīṅ nikāre piyā n banai ho tum rañḍuvā hoy jāv makanapur geṅḍuvā ho.
lai kaṅḍā piyā ḍoliyā ho koī aganī dai dev makanapur geṅḍuvā ho.
lai pisano piyā ḍoliyā ho koī pisano pīs dev makanapur geṅḍuvā ho.
lai lalanā piyā ḍoliyā ho loī kaurā dai dev makanapur geṅḍuvā ho.

The lemon tree is blossoming [wife is in her prime youth] in Makanpur.
My husband returned after spending twelve years on a business trip and is resting under a tree.
He sent a message to my home through an old woman who was collecting cowdung cakes.
The wife was sweeping the courtyard when the message of her husband's thirst came.
After cleaning the waterpot, she took cool water to her husband to drink.
Put the waterpot down on the ground, O dear wife, and let's talk about your days.
Your mother is very mean as she measures grain for grinding.
Your *bhābhī* is very mean as she counts the balls of bread dough.
Your sister is very mean as she counts all morsels of food.
Dear wife, it will not serve any purpose to ask my mother to leave, because with her the grandeur of old age will go.
Dear wife, it will not serve any purpose to ask my *bhābhī* to leave, becasue with her the seniority of the household will go.
Dear wife, it will not serve any purpose to ask my sister to leave, because her husband would turn around and leave.
Dear wife, all will be well if I ask you to leave, because all the bad luck will leave with you.
Dear husband, it will not serve any purpose to throw me out, as you will become a widower.
Dear husband, you will go with cowdung here and there asking for fire [for your pipe].
Dear husband, you will go here and there with grain to be ground.
Dear husband, you will go here and there with our son asking for food.

(LGT: 1989, Nandana)

अध्याय ५
छुटपुट गीत

केवट गीत

राम केवट संवाद

२४०.

राम लखन सीता सहित आये सुरसरि तीर
प्रेम सने अटपटे बचन कह निषाद गम्भीर॥
कह निषाद गम्भीर नाथ नहिं नाव चढ़ाऊँ
जाने का बाला कि चरण मह समझ न पाऊँ॥
बिकल निषाद दोऊ कर जोड़े ना चाहूँ उतराई
घाट तिहारे जब मैं आवहुँ मोहि उतार्यो साँई॥
बिन पौंवा धोये करिबै न पार हो नवरिया मोरी काठ की बनी
मोरे घरवा का ईहैइ अधार नवरिया मोरी काठ की बनी
गंगा तीरे खड़े पुकारैं केवट के रघुराई हो
बलकल बसन भसम तन धारे सिखा जटा बनाई हो
तापस भेष संगवा लीन्हें लखन और सिया माई हो
कहैं कि जल्दी पार उतारौ चित्रकूट हम जाई हो
भैया जल्दी हमें देहु न उतारि हो नवरिया मोरी काठ की बनी
केवट कहैं सुनहु रघुवर महिमा तुम्हार हम जानी हो
छुवतै चरण शिला भइ नारी साँचै साँच बखानी हो
जानि बूझि के हे स्वामी हम न करिबै नादानी हो
पहिले पाँव पखरिबै लइकै भर कठौतिया पानी हो
तबै गहिबै प्रभू जी पतवार हो नवरिया मोरी काठ की बनी
सुन अटपटी प्रेम की बानी रघुराई हरसाने हो
लखन सिया तन हेरि हेरि के बेरि बेरि मुसकाने हो
सुमिर पुरबुली कथा दुनो जन मन ही मन सकुचाने हो
आयुस पाय कठौता भर जल केवट जल्दी आने हो
प्रभु चरनन लिहेसि पखारि हो नवरिया मोरी काठ की बनी
पार उतर पूँछैं रघुराई कहौ तुम्हैं का देबैं हम

केवट सकुच कहै स्वामी तुमहीं बोलो का लेवैं हम
भवसागर तुम पार करौ नदिया नाला बस खेवैं हम
इहै हमार सत्य उतराई जलम जलम तक सेवैं हम
इहै अरजी का भीख ले हमारि हो नवरिया मोरी काठ की बनी ॥

rām lakhan sītā sahit āye surasari tīr.
prem sane aṭapaṭe bacan kah niṣād gambhir.
kah niṣād gambhīr nāth nahiṅ nāv caḍhāūñ.
jāne kā bālā ki caraṇ mah samaj n pāūñ.
bikal niṣād doū kar joṛe nā cāhūñ utarāī.
ghāṭ tihāre jab maiṅ āvahuñ mohi utāryo sāñī.
bin pauṅvā dhoye karibai na pār ho navariyā morī kāṭh kī banī.
more gharavā kā īhaii adhār navariyā morī kāṭh kī banī.
gaṅgā tīre khaṛe pukārain kevaṭ ke raghurāī ho.
balakal basan bhasam tan dhāre sikhā jaṭā banāī ho.
tāpas bheṣ saṅgavā līnheṅ lakhan aur siyā māī ho.
kahaiṅ ki jaldi pār utārau citrakūṭ ham jāī ho.
bhaiyā jaldī hameṅ dehu n utāri ho navariyā morī kāṭh kī banī.
kevat kahaiṅ sunahu raghuvar mahimā tumhār ham jānī ho.
chuvatai caraṇ śilā bhai nārī sāñcai sāñc bakhānī ho.
jāni būjhi ke he svāmī ham n karibai nādānī ho.
pahile pāñv pakharibai laikai bhar kaṭhautiyā pānī ho.
tabai gahibai prabhū jī patavār ho navariyā morī kāṭh kī banī.
sun aṭapaṭī prem kī bānī raghurāī harasāne ho.
lakhan siyā tan heri heri ke beri beri musakāne ho.
sumir purabulī kathā duno jan man hī man sakucāne ho.
āyus pāy kaṭhautā bhar jal kevaṭ jaldī āne ho.
prabhu caranan lihesi pakhāri ho navariyā morī kāṭh kī banī.
pār utar pūñchaiṅ rahurāī kahau tumhaiṅ kā debaiṅ ham.
kevaṭ sakuc kahai svāmī tumahīṅ bolo kā levaiṅ ham.
bhavasāgar tum pār karau nadiyā nālā bas khevaiṅ ham.
ihai hamār saty utarāī jalam jalam tak sevai ham.
ihai arajī kā bhīkh le hamāri ho navariyā morī kāṭh kī banī.

Ram along with Lakṣmaṇ and Sītā arrived at the bank of the river.
Niṣād [the boatman] seriously spoke in an affectionate but confused manner.
Nisād says that I will not take you on my boat.
I do not understand the mystery of your feet.
With folded hands, uneasy Niṣād says that he is not asking for a fare.
[I am requesting] When I come to ford, O my lord, that you take me across.
Without washing your feet, I will not take you across; my boat is made of wood.
For my household, it is the only support; my boat is made of wood.
Standing on the bank of the Ganges, Rām is calling Kevaṭ, the boatman.
Wearing the bark of tree, body smeared with ashes, and matted hair
In this ascetic garb, he is with Lakṣmaṇ and Sītā.
He is hurrying me to take him across as he is on his way to Citrakūṭ.
O dear brother, take me across quickly; my boat is made of wood.
"I know your grandeur, O Rām," says Kevaṭ.
Touching your feet a rock became a woman, I am speaking the truth.
Knowing all this, I will not act rashly.
First, I will wash your feet in a huge wooden tub.
Only then, will I hold my oars; my boat is made of wood.
Hearing such loving simple talk from Kevaṭ, Rām was amused.
Looking at Lakṣmaṇ and Sītā He smiled.
Remembering this old incident, both of them blushed.
Receiving permission, Kevaṭs hurriedly fetched a wooden tub full of water.
He was able to wash the Lord's feet; my boat is made of wood.
Reaching the other side of the river, Rām asked him what his fare was.
Ashamed, Kevaṭ replied, "you tell me, master, what should I ask?"
I only row across riverlets and river but You carry across the ocean of wordly existence.
"May I serve you life after life, that is my true toll."
"Please accept my humble request." My boat is made of wood.

(LGT: 218R: 1972-73, Kanpur, Boatmen)

अठंग

२४१.

कदम न धरना कुँवर पिछाड़ कर रण दिखाना चामत्कार।
कड़कि कर कहै सुभद्रा नार वीर अभिमन के सामने॥
खाड़ा खोनी कर में धार खा खा के दिल में तू खार
खटाखट बजाना खुब तलवार तुच्छ कौरव के सामने
गरजि कर दुश्मन के आगार गजब का मचाना मारा मार
गरूरी का गरूर कर झार गहरा जमाना अपना रंग
घुस घुस करना वार पै वार धसा धस गिरैं शूर सरदार
घेरे का तोड़ै मेरा कुमार घोर घमसान मचाना जंग
चहुँ दिश चितै चितै बन मान चलाना चोखे चोखे बान
चोटीले हो हो गिरैं जवान भगे रण छोड़ के मन हो दंग
छाँटना छटक छटक कर वीर छटा छट छोड़ भगैं रण को
छिपते फिरैं देखि कर दूर तुम्हारी सकल लड़न हो दंग
जम जम करना वार पै वार जालिमों के जा जा आगार
जा जोरो के करना वार द्रोण बम्हन के सामने॥
झटाझट झोंकी सी खंजर झूमना जिधर जाय सस्तर
झूमते उन्हें पड़े सस्तर ढूँढते फिरैं जयदरथ को
टूटना बाज सरहना भट्ट टिके न कोई सन्मुख सुभट्ट
टुक करना लाल झपट कुँवर दुशासन के रथ को
ठनाठन ठनक ठनक शमशीर ठाठ से चलाना तू रणधीर
ठाठ से चलाना तू रणधीर जा ठुकराना स्वारथ को
डपट गुरु दल का काटना मुण्ड डरे हों हजारों रण में रुण्ड
डर कर भगैं झुण्ड के झुण्ड देख तेरे कुल पुत्तर
ढाल से ढाल अड़ा कर लाल ढहाना ढूँढ ढूँढ बिकाल
ढाढस धर न सकैं भुपाल मेरे लालन से सामने॥
तेगि लै तड़प तड़प के शेर तड़क न करना तहाँ पर देर
तड़ा तड़ काटि काटि के ढेर लगाना रण में वीरों का
थक थक डार डार के सर थकित हो काँपें शेर थरथर
कि थेथर हो हो रण अन्दर पड़ा हो तन रणधीरों का
दनादन दौड़ दौड़ कर शान दिखाना बाणों का उसयान
देखकर दुश्मन हो हैरान लाल ये कमाल तीरों का

धड़ाधड़ अधर्मियों का धाड़ धड़ से धड़ करना पामाल
न दहसत खाना कहीं मजधार नुकीले नेजों का सम्हाल
नीधड़क बेटा करना वार दुश्शासन के सामने ॥
पैने पैने तीरों से लाल पापियों को करना पामाल
पड़े हों हजारों वीर बेहाल तड़पते घायल हों रण में
फँसाना घेरे में द्रगपाल फिर फिर फेर फेर तू डाल
फट फट वीरों का सम्हार करना बरबाद वार क्षण में
बहादुर मेरे वीर धनधार बढ़ बढ़ वीरों का ललकार
बढ़ बढ़ कर करना समर जाके ठुकराना वीरों का
भट रथ जिधर तुम्हारा जाय भय कर वीरों घबराय
भर भर वीर भगे भय खाय कि ऐसा शान रहे रण में
मजा छकके जाय चखाना मार दुष्टों का ढाहाना
मार पे मार मार मचाना दुरजोधन के सामने ॥
यही बातों पर रखना ध्यान यहाँ से जाय युद्ध दरम्यान
यादि ये रहे समर मैदान पीठ दिखलाना न कुँवर
रचा जो व्यहू गुरु महाराज तोड़ना जाकर फाटक आज
रखना बड़े सुवन का लाज तोड़कर व्यहू को करना समर
लाड़िले मेरे लड़ैते पिसर लड़ने को जाना अगर
लड़ना उससे भी बढ़कर न शंका लाना दिल अंदर
वीर क्षत्री का वीर कुँवर वहाँ पर दिखाना चामत्कार
यहँ वहँ वीर भगे भय खाय कि ऐसे शान रहे रण में
समर में होना न आधीर सर से छेदें सारा शरीर
सनासन चलाना अब भी तीर वीर दुष्टन के सामने ॥
हरावे जा दुश्मन के सर हर तरह समेझ अभिमन्यु को
हर्षित हो जावो रण को न देरी करो लाल क्षणभर
राम का रख करके साहारा रामधीन ने उच्चारा
राम चरण धर कर सनद करारा दिखाना अपना कुँवर
जालिम था तंग ककहरा साजा जानते हो तो समर में आजा
नहिं जाओ जल्दी लै बाजा पकड़ौ घर की डगर
मिसरा बनाया राजाराम मकान पदुमनाथपुर ग्राम
कि चोखू नित्य नया कालाम कहे भगवन के सामने ॥

kadam n dharanā kuñvar pichāṛ kar raṇ dikhānā cāmatkār.
kaṛaki kar kahai subhadrā nār vīr abhiman ke sāmane.
khāṛā khonī kar meṅ dhār khā khā ke dil meṅ tū khār.
khatākhaṭ bajānā khub talavār tucch kaurav ke sāmane.

garaji kar duśman ke āgār gajab kā macānā mārạ mār.
garūrī kā garūr kar jhār gaharā jamānā apanā raṅg.
ghus ghus karanā vār pai vār dhasā dhas giraiṅ śūr saradār.
ghere kā toṛai merā kumār ghor ghamasān macānā jaṅg.
cahuñ diś citai citai ban mān calānā cokhe cokhe bān.
coṭīle ho ho girain javān bhage raṇ choṛ ke man ho daṅg.
chāñṭanā chaṭak chaṭak kar vīr chaṭā chaṭ choṛ bhagain raṇ ko.
chipate phirain dekhi kar dūr tumhārī sakal laṛan ho daṅg.
jam jam karanā vār pai vār jālimoṅ ke jā jā āgār.
jā joro ke karanā vār droṇ bamhan ke sāmane.
jhaṭājhaṭ jhoṅkī sī khaṅjar jhūmanā jidhar jāy sastar.
jhūmate unheṅ paṛe sastar ḍhūñḍhate phiraiṅ jayadarath ko.
ṭūṭanā bāj sarahanā bhaṭṭ ṭike n koī sanmukh subhaṭṭ.
ṭuk karanā lāl jhapaṭ kuñvar duśāsan ke rath ko.
ṭhanāṭhan ṭhanak ṭhanak śamaśīr ṭhāṭh se calānā tū raṇadhīr.
ṭhāṭh se calānā tū raṇadhīr jā ṭhukarānā svārath ko.
ḍapaṭ guru dal kā kāṭanā muṇḍ ḍare hoṅ hajāroṅ raṇ meṅ ruṇḍ.
ḍar kar bhagaiṅ jhuṇḍ ke jhuṇḍ dekh tere kul puttar.
ḍhāl se ḍhāl aṛā kar lāl ḍhahānā dūñdh dūñdh bikāla.
ḍhāḍhas dhar n sakaiṅ bhupāl mere lālan ke sāmane.
tegi lai taṛap taṛap ke śer taṛak n karanā tahāñ par der.
taṛā taṛa kāṭi kāṭi ke ḍher lagānā raṇ meṅ vīroṅ kā.
thak thak ḍār ḍār ke sar thakit ho kāñpeṅ śer tharathar.
ki thethar ho ho raṇ andar paṛā to tan raṇadhīroṅ kā.
danādan dauṛ dauṛ kar śāna dikhānā bāṇoṅ kā usayān.
dekhakar duśman ho hairān lāl ye kamāl tīroṅ kā.
dhaṛādhaṛ adharmiyoṅ kā dhāṛ dhaṛ se dhaṛ karanā pāmāl
n dahasat khānā kahīṅ majadhār nukīle nejoṅ kā samhāl.
nīdhaṛak beṭā karanā vār duśśāsan ke sāmane.
paine paine tīroṅ se lāl pāpiyoṅ ko karanā pāmāl.
paṛe hoṅ hajāroṅ vīr behāl taṛapate ghāyal hoṅ raṇ meṅ.
phañsānā ghere meṅ dragapāl phir phir pher pher tū ḍāl.
phaṭ phaṭ vīroṅ kā samhār karanā barabād vār kṣaṇ meṅ.
bahādur mere vīr dhanadhār baṛh baṛh vīroṅ kā lalakār.
baṛh baṛh kar karanā samar jāke ṭhukarānā vīroṅ kā.
bhaṭ rath jidhar tumhārā jāy bhay kar vīroṅ ghabarāy.

bhar bhar vīr bhage bhay khāy ki aisā śān rahe raṇ meṅ.
majā chakake jāy cakhānā mār duṣṭoṅ kā ḍhāhānā.
mār pe mār mār macānā durajodhan ke sāmane.
yahī bātoṅ par rakhanā dhyān yahāñ se jāy yuddh daramyān.
yādi ye rahe samar maidān pīṭh dikhalānā n kuñvar.
racā jo vyahū guru mahārāj toṛanā jākar phāṭak āj.
rakhanā baṛe suvan kā lāj toṛakar vyahū ko karanā samar.
lāṛile mere laṛaite pisar laṛane ko jānā agar.
laṛanā usase bhī baṛhakar n śaṅkā lānā dil aṅdar.
vīr kṣatrī kā vīr kuñvar vahāñ par dikhānā cāmatkār.
yahañ vahañ vīr bhage bhay khāy ki aise śān rahe raṇ meṅ.
samar meṅ honā n ādhīr sar se chedeṅ sārā śarīr.
sanāsan calānā ab bhī tīr vīr duṣṭan ke sāmane.
harāve jā duśman ke sar har tarah samejh abhimanyu ko.
harṣit ho jāvo raṇ ko n derī karo lāl kṣaṇabhar.
rām kā rakh karake sāhārā rāmadhīn ne uccārā.
rām caraṇ dhar kar sanad karārā dikhānā apanā kuñvar.
jālim thā taṅg kakaharā sājā jānate ho to samar meṅ ājā.
nahiṅ jāo jaldī lai bājā pakaṛau ghar kī ḍagar.
misarā banāyā rājārām makān padumanāthapur grām.
ki cokhū nity nayā kālām kahe bhagavan ke sāmane.

Do not retreat, my dear child and show your miracles on the battlefield.
Thus forcefully says mother Subhadrā preparing her son, Abhimanyu, for the battle.
With your sharp swords and with great envy.
Display you wonderful swordmanship in front of worthless Kauravas.
Shouting in front of enemy, make wrathful killing.
Destroying the ego of egoist, you must establish your superiority.
Penetrate, attack and kill warriors and generals in the enemy line.
My young prince, break the enemy formation and wage a fierce battle.
Look in all directions, shoot your sharp arrow.
Wounded warriors fall and run frightended from the battlefield.
Selecting warriors, you attack them so that they flee from the battlefield.
Seeing your wonderful chivalrous art, the enemy flees.

Appearing in front of them, dispatch solid blows.
Fiercely attack in front of the brāhmaṇ Droṇ.
Display your quick moves with a dagger wherever the warriors run.
As they move, attack them and make them look for General Jayadrath.
Attack the enemy like a hawk so that none can stand to face you.
Break Duśāsan's chariot to pieces.
Linking with enemy swords O great warrier, let your sword dance.
Move with agility and kick the self-interested enemy.
Cut the heads of your teacher's army and cover the ground with thousands of headless bodies.
Scores of enemy warriors will flee upon seeing you art.
Propping your shield with enemy shields, make them lose feet.
The kings in the enemy line will lose their confidence to withstand you my son.
With electricity move your sword without delay.
Cutting enemy's head, make a heap on the battlefield.
Make the enemy exhausted and tired so they tremble in front of a lion
The whole battlefield should be covered with slain bodies.
In quick succession display the battery of arrows.
The enemy will be confounded upon seeing your wonderful display of archery.
Cutoff the heads of these deceitful enemies.
Don't become fearful in the middle of the battlefield and steady yourself from sharp spears.
Attack fearlessly, facing Duḥśāsan, my son.
With your sharp arrows, my dear child, make the sinful disappear.
Let there be thousands of wounded warriors on the battlefield.
Entrap Dragpal by encircling him.
Without delay, destroy the enemy's attack and kill them.
O my strong and virtuous warrior, step up and challenge the enemy warriors.
Agressively fight and strike at the warriors.
Whichever way your chariot goes, the enemy will be filled with fear.
Display such dignity on the battlefield that the warriors will run in panic.
Destroy these evil people and make them suffer the consequences.
Raise havoc of killing in front of Duryodhan.
Keep these advices in mind when you are on the battlefield.

Remember not to show your back on the battleground.
Break the gate of the battle tactics which respected teacher has arranged.
Keep the honour of elders by breaking the battle tactics and fight.
O my dear warrior son, go to battle.
Fight with conviction and do not let doubt enter your mind.
You are a son of a great warrior, so show your wonders there.
Make warriors run here and there, display such dignity.
Don't panic during war even if your whole body is pierced.
Even then, keep shooting your arrows at the evil warriors.
Go and defeat the enemy, thus [she] explained to Abhimanyu.
Go happily to the battlefield; do not delay even for a moment.
Have trust in Rām, thus said Rāmdhīn [the composer].
Keeping your authority in Rām, show your valour, dear prince.
This alphabet song was tough and if you know it then come to war.
Otherwise take your instrument and go home immediately.
This poetry was composed by Rājārām who lives in village Padumnāthpur.
Cokhu sings new poetry in front of god everyday.

(LGT: 219R: 1972-73, Kanpur, Boatmen)

चूँदर

२४२.

आयन गौने के परवाना तू तो हौ रंगरेज सयाना ॥
चूँदर तोसे एक रंगवाना हम ससुरारी जाबै ना
ऐसा रंग भरि दो दिलदार ढूँढे दोऊ जहाँ बाजार
पावैं नगद न उधार हम बलिहारी जाबै ना
सेवती चम्पा चमेली गुल चवन कचनार हो
सुरजमुखी कन्दैल कसरैया बेला खुसबूदार हो
सुरपती और गणपती और द्रोपदी अस नार हो
गणपती के संग में अरे लक्ष्मी तैयार हो
बेंदी राशि फूल औ चँदवा मजेदार राहै
ऐरन झुप्पेदार रहै करन फूल सिंगार राहै ना

गजानन कानन कुँडल पहिरे झलकदार राहै
चूहा पर सवार रहै कर लीहे कुठार राहै ना
अवध के सारा नक्शा सरजू निकट धार राहै
रामचन्द्र अवतार राहै दशरथ के घर बार राहै
कि देवन चढ़ विमान पर दशरथ का तैयार राहै
घर घर मंगलचार राहै अनहद के झँकार राहै ना
कौशिल गोदि खिलावै ललना लइके सुरज मनावै अँगना
बैठी झुला रही हैं ललना उनपे बारी जाबै ना॥
नारद का बीन बाजै गन्धर्वों का गान हो
सनकादिक मिरदंग बजावैं अप्सरों की तान हो
सरस्वती सीतार लेकर मोर पर सावार हो
बेद पढ़त ब्रह्मा रहैं और शिष्ट का परचार हो
अंडज पिंडज कुमज ये चारौ परकार राहैं
अस्थावर तैयार राहैं लखि चौरासी धार राहैं ना
गुरुनाम की नौका सत कै खेवनहार राहैं
मगर और घड़ियाल राहैं केछुवा खोपड़ेदार राहैं ना
लहर के अजो अजो पर मछरी एकातार राहै
पढ़िना मोछेदार रहैं केंकड़ा वेक पार रहैं
छापौ गंगा जमुना सुरस्ती की धार राहै
किला अछयबट दार राहै झँडा पँडेदार राहै ना
छापौ गदा लिहे हनुमाना औ फिर भी भरद्वाज अस्थाना
बासुकी का जानै जमाना हम हितकारी जाबै ना॥
चूँदरी में चित्र आला कृष्ण का परिचार हो
रहस लीला भी रहे और कुबरी तैयार हो
जमुना जी के निकट पर चढ़े कदम की डार हो
मुरली टेरत रहें और जल में नँगी नार हो
दाँत चूँदरी में कुबला के उखारि रहैं, पूतना का मारि रहैं,
कँसा का पछारि रहैं ना
छाप चूँदरी में वैद्यमान वारी रहैं, रूप मनिहारी रहैं
ललिता हाथि पसारि राहैं ना
छापौ कहीं कहीं पर नग पर गिरवरधारी राहैं
गज के प्राण उबारि राहैं गरुड़ पीठ सवारि राहैं ना
चूनर रहि है जो गल ताना एकौ चलिहैं ना बाहाना
देइहैं ससुरे में ताना हम तो मारी जाबै ना॥
जनक रहे स्वयंवर रहे और धनुष का विस्तार हो
विश्वामित्र लछिमन रहैं और राम तोड़नदार हो

जानकी जयमाल डाले फूलों की बौछार हो
टूटी धनुष का देखि कर परशुराम का खार हो
छापौ सिया हरण और रावण के दरवार राहैं
लंका सुमिरन दार राहैं समुन्दर वह पार राहैं ना
राम का सेतुबंध के कटक सहित वो पार राहैं
घेर चारौ द्वार राहैं लड़ने को तैयार राहैं ना
चकई तोता मैना सारस चोटीदार राहैं
छापौ कहीं कहीं पर रावण का सँघार राहै
बाघ सिंह सिंयार राहैं मिरगा सुवरणदार राहैं ना
छबि चूँदर में दिखलाना करैं ससुरे में सराहना
देखि कर मोहै सकल जमाना पिउ की प्यारी जाबै ना॥
चक्रव्यहू द्रोण रच्यो कि भीष्म रक्षाकार हो
करण सकुनी दिरजोधन जयदरथ भी तैयार हो
बीच में छापो कहीं कहीं अभिमन्यु लड़ने का तैयार हो
धोखे से हथियार छीना फिर भी मारा मार हो
रचि दो अंचल ऊपर शिव जी की बारात राहै
बीच में समुद्र मथन चौदहो रत्न जहिरात रहैं
मोहनी रूप देखात रहै केतनन बीना माथ राहैं ना
सोहागिन पहिन के चूँदर पिउ के घरवा जात राहै
दुश्मन देख घबड़ात राहै सोचै औ पछतात राहै ना
छापौ रामधीन भगवान गुरु एक साथ राहैं
कजरी में जहरात राहैं बैरी से अलगात राहैं ना
देखो सोच समझकर गाना और चूँदरी सी रंग मिलाना
नजर न चोखे से मिलाना नहिं निकारी जाबै ना॥

āyan gaune ke paravānā tū to hau raṅgarej sayānā.
cūñdar tose ek raṅgavānā ham sasurārī jābai nā.
aisā raṅg bhari do diladār ḍhūñḍhe doū jahāñ bājār.
pāvaiṅ nagad n udhār ham balihārī jābai nā.
sevatī campā camelī gul cavan kacanār ho.
surajamukhī kaṅdail kasaraiyā belā khusabūdār ho.
surapatī aur ganapatī aur dropadī as nār ho.
gaṇapatī ke saṅg meṅ are lakṣmī taiyār ho.
beṅdī rāśi phūl au cañdavā majedār rāhai.
airan jhuppedār rahai karan phūl siṅgār rāhai nā.
gajānan kānan kuñḍal pahire jhalakadār rāhai.

cūhā par savār rahai kar līhe kuṭhār rāhai nā.
avadh ke sārā nakśā sarajū nikaṭ dhār rāhai.
rāmacandr avatār rāhai daśarath ke ghar bār rāhai.
ki devan caṛh vimān par daśarath kā taiyār rāhai.
ghar ghar maṅgalacār rāhai anahad ke jhañkār rāhai nā.
kauśil godi khilāvai lalanā laike suraj manāvai añganā.
baiṭhī jhulā rahī haiṅ lalanā unape bārī jābai nā.
nārad kā bīn bājai gandharvoṅ kā gān ho.
sanakādik miradaṅg bajāvaiṅ apsaroṅ kī tān ho.
sarasvatī sītār lekar mor par sāvār ho.
bed paṛhat brahmā rahaiṅ aur śiṣṭ kā paracār ho.
aṇḍaj piṇḍaj kumaj ye cārau parakār rāhaiṅ
asthāvar taiyār rāhaiṅ lakhi caurāsī dhār rāhaiṅ nā.
gurunām kī naukā sat kai khevanhār rāhaiṅ.
magar aur ghaṛiyāl rāhaiṅ kechuvā khopaṛedār rāhaiṅ nā.
lahar ke ajo ajo par macharī ekātār rāhai.
paṛhinā mochedār rahaiṅ keṅkaṛā vek pār rahaiṅ.
chāpau gaṅgā, jamunā surastī kī dhār rāhai.
kilā achayabaṭ dār rāhai jhañḍā pañḍedār rāhai nā.
chāpau gadā lihe hanumānā au phir bhī bharadvāj asthānā.
bāsukī kā jānai jamānā ham hitakārī jābai nā.
cuñdarī meṅ citr ālā kṛṣṇ kā paricār ho.
rahas līlā bhī rahe aur kubarī taiyār ho.
jamunā jī ke nikaṭ par caṛhe kadam kī ḍāṛ ho.
muralī ṭerat raheṅ aur jal meṅ naṅgī nār ho.
dāñt cūñdarī meṅ kubalā ke ukhāri rahaiṅ, pūtanā kā māri rahaiṅ.
kañsā kā pachāri rahaiṅ nā.
Chāp cuñdarī meṅ vaiddhamān vārī rahaiṅ, rūp manihārī rahaiṅ.
lalitā hāthi pasāri rāhaiṅ nā.
chāpau kahīṅ kahīṅ par nag par giravaradhārī rāhaiṅ.
gaj ke prāṇ ubāri rāhaiṅ garuṛ pīṭh savāri rāhaiṅ nā.
cūnar rahi hai jo gal tānā ekau calihaiṅ nā bāhānā.
deihaiṅ sasure meṅ tānā ham to mārī jābai nā.
janak rahe svayaṁvar rahe aur dhanuṣ kā vistār ho.
viśvāmitr lachiman rahaiṅ aur rām toṛanadār ho.
jānakī jayamāl ḍāle phūloṅ kī bauchār ho.

ṭuṭī dhanuṣ ka dekhi kar paraśurām kā khār ho.
chāpau siyā haraṇ aur rāvaṇ ke daravār rāhaiṅ.
laṅkā sumiran dār rāhaiṅ samundar vah pār rāhaiṅ nā.
rām kā setubaṅdh ke kaṭak sahit vo pār rāhaiṅ.
gher cārau dvār rāhaiṅ laṛane ko taiyār rāhaiṅ nā.
cakaī totā mainā sāras coṭidār rāhaiṅ.
chāpau kahīṅ kahīṅ par rāvaṇ kā saṅghār rāhai.
bāgh siṁh siṅyār rāhaiṅ miragā suvaraṇadār rāhaiṅ nā.
chabi cūñdar meṅ dikhalānā karaiṅ sasure meṅ sarāhanā.
dekhi kar mohai sakal jamānā piu kī pyārī jābai nā.
cakravyahū droṇ racyo ki bhīṣm rakṣākār ho.
karaṇ sakunī dirajodhan jayadarath bhī taiyār ho.
bīc meṅ chāpo kahīṅ kahīṅ abhimanyu laṛane kā taiyār ho.
dhokhe se hathiyār chīnā phir bhī mārā mār ho.
raci do añcal ūpar siv jī kī bārāt rāhai.
bīc meṅ samudr mathan caudaho ratn jahirāt rahaiṅ.
mohanī rūp dekhāt rahai ketanan bīnā māth rāhaiṅ nā.
sohāgin pahin ke cūñdar piu ke gharavā jāt rāhai.
duśman dekh ghabaṛāt rāhai socai au pachatāt rāhai nā.
chāpau rāmadhīn bhagavān guru ek sāth rāhaiṅ.
kajarī meṅ jaharāt rāhaiṅ bairī se alagāt rāhaiṅ nā.
dekho soc samajhakar gānā aur cūñdarī sī raṅg milānā.
najar n cokhe se milānā nahiṅ nikārī jābai nā.

Messenger for my *gaunā* has come and you are a clever dyer.
I want a scarf dyed by you as I am leaving for my in-laws.
Dye it so beautiful that no one can find its like in both worlds' market.
No one can find it whether they pay cash or credit; I sacrifice to you.
Dye white rose, *campā,* jasmine, rose *cavan* (?), *kacanār*.
Colour beautiful sunflower, plantain, *kasaraiyā* (?), and jasmine.
Dye king of gods, Gaṇeś and woman like Draupadī.
Together with Gaṇeś Lakṣmī should be ready.
There should be a worship area with flowers and attractive canopy.
All kinds of jewellery should be there for make up.
In Gaṇeś's ears there should be shining earrings.
Riding on his mouse and carrying his axe.

Include a map of Avadh and the banks of river Sarayū.
Colour the story of Rām's incarnation and Daśaratha's household.
Daśaratha's preparation and observance by gods riding on their aerial vehicles.
Scenes of households singing congratulatory songs and wonderful music all around.
Kauśilyā playing with her son on her lap and worshipping the sun from her courtyard.
Sitting, she is putting her baby to sleep; May I sacrifice to her.
Sage Nārada playing his vīṇā and celestial musicians singing.
Angels singing songs to the accompaniment of Brahmā's son playing drum.
Riding on a peacock, Sarasvatī with her *sitār*.
Brahmā reading his Veda and propagating his creation.
Create all four types of creatures, born from an egg, born with life from the womb, and *kumaj* (?)
Asthavara (?) in readiness and eightyfour streams.
In the boat of Guru's name may there be the rower of truth.
Add crocodiles and turtles as well.
There should be a row of fish in the crest of each wave.
Fish with whiskers and many crabs.
Print Gaṅgā, Jamunā, and Sarasvatī rivers.
Also, add fort of Akṣayvaṭ and flags of priest.
Print Hanumān with his mace and the hermitage of Bharadvāj.
Everybody knows Vāsukī, chief of serpents; may I be kind to all.
In my scarf, there should a painting of Kṛṣṇa.
Add Kṛṣṇa's circular dance and Kubarī.
Depict, [Kṛṣṇa] sitting on a branch of a *kadam* tree on the bank of the Yamunā river.
Playing his music and [watching] naked women in the water.
[Print, Kṛṣṇa] taking out Kubalā's teeth and killing Pūtanā.
and defeating Kans
Print [Kṛṣṇa] as a doctor and bangle seller,
and Lalitā spreading her hands [for you to feel].
Print here and there Kṛṣṇa on snake's head.
Saving the life of the elephant and riding on the back of Garuḍ.
With such scarf on your body, one would not be able to make any excuse.

I will be an object of envy at my in-law's place.
There should be Janak, marriage [of Sītā] and details of bow.
Paint Viśvāmitra, Lakṣmaṇ and Rām breaking the bow.
Sītā putting the victory garland on Rām amidst a rain of flowers.
Show the anger of Paraśurām when he sees the broken bow.
Print, Sītā's abduction and the court of Rāvaṇ.
Print golden Laṅkā across the ocean.
Rām crossing the ocean with his monkey army over the bridge.
[His army] circling all the four gates and ready for a fight.
[Print] goose, parrot, starling and crane.
Print here and there killing of Rāvaṇa.
[Print] lion, tiger, jackal and golden deer.
Show your talent in my scarf so that it is praised at my in-law's place.
Let the whole world become enchanted looking at it; I will be a sweetheart to my husband.
[Print] Droṇa's strategical battle plan and Bhīṣm as its defender.
Show warriors like Karṇa, Śakunī, Duryodhan and Jayadrath ready for war.
Print at the centre, Abhimanyu ready for battle.
[Print] deceit by which [Abhimanyu's] weapons were spoiled and yet he fought.
At the border, paint the wedding party of Śiva.
At the centre, display the churning of the ocean and all the fourteen gems.
[Viṣṇu] in the form of a woman and deceiving many.
Wearing such a scarf, a married woman going to her husband's home.
Seeing [such a beautiful woman], all are envious and regretful [not realising devotion].
Print Guru Rāmdhin and god together.
Find jewels in singing [in praise of god] and remove oneself from enemies.
Sing with understanding matching the colours of the scarf.
Don't make eye contact with Cokhe [the singer] otherwise you will be thrown away.

(LGT: 221R: 1972-73, Kanpur, Boatmen)

राधा बिलाप

२४३.

कहती राधे जी बिलखाई कहवाँ गइले कुँवर कन्हाई,
पूँछें पेड़ बिरिछ से जाई बिन्द्रावन के सामने॥
ख्याल कर करील तू बतला दे हमरा श्याम तुही दिखलादे
चलकर बतादे प्यारे बिलख कहूँ बिरछन के सामने
गलती मत करना शहतूत साँची बता श्याम करतूत
कहवाँ गये नन्द के पूत चलौ बतलाने के लिये
घटिया न बनना तू आम कपट तज बता हमारा श्याम
उन बिन व्याकुल है ब्रजबाम अंग लगाने के लिये
चंचल चिहुक चितै चहुँओर निम्बू बता मेरा चितचोर
कटहल पैयाँ लागूँ तोर चलौ समझाने के लिये
छकाना न हमको आनार नहीं जस भूलूँगी तुम्हार
किधर को गये सजन हमार हमें ढुंढवाने के लिये
जल्दी जामुन दो बतलाई कैसे दर्श श्याम का पाई
मेंहदी बैठी मुँह छिपाई चल कदमन के सामने॥
झँझट हमरा दूर कराओ पाकड़ तुही भला बतलाओ
चलो मिलाओ दाया करके हमरा श्याम हे सुन्दर
टालो न खिन्नी और बेर बताओ जल्दी करो न देर
कहवाँ रहे मुरलिया टेर आज खाली मधुबन
खड़ी करती बिचार बता दे तू बरगद के झाड़
कित को गये सजन हमार छोड़ हमरा गोहन
डाट कर बोले बैन अस मोल काँधा हैं गूजर के फूल
बिरहा मारै जिया में हूल जरै हमरा बदन
ढंग कुछ नीम थकित बतलावै जिससे श्यामसुन्दर मिल जावै
बँसिया फूँक कै बजावै सब सखियन के सामने॥
तलपत मीन बिना जल नीर महुआ तुही बता जदबीर
कहाँ गै दिल के दावनगीर ढूँढन कहवाँ जाऊँ मैं
थकित होती हूँ खम्माज बता दे नन्द सुवन का साँच
बाँच कर बता दे प्यारे दिल दिलवर से नेह लगाऊँ मैं
दया कर अमरूद नवीना मोहन कहाँ बजाते बीना
गाफिल प्रतिदिन बदन मलीना कैसन पाऊँ मैं

धरकर धीर संतरा बोल तेरी सूरत है अनमोल
सुना दे श्यामसुन्दर का बोल गले लगाऊँ मैं
नाम का पता सेब बतलाना औ देखा हो तो नहीं छिपाना
दिखाते नहीं निठुर दीवाना इन नैनन के सामने॥
पता का बतलादे नवरंगी कित को गये रहस के ढंगी
संगी लरकइयाँ के छोड़ चल्यो सजनवा ना
फालसा संकट दूर कराओ हमरा श्याम तुही मिलाओ
न छिपाओ मानो मोरा तू कहनवा ना
बहाना करो न नासेपाती औ कित को गये मोर संघाती
पछताती बिना काँधा तोर सवनवा ना
भर आवाज लगाया नारा कित को गये हमारा प्यारा
तुही बतादे हरसिंगार सोचै मनवा मा
माँगन यहै बिरिछ आशोका औ तेरी जस फैली चहुँ लोका
मोका बतादे प्यारे मैं जाऊँ साजन के सामने॥
यहाँ से गये सजन हामार बेला जुही अदर मदार
गेंदा गुलाब खुशबुदार तेरी बलिहारी जाबै ना
राह तू केवड़ा बतलाई बेल से पूँछत है अकुलाई
काहे अब देरी लगाई पास गिरधारी जाबै ना
लतर नरगिस की नुकीली डार मदीना सुनि ले वचन हमार
कन्दैल सुरजमुखी बलिहार तेरी हितकारी जाबै ना
सफा बतलादे गल तोरइया तूने देखा कुँवर कन्हैया
नेवाड़ी तुही नहीं बतलइया किस फुलवारी जाबै ना
हर ते नेह लगा पछताती निराश हो फिर घर जाती
कि चोखे कहैं श्याम बिन घबड़ाती भावन के सामने॥

kahatī rādhe jī bilakhāī kahavāñ gaile kuñvar kanhāī.
pūñcheṅ peṛ birich se jāī bindrāban ke sāmane.
khyāl kar karīl tū batalā de hamarā śyām tuhī dikhalāde.
calakar batāde pyāre bilakh kahūñ birachan ke sāmane.
galatī mat karanā śahatūt sāñcī batā śyām karatūt.
kahavāñ gaye nand ke pūt calau batalāne ke liye.
ghatiyā n bananā tū ām kapaṭ taj batā hamārā śyām.
un bin vyākul hai brajabām aṅg lagāne ke liye.
cañcal cihuk citai cahuñor nimbū batā merā citacor.
kaṭahal paiyāñ lāgūñ tor calau samajhāne ke liye.
chakānā n hamako ānār nahīṅ jas bhūlūñgī tumhār.

kidhar ko gaye sajan hamār hameṅ ḍhunḍhavāne ke liye.
jaldī jāmun do batalāī kaise darś śyām kā pāī.
meṅhadī baiṭhī muñh chipāī cal kadaman ke sāmane.
jhañjhaṭ hamarā dūr karāo pākaṛ tuhī bhalā batalāo.
calo milāo dāyā karake hamarā śyām he sundar.
ṭālo n khinnī aur ber batāo jaldī karo n der.
kahavāñ rahe muraliyā ṭer āj khālī madhuban.
khaṛī karatī bicār batā de tū baragad ke jhāṛ.
kit ko gaye sajan hamār choṛ hamarā gohan.
ḍāt kar bole bain as mol kāñdhā haiṅ gūjar ke phūl.
birahā mārai jiyā meṅ hūl jarai hamarā badan.
dhaṅg kuch nīm thakit batalāvai jisase śyāmasundar mil jāvai.
bañsiyā phūñk kai bajāvai sab sakhiyan ke sāmane.
talapat mīn binā jal nīr mahuā tuhī batā jadabīr.
kahāñ gai dil ke dāvanagīr ḍhuñḍhan kahavāñ jāūñ maiṅ.
thakit hotī hūñ khammāj batā de nand suvan kā sāñc.
bāñc kar batā de pyāre dil dilavar se neh lagāūñ maiṅ.
dayā kar amarūd navīnā mohan kahāñ bajāte bīnā.
gāphil pratidin badan malīnā kaisan pāūñ maiṅ.
dharakar dhīr saṅtarā bol terī sūrat hai anamol.
sunā de śyāmasundar kā bol gale lagāūñ maiṅ.
nāma kā patā seb batalānā au dekhā ho to nahīn chipānā.
dikhāte nahīṅ niṭhur dīvānā in nainan ke sāmane.
patā kā batalāde navaraṅgī kit ko gaye rahas ke ḍhaṅgī.
saṅgī larakaiyāñ ke choṛ calyo sajanavā nā.
phālasā saṅkat dūr karāo hamarā śyām tuhī milāo.
n chipāo māno morā tū kahanavā nā.
bahānā karo n nāsepātī au kit ko gaye mor saṅghātī.
pachatātī binā kāñdhā tor savanavā nā.
bhar āvāj lagāyā nārā kit ko gaye hamārā pyārā.
tuhī batāde harasiṅgār socai manavā mā.
mañgan yahai birich āśokā au terī jas phailī cahuñ lokā.
mokā batāde pyāre maiṅ jāūñ sājan ke sāmane.
yahāñ se gaye sajan hāmār belā juhī adar madār.
geṅdā gulāb khuśabūdār terī balihārī jābai nā.
rāh tū kevaṛā batalāī bel se pūñchat hai akulāī.

kāhe ab derī lagāī pās giradhārī jābai nā.
latar naragis kī nukīlī ḍār madīnā suni le bacan hamār.
kandail surajamukhī balihār terī hitakārī jābai nā.
saphā batalāde gal toraiyā tūne dekhā kuñvar kanhaiyā.
nevāṛī tuhī nahīṅ batalaiyā kis phulavārī jābai nā.
har te neh lagā pachatātī nirāś ho phir ghar jātī.
ki cokhe kahaiṅ śyām bin ghabaṛātī bhāvan ke sāmane.

Weeping, Rādhā is asking, "where is my Kṛṣṇa.
She is asking trees and bushes all over Vṛndāvan.
Think, O bitter gourd and show me my Kṛṣṇa.
Come and tell me O dear, I beg you in front of all the trees.
Don't make a mistake, O mulberry and tell me the true doing of Kṛṣṇa.
Come with me to tell where Nand's son has gone.
Don't be cheap, O mango, without any trick tell me of Kṛṣṇa.
Without him this woman of Braj is longing to embrace him.
O clever lemon look around and tell me where is my heart-stealer.
O jackfruit, I touch your feet, come with me to convince him.
Don't tease me pomegranate otherwise I will forget your popularity.
Where has my husband gone making me search for him.
Hurry up jāmun and tell me how to see my Kṛṣṇa.
Don't hide your face henna, come in front of *kadam* trees.
Come fig and decide our skirmish and tell me.
Be kind and help me meet my dear Kṛṣṇa.
Come *khinnī* and berry and don't be evasive.
Where is He playing his flute? The Madhuban is empty today.
O banyan bush tell me as I stand here thinking.
Where has my husband gone leaving my company.
Kṛṣṇa is like the flower of *gūjar*, she said angrily.
This separation is paining my heart and my whole body is burning.
O, *nīm* tell me some way so that, tired as I am, I might find my Kṛṣṇa.
He could play his flute in front of all girlfriends.
I am restless like a fish without water; at least you, O *mahuā*, tell me some trick.
Where is the claimant of my heart and where should I search for him.

I am getting tired, O Khammāj (?) so tell the true whereabouts of the son of Nand.
O dear, calculate and tell me so that I can love my darling.
O guava, kindly tell me where Kr̥ṣṇa is playing his flute.
I am becoming senseless and my body is spoiled; how can I find him?
Peacefully, speak, O priceless-faced orange.
Let me hear Kr̥ṣṇa's voice so that I can hug him.
O apple tell me his whereabouts as you have seen him then don't hide.
Heartless [Kr̥ṣṇa] is not in front of my eyes.
O tangerine tell me which way the circular dance expert has gone.
My lover has left his childhood friends and has gone.
O *phālasā*, please remove my trouble and help me meet my Kr̥ṣṇa.
Don't hide and listen to my request.
O pear, don't make excuses but [tell me] which way my companion has gone.
O Kr̥ṣṇa, your moon is grieving without you.
"Which way has my dear gone," thus I shouted.
O *hārasiṅgār*, think in your heart and tell me.
O *aśok* tree, you are known in all four directions; I request only this.
O dear, tell me so that I come face to face with my husband.
My husband has gone from here, O dẹar jasmine, *jūhī*, *adār* and *madār*.
O fragrant marigold and rose, I sacrifice to you.
O *kevaṛā* and *bel*, confused, I ask you for guidance.
Why delay, I want to go near Kr̥ṣṇa.
O creeper *naragis* and *madīnā*, listen to my statement.
O well-wisher, plantain and sunflower, I will be obliged.
Tell me frankly, O zucchini, if you have seen my darling Kr̥ṣṇa.
Nevārī (?), you are not telling me in which garden I should go?
Regretting that she loved Hari, she returns home disappointed.
Cokhe [the singer] says, that she is scared in front of her home without Kr̥ṣṇa.

(LGT: 222R: 1972-73, Kanpur, Boatmen)

चक्की गीत

२४४.

रथ पर निरखत जात आज राम बन का गये हैं॥
रामा के पाइन चनन खड़ाऊँ इड़ियन चुअत गुलाल आज राम बन का गये हैं॥
रामा के हाथन चनन लकड़ियाँ अँगुरिन चुअत गुलाब आज राम बन का गये हैं॥
रामा के रथ पर सोने को सिंहासन धर्म धुजा फहराय आज राम बन का गये हैं॥
रामा के रथ पर सोने के कलशा, पचरँग पड़े हैं झंडा आज राम बन का गये हैं॥
जो मैं जनती रमैया छल करिहैं कर घुँघटा की ओट बात मन की कर लेती॥
जो मैं जनती रमैया बन जइहैं कर सोरह सिंगार झपट रथ पै चढ़ लेती॥

rath par nirakhat jāt āj rām ban kā gaye haiṅ.
rāmā ke pāin canan khaṛāūñ iṛiyan cuat gulāl āj rām ban kā gaye haiṅ.
rāmā ke hāthan canan lakaṛiyāñ añgurin cuat gulāb āj rām ban kā gaye haiṅ.
rāmā ke rath par sone ko siṁhāsan dharm dhujā phaharāy āj rām ban kā gaye haiṅ.
rāmā ke rath par sone ke kalaśā, pacarañg paṛe haiṅ jhaṅḍā āj rām ban kā gaye haiṅ.
jo maiṅ janatī ramaiyā chal karihaiṅ kar ghuñghaṭā kī oṭ bāt man kī kar letī.
jo maiṅ janatī ramaiyā ban jaihaiṅ kar sorah siṅgār jhapaṭ rath pai caṛh letī.

Riding on a chariot, Rām looked around as he proceeded towards the forest.
Rām is wearing sandalwood sandals and his heels are all red.
Rām is carrying a sandalwood staff and his fingers are red.
There is a golden throne on Rām's chariot from which flutters the flag of righteousness.
There are gold water-pots and colourful flags on Rām's chariot.
Had I known that Rām would leave me, I would have talked with him from behind my veil.

Had I known that Rām would go to the forest, I would have climbed onto the chariot donning my make-up quickly.

(LGT: 137R: 1972-73, Nandana, Brāhmaṇ Women)

२४५.

ई दोनों बालक किनके जनक पूँछैं मुनि सें ॥
ई दोनों बालक राजा जशरथ के, अवधपुरी घर इनके ॥
कोमल गात उमर लरिकाँई, धनुष बरोबर नाहीं ॥
जो इन हरि से धनुष न टूटै, खाई जहर मर जाई ॥
राम चितै लछिमन मुस्काने, अब सीता तजती हैं प्रान ॥
बाँये हाँथे धनुष उठाये, तोर करे दुइ खण्ड ॥
टूटे धनुष भीर भई भारी, जनक ने शीश नवाई ॥
धन्य हैं भाग्य तुम्हारे जानकी, राम सिया वर पाये ॥

i donoṅ bālak kinake janak pūñchaiṅ muni seṅ.
i donoṅ bālak rājā jaśarath ke, avadhapurī ghar inake.
komal gāt umar larikāñī, dhanuṣ barobar nāhīṅ.
jo in hari se dhanuṣ n ṭūṭai, khāī jahar mar jāī.
rām citai lachiman muskāne, ab sītā tajatī hain prān.
bāñye hāñthe dhanuṣ uṭhāye, tor kare dui khaṇḍ.
ṭūṭe dhanuṣ bhīr bhaī bhārī, janak ne śīś navāī.
dhanya haiṅ bhāgya tumhāre jānakī, rām siyā var pāye.

Janak is asking the sage about the identity of these two boys.
These two boys are sons of king Daśarath and their home is Ayodhyā.
They are tender and young in age; they don't even reach up to the bow in height.
If they fail to break the bow, I will eat poison and die.
Lakṣmaṇ smilingly looked at Rām and conveyed that Sītā is about to die [of grief].
He [Rām] lifted the bow with his lefthand and broke it in two.
Upon breaking the bow, there was great rejoicing; Janak bowed his head.
Blessed is your fate, Jānakī, that Rām is your husband.

(LGT: 138R: 1972-73, Nandana, Brāhmaṇ Women)

२४६.

अरे दादुल हमको लिखो है विदेश ॥
भइया बहिन दोनों एक कोंख जल्में, अरे दादुल पिये हैं एकै दूध
तुमकों तो बीरन मेरे ददुली बैठका, अरे बीरन हमकों लिखो है विदेश
गंगा के नीरे तीरे निकारी पलकिया, अरे दादुल कोयल शब्द सुनाये
अब का कोयल शब्द सुनावौ, छूटो है दादुल जी को देश ॥

are dādul hamakau likho hai videś.
bhaiyā bahin donoṅ ek koṅkh jalmeṅ, are dādul piye haiṅ ekai dūdh;
tumakoṅ to bīran mere dadulī baiṭhakā, are bīran hamakoṅ likho hai videś.
gāṅgā ke nīre tīre nikārī palakiyā, are dādul koyal śabd sunāye;
ab kā koyal śabd sunāvau, chūṭo hai dādul jī ko deś.

A foreign country is written in my fate, O dear father.
Brother and sister were born from the same womb; we drank the same milk, O dear father.
For you, my brother, father's sitting room is destined but, O brother, an outside country is in my fate.
As my palanquin went near the banks of the Ganges, O dear father, a cuckoo sang;
O cuckoo, why are you singing now, as I leave my father's village.

(LGT: 139R: 1972-73, Nandana, Brāhmaṇ Women)

धनुकिया दादरा

२४७.

मोर सइयाँ चले परदेश, सगुन लइ मैं खड़िव मोरे राजा ॥
मोर सइयाँ को मिट्टी दुपट्टा, खुटी मा वहु टँगो मोरे राजा ॥
मोर सइयाँ की ढ़ाल तरवरिया, खुटी मा वहु टँगी मोरे राजा ॥
मोर सइयाँ की लाली लाली घुड़िया, बड़ी मा वह बँधी मोरे राजा ॥
मोर राजा की ढ़ाल तरवरिया, खुटी मा वहु टँगी मोरे राजा ॥

mor saiyāñ cale paradeś, sagun lai main khaṛiv more rājā.
mor saiyāñ ko miṭṭī dupaṭṭā, khuṭī mā vahu ṭaṅgo more rājā.
mor saiyāñ kī ṛhāl taravariyā, khuṭī mā vahu ṭaṅgī more rājā.
mor saiyāñ kī lālī lālī ghuṛiyā, baṛī mā vah bañdhī more rājā.
mor rājā kī ṛhāl taravariyā, khuṭī mā vahu ṭaṅgī more rājā.

As my husband left for abroad, I stood with auspicious material.
My husband's scarf is left hanging on a hanger.
My husband's shield and sword are left hanging on a hanger.
My husband's red mare is tied in an enclosure.
My husband shield's and sword are left hanging on a hanger.

(LGT: 109R: 1972-73, Biraicamau, Dhanuk Men)

२४८.

रोय मरिबो चलि जइहौ बेदर्दी ॥
बड़ी बड़ी अँखियों में नान्हों नान्हों कजरा
भरि कै गंगा जल धोइ डरिबो ॥
नन्हीं नन्हीं दँतिया में कारी कारी मिसिया
लइ कै रुमाल पोंछ डरिबो ॥
गोरी गोरी बहियाँ में हरे हरे चुड़िला
धरि कै सिलबट्टा मा फोरि डरिबो ॥
घरि के डबिया में सारी धरी है
धरि के करिहाँ पर मसक डरिबो ॥

roy maribo cali jaihau bedardī.
baṛī baṛī añkhiyoṅ meṅ nānhoṅ nānhoṅ kajarā;
bhari kai gaṅgā jal dhoi ḍaribo.
nanhīṅ nanhīṅ dañtiyā meṅ kārī kārī misiyā;
lai kai rumāl poṅch ḍaribo.
gorī gorī bahiyāñ meṅ hare hare cuṛilā;
dhari kai silabaṭṭā mā phori ḍaribo.
ghari ke ḍabiyā meṅ sārī dharī hai;
dhari ke karihāñ par masak ḍaribo.

I will die from crying if you leave, O hard-hearted.

I have just a little black collyrium on my big eyes;
I will wash it away with Ganges water.
On my teeth, I have black *missi;*
I will wipe that out with my handkerchief.
I have colourful bangles on my fair skinned hands;
I will break them on a stone slab.
I have a *sārī* at home in a trunk;
I will tear it by putting it on my waist.

(LGT: 110R: 1972-73 Biraicamau, Dhanuk Men)

२४९.

पातरी मोहिं मारौ न राजा ॥
एक डबिया मा मिस्सी औ सुरमा,
एक डबिया मा बेंदी धरी चमकइहौ न राजा ॥
एक डबिया मा लहिआ रे बिछुआ,
एक डबिया मा बेंदी धरी चमकइहौ न राजा ॥
एक डबिया मा लँहगा औ लुगरा,
एक डबिया मा सारी धरी मसकइहौ न राजा ॥

pātarī mohiṅ mārau n rājā.
ek ḍabiyā mā missī au suramā,
ek ḍabiyā mā beṅdī dharī camakaihau n rājā.
ek ḍabiyā mā lahiā re bichuā,
ek ḍabiyā mā beṅdī dharī camakaihau n rājā.
ek ḍabiyā mā lañhagā au lugarā,
ek ḍabiyā mā sārī dharī masakaihau n rājā.

I am thin, don't beat me, my dear husband.
In one can there is *missī* and collyrium,
In another can *beṅdī*, with which I will decorate myself, dear husband.
In one can there is an ankle bracelet and toerings,
In another can *beṅdī*, with which I will decorate myself, dear husband.
In one can there is a long skirt, in another a scarf,
In another there is a *sārī*, with which I will decorate myself, dear husband.

(LGT: 111R: 1972-73, Biraicamau, Dhanuk Men)

बेलवरिया

२५०.

गरजैं हनुमान कैसे लखन मरि जइहैं ॥
आयु गई है उराई ब्रह्मा ढिग जाय खैंच जमी पर लइबै
देंबै बढ़वाय अजर अमर बुलवइबै
आज्ञा को पाय नाथ दया कर दीजे, हे कृपानिधान कैसे लखन मरि जइहैं ॥
इन्द्रासन को धाऊँ संग इन्द्र उठाय सूर्यदेव को रोंकूँ
शंकर ढिग जाय अमृत लाय पिलाऊँ
यमपुर को धाय काल बली को मारूँ, ना जाई जान कैसे लखन मरि जइहैं ॥
कृपा नाथ करि दीजे आज्ञानुसरा लंकापुरी को धाऊँ
दसमुख को मार भुजा आकाश को
गिर लेऊँ उखार लाऊँ संजीवन बूटी दूँ फौरन आन कैसे लखन मरि जइहैं ॥
सुन प्यारे का मंजबू हो हरि गे घबिराय दीला बनारस वाला
पहुँचा है आज कवि भुल्लन का चेला
लिख दिया बयान कैसे लखन मरि जइहैं ॥

garajaiṅ hanumān kaise lakhan mari jaihaiṅ.
āyu gaī hai urāī brahmā ḍhig jāy khaiṅc jamī par laibai.
debai baṛhavāy ajar amar bulavaibai.
ājñā ko pāy nāth dayā kara dījai, he kṛpānidhān kaise lakhan mari jaihaiṅ.
indrāsan ko dhāūñ saṅg indr uṭhāy sūryadev ko roṅkūñ;
śaṅkara ḍhig jāy amṛt lāy pilāūñ;
yamapur ko dhāy kāl balī ko māūñ, nā jāī jān kaise lakhan mari jaihaiṅ.
kṛpā nāth kari dījai ājñānusarā laṅkāpurī ko dhāūñ;
dasamukh ko mār bhujā ākāś ko (?)
gir leūñ ukhār lāūñ sañjīvan būṭī dūñ phauran ān kaise lakhan mari jaihaiṅ.
sun pyāre kā mañjabū ho hari ge ghabirāy dīlā banāras vālā;
pahuñcā hai āj kavi bhullan kā celā.
likh diyā bayān kaise lakhan mari jaihaiṅ.

"How will Lakṣmaṇ die?" Hanumān shouted.
If his age is finished, then I will go to Brahmā and drag him to the ground.

And will make Brahmā increase his life to make him immortal.
Give me permission, O abode of compassion.
I will go to the kingdom of Indra and will wake him to stop the rising of sun;
I will go to Śaṅkar and bring nectar for him to drink;
I will go to the city of death and will kill death itself but will not let Lakṣmaṇ die.
Give me permission to go to Laṅkā;
I will kill Rāvaṇ... (?)
I will tear the mountain and will bring the *sañjīvanī* herb immediately.
Listening to such feelings from his loved one, Rām was afraid, thus says the poet from Banāras.
Poet Bhullan's disciple has arrived today.
I have thus written my account. How will Lakṣmaṇ die?

(LGT: 168R: 1972 73, Karmi, Mixed Men)

लचक

२५१.

नशेबाज का सुनौ माजरा कहै चतुर चारिव नारी ॥
पहली नार दिलों से बोली मोरे पिया हैं गँजेड़ी
राति दिना मा सौ सौ चिलमैं बदन मलीना कै डारी
संपत्ति रहै नशे मा गँवाइन खाँसी खुर्रा भा जारी ॥
दुसरी नार दिलों से बोली मोरे पिया हैं भंगेड़ी
होत भोर लै कुँडी सोंटा तापर भाँग करैं जारी
भाँग खाय भकुवा होइ बैठे कौन करै खेती बारी ॥
तिसरी नार दिलों से बोली मोरे पिया हैं अफीमची
पिये अफीमा घूमैं बावरा लसर पसर की तैयारी
खाँड़ चिरौंजी के भोजन न पावैं पटकि दिहेन लोटा थारी ॥
चौथी नार दिलों से बोली मोरे पिया हैं मदप्याला
पिये मदा ई घूमैं बावरा जाय गिरे नारी नाला

कहे सुने से गइवँ उठावै मुझे देत लाखिन गारी ॥
कहैं कबीर सुनौ भइ साधो चारौ नशेन की बलिहारी ॥

naśebāj kā sunau mājarā kahai catur cāriv nārī.
pahalī nār dilon se bolī more piyā hain gañjeṛī
rāti dinā mā sau sau cilamain badan malīnā kai dārī.
sampatti rahai naśe mā gañvāin khāñsī khurrā bhā jārī.
dusarī nār dilon se bolī more piyā hain bhangeṛī;
hot bhor laī kuñḍī sonṭā tāpar bhāñg karain jārī;
bhāñg khāy bhakuā hoi baiṭhe kaun karai khetī bārī.
tisarī nār dilon se bolī more piyā hain aphimacī;
piye aphīmā ghūmain bāvarā lasar pasar kī taiyārī;
khāñṛ ciraunjī ke bhojan n pāvain paṭaki dihen lotā thārī.
cauthī nār dilon se bolī more piyā hain madapyālā.
piye madā ī ghūmain bāvarā jāy gire nārī nālā;
kahe sune se gaivañ uṭhāvai mujhe det lākhin gārī.
kahain kabīr sunau bhai sādho cārau naśen kī balihārī.

"Listen to the happenings of a drunkard!", say four clever women.
First woman said that her husband is a drug addict;
Night and day, he smokes hundred of pots and has made his body filthy.
He lost his wealth in drugs and now he is suffering from cough ailments.
Second woman said that her husband is a hemp drinker;
Early in the morning he prepares his hemp on slab stone;
After eating his hemp, he sits like an idiot and who will do farming.
Third woman said that her husband is an opium addict;
After smoking opium, he wanders around insane;
If he does not get to eat rich food, then he throws his plate and drinking vessel.
Fourth woman said that her husband is a wine drinker.
Drunk, he wanders insane and falls in gutters;
Hearing this state, I went to pick him up and in return he abuses me.
Kabīr says, "Listen good soul, this is the story of four intoxicants.

(LGT: 122R: 1972-73, Akohariya, Ahīr Man)

२५२.

उमरिया कैसे कटै बारी॥
आम पके महुआ गदराने, छाई अनारों में लाली
जब नेबुलन मा रसि भरि आवा, छोड़ि चला माली॥
ससुरे गई घैरे जो गइली, घर से सासु निकाली
कवहिं के लाये ननदिया ठाढ़ी, सैंया से चुगली करै सारी॥
एक तौ रहौं बिरहा की मारी, दूजे गोसइयाँ बिपदा डारी
तीजे गोद रहा खाली॥

umariyā kaise kaṭai bārī.
ām pake mahuā gadarāne, chāī anāroṅ meṅ lālī;
jab nebulan mā rasi bhari āvā, choṛi calā mālī.
sasure gaī gharai jo gailī, ghar se sāsu nikālī;
kavahin ke lāye nanadiyā ṭhāṛhī, saiṅyā se cugalī karai sārī.
ek tau rahauṅ birahā kī mārī, dūje gosaiyāñ bipadā ḍārī;
tīje god rahā khālī.

How will my adolescent age pass?
My body is ripe like mango and *mahuā* and red like pomegranate;
The gardener left when the lemons [breasts] were full of juice.
At in-law's home, my *sāś* threatens to throw me out of the house;
My *Nanad* is standing at the gate to say bad things about me to my husband.
Thus, I was suffering and now the god has put another problem on me;
Third, I am childless.

(LGT: 123R: 1972-73, Akohariya, Ahīr Man)

लाचारी

२५३.

कै बंशी वाले मनमोहना की बंशी नेक बजा
तेरी बंशी मन हरे कि घट अंगना न सुहाय

कै नन्दलाला मदन गोपाला जुलुम किया बालेपन मा
पहिरे माला ओढ़े दुशाला काला काजर नैनन मा
औ बंशी बजावै तान सुनावै धेन चरावै कुंजन मा
सखी बेलमावैं रारि बढ़ावैं कैंच लगावैं नैनन मा
ग्वाल बाल गोपाल साथ लै जाई के घ्यारय सखियन का
चंचल चपल छैल नटनागर र्वाकै गैल सखिन केरी॥
ओरहन लेव जसोदा माई कहन लाग बृषभान लली
मैं जमुना जल भरन जाति थी मिले कन्हैया कुँज गली
ना कुछ बोले ना कुछ चाले पाय अचानक हमैं चली
मोर गागर फोरी बाँह मिरोरी चोली फारि के कूच मली
कहाँ तके हम हाल बतइबै हमें बनावत है चेरी॥
कहैं जसोदा सुनौ ग्वालिनी तुझे बात न लगी शरम
ये चार दिना का मेरा बालक है वो क्या जाने बुरा करम
तेरी है अलमस्त जवानी बदन मा छाई तेरे गरम
तुम जाय के अरझौ झगड़ा ठानौ आयके हमसे कहौ मरम
रस की माती तु अठलाती बेगड़ गया है तेरा चाल चलन॥
तब कहै ग्वालिनी सुन लेव जसोदा तुम तो कहती है छोटा
ये जितना छोटा कुँवर कन्हैया उतना ज्यादा है खोंटा
जैसे साँड़ गलिन मा घूमै खाय खाय फिरता मोटा
है ऐसा तेरा कुँवर कन्हैया छैल छबीला है ढोटा
बुद्धा कहै किशन के लीला सुख देती नत बेरिन मा॥

kai baṅśī vāle manamohanā kī baṅśī nek bajā;
terī baṅśī man hare ki ghaṭ aṅganā n suhāy.
kai nandalālā madan gopālā julum kiyā bālepan mā;
pahire mālā oṛhe duśālā kālā kājar nainan mā;
au baṅśī bajāvai tān sunāvai dhen carāvai kuñjan mā.
sakhī belamāvaiṅ rārī baṛhāvaiṅ kaiṅc lagāvaiṅ nainan mā.
gvāl bāl gopāl sāth lai jāī ke ghyāray sakhiyan kā;
cañchal capal chail naṭanāgar rvākai gail sakhin kerī.
orahan lev jasodā māī kahan lāg bṛṣabhān lalī;
maiṅ jamunā jal bharan jāti thī mile kanhaiyā kuñj galī;
nā kuch bole nā kuch cāle pāy acānak hamaiṅ calī;
mor gāgar phorī bāñh mirorī colī phāri ke kūch malī;
kahāñ take ham hāl bataibai hameṅ banāvat hai cerī.
kahaiṅ jasodā sunau gvālinī tujhe bāt n lagī śaram;

ye cār dinā kā merā bālak hai vo kyā jāne burā karam;
terī hai alamast javānī badan mā chāī tere garam;
tum jāy ke arajhau jhagaṛā ṭhānau āyake hamase kahau maram;
ras kī mātī tū aṭhalātī begaṛ gayā hai terā cāl calan.
tab kahai gvālinī sun lev jasodā tum to kahatī hai choṭā;
ye jitanā choṭā kuñvar kanhaiyā utanā jyādā hai khoṅṭā;
jaise sāñṛ galin mā ghūmai khāy khāy phiratā moṭā;
hai aisā terā kuñvar kanhaiyā chail chabīlā hai ḍhoṭā;
buddhā kahai kiśan ke līlā sukh detī nat berin mā.

O flute player Kṛṣṇa, play your flute a little;
Your flute seizes my mind so much that I do not like my home or courtyard.
O son of Nand, you were outrageous in childhood;
Wearing a garland, covering yourself with a shawl and mascara in your eyes;
You played flute while tending cows in the groves;
You linger with girlfriends and thus create trouble; your eyes are like scissors.
Together with your friends, you blockade girlfriends;
Naughty and clever Kṛṣṇa blocks passages to girlfriends.
"Listen to my complaint mother Yaśodā", said daughter of Bṛṣbhān;
I was on my way to Yamunā to fetch water when Kṛṣṇa met me at the bower;
Seeing me going alone, he didn't talk or do anything;
He broke my pot, twisted my arms, tore my bodice and fondled my breasts;
How much should I tell you? He is making me a servant.
Yaśodā replied thus, "O milkmaid, aren't you ashamed saying all this?"
My child is very young and does not know such bad deeds;
You are excited in your coming of youth;
You yourself go and tangle with him and later come to tell me;
You are coquettish and your character has become bad.
In response, milkmaid said, "Listen Yaśodā, you tell me that he is small!"
However small your darling Kṛṣṇa may appear, he is just as naughty;
He is like a wandering bull, getting fat from eating everywhere.
Your darling Kṛṣṇa is a dandy and handsome child;
Buddha [composer] says, "Kṛṣṇa's pastimes always give pleasure."

(LGT: 5R: 1976, Sheoli, Dhobī Men)

२५४.

हाल सुनावौं उइ नर का जो रंडिन के घर जाते है॥
ठाट बनाके घर से निकले बाँध कलाई मा एक घड़ी
एक हाथ मा सिगरेट मुँह में और दूसरे हाथ छड़ी
है कोट अस्तुओं की जेबों में दिखलाते हैं चैन पड़ी
तरह तरह के फैशन उनके बातैं करते बड़ी बड़ी
चौक में पहुँचे जो देखा रंडियों ने एक बार
आँख से करके इशारा दिया मोहनी उन पर डार
बात करने को चढ़े छज्जे पर फिर ओ घोर गँवार
धरम के जाने वा रहने का नहीं जिनको है विचार
हुए अधर्मी पापी बिल्कुल जरा नहीं शरमाते हैं॥
पहुँचे जब कमरे के ऊपर पूँछन लागे नाम निशान
मुस्क्या कर रंडी यों बोली नाम हमारा नन्हीं जान
आवभगत करिके बैठाला गया जेब पर फौरन ध्यान
तब प्रेम भरे लहजे में बोली बाबू जी खिलवा दो पान
था वहाँ मौजूद भडुवा सबसे भी हुशियार है
पान लाने के लिये होता वो चट तैयार है
माँग कर दो चार पैसे जाता फिर बाजार है
बाँध कर तागे में लाता फिर गिलौड़ी चार है
लगे मुसलमानों के हाथ के पान मजे से खाते हैं॥
बातचीत में फीस हुई तय रहे रात रंडी के पास
पीकर बोतल छै नम्बर की फिर कहते उससे स्याबाश
हो मदाद में राज ठाठ से किया धरम का सत्यानाश
थोड़े दिन में ही बन जाते वो पूरे रंडी के दास
छीन कर औरत का जेवर जाके रंडी को है दिया
बाप दादे किये कमाई फूँक फिर ऐसा दिया
घर को अपने सेठ के घर जाके गिरवीं लिखै दिया
और रूपया लेके सब रंडी के आगे धर दिया
खुद रहते रंडी के घर में नारी को नित तरसाते हैं॥
नारी दिल में सोचती है सोचै अपने दिल दरम्यान
मिला कुकर्मी पति है हमको यतन करूँ मैं क्या भगवान
छल्ला छल्ला मेरा लेकर फूँक दिया कुल किया नसान
भीख माँग कर अब क्या खाऊँ या मैं अपने तज दूँ प्रान
नारी निसदिन सोचती यूँ ये मल्हारें गा रहे

साथ भडूवों के शरम तज खूबै मौज उड़ाय रहे
हाथ मदिरा ही नहीं कोकीन भी हैं खा रहे
देखकर इनकी ये दशा घर द्वार सब चिल्ला रहे
नहीं किसी की सुनते अब अपनी हँसी जगत मा करवाते हैं ॥
सुनौ फायदा जो रंडी के रखने से होता है हाल
बीज तुम्हारे से जो लड़की पैदा हुई हुई हुस्नदार
बनते हैं दामाद हजारों करते नाहीं जरा बिचार
हुआ जो लड़का भडुवा होकर करै दलाली सरे बजार
और भी जो रोग होते हैं जरा सुन लीजिये
हो गई कहीं सुजाक तो जीवन भर दवाई कीजिये
पड़ गई जिसम में गर्मी निकली ध्यान इस पर दीजिये
नीम टोहनी हाथ ले मक्खियाँ उड़ाया कीजिये
बुद्धालाल कहैं तजौ रंडी का मजा कौन इनमा पाते ॥

hāl sunāvauṅ ui nar kā jo raṇḍin ke ghar jāte haiṅ.
ṭhāṭ banāke ghar se nikale bāñdh kalāī mā ek ghaṛī;
ek hāth mā sigareṭ muñh meṅ aur dūsare hāth chaṛī;
hai koṭ astuoṅ kī jeboṅ meṅ dikhalāte haiṅ cain paṛī;
tarah tarah ke phaiśan unake bātaiṅ karate baṛī baṛī
cauk meṅ pahuñce jo dekhā raṇḍiyoṅ ne ek bār;
añkh se karake iśārā diyā mohanī un par ḍār;
bāt karane ko caṛhe chajje par phir o ghor gañvār;
dharam ke jāne vā rahane kā nahīṅ jinako hai vicār;
hue adharmī pāpī bilkul jarā nahīṅ śaramāte haiṅ.
pahuñce jab kamare ke ūpar pūñchan lāge nām niśān;
muskyā kar raṇḍī yoṅ bolī nām hamārā nanhīṅ jān;
āvabhagat karike baiṭhālā gayā jeb par phauran dhyān;
tab prem bhare lahaje meṅ bolī bābū jī khilavā do pān;
thā vahāñ maujūd bhaḍuvā sabase bhī huśiyār hai;
pān lāne ke liye hotā vo caṭ taiyār hai;
mañg kar do cār paise jātā phir bājār hai;
bāñdh kar tāge meṅ lātā phir gilauṛī cār hai;
lage musalamānoṅ ke hāth ke pān maje se khāte haiṅ.
bātacīt meṅ phīs huī tay rahe rāt raṇḍī ke pās;
pikar botal chai nambar kī phir kahate usase syābāś;
ho madād meṅ rāj ṭhāṭh se kiyā dharam kā satyānāś;

thoṛe din meṅ hī ban jāte vo pūre raṇḍī ke dās;
chīn kar aurat kā jevar jāke raṇḍī ko hai diyā;
bāp dāde kiye kamāī phūñk phir aisā diyā;
ghar ko apane seṭh ke ghar jāke giravīṅ likhai diyā;
aur rūpayā leke sab raṇḍī ke āge dhar diyā;
khud rahate raṇḍī ke ghar meṅ nārī ko nit tarasāte haiṅ.
nārī dil meṅ socatī hai socai apane dil daramyān;
milā kukarmī pati hai hamako yatan karūñ maiṅ kyā bhagavān;
challā challā merā lekar phūñk diyā kul kiyā nasān;
bhīkh māñg kar ab kyā khāūñ yā maiṅ apane taj dūñ prān;
nārī nisadin socatī yūñ ye malhārai gā rahe;
sāth bhaḍūvoṅ ke śaram taj khūbai mauj uṛāy rahe;
hāth madirā hī nahīṅ kokīn bhī haiṅ khā rahe;
dekhakar inakī ye daśā ghar dvār sab cillā rahe;
nahīṅ kisī kī sunate ab apanī hañsī jagat mā karavāte haiṅ.
sunau phāyadā jo raṇḍī ke rakhane se hotā hai hāl;
bīj tumhāre se jo laṛakī paidā huī huī husnadār;
banate haiṅ dāmād hajāroṅ karate nāhīṅ jarā bicār;
huā jo laṛakā bhaḍuā hokar karai dalālī sare bajār;
aur bhī jo rog hote haiṅ jarā sun lījiye;
ho gaī kahīṅ sujāk to jīvan bhar davāī kījiye.
paṛ gaī jisam meṅ garmī nikalī dhyān is par dījiye.
nīm ṭohanī hāth le makkhiyāñ uṛāyā kījiye.
buddhālāl kahaiṅ tajau raṇḍī kā majā kaun inamā pāte.

I tell you the condition of men who frequent the prostitute's home;
All dressed, he comes out of his home with a watch on his wrist;
In one hand he carries a cigarette in and out of his mouth; in the other hand
he carries a walking stick.
He displays a chain coming from his jacket's pocket;
He dresses in different fashion and talk big;
As he reached main area and the prostitutes look at him;
With her eyes she signalled and captivated him;
Utterly stupid, he climbed on the railing to talk with her;
He doesn't think about keeping or not keeping his religious way of life;

He became an unrighteous sinner but he is not ashamed.
Once in her room, he asked her name;
Smilingly, the prostitute said that her name is Nanhin Jān (little soul)
She welcomed and offered him a seat and immediately thought about his purse;
She lovingly asked him to get some betel leaves for her to eat;
A clever pimp was present there;
He gets ready to bring betel leaves immediately;
Asking for a few coins, he goes to market;
He brings four betel leaves all tied;
Delightfully, he eats betel leaves prepared by a Muslim
During conversation they set a price and he spends his night with the prostitute;
After drinking wine "Number Six," he encourages her;
Thus getting drunk, he ruins his righteousness;
In a few days, he becomes a total servant of the prostitute;
He snatches his wife's ornaments and gives them to the prostitute;
He wastes the earnings of his father and grandfathers;
He mortgages his house to a lender;
He took all the money and placed it in front of the prostitute;
Living at the prostitute's home, he causes longing for his wife.
His wife constantly thinks in her heart;
I have begotten a bad person like my husband; O god what should I do?
He has taken every penny and jewellery and has ruined my family;
Should I beg to eat now or should I kill myself;
His wife thinks like this everyday while he is merrymaking;
Shamelessly, he is enjoying in the company of pimps;
Not only does he have wine in his hand but now he uses cocaine too;
Seeing him in this condition, all his family members are crying;
He listens to nobody and has become the laughing stock of his neighbourhood;
Listen to some advantages of going to the prostitute;
If a beautiful daughter was born from your seed;
Don't you think that you will have thousands of sons-in-law;
If you had a son, he will become a pimp and do his business openly in the market.

Listen to the list of illnesses which are prevalent [with such associations].
If you picked up gonorrhaea, it will take lifelong medication.
Keep in mind that you might get syphilis.
It will take a lifetime to get rid of flies with a *nīm* twig.
Buddhalal (the composer) says to abandon prostitutes. What pleasure can you get from them?

(LGT: 6R: 1976, Sheoli, Dhobī Men)

२५५.

उठो अलबेली नार झारि डारौ अँगना ॥
झारि डारौ अँगना बटोरी डारौ धामा ॥
काहे की बढ़िनी काहे केरो बँधना, काहे के लागे फुँदना ॥
मन केरी बढ़िनी सुरति केरो बँधना, सोने के लागे फुँदना ॥

uṭho alabelī nār jhāri ḍārau añganā.
jhāri ḍārau añganā baṭorī ḍārau dhāmā.
kāhe kī baṛhinī kāhe kero bañdhanā, kāhe ke lāge phuñdanā.
man kerī baṛhinī surati kero bañdhanā, sone ke lāge phuñdanā.

Get up, O beautiful woman, and sweep your courtyard.
Sweep the courtyard and your home.
What are your broom and rope made of and what kind of tassels are on it?
The broom is made of the mind, the rope of reflections, and the tassels are made of gold.

(LGT: 90R: 1972-73, Tahirapur, Camār Men)

२५६.

बारे मा दुइ भाँटा बोइ देव कि अण्डा और उँखारी
कोठे के ऊपर नचै बुढ़उना तोरे डारति छानी
खटमल कटै नींद नहिं आवै उठि के मार मोर सैंयाँ ॥
जब मोर बुढ़उनै कइहौ बुढ़उना, तेहिके जुवनवै खाऊँ ना
अपने बुढ़उनै दाबूँ बगल मा सकिल भुसउरी जाउँ ना ॥
जब हमरो बुढ़उना ऐस बिषकर्मी, दूध भात ना खाति है

जेहिकी देखै नीकी मेहरिया हुँवइ सकिल के जात है ॥
जब आँगन मइहाँ सासु परी है भीतर परी देउरानी
तनिक सासु मेरो लरिका लइ लेव सइयाँ मजा लइ लेय ॥

bāre mā dui bhāñṭā boi dev ki aṇḍā aur uñkhārī.
koṭhe ke ūpar nacai buṛhaunā tore ḍārati chānī.
khaṭamal kaṭai nīṅd nahiṅ āvai uṭhi ke mār mor saiṅyāñ.
jab mor buṛhaunai kaihau buṛhaunā, tehike juvanavai khāūñ nā.
apane buṛhaunai dābūñ bagal mā sakil bhusaurī jāuñ nā.
jab hamaro buṛhaunā ais biṣakarmī, dūdh bhāt nā khāti hai;
jehikī dekhai nīkī mehariyā huñvai sakil ke jāt hai.
jab āñgan maihāñ sāsu parī hai bhītar parī deurānī;
tanik sāsu mero larikā lai lev saiyāñ majā lai ley.

In the front, sow two eggplants and take care of them as eggs and sugarcane.
On top of the house, my old husband is dancing and breaking the thatched roof.
I can't sleep because bed bugs are biting; O dear husband, get up and kill them.
If you call my old man old, I will flirt with your young husband.
I will carry my old man under my armpit and will hide with him in the strawroom.
My old man is wicked and refuses to eat his milk and rice.
Whatever beautiful woman he sees, that's where he hovers around.
In the courtyard my *sās* is sleeping, inside my *nanad*;
O *sās*, take care of my child for a while so that my husband can enjoy me.

(LGT: 116R: 1972-73, Ganj Muradabad, Dhobī Men)

२५७.

अपने त गइला राजा पूरुबवा वोही लालरिया के देशवा ॥
अपने त ललरी देखी लोभइला, हमें टीकउनो के सापना ॥
अपने त ललरी देखी लोभइला, हमें चूनरियो के सापना ॥
अपने त ललरी देखी लोभइला, हमें झूलउवौं के सापना ॥

apane t gailā rājā pūrūbavā vohī lālariyā ke deśavā.
apanė t lalarī dekhī lobhailā, hameṅ ṭīkauno ke sāpanā.
apane t lalarī dekhī lobhailā, hameṅ cūnariyo ke sāpanā.
apane t lalarī dekhī lobhailā, hameṅ jhūlauvauṅ ke sāpanā.

O dear husband, you went east to the country of red women.
You became obsessed with red women and for me there is no gift not even in dream.
You became obsessed with red women and for me even a scarf has become a dream.
You became obsessed with red women and for me even a swing has become a dream.

(LGT: 152R: 1972-73, Nayapurva, Varanasi, Ahīr Women)

लावनी

२५८.

सुर बिन मिलै न सुरसती औ गुरु बिन मिलै न ज्ञान
गुरु बिन मिलै न ज्ञान खड़े दंगल मा गावौं
लेके गुरु का नाम सभा मा शीश नवावूँ खता कबहूँ न पावौं
कह गिरधर कविराज गुरुनन के स्यावव चरन
कहते बुद्धालाल बैठ सिंहासन गुरू अपना॥
हरदम हरि का भजन करौ हिरदे मा मालिक को पहिचान॥
क्यों भटके तुम फिरौ दिवाने घट मा बिराजै श्री भगवान
दरशन करना चाहौ राम का तुम भी अगर तलाश में हौ
कहीं न तुमको पता मिलेगा भूला किसकी आश में है
नहीं मिलै हरि गये द्वारिका नहीं काशी कैलाश में हैं
नहीं मिलै प्रभु मक्के मदीने नहीं काबे के पास में हैं
नहीं मिलै हरि बुतखाने में नहीं मिलेंगें कबुरुस्तान॥
नहीं मिलै हरि गये द्वारिका नहीं काशी कैलाश में हैं
नहीं मिलै हरिद्वार गये से नहीं तीरथ गंगा जल में
दिल की दुबिधा दूर करौ तो प्रभू मिलैंगे एक पल में

चित धरिकै हरि नाम जपौ तब तुम्हें मिलैगे कृपानिधान॥
नहीं मिलै हरि गिरजा मस्जिद नहीं मन्दिर दीवार में हैं
नहीं मिलै हरि तिलक दिये और नाही खाक लगाने से
नहीं मिलै माला तसबी में नहीं जटा के रखाने में
नहीं मिलै घर बार तजे नहीं तोंदी के लटकाने से
नहीं मिलै घर बार तजे नहीं मुलुक मुलुक रम जाने से
नहीं मिलै हरि भेष बनाये मिलैंगे हरि गुन गाने से
दिल से नाम भजो दिलवर का नाहक होते तुम हैरान॥
तीन लोक चौदहो भुवन संसार सकल फिरि आओगे
कहीं न तुमको पता मिलैगा ढूँढ़ ढूँढ़ मर जाओगे
काया ये अपनी निर्मल करिकै प्रभु से नेह लगाओ तुम
फिर दिनदयाल प्रसन्न जो होइहैं सहजि मा दर्शन पाओगे
बुद्धा कहे प्रीत करि हरि से तज करिकै अपना अभिमान॥

sur bin milai n surasatī au guru bin milai n jñān.
guru bin milai n jñān khaṛe daṅgal mā gāvauṅ;
leke guru kā nām sabhā mā śīś navāvūñ khatā kabahūñ n pāvauṅ.
kah giradhar kavirāj gurunan ke syāvav caran;
kahate buddhālāl baiṭh siṁhāsan gurū apanā.
haradam hari kā bhajan karau hirade mā mālik ko pahicān;
kyoṅ bhaṭake tum phirau divāne ghaṭ mā birājai śrī bhagavān.
daraśan karanā cāhau rām kā tum bhī agar talāś meṅ hau.
kahīṅ n tumako patā milegā bhūlā kisakī āś meṅ hai.
nahīṅ milai hari gaye dvārikā nahīṅ kāśī kailāś meṅ haiṅ.
nahīṅ milai prabhu makke madīne nahīṅ kābe ke pās meṅ haiṅ.
nahīṅ milai hari butakhāne meṅ nahīṅ mileṅgeṅ kaburustān;
nahīṅ milai hari gaye dvārikā nahīṅ kāśī kailāś meṅ haiṅ.
nahīṅ milai haridvār gaye se nahīṅ tīrath gaṅgā jal meṅ;
dil kī dubidhā dūr karau to prabhū milaiṅge ek pal meṅ.
cit dharikai hari nām japau tab tumheṅ milaige kṛpānidhān.
nahīṅ milai hari girajā masjid nahīṅ mandir dīvār meṅ haiṅ.
nahīṅ milai hari tilak diye aur nāhī khāk lagāne se.
nahīṅ milai mālā tasabī meṅ nahīṅ jaṭā ke rakhāne meṅ.
nahīṅ milai ghar bār taje nahīṅ toṅdī ke laṭakāne se.
nahīṅ milai ghar bār taje nahīṅ muluk muluk ram jāne se.

nahīṅ milai hari bheṣ banāye milaiṅge hari gun gāne se.
dil se nām bhajo dilavar kā nāhak hote tum hairān.
tīn lok caudaho bhuvan saṅsār sakal phiri āoge.
kahīṅ n tumako patā milaigā ḍhūñṛh ḍhūñṛh mar jāoge.
kāyā ye apanī nirmal karikai prabhu se neh lagāo tum.
phir dīnadayāl prasann jo hoihaiṅ sahaji mā darśan pāoge.
buddhā kahai prīt kari hari se taj karikai apanā abhimān.

There is no Sarasvatī without voice and there is no knowledge without a teacher.
There is no knowledge without a teacher, I proclaim this in an assembly.
After remembering my teacher, I bow to the whole assembly; I do not make mistake.
Poet Giradhar says to service guru's feet;
Buddhalal (the composer) says to keep your teacher on the throne.
Constantly recite God recognising him in your heart.
Why are you wandering like a madman when God resides within you.
If you are looking for Rām and want to see him.
You will not find him anywhere. What hope do you have.
You will not find God by going to Dvārikā, Kāśī or Kailāś.
God is not in Mecca, Madinā nor near the Kābā.
God is not in a house of idols nor at the cremation ground;
You will not find God by going to Dvārikā, Kāśī or Kailāś.
You will not find him by going to Hardvār nor by the Ganges water.
Abandon all doubts from your heart and you will find God in a moment.
Recite his name sincerely and you will find the Master of Kindness.
God is not in church, mosque, and temple.
You do not find God by applying *tilak* or smearing your body with ashes.
You do not find God in rosary or photo and not by keeping matted hair.
You do not find God by abandoning your family and not by growing your belly.
You do not find God by abandoning your family and roaming from country to country.
You would not find God by dressing up; you would find God by reciting his glory.

Recite his name sincerely, my beloved; There is no need to worry.
You would travel the three worlds and fourteen terrestrial planes.
You would die searching but you would not find his whereabouts.
Make your body and mind pure and then love God.
Then Merciful to the poor would be pleased with you, and you would see him easily.
Buddha (the composer) says, "Love God by renouncing your pride".

(LGT: 3R: 1976, Sheoli, Dhobī Men)

२५९.

घर के दीपक दीयना और दिन के दीपक भान
राति के दीपक चन्द्रमा इस तन के दीपक ज्ञान ॥
कहै मन्दोदरि सुनौ पिया तुम्हें यही काम करना चाहिये
यही काम करना चाहिये प्रभु के चरनन पड़ना चाहिये
रामचन्द्र को नर मत जानो घट घट व्यापक हैं भगवान
माया ममता छोड़िकै रामचन्द्र का धर तू ध्यान
मन्दोदरि का वचन लगा रावण के मन में तीर समान
होत प्रात ही जा बैठा है है ऐसा मूरख अज्ञान
महा मूढ़ मूरख अज्ञानी राम बिमुख चाहे कल्यान
ध्यान मन्दोदरि का है राम पे रामचरित कहना चाहिये ॥
जब देश देश के भूपति आये जनक सभा मा सुनौ पिया
नहीं किसी से उठा धनुष तो सभी सभा को हार दिया
कौतुक में श्री रामचन्द्र ने तीन खण्ड धनु तोड़ दिया
धनुष तोड़ के रामचन्द्र ने तहाँ जानकी व्याह लिया
जब लिया जानकी व्याह राम ने तब क्यों नहीं संग्राम किया
हठ का छोड़ दशानन मिलौ राम लय संग सिया
कीन्है सूपनखई नाक बिन खरदूषन को नाथ
एक बान में बाली के निकर गई तन साँस
ऐसे हैं बलधाम राम जी उनसे तुम्हैं पिया डरना चाहिये ॥

ghar ke dīpak dīyanā aur din ke dāpak bhān;
rāti ke dīpak candramā is tan ke dīpak jñān.
kahai mandodari sunau piyā tumheṅ yahī kām karanā cāhiye.
yahī kām karanā cāhiye prabhu ke caranan paṛanā cāhiye.

rāmacandr ko nar mat jāno ghaṭ ghaṭ vyāpak haiṅ bhagavān.
māyā mamatā choṛikai rāmacandr kā dhar tū dhyān.
mandodari kā vacan lagā rāvaṇ ke man meṅ tīr samān.
hot prāt hī jā baiṭhā hai hai aisā mūrakh ajñān.
mahā mūṛh mūrakh ajñānī rām bimukh cāhe kalyān.
dhyān mandodari kā hai rām pe rāmacarit kahanā cāhiye.
jab deś deś ke bhūpati āye janak sabhā mā sunau piyā.
nahīṅ kisī se uṭhā dhanuṣ to sabhī sabhā ko hār diyā.
kautuk meṅ śrī rāmacandr ne tīn khaṇḍ dhanu toṛ diyā.
dhanuṣ toṛ ke rāmacandr ne tahāñ jānakī vyāh liyā.
jab liyā jānakī vyāh rām ne tab kyoṅ nahīṅ saṅgrām kiyā.
haṭh kā choṛ daśānan milau rām laya saṅg siyā.
kīnhai sūpanakhaī nāk bin kharadūṣan ko nāth.
ek bān meṅ bālī ke nikar gaī tan sāñs.
aise haiṅ baladhām rām jī unase tumhaiṅ piyā ḍaranā cāhiye.

The lamp of home is a light and the lamp of the day is the sun;
The lamp of the night is the moon and knowledge is the light of this body.
Mandodarī is saying to her husband that that's what you should do.
You should prostrate at the feet of God.
Do not think of Rām as a human being; he is god who is prevailing everywhere.
Abandon ignorance and greed and meditate on Rām.
Like an arrow, Mandodarī's statement pierced Rāvaṇ's mind.
He is so stupid and ignorant that he went and sat on his throne at early dawn.
He is so foolish and ignorant that he thinks of his well-being by opposing Rām.
Mandodarī is thinking of Rām and that we should listen to the story of Rām.
When kings from many countries came to Janak's assembly, listen my husband.
When nobody could lift the bow, then he defeated everyone.
In curiosity, Rām broke the bow into three pieces.
After breaking the bow, Rām wed Jānakī.
When Rām wed Jānakī then why didn't you fight with him?

Leave obduracy, O Ten headed, and go alongwith Sītā to meet Rām.
He cut off Śūrpanakhā's nose and killed Kharadūṣaṇ.
With his one arrow Bālī lost his life.
Rām is such an abode of strength and, my dear, you should fear him.

(LGT: 4R; 1976, Sheoli, Dhobī Men)

सारवी

२६०.

अरे भैंस चलै खुरु धमकति आवै सँवलिया, यह लोधइनी शब्द ओनाय।
अरे बारे लोधउना तोरे म्वाछा उखरिबे, हम जइबे अहिर के साथ॥
अरे गउवन कै चरवइहा छूटिगे रसिया, हिंयाँ छूटे सागरा के नहान।
अरे भरे कटोरा दूध के छूटे रसिया, हिंयाँ छूटे सखियन व्योहार॥
अरे बिना पात यह छूली र्वावै सँवलिया, बिन र्वावै चरवाहे गाय।
अरे बिना पुरूष यह र्वावै तिरिया, मुलउ रो रो करै भिनसार॥
अरे जब से पिया तुम गयेव परदेशवा, हियाँ तीन काम तज दीन।
अरे आँखी का कजला माँग का सेंदुरा, यह सेजियौ दुलभ कै दीन॥

are bhaiṅs calai khuru dhamakati āvai sañvaliyā, yah lodhainī śabd onāy.
are bāre lodhaunā tore mvāchā ukharibe, ham jaibe ahir ke sāth.
are gauvan kai caravaihā chūṭige rasiyā, hiṅyāñ chūṭe sāgarā ke nahān.
are bhare kaṭorā dūdh ke chūṭe rasiyā, hiṅyāñ chūṭe sakhiyan vyohār.
are binā pāt yah chūlī rvāvai sañvaliyā, bin rvāvai caravāhe gāy.
are binā puruṣ yah rvāvai tiriyā, mulau ro ro karai bhinasār.
are jab se piyā tum gayev paradeśavā, hiyāñ tīn kām taj dīn.
are āñkhī kā kajalā māñg kā seṅdurā, yah sejiyau dulabh kai dīn.

The water buffalo comes with thumping hooves; [similarly] one hears the words of a *lodhain*.
"O *lodh*, I will pluck your moustache [to humilate you] and will run away with a milkman".

The friends with whom I grazed cattle are left behind and so is the freedom of bathing in the tank.
Eating and drinking in plenty is left behind and childhood friends are left behind.
Without leaves, a tree cries, as without a herdsman a cow wanders.
Without a man, a woman cries all night until dawn.
From the time, O husband, you went out of town, I have abandoned three things.
Application of collyrium to my eyes, putting *seṅdūr* on the part of my hair, and sleeping on my bed.

(LGT: 121R: 1972-73, Akohariya, Ahīr Man)

हाहू

२६१.

कान्ह कहुँ खेलन मति जाओ बसै बृन्दावन में हाहू ॥
गयो खेलन बालक नादान, काट लीन्हें हाहू ने कान
इसमें सुना देखा नहीं हाहू बाको नाम, ताते तात बात मेरी मानो
बार बार बलि जाऊँ कृष्ण घर खेलौ बलदाऊ ॥
प्रबल बाराह रूप धार्‌यो, बिकट हिरणाक्षन को मार्‌यो
प्रबल नरसिंह खम्भ फार्‌यो, बिकट बट हरणाकुश मार्‌यो
राज दियो प्रहलाद को निशचर भये प्रहीन
तहाँ न देखो हम हाहू को कैसो प्रबल प्रवीन, बसै कहाँ मोको बतलाओ ॥
कच्छ रूप सागर मथो चौदह रतन निकार
पाई सुधा सकल देवन ने रूप मोहिनी धार
सुदरशन हन्यो चक्र राहू ॥
लियो अवतार आय बामन गयो बलि द्वार दान माँगन
बिराट रूप धारन कियो नाप लियो तिहुँ लोक
तहाँ न देखो हम हाहू को कैसो प्रबल प्रवीन, बसै कहाँ माको बतलाओ ॥
परशुराम अवतार लय कियो द्विजन को छाड़
इकईस बार मार क्षत्रिन को
पृथ्वी करी निक्षत्री बसै कहाँ मोको बतलाओ, पकरि मारौं सारे को खेद ॥

धर्‍यो तन त्रेता में हम राम सुफल मख लिये गुरू के धाम
धनुष हम तोड़ो मिथिला ग्राम बरी सीता करि पूरण काम
कुम्भकरण रावण हन्यो राज भभीखड़ दीन्ह
तहाँ न देखो हम हाहू को कैसो प्रबल प्रवीन, पकरि मारौं सारे को खेद ॥
धर्‍यो तन द्वापर में अवतार उतारन कारण पृथ्वी भार
कंस बध आदि असुर सँहार अलौकिक लियो बौध अवतार
ई दस लीला अवतार की काहू के मित गाय
कहैं गणेश परसाद कृष्ण रस आनन्द बरसाऊँ ॥

kānh kahuñ khelan mati jāo basai bṛndāban meṅ hāhū.
gayo khelan bālak nādān, kāṭ līnheṅ hāhū ne kān;
isameṅ sunā dekhā nahīṅ hāhū bāko nām, tāte tāt bāt merī māno.
bār bār bali jāūñ kṛṣṇ ghar khelau baladāū.
prabal bārāh rūp dhāryo, bikaṭ hiraṇākṣan ko māryo.
prabal narasiṅh khambh phāryo, bikaṭ baṭ haraṇākuś māryo.
rāj diyo prahalād ko niśacar bhaye prahīn.
tahāñ n dekho ham hāhū ko kaiso prabal pravīn, basai kahāñ moko batalāo.
kacch rūp sāgar matho caudah ratan nikār.
pāī sudhā sakal devan ne rūp mohinī dhār,
sudaraśan hanyo cakr rāhū.
liyo avatār āy bāman gayo bali dvār dān māñgan.
birāṭ rūp dhāran kiyo nāp liyo tihuñ lok.
tahāñ n dekho ham hāhū ko kaiso prabal pravīn, basai kahāñ moko batalāo.
paraśurām avatār lay kiyo dvijan ko chāṛ.
ikaīs bār mār kṣatrin ko,
pṛthvī karī nikṣatrī basai kahāñ moko batalāo, pakari māraun sāre ko khed.
dharyo tan tretā meṅ ham rām suphal makh liye gurū ke dhām.
dhanuṣ ham toṛo mithilā grām barī sītā kari pūraṇ kām.
kumbhakaraṇ rāvaṇ hanyo rāj bhabhīkhaṛ dīnh.
tahāñ n dekho ham hāhū ko kaiso prabal pravīn, pakari māraun sāre ko khed.
dharyo tan dvāpar meṅ avatār utāran kāraṇ pṛthvī bhār.
kaṅs badh ādi asur sañhār alaukik liyo baudh avatār.
ī das līlā avatār kī kāhū ke mit gāy;
kahaiṅ gaṇeś parasād kṛṣṇ ras ānand barasāūñ.

Kṛṣṇa do not play outside as there lives a Hāhū ogre in Vṛndāvan.
The innocent child went out to play and the Hāhū ogre cut his ears.
There is nothing which I have seen or heard but his name is Hāhū so dear child listen to my advice.
O dear Kṛṣṇa, I sacrifice on you, play at home with brother Baladāū.
I incarnated as Barāh and killed terrible Hiraṇākṣa.
From the pillar, I appeared as Narasiṁha and killed terrible Hiraṇākuṣa.
I gave the kingdom to Prahlād and made demons weak.
There, I did not see this terrible Hāhū, Tell me, where does he live?
As a tortoise, I churned the ocean and brought out fourteen gems.
All gods received nectar from me disguised as an enchanting woman,
Killed demon Rāhū with discus.
In my incarnation as Vāman, I went to the gate of King Bāli.
[After receiving the word] Transforming into a huge form, I measured the three worlds.
There, I did not see this terrible Hāhū. Tell me, where does he live?
In my incarnation as Paraśurām, I made brāhmaṇs invincible.
I killed warriors twentyone times,
And made this earth warriorless. So tell me so that I can chase and kill him.
In Tretā, I incarnated as Rām and stayed at my *guru*'s home.
I broke the bow in the town of Mithilā and completed the wedding with Sītā.
I killed Kumbhakaraṇ and Rāvaṇ and gave the kingdom to Vibhīṣaṇ.
I did not see this terrible Hāhū there. Tell me, so that I can chase and kill him.
In *Dvāpar*, I have incarnated once more to remove the burden from this earth.
I killed Kaṁsa and other such demons and then I incarnated as the phenomenal Buddha.
Singing thus the story of god's ten incarnations;
Gaṇeśa Prasād says, "I sing the blissful rain of Kṛṣṇa's love."

(LGT: 235R; 1972-73, Ganj Muradabad, Sunār Woman)

Glossary

Abīr : The glistening red powder which people throw on eah other during the *Holī* festival.

Adār : A kind of tropical bush.

Agahan : The ninth month of the Hindu year.

Ajavāin : An aromatic seed used in Indian cooking; also used as the title of a song sung after chidbirth.

Ājā : Father's father.

Ājī : Father's mother.

Annaprāśan : A ceremony of first feeding of solid food (most often *khīr* which is made of rice and sugar cooked in milk) to the child, usually when a child is six months old.

Aṅtakarm : Death and related ceremonies.

Āratī : A ceremony performed during worship by moving a lighted lamp (usually burning camphor) in a circle in front of the idol; a bride's father performs this ceremony on the groom at the time of the wedding to show the bride's family's respect for the groom and his family.

Āsāṛh : The fourth month of the Hindu year.

Aśok : The *jonesia aśoka* plant.

Bābā : Father's father.

Bahanoī : Sister's husband.

Bahū : Son's wife.

Baiśākh : The second month of the Hindu year.

Baṛhaī : A caste which does carpentry; a member of this caste.

Baraī : A caste which prepares and sells betel leaves; a member of this caste.

Bārī : A caste which prepares and sells items (bowls, plates, etc.) made of leaves; a farm labourer.

Bārin : The wife of a Bārī.

Barua : A boy who is undergoing the sacred thread ceremony.

Bauriyā : See Bārī.

Bel : A creeper.

Belā : A jasmine flower.

Beṅdī : See Biṅdī.

Bhābhī : Brother's wife.

Bhādau : The sixth month of the Hindu year.

Bhaṅgī : A caste which sweeps streets and cleans latrines; a member of this caste.

Bhaujī : See Bhābhī.

Biṅdī : A red dot worn by a woman on her forehead; traditionally applied with red powder or liquid; nowadays self-adhesive plastic dots in many colours and designs are available.

Buā : Father's sister.

Cācā : Father's brother.

Cācī : Father's brother's wife.

Cait : The first month of the Hindu year.

Cakiyā : A stone-mill used for hand-grinding grain.

Cakor : A red-legged partridge which is said to eat fire and to be in love with the moon.

Camār : A caste which disposes of dead animals and works with leather; a member of this caste.

Campā : The fragrant, yellow flower of the *michelia champacca* tree.

Camelī : The jasmine plant; its fragrant flower.

Caṛhāvā : *Sārīs*, ornaments, make-up, combs, and other materials for grooming, etc., presented to the bride on the day of her marriage.

Caruā : A ceremony which is performed by a woman's *sās* after the birth of a child. After polishing the outside of an earthen pot with cow-dung, the *sās* puts it on the fire, to boil water and a few spices, to make a drink for the *jaccā*. For doing this, the *sās* has the right to demand a gift from her *bahū*.

Chaṭhī : The ceremony performed on the sixth day after childbirth. The *nanad* prepares the ritual ingredients.

Chedan : See *Karṇavedh*.

Choṭī : Younger brother's wife.

Cūṛākaraṇ : The ceremony of shaving of a child's head.

Dādī : See *Ājī*.

Devar : Husband's younger brother.

Devarānī : Husband's younger brother's wife.

Dhānuk : A caste which threshes rice and farms; a member of this caste.

Dhobī : A caste which washes clothes; a member of this caste.

Ḍholak : A two-headed cylindrical drum.

Dhotī : A man's garment, consisting of a long piece of cloth draped around the lower part of the body. Also, a woman's garment, similar to the *sārī*, but made of cotton and worn for everyday use (a *sārī* is usually made of silk and worn only on special occasions).

Ḍom : A scavenger class among the Hindus, a caste which takes care of dead people; a member of this caste.

Dulahin : A bride; a *sās* and *sasur* often use this affectionate term for their son's wife.

Fālaśā : A tropical fruit (*grewis asiatica*).

Gaṛariyā : A caste which herds animals; a member of this caste.

Garbhādhān : A ceremony performed when it is known that a woman has become pregnant.

Gaunā : The ceremony of taking a bride to her husband's house for the first time after marriage. Early marriage was, and is still to some extent, common in India. After marriage, the girl remained in her parents' house until the age of puberty, after which, with the performance of the *gaunā* ceremony, she was taken to her husband's house.

Gavan : See *Gaunā*.

Ghī : Clarified butter.

Godān : See *Kesant*.

Gūjar (*Gūlar*) : A wild fig tree.

Gulāl : Red farinaceous power which people throw on each other during the Holī festival.

Hārasiṅgār : The weeping nyctanthes; its flower.

Harīra : A special dish made for a mother after the delivery of a child; spices such as *jīrā* (cumin seed), *pīpar* (a kind of long pepper), *ajavāin* (an aromatic seed), *soṅṭh* (dry ginger), and *haldī* (turmeric) are mixed with dried fruit in a syrup of *guṛ* (raw sugar).

Jaccā : A woman who has given birth to a child.

Jāmun : A kind of black plum with purple meat and a sweet and sour taste.

Janeū : See *Yajñopavīt*.

Jātakarm : A ceremony performed at the birth of the child.

Jeṭh : Husband's elder brother; the third month of the Hindu year.

Jeṭhānī : Husband's elder brother's wife.

Jhāñjh : A cymbal approximately 4 inches in diameter.

Jhoñjhiyā (*Jhuñjhiyā*) : A baked round clay pot into whose body decorative designs (of flowers and leaves, etc.) have been cut. When a clay lamp is lit inside this pot, the light creates a pattern of dark and light.

Jījā : Sister's husband.

Jījī : Elder sister; husband's elder brother's wife.

Juhī : A kind of fragrant flower.

Kacanār : The tree *banbinia variegata*; the flower of this tree, which are used as a vegetable.

Karṇavedh : The ceremony of piercing a child's ears.

Kāchī : A caste which grows vegetables; a member of this caste.

Kadam : The tree *neculea cadamba*; a plant sacred to Kṛṣṇa devotees, because Kṛṣṇa played many games under this tree.

Kahār : A caste which bears palanquins and draws water from wells for their clients.

Kahārin : Wife of a *kahār*; see *kahār*.

Kājal : A childbirth ceremony, observed on the fifth or sixth day after delivery. The *nanad* applies *kājal* to the newborn child's eyes for the first time. *Kājal* is a black paste made out of lampblack and other ingredients. It is widely used in India and applied to children's eyes and foreheads everyday, since it is believed that this will protect the child's eyes and keep him safe from evil eyes. In this ceremony, the *nanad* applies *kājal* to one of the child's eyes and then pretends that her fingers hurt and she cannot apply *kājal* to the other eye. The *jaccā* and other family members then try to persuade her by giving her some gifts. Only after the *nanad* gets what she wants does she apply the *kājal* to the child's other eye.

Kajarī (or *Kajalī*) : A song-form sung during the rainy season.

Kakarī : A kind of long thin cucumber.

Kalamī : A grafted succulent variety of mango which has custard-like flesh.

Kaṅdail : The plantain tree; its fruit.

Kaṛhī : A soup-like preparation made with chickpea flour and buttermilk.

Kātik : The eighth month of the Hindu year.

Keśāṅt : The ceremony of shaving a young man's beard and/or giving the gift of a cow as a token fee to a spiritual preceptor near the end of Vedic studies.

Kevaṛā : The plant *pandarnus odoratissimus*; its perfume.

Khaur : An ornament worn on the head; a mark of sandalwood paste on one's forehead.

Khicaṛī : A dish of rice and lentils cooked together.

Khinnī : A kind of fruit.

Kohabar : The room in which family deities are kept at the time of marriage.

Kos : A distance of two miles (about 3520 yards).

Kumakum : Coloured powder.

Kuñjaṛā : A caste which grows and sells vegetables and fruits; a member of this caste.

Kuramī : A caste which does farming; a member of this caste.

Kuś : A kind of grass, sacred to Hindus and used in rituals.

Kvañr : The seventh month of the Hindu year.

Laḍḍū : A kind of sweet.

Laṅgūr : A boy who maintains a temple sanctuary and garden; a kind of monkey.

Lodh : A caste which takes care of domestic animals and does farming; a member of this caste.

Lodhain : Wife of a *Lodh*; see *Lodh*.

Lohār : A caste which makes and repairs iron tools; a member of this caste.

Madār : The plant swallow wort, *calotrapis gigantea*.

Māgh : The eleventh month of the Hindu year.

Maharī : Female form of *maharā*, a caste group whose profession is to clean the pots and pans of a household and fetch water from the well for the family's consumption; a member of this caste.

Maheriyā : A dish prepared in sour buttermilk or boiled milk.

Mahuā : The tree *Bassia latifolia*, which bears sweet flowers, used in the preparation of a spirituous liquor; its dried flowers are eaten during fasting.

Māīñ : Mother's brother's wife.

Māmā : Mother's brother.

Māmī : See *Māīñ*.

Man : A unit of measurement.

Manihār : A caste which makes and sells glass bangles; a member of this caste.

Mañjīrā : Cymbals.

Meṅhadī : A myrtle plant, the leaves of which are ground into a paste and used by women to dye their hands and feet in decorative designs.

Missī : A black powder which females use to tinge their teeth.

Mṛdaṅg : A barrel-shaped drum.

Muṇḍan : See *Cūḍākaraṇ*.

Nagāṛā : A kettledrum.

Nāmakaraṇ : The ceremony of naming a child.

Nanad : Husband's sister.

Nīm : The *margosa* tree.

Niṣkramaṇ : The ceremony of taking a child out of the house for the first time, usually at the age of four months.

Paṅsāsār : See *Paṅsāsārī*.

Paṅsāsārī : A simple game played between bride and groom, after the main marriage ceremonies. The *sarahaj* throws a piece of gold or silver into a bowl of water and the bride and groom try to retrieve it. This is done seven times: whoever fetches it the most is the winner; the loser is teased. It is also believed that whoever wins will dominate the household.

Papīhā : The sparrow hawk.

Pasanī : See *Annaprāśan*.

Paṭavā : One who entwines ornaments, beads, etc., with silk, cotton, or colourful thread.

Phāgun : The twelfth month of the Hindu year.

Phūlageṅdavā : Lit., a ball made of flowers; a type of necklace with flower designs.

Phūphā : Father's sister's husband.

Pīpar (also *piparī*) : A long pepper used in herbal preparations for a new mother.

Piparāmuṛh : The root of a long pepper used in medicine.

Piyarī : A *sārī* dyed in turmeric colour. It is customary for a bride's parents to send a *piyarī* and other gifts for all ceremonies that take place at their daughter's husband's house.

Puṅsavan : A ceremony performed in the third month of pregnancy, in order to assure that a male child will be born.

Pūs : The tenth month of the Hindu year.

Rocanā : Turmeric and lime or sandalwood paste applied on the forehead during a ceremony or at the time of leave-taking, as a mark of good luck.

Śādī : See *Vivāh*.

Śahanāī : A double-reed instrument.

Sālā (or *Sārā*) : Wife's brother.

Sālī (or *Sārī*) : Wife's brother's wife.

Salīno (or *Sanino*) : A Hindu festival observed on the full moon day of the month of *Sāvan*.

Samāvartan : A ceremony performed at the end of Vedic studies, when a son returns home after finishing his studies.

Sañjīvanī (also *Sañjīvan*) : The root of a bush used as a medicine, reputed to have the power to restore a dead person to life.

Sāṛī : A long piece of cloth worn by Indian females around the waist, passing over one or both shoulders and sometimes the head; wife's brothers wife (*salī*).

Sarahaj : Wife's brother's wife.

Sāraṅgī : A bowed instrument.

Sās : Wife's husband's mother.

Sasur : Wife's husband's father.

Satiyā : A wall painting made by *nanad*, to be worshipped by the new mother, to assure the health of the newborn child.

Sāvan : The fifth month of the Hindu year; a song form.

Seṅdhurā (or *Siṅdhaurā*) : A box containing toiletries presented to a bride.

Seṅdūr (also, *Siṅdūr*) : A special red power worn by a married woman in the part of her hair.

Sīmantonayan : A ceremony performed in the fourth, sixth, or eighth month of pregnancy, to protect the pregnant woman from evil spirits.

Sitār : A popular stringed instrument used in Indian classical music.

Snān : See *Samāvartan*.

Sohāg : The happy state of a wife when her husband is alive; a marriage ceremony during which the bride-to-be pays her respects and asks seven married women individually for their blessings. In return, each woman puts some *siṅdūr* in the part of her own hair and then applies it to bride-to-be's part three times.

Surajamukhī : A type of sunflower.

Tablā : A two-piece set of drums.

Tāī : Father's elder brother's wife.

Tāū : Father's elder brother.

Tīj : A Hindu festival.

Ṭesū : A kind of wildflower.

Tilak : A mark on the forehead.

Upanayan : See *Yajñopavīt*.

Vidyārambh : A ceremony performed at the commencement of a child's reading and writing the alphabet.

Vivāh : Marriage.

Vedāraṃbh : A ceremony performed at the beginning of Vedic studies.

Yajñopavīt : The sacred thread ceremony.

Bibliography

Crooke, William

1896, *The Popular Religion and Folklore of Northern India*, Delhi: Munshiram Manoharlal.

Gupta, B.A. Rai Bahadur

1919, *Hindu Holidays and Ceremonials*, Calcutta: Thacker, Spink & Co.

Pandeya, Rajbali

1966, *Hindu Saṁskāra: The Social and Religious Study of the Hindu Sacraments*, Varanasi: Chowkhambha Vidyabhawan.

Prasad, Vishwanath

1962, *Magahi Saṁskāra Geet*, Patna: Bihar Rastrabhasa Parishad.

Sanyal, M. (tr.)

n.d., *The Śrīmad Bhāgavatam*, Calcutta: Oriental Publishing Co.

Shastri, Hari prasad (tr.)

1962, *The Rāmāyaṇa of Vālmikī*, London: Shanti Sadan.

Tewari, Laxmi G.

1991, *Folk Music of Uttar Pradesh, India*, "Traditional Music of the World Series," Berlin: International Institute for Comparative Music Studies.

1982, "The Folk Festival of Jhonjhi-Tesu" in *Asian Folklore Studies* 41(2) : 217-30.

1975, *Folk Music of India: Uttar Pradesh*, New York: Lyrichord Discs.

Williams, Sir Monier

1916, *Religious Life and Thought in India* as quoted in Abhay Charan Mukerji, *Hindu Fasts and Feasts*, Allahabad: Indian Press, 1916:ii.